HOW TO BUILD AND MODIFY
CHEVY NOVA
1968–1974

Wayne Scraba

CarTech®

CarTech®

CarTech®, Inc.
838 Lake Street South
Forest Lake, MN 55025
Phone: 651-277-1200 or 800-551-4754
Fax: 651-277-1203
www.cartechbooks.com

© 2017 by Wayne Scraba

All rights reserved. No part of this publication may be reproduced or utilized in any form or by any means, electronic or mechanical, including photocopying, recording, or by any information storage and retrieval system, without prior permission from the Publisher. All text, photographs, and artwork are the property of the Author unless otherwise noted or credited.

The information in this work is true and complete to the best of our knowledge. However, all information is presented without any guarantee on the part of the Author or Publisher, who also disclaim any liability incurred in connection with the use of the information and any implied warranties of merchantability or fitness for a particular purpose. Readers are responsible for taking suitable and appropriate safety measures when performing any of the operations or activities described in this work.

All trademarks, trade names, model names and numbers, and other product designations referred to herein are the property of their respective owners and are used solely for identification purposes. This work is a publication of CarTech, Inc., and has not been licensed, approved, sponsored, or endorsed by any other person or entity. The Publisher is not associated with any product, service, or vendor mentioned in this book, and does not endorse the products or services of any vendor mentioned in this book.

Edit by Bob Wilson
Layout by Monica Seiberlich

ISBN 978-1-61325-330-4
Item No. SA392

Library of Congress Cataloging-in-Publication Data Available

Edited and designed in the U.S.A.
Printed in China
10 9 8 7 6 5 4 3 2 1

Title Page:
Whether building for the strip or the street, the Nova is an excellent and attractive platform.

Back Cover Photos

Top:
This is where four-link tuning gets interesting! As you can see, there are several ways to come up with the same instant center (or at least instant centers that are close). One tends to wheelstand and/or rattle the tires. The other does not. (Illustration Courtesy Jerry Bickel Race Cars)

Middle Left:
The spring might look "bowed" in this photo, but it's not. What worked for this Nova was a stock small-block spring for a car with power steering and a few other options. The car will eventually receive a big-block.

Middle Right:
The RobbMC -8 AN pickup for a Nova measures 1/2 inch in diameter. Note there is no problematic sock filter. This means an inline filter of some sort is mandatory.

Bottom:
Cores for a Davis radiator are of proprietary design. They're Nocolok furnace brazed and, whereas most companies offer one fin count, Ron Davis Racing Radiators sizes the fin count and thickness to the application. Davis incorporates quality Spal fans in the package. Note the way the fans are completely sealed to the radiator by way of the aluminum shroud.

DISTRIBUTION BY:

Europe
PGUK
63 Hatton Garden
London EC1N 8LE, England
Phone: 020 7061 1980 • Fax: 020 7242 3725
www.pguk.co.uk

Australia
Renniks Publications Ltd.
3/37-39 Green Street
Banksmeadow, NSW 2109, Australia
Phone: 2 9695 7055 • Fax: 2 9695 7355
www.renniks.com

Canada
Login Canada
300 Saulteaux Crescent
Winnipeg, MB, R3J-3T2 Canada
Phone: 800 665 1148 • Fax: 800 665 0103
www.lb.ca

CONTENTS

Introduction 4

Chapter 1: Starting from Scratch 6
Reference Material 6
Stripped Ease 9

Chapter 2: Getting Framed 17
Bare Bones 17
Mounting Points 21
A-Arms 22
Installing the Rest 28
Frame Connectors 29

Chapter 3: Rear Axle 31
12-Bolt 31
Ford 9-Inch 34
Dana 60 40
Gear Sets 41
Axles 42

Chapter 4: Rear Suspension 50
Bolt-On Bars 50
Tuning CalTracs 52
Four-Links and Ladder Bars 54
Chassis Instant Center 55
Pinion Angle 57
Laterally Linked 59
Controlling the Roll 60
Torque Rotation 61
Solutions 62
Rod Ends 63

Chapter 5: Springs and Shock Absorbers 67
Springs 67
Shock Absorbers 70
Shackles and Bushings 75

Chapter 6: Brakes 77
How to Build Drum Brakes 82
Master Cylinder and Proportioning Valves 86
Roll Control 87
Brake Flex Hoses 89
Brake Hard Lines 91

Chapter 7: Engine Swaps 94
Frame Mounts 94
Motor Mounts 96
Transmission Crossmembers 96
Transmission Mount 96
Flywheels, Flexplates and Starters 97
Clutch Linkage 98
Alternators, Water Pumps and Pulleys 102
LS Drives 102
Throttle Linkage 103
Heater 104
Ignition Controls 104
Headers 104

Chapter 8: Wheels and Tires 107
Critical Parts of a Wheel 107
Stuffing Fenders 110
Wheel Studs 113
Drag Radials 115

Chapter 9: Fuel System 119
Gas Tanks and Fuel Cells 119
High-Flow Pickups for Stock Nova Tanks 126
Mechanical Fuel Pumps 127
Electric Fuel Pumps 129
Fuel Pressure Regulators 130
Fuel Filters 132

Chapter 10: Radiators and Electric Fans 134
Radiator 134
Cooling Fans and Shrouds 137

Source Guide 143

INTRODUCTION

Over the past 40 years or so, I've had four Novas in my shop(s) along with five of their close cousins, the first-gen Camaro. I like these cars a lot (and you probably do too, considering you're reading this!). There's a good reason: They're simple and easy to work on. They have massive aftermarket support (both from a high-performance and restoration point of view). They're light. They have a huge engine compartment (which means they can pretty much swallow any performance engine Chevrolet ever built). They accept almost any gearbox Chevrolet built. Choices for rear ends are similar: You have a ton of options. Compared to the Camaro, they have a smaller rear wheelwell, but for drag duty, they make up for it with rear overhang (rear weight bias). The cars are narrow too. That doesn't make them great for burning corners, but light, narrow, and a good rear overhang is the right recipe for street/strip or dragstrip duty. They also make for an "okay" Pro Touring combination, but honestly, a Camaro is likely a far better choice.

The biggest issue with a Nova is the room for rear rubber; they're tire limited. Sure, you can mini-tub the car to make room for big tires, but when you do that, you must move the rear shocks inboard. You must replace the shocks with Camaro models too. The springs must be moved. That means you need to weld new perches on the rear end. And finally, you need to either section the gas tank or install a narrow job. That's a lot of fab work. Certainly there's the odd kernel of knowledge in here for someone building a Pro Touring car, but this book is geared toward street and street/strip Novas. Finally, 1968–1974 Novas are still somewhat affordable. Do your homework and you can find one to fit almost any budget.

The way a car feels isn't mentioned much when discussing car builds. To me, the Nova feels just right. Aside from occasionally knocking your head as you enter, a 1968–1974 Nova has a great seating position. With something such as a stick shift combination, the pedal and shifter relationship is great. And your view of the road is, well, commanding; just like in a pickup truck! But the real bottom line here is, these cars were made for banging gears. I love 'em!

Every one of my Novas was built in my own shop. That shop has, over the years, changed considerably. It grew to accommodate some of my old racing endeavors and then shrunk when I decided the time was right to downsize. Today that shop is a two-car garage attached to my house. I don't think it exceeds 500 square feet. There's no lift (the ceiling is too low) and, honestly, no fancy tools either. Just a collection of tools that fit inside an old Snap-on rollaway cabinet and chest along with a larger Mac rollaway cabinet. And my guess is that's pretty close to what many of you have. It might not be fancy, but the truth is, it's sufficient to build a nice Nova. I'll get to that in a bit.

Fair enough. I've probably mentioned a lot of things you already know! But what can this book do for you? Remember those Novas and Camaros I worked on over the years? Well that trail of Chevys taught me a lot about car building in general and Novas in particular. I made mistakes along the way (the truth be told, a lot of them!). But at the same time, I also came up with a good number of solutions. It's all about education, and it's my plan to share that learning with you.

What kind of projects can benefit from this book? Is it limited to restorations? Heck no. I've built race cars, hot rods, restorations, and street machines over the years. And I've learned that they have one thing in common. They all take the same path during preliminary construction: Strip it. Clean it. Catalog it. Inventory it. Refurbish it. Store it. Reinstall it. It really doesn't matter what kind of project you have; this book provides insight into how and where to begin.

You'll find an abundance of do-it-yourself paint and body books out there. Some good (S-A Design has some really, really good ones; I dig Pat Ganahl's *Paint Your Car on a Budget*). Some decidedly crappy. What really bugs me is that most of them forget that you must somehow get to either the paint and body or the chassis shop. The car didn't fall apart by itself and say "Paint Me" or "Tub

INTRODUCTION

Me"! A huge amount of work comes first. And if you haul the beater directly to the body or chassis shop, guess who's going to pay for the labor? Besides, I think there's a good amount of satisfaction involved in doing this stuff yourself and simultaneously, you'll be certain the work is done right. After all, there's no one else to blame, right?

The issue of cost is something everyone must address sooner or later in a car project. Sure, with a full-tilt frame-off build you can amortize the costs over several years, but for most folks (me included), paying as much as $100 per hour to peel apart a car and then put it together is simply gut wrenching. I can appreciate paying skilled labor to paint a car, but gee whiz, coughing up that kind of dough to pay a kid to do the work for the shop makes me, well, anxious! And especially so if that same kid has a regular job of sweeping the floor in the shop and he's called in to strip cars on occasion. One of the primary ideas behind this book is to show you how to save money. Trust me, by doing the dirty work yourself you can save a ton. You also save plenty of frustration in the end.

Speaking of saving (cash), one itsy-bitsy detail plenty of folks overlook is the value of their junk. You might be pleasantly surprised at how much value there is in the used, unwanted hardware you peel off a project car. Case in point: I once sold a Nova (I had moved on to other things and this deuce was excess baggage) to a buyer who didn't want the rubber floor mat that originally came with the car. On a lark, I placed it on eBay with what I thought was a ridiculously high reserve. Yeow! Two, ughm, well-heeled collectors went after the floor mat. Yes, it was mint, but I didn't think it was $1,500 mint. To a little guy like me, that was a considerable bonus. And it just goes to show how much value there might be in your Nova junk.

Notice that I have left out engines and transmissions in the book. What's up with that? It's very simple. The good folks from S-A Design have given me 144 or so pages to write about building Novas. If I include engines and transmissions in the book, I take away from the total. You and I both lose valuable room for valuable information. And to be honest, I can't tell you how to build an engine in a chapter. Nor can I show you how to go through any number of transmissions (automatic and stick) in a chapter. Instead, you should pick up one of S-A Designs engine books for that info. There's no shortage of good Chevrolet engine books in the CarTech catalog!

When everything is said and done, you have to consider the difficulty of actually doing this stuff. Just how difficult is it? Not very. The truth is, there's probably more to the actual organization than there is to turning wrenches. Certainly you must be a wee bit more advanced than the righty-tighty, lefty-loosey crowd, but I think anyone with the desire can perform the mechanical work. Sure, I've been involved with car construction for probably too long (more than 45 years and counting—Yikes!), so some of the tasks have become second-hand, but I'm quite confident someone just starting out can get the job done by reading and following this book. It's not a blow-by-blow how-to publication though (there's not enough room in a 144-page book to accomplish that). Be sure to couple this book with a good shop manual (Chevy's OEM Service and Overhaul manuals along with an OEM Fisher Body Manual are good examples, and so is a reproduction Chevrolet Assembly Instruction Manual). Those manuals certainly help you get the job done. There's more too: This is a hobby. That means it is supposed to be enjoyable. Don't sweat it if you come across a stumbling block. Remember, nothing involved in building a Nova is insurmountable. In fact, I'm pretty sure all of you will come away with a smile on your face when you're working on your project. I do.

In a nutshell, that's the entire premise of this book: how to build a high-performance Nova and have fun and save money doing it. I know what follows is something you can use. And I trust both of us will have a good time as we go through the various chapters. Check it out. You won't regret it.

CHAPTER 1

STARTING FROM SCRATCH

Okay. You have the project Nova. Now what? It's obvious you can start tearing it apart to begin your build, but first things first: You should gather reference material for your project.

Reference Material

When it comes to information, you never get enough. The reality is, if you're armed with information on basic mechanics and high performance the work will proceed in a much smoother fashion. But what information should you get?

You need to come up with a selection of resource books, factory service publications, and just as important, catalogs from the various aftermarket companies. Knowledge of your particular Nova is one thing, but when it comes time to disassemble a specific component, restore or rebuild it, and then reassemble it, you often require more than a knack with hand tools. Before one screw or bolt is loosened on your car, do yourself a favor and purchase (or scrounge where necessary) the publications noted below.

Factory Service Manual

Chevrolet printed factory service manuals for each model year of the Chevrolet passenger car(s), Novas included. They're not easy or light reading, but they do deal with minor service procedures, vehicle maintenance, and component adjustment. In addition, they also show the correct way to remove and replace various components and subassemblies. The service manuals cover all Chevrolet passenger cars as well as Corvettes.

Factory Overhaul Manual

In GM Land, the Overhaul Manual takes over where the Service Manual ends. It details the repair and replacement of major components.

Don't be fooled into thinking the World Wide Web can provide you with all of the technical details you need to build and rework a vintage Nova. What you see here is a good collection of "must have" books and manuals.

Building a car such as a Nova doesn't necessarily mean that you need a huge-by-large shop. With a little bit of planning you can get by with a workspace that measures less than 600 square feet.

---

6 CHEVY NOVA 1968–1974: HOW TO BUILD AND MODIFY

STARTING FROM SCRATCH

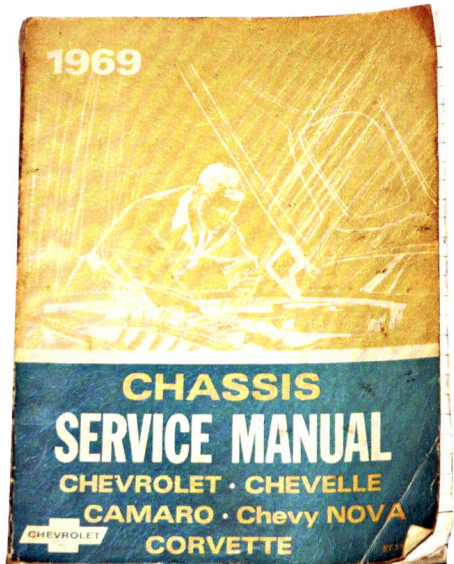

Nothing can replace a Chevrolet factory Service Manual. The original equipment Service Manuals handle minor service, adjustment, tune up, and other repairs.

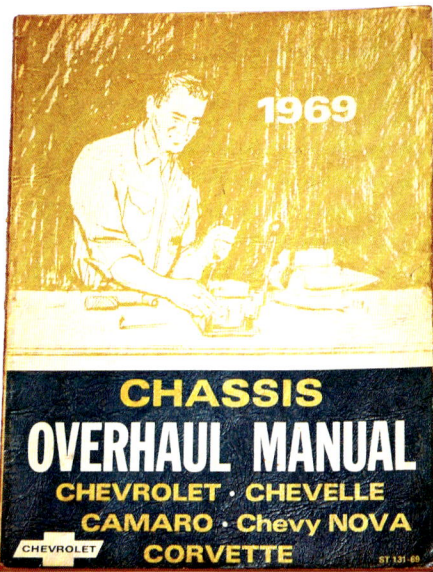

For more comprehensive repairs, Chevrolet issued an Overhaul Manual. It is a supplement to the Service Manual. As you might have guessed, it looks at how to completely rebuild major components.

GM's Fisher Body Division also printed repair manuals for various automobiles, including Novas. If you're befuddled about how to remove a piece of trim or adjust a window (or any number of body-related topics), you need this.

While the Service Manual deals with minor repairs, this book examines the down and dirty hard jobs. This manual is designed for use in conjunction with the Service Manual. And like the other publication, it covers all passenger cars and Corvettes.

Body Service Manual

General Motors had a special manual that examined topics that were not covered in either the service or overhaul publications. If you're left scratching your head about how to fix something, the Fisher body service manual might solve it. For example, the General may have included one type of molding clip on all vehicles. This manual tells you how to remove and replace that clip. It might be generic, but it shows how the task is done. Fisher Body Service Manuals for a given year cover all passenger cars (Chevrolet, Pontiac, Olds, Buick, and Cadillac).

Assembly Instruction Manual

Reprinted Assembly Instruction Manuals, or "AIMs," are available for almost all older Chevys. These are the manuals used on the assembly line during vehicle construction. Examples are printed in a loose-leaf format and feature large, sometimes-exploded, drawings of all components and sub-assemblies that are pieced together during the manufacturing process. These drawings show where the parts go and how they go together.

Part numbers are included, but these are production numbers, not service (replacement or dealership parts department) numbers. The AIM also shows you where and how components are glued together, correct fastener installation, proper clamp location and orientation, the correct location of pierced holes, and ride height specifics. Production options are included along with location mounting points and special torque specifications for almost all parts of the Nova.

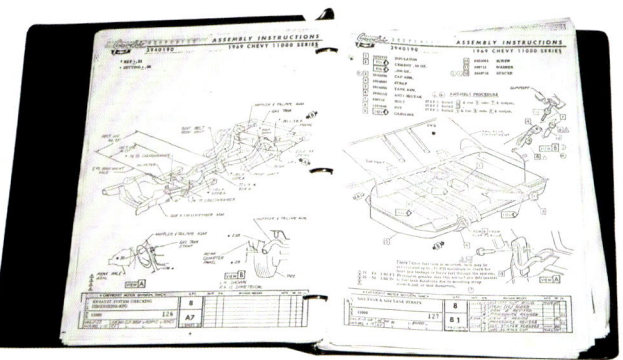

Most Nova enthusiasts know what an "AIM" is. It's the Assembly Instruction Manual that Chevrolet used on the assembly line to build a Nova. The factory AIM is loaded with assembly drawings, descriptions of options, and more.

CHAPTER 1

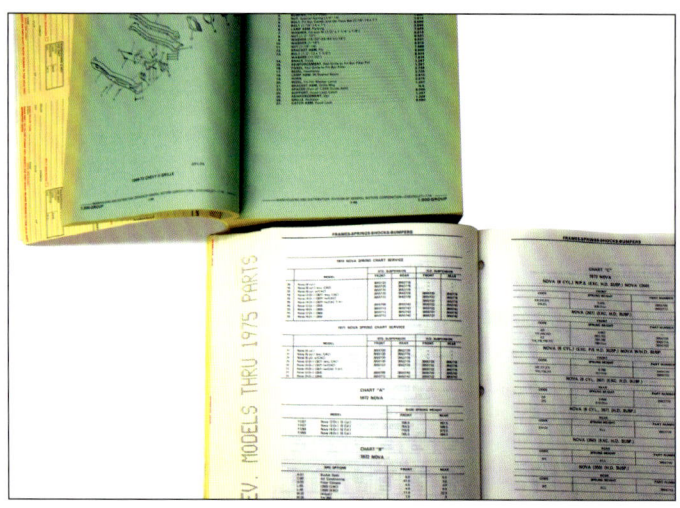

Chevrolet Parts Catalogs are important. They're usually made up of an illustration catalog (or section) along with a parts book. You need them both. If you dig around, you can find reprints or lightly used originals.

Wrecking yards originally used this old monster book to identify parts and show interchanges. Hollander publishes them. The company still prints manuals and it even has smaller examples dedicated specifically to one line of car (for example, 1968–1979 Novas). Honestly, this is the go-to book when scrounging for parts.

The AIM is broken down into two parts. The first part covers approximately one dozen basic assembly areas that range from labels to stickers to complete electrical installation. This portion of the Assembly Instruction Manual is called the "Uniform Parts Classification." Following the UPC section is the RPO, or "Regular Production Option," portion of the book.

Factory (OEM) Parts Catalog

Reprints of vintage Chevrolet parts catalogs (or originals) are readily available if you do a bit of digging. These catalogs not only list the part numbers for various components, they also feature blow-up illustrations of many parts. If you're dealing with, say, a 1970 Nova, among the best bets for a parts catalog is the reprinted 1971 versions (if your Nova is a 1971 or older model). They cover all years of Chevrolets through 1971. Obviously, almost all the part numbers have been discontinued and the few remaining have been changed in the past decades.

Hollander Interchange Manual

Scrounging parts for your car can sometimes feel like an impossible dream. Fortunately, many pieces are direct interchanges with similar (or not so similar) "corporate" offerings. As an example, a Nova four-door sedan or even something such as a Buick Apollo can supply a host of goodies for your SS396 project. Items such as suspension pieces, electrical components, some transmission components, and even certain trim parts and myriad accessory or RPO components are virtually identical.

So how in the world do you know which parts interchange and which don't? The big parts are by far the easiest. A company called Hollander provides massive manuals to wrecking yards that outline the various interchanges between respective marques. Hollander manuals are typically 4 inches thick and include information on all "hard" parts, including identification of those components. Small items, such as trim pieces, are not included.

For a Nova, consider Volumes 1 and 2 of the 1964–1974 issue. This is an expensive package, but the dollars saved during the restoration will be well worth the expense.

If the high price scares you off, try searching for a used "41st Auto-Truck Interchange Edition" (such as the one shown in the accompanying photos). It covers domestic vehicles from 1965 to 1975 and, as a result, encompasses all Chevrolets of that era. Where do you find used Hollanders? Your local wrecking yards are good bets. The Hollander Interchange Manual is considered the "bible" of the dismantling business. Any reputable wrecker knows what you're talking about. Wreckers don't have much need for an old Hollander if no older cars are left in their yard. You can also try online sources such as eBay.

Aftermarket Support

Some cars have great aftermarket support. Our old Novas are among these. Before you begin the build (and long before you buy a car), you contemplate things including reproduction parts, NOS parts, and aftermarket parts availability. With good resources such as these, it's a whole bunch easier to piece together a good

8   CHEVY NOVA 1968–1974: HOW TO BUILD AND MODIFY

STARTING FROM SCRATCH

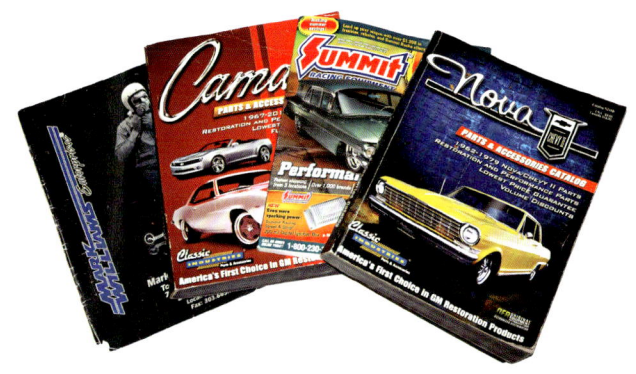

Sooner or later you'll need help from the restoration or high-performance aftermarket. These are just a few catalog examples. A Camaro parts catalog is a good idea for your Nova too, because there's a lot of interchange between Novas and Camaros. Sometimes a Nova reproduction isn't available but a Camaro piece is. Keep that in mind.

Should you decide to remove all the front sheet metal on a Nova, options are limited. The hood must come off before the fenders. To warm up to the idea (and the job), remove the trim first. Besides, the anodized aluminum is rather fragile, so it's best to get it out of the way first.

car. The bottom line here is, gather up as many pertinent catalogs from various vendors as possible. Some of the vendors offer decent discounts to regular customers too. When it comes to aftermarket vendors, some are good, some are great, and some are not so good.

Stripped Ease

Conventional wisdom states you should drain the fluids, peel out the engine, the radiator, and the rest of the power train, and start from there. That works, but there's another way that might be better: Consider removing the sheet-metal parts and other bits that you know need replacing well before stripping out the mechanicals. Here's why: If you have a small shop, space is always at a premium. When you take out heavy, messy stuff such as the engine and transmission, you'll be tripping over it. The option of moving the car (driving it) while removing bulky (and sometimes delicate) sheet-metal pieces can be advantageous. Honestly, it works very well in a crowded garage.

Remove the Hood

Nova hoods are usually a pain in the you-know-where to remove. They're heavy and bulky, and if you're not careful, they can slide backward and take out the windshield. Here's a system you can use to do most of the heavy lifting by yourself (although for a big hood you have to enlist your wife, girlfriend, kid, or the guy next door for a few minutes):

Place a couple of 2 x 4s (1½ to 2 feet long) between the hood, front fenders, and the windshield. Depending upon the car and the state of the paint you might want to wrap each board with a heavy terry towel. When you remove one side of the hood, it can slide down to the 2 x 4 without contacting the windshield. You can slowly remove the other side using a ratchet and appropriate socket (it is difficult with a regular combination wrench). With a Nova, you need help for the second side. The only thing that your helper has to do is to hold

This placement of lumber (2 x 4s) is very useful when removing the hood. Softwood doesn't damage the paint if you're careful, but if you think you'll lose sleep over the process, wrap the lumber with heavy terry towels. With a bit of care, the 2 x 4s will help you remove the hood without any damage to the car.

A car can be stripped using a variety of methods. Some just happen to be better than others. If it's coming down to a full-bore restoration, the car must be stripped completely, as with this example.

CHEVY NOVA 1968–1974: HOW TO BUILD AND MODIFY

CHAPTER 1

Frozen Fasteners

On some cars, you soon discover that the odd fastener (or maybe the majority) is frozen solid. The cure is simple; plenty of folks use PB Blaster as a penetrating oil. Give the stubborn nut/bolt/washer a blast with the goop and let it soak. In most cases it should loosen. If the penetrating oil doesn't work, it's time for more aggressive tactics. Use a good old-fashioned propane torch and heat the fastener. If it's been thoroughly coated with penetrating oil, you know it because it smokes and stinks! As soon as it's hot, try turning out the fastener. By the way, this works perfectly for super-stubborn Phillips-head screws (such as the type General Motors used for door latches). They can be problematic to remove, but if you use the above process and whack the fastener with an impact screwdriver, it will loosen.

One thing is certain when you're working on any old car: Sooner or later you run into a frozen fastener. These are the tools of the trade when it comes to removing stubborn bolts and screws. Sometimes penetrating oil works. And sometimes you have to resort to heat.

Up close are two tools you can't do without on a Nova rebuild: an impact driver and the hammer you need to run it. The impact driver can be set up to both tighten and loosen, and that's something some folks overlook. If you have a frozen screw or other small fastener, this thing works wonders.

the hood upright on the hinges while you loosen and remove the fasteners. After the bolts are removed, you can slide the hood backward toward the windshield where it can contact the 2 x 4s. At this point you can safely lift it off the car and set it aside. By the way, it's a good idea to remove the hood from the hinges, and then remove the hinges separately. It's easier that way.

Peel Out the Powertrain

Right about now, your project car should be staged and ready for engine and transmission removal. What you need here is a cherry picker (engine hoist), a floor jack, a couple of axle stands, a small collection of hand tools, and a good-sized drain pan. Depending upon how you chose to remove the engine (with the front sheet metal removed or with it on the car) you might need a set of ramps.

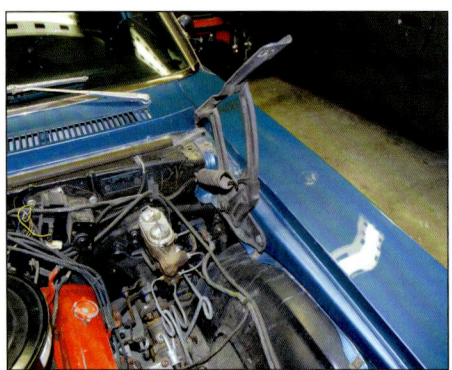

You need a helper to balance the hood while you remove the two bolts per side. Remove one side, set the hood down on the 2 x 4, and then go to the other side of the car. It works and you never damage a windshield or cowl vent panel with this process.

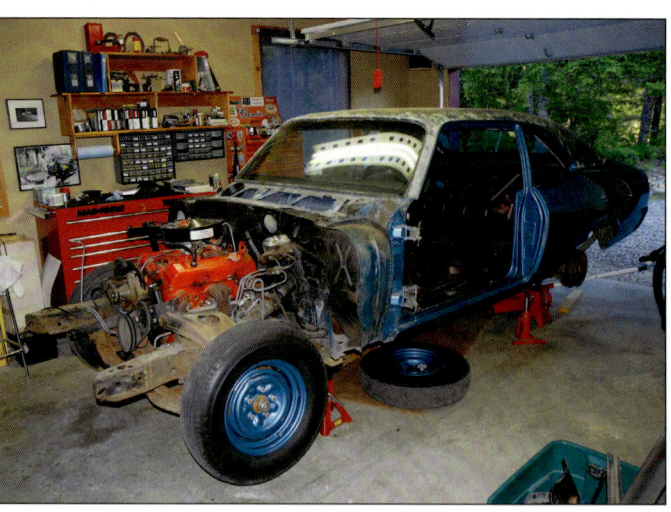

Now you're getting somewhere in the disassembly process. If you leave a Nova in a running (or a least rolling) mode as long as possible, it makes life easier (and less cluttered) in the shop. Right about now, though, it's time to change that. Check it out.

10   CHEVY NOVA 1968–1974: HOW TO BUILD AND MODIFY

Drain the Fluids

The subtitle of this section should probably read, "Drain the Appropriate Fluids." Truth be known, you don't need to drain everything. The rear axle doesn't need to be emptied, especially if you're swapping in another. Ditto with the engine oil. The engine oil isn't going anywhere unless you manage to turn the whole thing upside down, and that sure isn't likely (fingers crossed). That leaves three things to drain: the cooling system, the fuel system, and the transmission fluid. You don't necessarily have to drain the transmission if it's a stick, but if it's an automatic, fluid goes everywhere, no matter what you do.

When it comes to gasoline, ensure the car didn't have much in the tank to begin with. The reason is that 15 or so gallons of fuel are difficult to deal with. You'd rather deal with 1 gallon. Aside from the question of where to keep the extra gas, you also must concern yourself with weight. A U.S. gallon of gas weighs roughly 6.2 pounds; therefore, 15 of them tip the scales at 93 pounds. If you drop the tank with an extra 93 pounds of fuel in it, you appreciate why it's a good idea to work with a nearly empty tank! Of course, the hazard of slopping around with a lot of raw gas in the general vicinity is something that should be avoided too.

If there's a bit more gas in the tank than you care to have, it's a good idea to push the car outside the shop door to drain it. It's safer, and you don't have to worry about raw gas flowing all over the shop floor. It also saves on making a stink.

To drain the gas tank, it's likely easiest to remove the lines. All Novas have a "soft" (rubber) flex connection on the frame rail rear of the passenger-side rear tire, and that's as good a spot as any to initiate the draining process. Use a clean drain pan and pour the collected fuel into a sealed (clean) fuel jug. It's now gasoline for your lawn mower.

With the tank close to empty, you can unhook the tank straps and lower the gas tank to the ground. At this point, you can completely unhook any fuel lines (return or feed lines) if you haven't already done so. The tank should come out easily, provided nothing is caught. At this stage, you can just tip it over and drain the works into the "lawn mower" fuel jug.

The next big mess (no kidding) is the coolant. First things first: Chase your dog and/or your cat out of the shop. Keep the shop off limits to them until you're done. Most of you know the reason: Antifreeze (coolant; call it what you will) can kill animals if ingested.

It's best to drain the radiator first, and then follow up by draining the cylinder block. Be sure the engine is dead cold. Being scalded by hot coolant is never fun. Slide a big drain container under the radiator and open the petcock. It starts as a trickle. Loosen the radiator cap. Now a torrent of coolant should come out. Keep in mind that coolant is slippery, foul-smelling stuff. If there's an appreciable spill, you have an equally big cleanup. For that, you need plenty of floor dry absorbent.

When the radiator has stopped dripping, you can drain the block. Chevy drains are near the oil pan rails (sometimes they're hard to see because they can be obscured by the exhaust manifolds). Usually these drains have a hex head that you can

What to Do with Old Fluids

You now probably have more old waste fluid than you ever dreamed possible. What do you do with this stuff? First and foremost, don't toss it in the ditch, over the fence, or in the neighbor's back yard.

The environment is important. That's a no-brainer because it's the only one we have. So what's the best way to get rid of waste oil and coolant? In some jurisdictions, the folks who sell oil and coolant are obliged to accept it as waste at no charge. Collect a couple of older race fuel jugs (5 gallons each). Designate them for used oil and used coolant (don't mix them up). When you fill them, simply transfer the contents to the drop-off facility tank. Check it out. It's most often free. And the bonus is, it's usually pretty clean.

No matter what you're doing with a project Nova, sooner or later you'll be faced with getting rid of stuff such as used oil, antifreeze (coolant), transmission fluid, and rear-end lube. It is your social responsibility to get rid of this mess the proper way. Recycle it.

CHAPTER 1

Keeping Track of Your Stuff

When you're slaving over a big project such as a complete Nova build, it's easy to lose track of parts. A lot of them can go missing, and it becomes particularly painful when the time comes to reassemble the car. The best solution is to get organized. To keep things under control consider using temporary folding tables to store parts. These are particularly useful for large and perhaps fragile pieces. FYI: You can buy inexpensive folding tables from Costco.

Rubbermaid Totes are perfect for small-parts storage. For most Nova projects, the 21 x 15.5 x 9–inch size (shown) work well and happen to be the most manageable (bigger bins get pretty heavy when filled with parts).

As bits and pieces are removed from the car, tag and bag them. For smaller parts, sandwich bags are best. Bigger parts can be stored in freezer bags. If the part is too big, simply tag it using a parts tag. Include the fasteners that go with the part in the bag. If the part is too big to bag, fasten the accompanying hardware bag right to it and tag it.

Save almost all parts, even if they will be replaced eventually. A good example is a set of fasteners you know you never will use. Mark them as "replace" on the tag. Then add the respective fasteners to your "want list." This way, you can keep track of what needs replacing instead of searching for new hardware and pieces at the last minute. Keep the originals for reference in the event the replacements are not the same.

Mark "for sale" the parts you're confident you can sell and where you're positive the replacement is a perfect fit (for example, marker lamp assemblies). Eventually, you can start a dedicated Rubbermaid bin with "for sale" stuff.

Finally, a little luxury most of us can afford today is an inexpensive digital camera or a cell phone that has a decent built-in camera. Even a cheap job such as this old Nikon Coolpix is adequate. Basically, if you shoot photos along the way, it makes reassembly much easier (and in some "scratch-your-head" instances, a whole lot easier). ■

With any major project, you're going to end up with a bunch of loose parts. Keeping track of them is incredibly important. And that's what this sidebar is all about. This is a metal storage rack used just for that purpose. This is where the loose parts stay until they're needed.

A few big Rubbermaid bins go a long way toward keeping things tidy. Keep parts separated: those that are restored or rebuilt, those that need to be rebuilt, and those that you plan to sell.

Bag, tag, and ID everything. As time wears on with the project, you might not remember where every part goes on a car. You'd be surprised how much easier it is to reassemble a car when the parts are all identified.

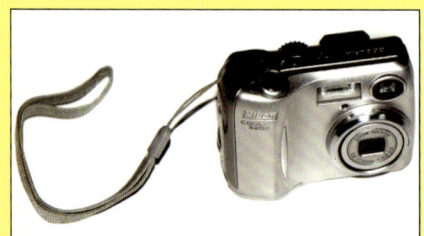

When you take something apart, it's easy to forget exactly how it went back together. An inexpensive digital camera takes great photos (better than a cell phone) and it's equally easy to download those images to your computer.

12 CHEVY NOVA 1968–1974: HOW TO BUILD AND MODIFY

get an open-end wrench onto. Place a pan under the block drain and allow gravity to do its thing. Repeat with the drain on the opposite side of the block. You might be surprised at how much coolant remains in the block after the radiator is drained.

Last on the list of stuff to drain is the transmission (as pointed out above, there's little need to drain a stick). Some automatics have a drain plug (lucky you). Others don't. Typically, the drain plug is located on the transmission pan. If there is no drain plug, the only way to drain the automatic is to remove the pan. Try to drop one corner (obviously the lower) to drain it. There could be more oil than you would expect. If there is no drain plug, expect a (big) mess.

Peel Out Pieces

You should be ready to start peeling out pieces. First things first: Remove the radiator. Remove the fan too, simply because slicing yourself with sharp objects while you're toiling away isn't fun. Pulling this stuff off also provides you with a load of elbowroom. You should also remove accessory connections at the engine. You're probably saying, "Like what?" There's more hardware here than you might think. Here's a thumbnail of what must be unhooked and/or removed, and this is just for a basic Nova (in no particular order).

Radiator and heater hoses: Usually a wire Corbin clamp or a good old-fashioned screwdriver hose clamp. If the hoses are stubborn (frozen on the fittings) you might have to cut them off.

Fuel line connections: The best place to unhook it is at the fuel pump. Unhook the line from the frame rail to the pump. This means that the pump can come out with the engine. FYI, you should use a flare wrench on the fitting.

Automatic transmission cooler lines: Such as the fuel line, you should use a flare wrench here. Years of use, heat cycles, and corrosion can make the flare nuts difficult to crack. If you've tried everything and you're finding the hex on the nut is getting rounded, try Vise-Grips. The flare nut (and, most likely, the line) will be finished, but you should be able to remove the lines. It is possible to remove the fittings at the radiator and take the lines off the trans when it's out of the car, but this only works if the engine and transmission are removed in one piece.

Power brake vacuum hose: This frequently amounts to a hose clamp on an intake manifold fitting.

Throttle linkage: Another easy job that often is either a single nut or a little clip that has to be unfastened or released. In the odd case, there's also a bracket that can be attached to the intake or carb that supports the linkage. That might have to be removed too. When it's unhooked, tie up the cable or hard linkage so that it doesn't get hung up when pulling the engine.

Transmission and kick-down linkage: Depending upon the car, you either have a column shift or floor shift linkage to remove. It doesn't matter if it's a stick or an automatic; the linkage must be removed. Some cars have a back drive/interlock setup that maintains the transmission in park or neutral for starting. That must be removed too (it's attached to the steering column). On floorshift-stick cars, you can simply remove the shifter handle, but on others where clearance is tight, the entire shifter mechanism must come out.

Here's the objective: an empty engine compartment. For this Nova project the fenders and front sheet metal remained, but after pulling the engine the subframe looked far too crusty. Everything eventually came out.

After the fluids are drained, you can remove the various hoses. Most of the time, they're relatively easy to remove. Don't concern yourself with saving hoses or hose clamps (unless you're a matching-numbers type). You can simply cut off a hose if it's stubborn.

CHAPTER 1

Before peeling out the engine, don't forget about the ground straps; a few more than just the battery cable ground are shown here. Depending upon the options, the Nova can have from almost none to three or four engine grounds.

Old, sometimes frozen hard lines (fuel line, trans cooler, etc.) are often a royal pain. If a flare wrench slips during disassembly, try clocking it another direction. If that fails, the best suggestion is to get out the Vise-Grips! Otherwise you'll have to cut off the hard line.

Speedometer cable: The cable unhooks at the transmission tailshaft. When free from the tailshaft, pull the entire thing out, or tie it out of the way.

Clutch linkage: This is pretty much a basic unbolt situation. The cross shaft hooked between the frame and the engine must be removed. Attachment clips are similar to those found on shifter rods.

Ground straps: More than one ground strap has caused an engine to hang up during removal. The straps often go from the engine to the body and/or the frame. Sometimes they're hidden between the engine and the firewall.

Battery cables: Two heavy cables run to the engine, a positive cable to the starter and a negative cable going somewhere to ground on the engine. In addition, you may find smaller wires going directly from the positive battery cable to one or more power blocks.

Starter and ignition wiring: A few wires must be removed at the ignition (coil) as well as the starter. These aren't difficult to find, but Novas usually incorporate a clamp at the back of the engine to retain the wiring harness. Remove it.

Alternator or generator wiring: A plug at the back of the alternator requires removal. These are simple clip-on devices that can be unfastened with a flat-blade screwdriver.

Sending unit wiring or hard lines: The oil pressure sender has an electrical connection that requires unhooking. Ditto with an electric water temperature gauge or idiot-light connection. For the most part, these are simple clip-on jobs that remove with a flat-blade screwdriver. If the car has mechanical gauges, you must remove the fittings on the engine. Be careful (and gentle) with mechanical water-temperature gauge fittings. They regularly bind, and during the removal process you can damage (or destroy) the gauge line. Most often, there is no easy fix and the entire gauge must be replaced.

Power steering pump: Some folks remove the hoses now, but it's often more convenient to simply remove

Unhooking the exhaust usually follows the same path as dealing with frozen hard lines. Soak the respective fasteners with PB Blast before leaving the shop at night. The next day, the bolts should be ready to cooperate. If not, an impact wrench does wonders.

CHEVY NOVA 1968–1974: HOW TO BUILD AND MODIFY

the pump from the engine and tie it aside (on the frame). With this approach, you can remove the hoses later. If you choose to remove the hoses right now, keep in mind that a flare wrench makes life a bit easier. Sometimes it takes quite a bit of force to crack open the flares.

Exhaust manifolds/headers: You must unhook the exhaust whether it's header- or manifold-equipped. With manifolds, the connections to the exhaust pipes can regularly be a pain to break free. Penetrating oil is a good idea. Allow the fasteners to soak overnight. An air-powered impact wrench is your best friend in this situation. As far as headers are concerned, you must look at your car. In some cases, after you remove the headers from the engine (at the cylinder heads), they can remain in the engine compartment (tied away so that the engine can come out). In other cases, you must remove the headers (or the bigger parts of them) before the engine can come out.

Driveshaft: The driveshaft must be removed before the engine and transmission can come out. Typically, it is mounted with four nuts on U-bolts fitted over the rear universal joint. Remove the bolts and drop the shaft downward. Tape the U-joint caps so they don't fall off. Why? If the caps fall off, you'll be chasing more than a few needle bearings across your shop floor. After it's taped, pull the shaft (front yoke and all) away from the transmission.

Transmission crossmember/mount cushion: When removing the engine and transmission in one piece, you can remove the entire transmission crossmember at this stage of the game. Some folks just remove the transmission mount cushion and pull the engine forward, but it's far easier to pull the engine and transmission with the crossmember out of the way. You need to support the transmission (a floor jack under it works). Then remove the cushion bolts along with the crossmember fasteners. Next, slide the crossmember out of the way. You can leave the floor jack in place under the transmission for the time being.

This is a major step in the disassembly process. The old lump is coming out! No real tricks are needed for this job, and as you can see; you don't even need a fancy engine leveler. The engine can come up and out. The process is the same with or without the front sheet metal installed.

Distributor and/or cap: Remove the cap or the complete distributor before pulling the engine. Why? The cap is inevitably crunched against the firewall sometime during the engine removal process.

Motor mount bolts: Take the nuts off the motor mount bolts (this is the lone bolt that joins the rubber mount to the steel mount). You can't remove the bolt completely until you take weight off it.

Break Out the Cherry Picker

The engine can be removed either with or without the transmission attached. If the nose of the Nova is still covered with sheet metal, you can get the engine and transmission out in one piece, but you must lift the entire car quite a bit to allow for clearance between the transmission tailshaft and the floor. Figure it this way: To clear something such as the radiator support, the engine and trans must come out at a big angle. If you don't have the front of the car high enough off the ground, the trans tailshaft will hit the floor and you will be stuck. The solution is to place a set of wheel ramps under the front wheels. In most cases, you have enough room to pull the engine with the transmission attached. Keep in mind that this also means the cherry picker has a much higher lift.

The other option is to pull the transmission and engine separately. Remember that a transmission can be heavy. That's why shops use transmission jacks. If you choose this

CHAPTER 1

route, you must lift the Nova quite a bit to allow the transmission and the jack to roll out from underneath. This certainly isn't insurmountable. In most cases, a set of axle stands set on "high" get the job done. It should go without saying, but no matter what, always give the car a good shake when it's on axle stands before climbing underneath. If it's going to fall off it may as well do it when you're not under the car.

To pull the transmission separately, you must support it and the back of the engine. A floor jack with an adapter works for the transmission. For the engine, use a bottle jack with a piece of 2 x 4 board sandwiched between the oil pan and the jack for support. The jack also allows you to drop the rear of the engine down a bit for extra bellhousing bolt access. With an automatic, remove the torque converter dust shield to gain access to the bolts that hold the torque converter to the flex plate. Remove those and then remove the transmission bellhousing–to–engine mount bolts. You should be able to roll the jack backward with the transmission attached, although it might take bit of persuasion (with a big flat screwdriver) to break it free. No matter how careful you are when draining an automatic, you still get fluid on the floor because there is ATF inside the torque converter that can't drain. Expect it to leak and have floor dry on hand.

For a stick-shift Nova, you don't have to remove the bellhousing. You still must support the back of the engine and the transmission. In this case, you simply remove the transmission-to-bellhousing bolts and then slide the gearbox backward. A straight pull backward is required to clear the pilot bushing and clutch assembly.

In either case (stick or automatic) you can now lower the floor jack and pull the transmission out the side of the car. You see why you need the car lifted high on axle stands to get the works out.

Pulling the engine is pretty easy after all (or most of the above) is completed. If the sheet metal is removed from the nose, it's even easier. Basically, hook up your engine hoist.

Back to the lift. After you have the chain attached, lift the engine slightly to get the weight off the motor mount bolts. Then it should be a simple matter to pull out the fasteners. With that out of the way, you can pull the engine up and forward. You need some room to get the engine out of the engine compartment. It's not uncommon to roll the car backward a bit as the engine (and transmission) comes out. When it's clear of the car, you can maneuver the engine along with the transmission easily with a cherry picker.

Give yourself a big pat on the back. You've pretty much mechanically stripped the car.

The Nova engine came out with the Powerglide attached. Because the front sheet metal (including the rad support) was already out of the way, pulling the engine and trans in one piece wasn't difficult.

Right about now is a good time to give yourself some credit. Your Nova project is getting a lot closer to being completely stripped and ready to rebuild and rework. This car was stripped clean, ready for new paint. You don't always need to go this far in the disassembly process.

CHAPTER 2

GETTING FRAMED

Getting down the road or getting down the dragstrip isn't just a matter of building power, bolting it in, and pointing the car in the right direction. The rear-suspension setup and balance of the power train are certainly critical, but the part of the Nova that seldom gets respect is the front end. Sure, you can go with a standard setup procedure, but with the technology available, you can bolt together a pretty trick front end (no fabrication necessary) to make your Chevy quicker, faster, and able to handle and stop better (on the street or the strip). Follow along to see how to set up a Nova front end for street and strip duty.

Bare Bones

You have to start somewhere. Unless you're lucky, the subframe in your Nova is the usual crusty mess. It's a good idea to strip everything out of the subframe: A-arms, motor mounts, steering linkage, sway bar, springs, shocks, steering box, etc., and then drop it out of the car. It's a matter of removing six bolts: four subframe-to-body bolts and two subframe-to-radiator support bolts.

With the subframe naked and out of the car, drag it outside, coat it in degreaser, and then pressure wash it. Scrape off any undercoating. Here, a propane torch, a putty scraper, and a brace of wire brushes (in varying sizes) work wonders. After the grease, grime, and undercoating are gone, consider grinding the factory welds and weld splatter. FYI: this is a dirty job, but the only way to get it done is to grind it with an angle grinder and a die grinder, and then finish it

It's no secret the subframe on a 1968–1974 Nova is fundamentally the same as the subframe on a 1967–1969 Camaro. That means huge aftermarket support: A-arms, springs, shocks, steering, brakes, and so on.

You don't have to completely remove the front sheet metal on your Nova to get at the subframe, but it sure does make it easier to work on. The condition you see here is typical. This car sat unused for decades.

CHAPTER 2

The back four body mount bolts are easy to access. Note that the OEM body mounts are still intact in this photo. The other two body mount bolts (total of six) are actually radiator support mounts.

Stripped! The subframe can be totally stripped by using hand tools, but access to a good air compressor and impact gun makes disassembly super easy.

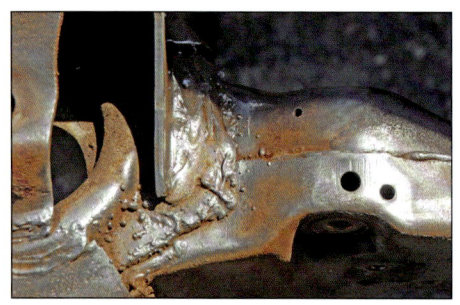

This welding mess is typical of these cars. The robot welders used back then weren't exactly sophisticated, and, as a result, welding splatter is everywhere.

This is the same area on the subframe from a slightly different angle. The welding splatter is removed with a combination of a 4½-inch angle grinder and a small air-powered die grinder. Sharp edges should be taken into consideration too.

This subframe is back from the powder coating shop and fit with the top half of a Detroit Speed solid body mount set. As you can see from this close-up, time spent prepping the subframe with a grinding wheel is well worth it. Copy this. Your hands will appreciate the lack of sharp edges!

off with a wire wheel. It works, but it takes time. You can also grind down sharp edges on these subframes (there are a lot of them). Why bother? To minimize the chance of tearing up your skin while working on the car. When that is complete, it's ready to be sandblasted. From there, it can go to your favorite powder coater, or you can paint it.

Speaking of powder coating, its reputation is that of a remarkable coating. Although accurate for the most part, it's not enchanted and it's certainly not without faults.

After you paint or powder coat the subframe, you can reunite it with the body. You can use OEM-style rubber cushion mounts or solid mounts. Solid body mounts eliminate flex between the body and subframe connection. The overall performance of the car improves with this extra chassis stiffness.

The accompanying photos show the use of Detroit Speed mounts. They're CNC-machined from billet aluminum and hard-coated (not bright anodized). Hard coating resists corrosion that occurs between steel and aluminum surfaces. CNC-machined stainless-steel bevel washers are included. They're also available in 1/2-inch-height sizes. Half-height mounts lower the car (obviously), but they also bring their own issues (dimensions for things such as the rag joint stack up). Nova applications have two cowl area bolts that are 1/2 inch longer than a Camaro's, and they also include a special spacer that fits above the first body mount at the cowl. The kits are complete with a similar set of solid radiator core support mounts, and the optional stainless-steel ARP bolt kits are available. Solid mounts

Detail Plating and Coating

When you're building your Nova, quite a few parts lend themselves to chrome plating, cad plating, zinc dichromate plating, and powder coating. When it comes to chrome (and its close cousin, nickel plate), the respective processes are much the same.

Chrome Plating

Almost any metal can be chrome plated, including "pot metal," common carbon steel, and even aluminum. Prior to plating, the metal must be completely cleaned, most often in a hot alkaline immersion. Previously plated parts (such as bumpers) must be "un-plated," which involves immersion in a tank containing sulfuric acid. Direct current is applied and the old plate is drawn into a lead cathode. Rusty pieces are placed in a tank containing hydrochloric acid (sometimes referred to as the "acid pickling" tank). Unfortunately, the extensive use of corrosive and caustic chemicals can have a drastic effect on die-cast components. If handled without care, they simply disappear into the acid bath.

After stripping, the component is buffed. The buffing procedure smooths the surface, removing high and low spots, and gives the surface a high luster, or sheen. This is the key to good chrome plating.

After buffing, the component is copper electro-plated. The part is centered in a tank containing a mixture of cuprous cyanide, sodium cyanide, and sodium thiosulfate. Heated to 104 degrees F, the tank is charged with DC current. Depending upon the construction or condition of the part, it must remain in this environment approximately 20 minutes (longer if it is heavily pitted or previously corroded).

The part is removed from the tank, completely rinsed, and re-polished. The buffing or polishing stage is again critical.

The next stop is the nickel tank. The most common "bath" is called the Watts Composition, which is a mixture of nickel chloride, nickel sulfate, and boric acid, as well as other small composites. Approximately 30 minutes later, the part emerges from the nickel tank. Re-polishing is not necessary, and for the most part, not possible at this stage because the nickel plate is very thin (on the order of .001 inch thick). The part is rinsed and readied for a final bath in the chrome tank.

The part looks perfect after leaving the nickel tank. The use of chrome is for protection; it prevents the nickel from tarnishing. The chemical solution in the chrome tank includes sulfuric acid and chromic acid. The final chrome plate is extremely thin (approximately 40 millionths of an inch).

Cad and Zinc Plating

What about cad plating or zinc dichromate plating? Cad plating provides a dull gold or silver color to your parts and slightly better protection from corrosion than zinc plate. It was much more common in the past, but due to the toxicity of the process (and, consequently, the environmental issues), it isn't used much. It's easy to confuse cad with zinc plate.

Zinc dichromate plating is composed of a thin coat of zinc applied mechanically or by way of electroplating. A chemical chromate conversion is used in the process, which can either be a clear with a blue tinge, or iridescent yellow. The yellow or "gold" on cadmium-plated parts is solid, while zinc plate has a sort of rainbow effect.

Decorative Plating

Not all is bliss with plated parts (and this is particularly important when it comes to high-performance applications). Decorative plating creates a byproduct called "hydrogen

Powder coating something such as a subframe makes for a neat, clean finish. This coating method provides protection for the inside of the component as well as the outside. Just keep in mind that while powder coating is durable, it's not "bulletproof"!

Although this 1969 Nova front bumper has been detailed and assembled with park lamps and bumper brackets, it has also been re-plated. In the process, the bumper is pickled in a sulfuric acid bath. Plenty of corrosive chemicals are used in the plating process, and, as a result, costs for chrome plating have escalated over the years.

Detail Plating and Coating CONTINUED

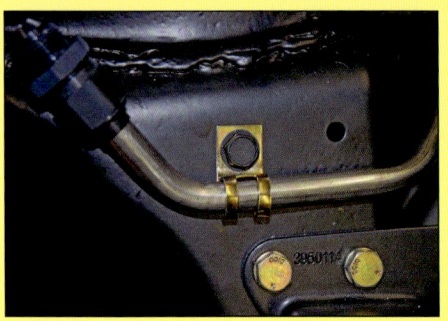

The AN (aircraft) bolts at the bottom of the photo (on the motor mount) are factory zinc-plated. The clamps have been re-plated in zinc. Zinc plating differs from cadmium plating in that the finish has a sort of rainbow effect.

embrittlement." Fasteners above SAE Grade 5 are susceptible to hydrogen embrittlement in the cleaning and coating processes (particularly the electroplating aspect). Because of the various forms of acid involved in the prep stages of chrome plating, a hydrogen byproduct is released into the tank; it is absorbed by the metal part being cleaned. When a current is applied to a parent metal, it too can create brittleness. As the name implies, hydrogen embrittlement causes the parent metal to become brittle, and eventually it can crack under stress.

Certain methods of heat-treating can lessen the chance of hydrogen embrittlement. The most common involves baking the chrome-plated part in a special oven at approximately 375 to 400 degrees F for a predetermined length of time. Theory is that the heat pulls the free hydrogen atoms from the metal pores, reducing the chance of embrittlement. It is clear that decorative plating of load bearing members isn't desirable. Springs, stressed suspension components, steering parts, and so on should never be chrome plated.

Powder Coating

Fair enough, but what if you need some form of tough external protection for various pieces on your Nova? Consider powder coating. Powder coating involves the use of special plastic or epoxy powders sprayed onto a subject component with a special spray gun. The component is given a negative charge (grounded). As the powder is discharged through the spray gun, it receives a positive electrical charge. Next, the component is baked in a proprietary oven (set at 300 to 400 degrees F) for approximately 25 minutes so that the powder solidifies. By the way, stripping (as in Redi-Strip), sandblasting, or glass beading a component produces a squeaky clean surface for the powder to adhere.

The real beauty of powder coating is its inherent durability. Powder coatings are almost impervious to automotive chemical spills, except for brake fluid. Powder coating has gained a reputation as a remarkable coating, but it's not infallible. We've all heard the sales pitch claiming you can smack a coated part with a hammer and it doesn't chip. Fascinating, but not exactly true. Powder coating is durable, but not invincible! It also has drawbacks. For example, it cannot be used on a part that cannot withstand the baking process. The baking process can distort certain critical machined surfaces (in the same way a heat treatment can). In addition, some items may have to be re-machined after powder coating. ■

What's up here? This is an "inventory" photo. If you send out a bunch of parts for powder coating or chroming, it's an extremely good idea to take a photo of all the pieces. This way, if something goes missing (and it seems like it always does), you can identify it.

Almost every major component has been powder coated on this Nova subframe. You find that it's often better not to have some items powder coated. Spindles are a good example. They get beat up during the assembly process and chip easily. Sometimes, good old-fashioned rattle-can paint is hard to beat!

install the same as cushion jobs, but you must use anti-seize on all stainless bolt threads. You'll be cursing yourself if you don't.

When the subframe is installed, do not torque to specs. The subframe must be squared in the car. Here's a quick way to do it at home: At the rear of the body (ahead of the front spring eye) is a body crossmember with two trammel alignment holes. They're easy to spot: They measure approximately 5/16 inch in diameter and they're near the rocker panel. With the car level to the floor, drop a plumb line down from the center of each of these trammel holes. Mark that point with a piece of tape on the floor. Beside the forward body mount point on the subframe is an extra hole (see the photos). Drop a plumb line down from the center of this hole. Mark that location on the floor with another piece of tape. Measure front to back on both sides. Then measure diagonally from the passenger-side rear trammel hole to the driver-side plumb line mark. Do the same from the driver-side rear trammel hole to the passenger-side subframe plumb line. What you need to do is get the front-to-back and diagonal measurements as close to the same as possible. That will mean that the subframe is square in the car. Keep in mind these are old production line cars and might be out 1/8 inch or so over 6 feet. When done, you can torque to specs (typically 90 ft-lbs) and move forward on the build.

The Detroit Speed body mount package includes an upper and a lower mount manufactured from aluminum. The spacer on the left is a factory Chevrolet piece that has been powder coated. It mounts above the top "biscuit," next to the body mount bracket. Detroit Speed includes a thick, hard-anodized aluminum spacer with its Nova body mount kits. This is the primary difference between a Camaro and a Nova from a subframe mount perspective. Camaros don't use the spacer.

This hole next to the body mount opening in the subframe is for a factory alignment pin that was used during assembly to mate the body to the subframe. A large punch (or the jack handle from the car) can be used to replicate the initial body-subframe alignment process. It's also a good point to measure from when squaring the subframe.

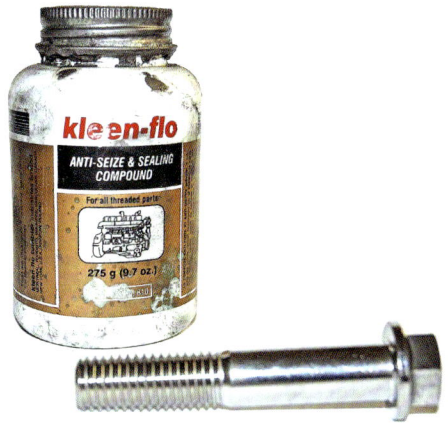

Anytime you use a stainless-steel fastener, you must use anti-seize; otherwise, the dissimilar materials will gaul. If they do gaul, the fastener will freeze up. You might be surprised at how difficult they are to remove after they have seized.

What's with the "X" on the floor? The plumb line has been dropped from a rear body trammel point. It's a point from which to measure diagonally to the opposite side of the car when squaring the subframe to the body.

Mounting Points

The upper A-arms are held in place with a set of studs. They have knurls near the head, like those on a wheel stud. Most used jobs are well past their "best before" date. New examples are the way to go. Classic Industries and others sell them, and they're easy enough to install: Slip them in from the back and lightly tap the head with a hammer and punch to seat them. When you install the upper A-arm, the nuts pull the studs into place as you tighten them.

It's a good time to install the engine frame mounts. On a Nova, the hardware for the mounts proves to be far easier to install before the

CHAPTER 2

With the subframe apart, it's a good time (and a very good idea) to replace the A-arm studs on your Nova. These studs resemble wheel studs: hex head on one end with a knurl under the head. These examples are from Classic Industries.

Another tip is to install the engine frame mounts before the lower A-arms are installed on your Nova subframe. This is because the nuts on the backside are more difficult to reach with the lower A-arms installed. FYI: Those are AN (aircraft) bolts you see here.

Three bolts are used to install the stock Nova steering box. The box is actually threaded. Note the thick washers used under the bolt heads. They're required because of the fastener torque. This car includes a new Delphi manual steering box from Classic Industries.

A-arms go on. To learn more about the mounts, go to Chapter 7, Engine Swaps, Mounts and Hardware. You'll be glad you did.

Consider how you'd like to steer your car. Sure, you can swap to a rack and pinion arrangement. It offers a lot of advantages, but a rack swap isn't exactly a bolt-in. Plenty of Novas were factory-fit with power steering. If you don't want or need the heft or complexity, consider replacing it with a manual box. Classic Industries offers brand-new Delphi steering boxes with a simple bolt-in arrangement. Remove three bolts from the frame, drop out the old steering box, and reinstall the new box. Unfortunately, manual steering box pitman arms aren't exactly wrecking yard parts anymore. You need a good reproduction. Before you install it, center the steering box (basically, mark the shaft, count the turns lock to lock, and turn it back halfway). Point the wheels straight ahead, and only then should you install the pitman. It needs big torque to tighten to specs (140 ft-lbs according to a Chevy service manual). It's a good idea to use a new lock washer here.

Next up is the idler arm. It's a good time to replace it. Note in the photos, the idler was installed with 6AN fasteners (lock nuts, bolts, washers). The bolts are "backward," heads to the engine compartment side. This adds clearance for headers (and hands) within the engine compartment.

A-Arms

It should be no secret that bolt-in A-arms for the nose of a purpose-built car are readily available from plenty of sources. Why the need for aftermarket upper and lower control arms? Simple: The stock front suspension components bolted to the nose of your Nova as it rolled down the Detroit assembly line were never optimized for quarter-mile use or for burning corners. Vehicle manufacturers were typically conservative when it came to built-in caster. Chevrolet was certainly no exception.

Let's stop right here for a minute. What's caster? Caster is the backward

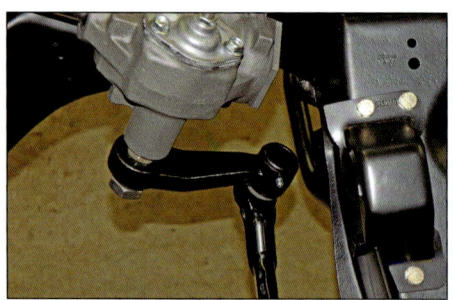

The steering should be centered, and then you can install the pitman arm. The pitman arm and the pitman arm shaft are splined, and they can only mate one way. A lock washer is between the pinion nut and the pinion arm. Torque for the nut is honking at 140 ft-lbs.

Nova idler arms are easy to install via two large access holes on the outside of the frame for the fasteners. Here, two more AN bolts have been used and, as pointed out in the text, they're actually installed backward. See the text for more information (there's a good reason for doing it this way).

The selection of A-arms out there is absolutely massive, ranging from reproduction factory-style pieces to road components to drag race hardware. These A-arms are TRZ Motorsports components from the drag racing end of the equation. They offer much improved geometry when compared to the stock A-arms.

Obviously, this is not a Nova, but look at the wheel camber! You can well imagine how the landing feels through the steering wheel on this Chevelle. Camber change on a vintage Nova is very similar. And it's not a good feature.

or forward tilt of the spindle as you view it from the side of the wheel and tire. When caster is positive, the spindle tilts backward, which places weight behind the tire contact patch. If the caster is negative, the top of the spindle is tilted forward, which places weight in front of the tire contact patch. Caster is expressed in degrees and measures the amount the centerline of the spindle is tilted from true vertical. For the most part, OEM caster figures seldom go beyond –3/4 degree (negative), but in almost all drag race applications, positive caster is required. Why? Consider positive caster a way to "self-center" the steering. Ponder bicycles for a minute. A comfy long-distance touring bike has a fork that's kicked out. This fork "kick out" provides a big chunk of positive caster. In turn, the bicycle experiences a significant amount of directional stability. Then look at a mountain bike. Here the fork is much closer to vertical. The benefit of the mountain bike is that it can turn very quickly; however, it definitely lacks directional stability. The bottom line is, you can easily ride a touring bicycle with your hands off the handlebars. It's not that easy with a mountain bike.

Camber is the tilt of the wheel at the top (tilting in or tilting out). Camber is expressed and measured in degrees and looks at the tilt of the wheel from true vertical. If the wheel and tire package tilt out at the top, it means that the camber is positive. If the top of the wheel and tire package tilt in, camber is negative. The idea behind camber is to keep the tire planted squarely on the pavement. This creates maximum front tire grip. In theory, zero degrees of camber seems like a good idea, but that isn't always the case for Novas that were originally production-line cars (not purpose-built as in a tube frame car). Most production line cars require different camber figures (while at rest) so that good grip and tire wear are maintained as the car travels down the road. Typically, a car with a small amount of negative camber exhibits better dragstrip handling characteristics without killing the tire.

A typical stock 1968–1972 Nova has a factory caster specification of ± 1/2 degree. To adjust the caster in a stock Nova, transfer shims front to rear or rear to front. If you transfer one shim (1/32 inch) from the rear bolt to the front it decreases positive caster by approximately 1/2 degree. The opposite (transferring one shim from the front bolt to the rear bolt) increases positive caster by approximately 1/2 degree. That same vintage Nova has a camber specification of 1/4 degree, ± 1/2 degree. To set camber you must add or subtract an equal number of shims from the front and the rear bolts on the A-arm cross shaft. One shim (again, 1/32 inch) at each location changes the camber by approximately 1/5 degree. Adding a shim at each end decreases positive camber.

Camber and caster are usually set together. In a high-performance application, you will probably run out of room to properly adjust the caster and camber on a car with stock A-arms. This becomes very apparent when you try to get a reasonable (for

CHAPTER 2

Camber and caster are set by way of shims on the top A-arm cross shaft. More positive caster leads to better tracking at speed. You add and subtract shims to get to the desired settings. You can only do so much with the stock setup or with an offset cross shaft (as shown here). In the end though, you usually end up with a compromise in the settings.

Aftermarket A-arms such as these uppers from TRZ offer a big benefit with improved caster built in. These examples allow for 5 to 7 degrees (depending upon the setup). Similar A-arms from Detroit Speed and a few others also offer improved caster.

drag racing) caster number in a 1968–1974 Nova. To get something such as 5 or 6 (or even 7) degrees of caster is difficult, if not impossible. That's one big reason why an aftermarket A-arm package is a serious problem solver for drag race applications. When TRZ Motorsports engineered the control arms shown in the photos, they built in 5 to 7 degrees of positive caster. TRZ points out, "Caster varies on cars that have different ride heights. If the rear of the car is higher than the front, it then has less caster. In some cases people can only get 5 degrees or so due to variances in the frames, prior accident damage, front frame damage, or the rear of the car sitting too high." It all means it's possible to come up with way more positive caster than stock. With a lot of caster your car won't like backing up so much, but it sure will track well at speed.

The 1968–1974 Nova has considerable camber change as the front end goes through its travel. In an all-out drag car, you can really see the change as the car dangles the front end in a wheelstand. But the situation worsens when the car drops back down to the tarmac. The take-off and flight part of a wheelstand is easy. Landing isn't. The result is often a series of hairline cracks on factory A-arms. That's a big reason quality materials are important when it comes to front suspension hardware. The same applies to the welds and component finishing. A-arms are no place for lousy material choices. Or for backyard welding.

Speaking of welding and materials, the TRZ upper and lower control arms shown in the accompanying photos are manufactured from 4130 chrome moly tubing and they're TIG welded. Depending upon the model of car you have, they can reduce the weight of the control arm package (upper and lower) by 15 pounds per side; that's a total diet plan of 30 pounds if you're keeping track. And half of it is unsprung.

Another (huge) part of the front-end equation involves the front bushing choice. You find some A-arms out there that make use of bushings that just don't work for drag racing or other forms of motorsports. If you've been around the block with race car suspension, you've discovered that the road-style urethane bushings have a tendency to seize or stick (or as Penske and other big-time suspension folks refer to it, "stiction"). When the suspension system in a race or performance car has this stiction, it means the shock can't do its job effectively.

A-arms that make use of a bearing (rod end) or use some form of Delrin bushing (Delrin, by the way, is a form of very hard "plastic" material) are far better suited to high-performance applications. Delrin does not have

Aside from geometry, what do you look for in aftermarket A-arms? Material choice is important, as is material thickness. Weld quality is critical (check out the high-quality welds on these TRZ A-arms). Bushing and ball joint selection is equally important.

GETTING FRAMED

Dialing in Caster, Camber and Toe for Drag Duty

If you decide to drag race your Nova, try adding more caster. Keep an eye on the car's toe-change through its travel while the car is jacked. Toe-in change must be kept to a minimum. The very last thing you need is toe-out as the front end travels. Before you do a wheel alignment, place weight in the driver's seat that is equal to the driver's weight. Shot bags or weight-lifting equipment work. Be sure to top the fuel tank with the appropriate level of gasoline. Set the tire pressures to the level you normally race with (i.e., high pressure on the nose, and lower pressures at the rear). With the car on the alignment rack, jack the nose up to duplicate a normal race "attitude" (an inch or two seems to be about right). Jack and block the back of the car to compensate for the height of the front-wheel-alignment turn tables. The car is ready for the alignment.

Remember that every car is slightly different, but here are the OEM alignment figures.

Because every car in competition is different, use the following basic guidelines for your Nova wheel alignment.

- Camber should be set at zero; you should try to keep the front wheels straight up and down.
- Toe-in should be as close to zero as possible on a production line chassis. Watch for toe-out while the nose is in the air.
- Caster should be between 3 and 6 degrees. As the speed of the car increases, the need for more caster also increases. This stabilizes your car at speed. You likely need aftermarket A-arms to gain this much caster. ■

Stock Production Line Wheel Alignment Specs

	Typical	Nova
Caster (degree)	1/2	± 1/2
Camber (degree)	1/4	± 1/2
Total Toe (inch)	1/8	± 1/4

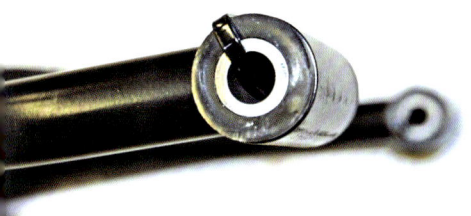

This is a Delrin bushing insert. Delrin is a hard plastic type of material that is naturally self-lubricating. Note that a steel sleeve is pressed inside the bushing, and that's where the lower attachment bolt passes through.

cold flow tendencies, and, as a result, maintains alignment over time. It is also oil-impregnated. When it encounters friction, it releases its own lubricant. That's what makes it a good choice for high-performance applications. In construction, quality Delrin bushings are multi-piece affairs. For example, the bushing layout found in the TRZ lower A-arms (shown in the accompanying photos) consists of a chrome-moly housing.

Inside is a Delrin insert, and inside that (where the bolts pass through) is another metal sleeve. The way it's designed, the Delrin also acts as a thrust washer, which controls the fore and aft movement of the A-arm without binding.

The TRZ upper A-arms are engineered with 1/2-inch rod ends that mount on the respective cross shafts (instead of bushings). There is (obviously) no stiction with a rod end, and in terms of strength, a typical 1/2 x 1/2–inch rod end has a radial static load rating of more than 6,500 pounds (each!). You never experience those sorts of forces in any high-performance application. There is zero deflection without any sort of suspension bind. Some of the pieces aren't really dedicated drag-race components. Some are road-race inspired. A few of them can pack plenty of sophistication.

A big issue with any A-arm (stock or aftermarket) is controlling suspension travel. It's no secret that, for quarter-mile applications, huge suspension travel can be a good thing on low-powered cars or on greasy tracks, but if the horsepower wick is turned up and/or there's some bite in the track surface, adjustability in the A-arms becomes rather important. In those cases, a means to control the travel so that you can limit a wheel-stand is important.

Most early GM production-line cars (including Novas) feature a system of limiting the downward movement of the front control arms. In a race car (especially a low-horsepower race car), you need as much front-end travel as possible. Front-end travel in these vehicles can be increased without the addition of ball joint extensions (which in most sanctioning body rule books are illegal). Chevrolet used a rubber snubber mounted to the upper control arm to limit A-arm travel. If the snubber is trimmed, the front end of the car has more travel. Keep trimming the snubber until the car slows down (of course, in some cases, you must remove the snubber altogether). If you trim too much of the snubber away, swap the snubber for a common traction-bar component. When trimming snubbers, watch the brake flex line. You can go too far!

Certain limitations come into play as well. If you need to reduce the travel, you have no choice but to re-install a new snubber. Moreover, at the best of times, that stock snubber is too short for a high-power car running on a track with "teeth." The aftermarket provides fixes for this (some involve cables attached to the chassis; some are based upon steel snubbers), but with some of the drag race–inspired A-arms (such the TRZ jobs in the photos), it's not an issue. They already come assembled with adjustable travel limiters (basically, a Grade-8 bolt). The bolts thread into a boss on the upper A-arm and you adjust the travel you need for your car on the track you're running from the topside. It's a simple nut/jam nut operation. And you can do the tuning with a couple of common 3/4-inch wrenches.

Virtually all aftermarket road race/Pro Touring–style A-arms for Novas come equipped with mounting tabs for front sway bars. In drag racing, corners don't count. The front bars restrict control arm movement, effectively linking both sides of the front suspension. Disconnecting or removing the sway bar allows the suspension to rise and fall rapidly; that, in turn, translates to better launch capabilities. The solution is simple for Novas that see dragstrip duty: Dump the sway bar.

When contemplating aftermarket A-arms, consider a couple of other factors: one, the cross shaft found on the upper A-arm. The many manufacturers of A-arms don't rely upon the stock (heavy) steel shaft. Instead, they use a cross shaft that is milled from billet aluminum. It shouldn't be an issue because the loads experienced in a street/strip car aren't sufficient to compromise the structure, even when you take regular wheelstands and, particularly, landings into consideration.

Another consideration when buying aftermarket A-arms (drag race or otherwise), is the respective

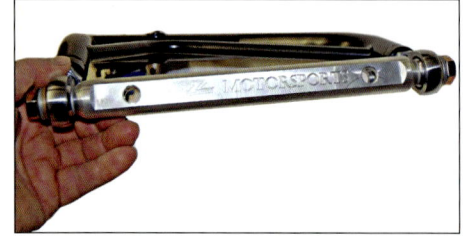

The upper cross shaft found on many aftermarket A-arms is machined from billet aluminum. Aluminum can be used here, because the loads experienced aren't that great. Note too the use of aircraft-style (three-piece) rod ends rather than bushings. They eliminate stiction and make large geometry adjustments rather simple (although you can still use conventional shims for minor adjustments).

ball joints. Extended ball joints are available today for stock A-arms, but they're not required in aftermarket A-arms simply because they already incorporate geometry that has been "fixed." You should be able to service a good aftermarket A-arm easily (without going out of your way to find replacement parts). It's a good idea to use aftermarket A-arms built to accept replacement ball joints for the given car (for example, 1970

In this photo, you can see the large Grade 8 bolt protruding through the upper A-arm. This is a suspension travel limiter. The idea here is to have control over how much the suspension travels at the dragstrip. Cars with big power don't need as much suspension travel as low-horsepower cars, and this bolt provides the necessary adjustment.

Don't overlook the obvious when shopping for aftermarket A-arms. Service items such as easily replaceable ball joints are important. Here, the upper joint is a conventional bolt-in and it installs with four simple fasteners.

Longer Ball Joints and Taller Spindles

Some ball joints are available with a longer-than-stock pin length to correct roll centers. These longer-pin ball joints feature hardened pins in stock-type housings; they are not rebuildable. Fair enough. What is the advantage?

The Nova (along with its Camaro brethren) suffers from a too-short spindle. This prevents the tire from cambering properly when powering through a corner (the top of the tire cambers out too long before it starts pulling in). In turn, this causes the tire to scrub on the outside instead of running on the complete tire contact patch.

Tall ball joints add spindle height by increasing the distance between the two pivot points. Essentially, they're a quick way to get 1/2 inch or so additional spindle height.

Taller upper ball joints have no effect upon the ride height of the car because the upper arms are not weight bearing.

On the other hand, a taller spindle has a higher overall height than the factory spindle. This is designed to relocate the upper ball joint pickup points to achieve better front-end geometry. The taller spindle height improves handling by modifying the camber curve. The result is a negative camber gain during suspension compression (when carving a corner). Some aftermarket spindles (for example, a Belltech) are simply lowered; they're not taller. You can find taller-than-stock spindles without any drop or you can get spindles that are both dropped and tall (for example, certain spindles from Detroit Speed).

It is possible to purchase longer-than-stock upper ball joints for vintage Novas. The purpose is to fix the camber curve. You don't gain much spindle height with the swap (perhaps 1/2 inch total), but for these cars, every little bit helps.

Nova A-arms use replacement ball joints for a 1970 Nova). Service parts are available just about anywhere.

What about spring types? I look at springs in Chapter 5, but you can source A-arms in two configurations: one with a stock lower-spring pocket and another for coil-over shock applications. For Novas, you need to make a modification to the shock mount on the upper frame for most coil-overs. TRZ offers a kit just for that application. If you're using a stock-style spring, the A-arms are a simple bolt-in.

Before leaving A-arms, the final thing you should think about (particularly when it comes to aftermarket A-arms) is the lower shock absorber mount. The problem here is the size of some aftermarket shock absorber bodies, particularly the adjusters. Plenty of these aftermarket shocks have big adjusters on either side of the shock, and they don't fit inside stock A-arms. Many aftermarket A-arms have a shock opening in the lower A-arm that needs to be ground away so that you can fit the shock body. That's not the end of it, either. In many cases, after you get the shock in, you cannot access the shock adjuster (which is a wee bit counterproductive). Look for A-arms with the largest possible opening for the adjusters to pass through, and where the inner pocket that surrounds the shock has been relieved to free space for the adjuster knobs. Finally, look for lower shock mounts that are designed with built-in weld-nuts. This will eliminate the need to stick a wrench inside the control arm to fasten the shock.

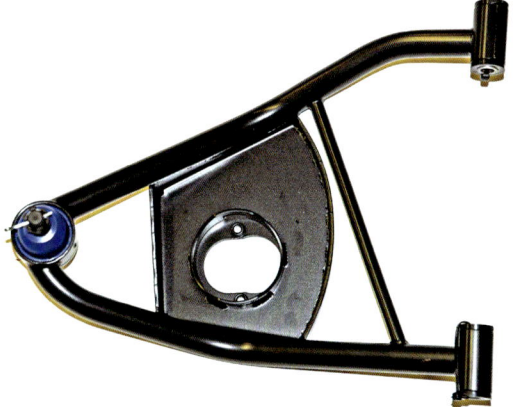

Downstairs, this A-arm from TRZ is engineered to work with a factory coil spring. You can specify coil-over shocks for many A-arms, but keep in mind that coil-overs do not store as much spring energy as a stock spring (which is important for a relatively heavy car such as a Nova when traversing the quarter-mile). Note too, the shock opening is large enough to accept an aftermarket shock with external adjuster knobs.

CHAPTER 2

Installing the Rest

Aftermarket A-arms install just like factory parts; they bolt right in. You need a spring compressor for the coil springs (more on spring selection in Chapter 5). Always watch where the spring is pointed when you're compressing it. Always heavily lube the threads on the spring compressor too, and always make it a practice to heavily lube the threads during the tightening process. Finally, watch the spring compressor to make sure it's centered in the spring. They can dance around and move off-center while tightening. In most cases, the rod of the spring compressor must protrude through the upper shock stud hole in the subframe during installation. If it's off-center in the spring, it won't fit and you'll have to start all over again (it can also slip when compressing the spring).

Inspect the spindle carefully. Over time they can develop fractures, and of course, they can wear, particularly on bearing surfaces. For tie rod ends, source new inners and outers. To join them, consider using solid tie-rod sleeves. The setup from Hotchkiss includes machined hex bodies (so you can easily turn them

New tie rod ends are a must in any high-performance build. These are from Classic Industries. Another important (but seemingly minor) piece is the tie rod sleeve. The factory pieces are flimsy. Period. These billet jobs from Hotchkiss make toe adjustment easy; they're also beefy.

This is an overall look at a finished built-for-performance Nova subframe. Almost every critical fastener was replaced with either a new reproduction or a new AN component. It's not difficult to copy this plan, but it does take time to complete.

In this example, the spindle is a stock Chevrolet piece. Be doubly cautious when it comes to OEM spindles. Some can fatigue to the point that they develop stress cracks. It's not a bad idea to have them Magnafluxed.

In this side view of the same finished subframe you see that several fasteners and brackets were either zinc plated or powder coated. Those treatments might not make your Nova quicker or faster, but they sure make it easier to work on.

GETTING FRAMED

Solid Body 149.99

Eliminate the Back Drive

Every Nova 1969–on was fitted with a steering-mounted ignition switch along with a steering column/ignition key interlock/back drive (of some sort) for the transmission. What this did was ensure the car was in park or reverse before it was started. In turn, the linkage insured a moveable collar on the steering column was positioned fully counterclockwise. Only then could the ignition key be installed or removed. When you moved the shifter, the collar on the steering column moved. It meant that you couldn't remove the ignition key while the car was being driven.

Fair enough, but the maze of mechanical links also fouls up a header installation in a big way and, for the most part, doesn't allow for the install of any headers. The same applies to the install of an aftermarket floor shifter. That's the conundrum. So how do you make it all work together? It's not that difficult. What has been done since the beginning of time is to disable the interlock. Simply remove the back drive completely and then wire up the remaining interlock rod(s) on the base of the steering column so that the collar on the column can't move from the counterclockwise position.

Drill a small hole in the column jacket (as shown in the accompanying photo), and then wire the column back-drive lever in one spot. The wire used in the example is stainless-steel aircraft safety wire. Double up the wire and twist it as shown. This ensures the collar on the column doesn't move. The only catch is that you can start the car without it being in the appropriate gear. Just remember that.

Vintage Novas (and most vintage Chevys, for that matter) use a back drive system that links the steering column to the transmission linkage. The trouble is, it fouls up a header installation. The obvious cure is to eliminate it. The key is to secure the column so that the steering column collar (at the ignition key switch) doesn't flop around without the back drive. This photo shows a good way to wire it in one place.

to adjust toe with a basic open-end wrench) and matching jam nuts. They're powder-coated gloss black and install the same as stock.

Frame Connectors

The Chevy Novas we love were built as simple machines. Carving corners or traversing the quarter-mile with the performance seen today wasn't even a twinkle in the engineer's eye when these things came off the assembly line. The truth is, these old cars, with their big honking bolt-on front subframe mated to a unit construction body were pretty much flexi-fliers. After all, that big front subframe was simply bolted to the body in only four spots. Making it worse was the fact that the four bushings attached by those four bolts deteriorated with age and use. When you pounded on the cars, the bodies moved around. Sometimes they moved around a lot! So much so that door and trunk gaps could permanently change. Doors often didn't close correctly. You might even have seen some with a heavily cracked and buckled floor pan. It's not good.

Here's a look at a set of Competition Engineering bolt-in frame connectors installed in a 1970 Nova. They're a relatively straightforward bolt-in.

Detroit Speed 199.99

The front of the connector slides into the OEM subframe, as shown here. To install it, you must loosen the rear subframe bolts. When that's done, you can slide the front of the connector in place.

CHAPTER 2

Detroit Speed's Hydroformed Subframe

As Nova enthusiasts, we're lucky because the subframe on our favorite car is pretty much identical to the one used by the incredibly popular first-gen Camaro. For all intents and purposes, the subframes are a direct interchange. That means a lot of high-quality, high-tech aftermarket components are out there. If you're set to burn corners, a great choice is the subframe from Detroit Speed. What sets the Detroit Speed subframe apart from the others is the fact the rails are hydroformed. Hydroforming is a process that uses fluid to help form the metal. First, a blank section of tubing is cut to length and then bent to the approximate shape of the subframe rail. The blank is placed into the lower half of a die situated in a huge-by-large hydraulic press. The blank is pressurized with a mix of water, lubricant, and corrosion inhibitor. The press closes the upper half of the die. A mix of external pressure (from the press) and internal pressure (the water mix inside the blank) forms the rail. No heat is added. This creates a subframe rail that has constant wall thickness, is free of wrinkles, and is not compromised by added heat.

After it is hydroformed, Detroit Speed welds in custom-stamped front crossmember assemblies and adds the respective mounts for the front suspension system, along with provisions for the rack-and-pinion steering. Those mounts allow for the installation of their TIG-welded upper and lower A-arms that work in concert with their own forged front spindle. The upper and lower control arms are fitted with Delrin bushings and, as you can see, they're heavily gusseted. The overall geometry allows for more positive camber than stock.

Springs are of the coil-over variety while the accompanying shocks can be single adjustable, double adjustable, or remote canister types. Spring rates are worked out for you depending upon the engine combination you select. The steering is a specifically tuned power rack package, while the sway bar is a splined NASCAR-style job. Sway bar bushings are formed of custom composite Delrin. The package accepts any stock or aftermarket C6 Corvette brake package. It mandates 17-inch-or-larger front wheels (minimum inside diameter of 16.250 inches).

Detroit Speed has thought of everything that a corner-carving Nova enthusiast wants in a high-tech subframe. It's not inexpensive, but the quality is outstanding. If you take that complete, preassembled route, you have only four body mounts and two radiator support mounts to remove and replace to install the subframe. It can't get much simpler.

The back of the connector sandwiches in between the rear subframe and the forward leaf spring perch. You must trim the connector slightly to clear the perch.

This is a good look at how the connector fits the Nova. It's unobtrusive; you really have to look to see it (or know what you're looking at).

What can you do about it? The fix is not difficult. Add frame connectors to stiffen the car, and replace the body mount bushings. These pieces add rigidity to the Nova, eliminate the buckling and cracking, and allow the door gap and panel gaps to remain consistent. In addition, they make the car quicker and faster. You don't lose forward energy that would otherwise be spent twisting the car. As a bonus, that old Nova might just prove to be more fun to drive.

Connectors are available in weld-in, bolt-in, square-, rectangular-, and round-tube configurations. You have a lot of choices, and the truth is, the bolt-in jobs aren't as bad as you might think. The reason is, you can do the work at home and you don't need to cut the car up. Better still, a bolt-in connector is reversible. If you (or someone else) want to return the car to stock, or very close to stock, it's possible.

If you examine the accompanying photos, you can see a set of bolt-in Competition Engineering frame connectors installed in a Nova. They fit nicely, but it is necessary to trim the connector bracket at the spring perch. It's not a big job, but it does take some time.

CHAPTER 3

REAR AXLE

You'd think that selecting a rear end for your Nova would be easy. It's not. There are almost too many choices! From the factory, 1968–1974 Novas were fitted with 8.20-inch-diameter ring-gear 10-bolts, 8.50-inch-diameter ring-gear 10-bolts, and 8.875-inch-diameter ring-gear 12-bolts. On the aftermarket side, custom 12-bolts are available along with Dana 60 models and, of course, 9-inch Fords. Options are many.

While it is possible to make the pair of 10-bolts live in a high-performance Nova application, you're far better off with a 12-bolt, a Dana, or a 9-inch. The reasons are manifold and they range from outright strength to parts availability. Equally important, the aftermarket now has you covered when it comes to the "Big Three" of rear axle assemblies. You don't have to scrounge junkyards for any of them. And you don't have to mess with worn-out 40-year-old components either. In no particular order, here's the inside scoop on the three best choices.

12-Bolt

Quite possibly, the strongest iron-case 12-bolts on the planet come from Mark Williams Enterprises. Mark Williams starts with a custom case. This setup (which is basically like starting from scratch in the design) fixes all the shortcomings of the 12-bolt and then mixes in the right mounting system for any number of new or vintage General Motors (or other manufacturer) vehicles, including Novas. As you see in the accompanying photos, the housing looks pretty much like a conventional 12-bolt. But looks can be deceiving. For example, the area behind the rear caps in a stock GM 12-bolt casting is heavily scalloped (basically hollow). This compromises strength. In the Mark Williams housing, the area surrounding the caps is solid. The actual caps are much larger than those found in a stock GM casting. Why go to all this trouble? Simple. The hypoid action of the rear end tries to force the carrier backward, out of the housing. By increasing the beef in the housing, the fore and aft movement is stopped cold with no need for a billet cap (a common fix for 12-bolts and Dana 60 rear ends).

Mark Williams can build the iron case for a conventional 30-spline (or 33-spline) axle. If you need brute strength, it can be manufactured to accommodate a honking 35-spline axle. The bore size of the case determines the axles you can use. Keep in mind that when an axle spline is increased, the diameter of the axle

This 12-bolt looks tame sitting up inside the Nova, but in reality, this is one trick piece with many improvements over stock.

CHAPTER 3

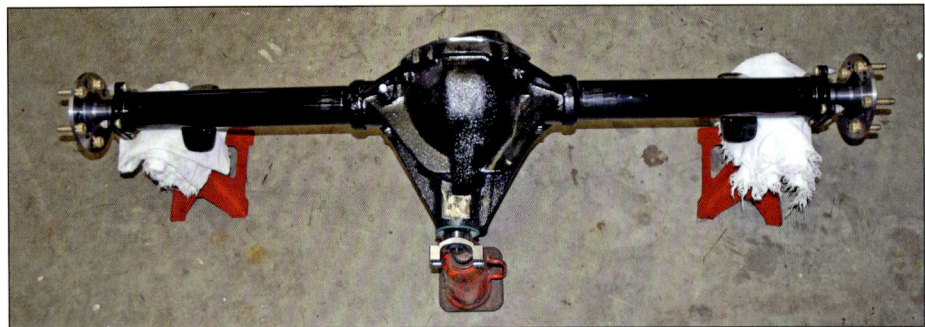

What you're looking at is quite possibly the ultimate iron-case 12-bolt for street/strip applications. Mark Williams custom builds these rear-end assemblies to order.

This 12-bolt from Mark Williams is built with light, strong chrome-moly (4130) axle tubes. The housing ends are engineered to accept an extremely large 45-mm axle bearing. The axle incorporates an external bearing retainer and therefore does not rely upon a C-clip for axle retention.

shaft increases (which in turn dictates the need for a special large-bore case). The 35-spline axle is massive. How massive? Think Dana 60.

Mark Williams can supply the housing with either mild steel or chrome-moly steel tubes. For the housing shown in the accompanying photos, Mark Williams included chrome-moly tubes. Mark Williams fully welds the axle tubes to the center section. In a stock 12-bolt, the tubes are only held in place by way of plug welds. When looking at vintage 12-bolts, you find that in many cases the factory GM welds were not sound, and under close examination, pinholes in the respective welds become evident. This isn't of much consequence in the strength department on a housing such as this (since the tubes have been totally welded to the center section), but there is one small problem: The factory spot-weld system often leaks or "weeps" lubricant. Because of this problem, many a 12-bolt has had seals replaced, gaskets replaced, and drain plugs swapped, only to find that the leak was at a factory spot weld. The solution is rather simple in nature, but is time consuming to accomplish. Each of the tube spot weld locations is filled with a plug weld or "rosette" weld process. The result is a clean, leak-free housing.

One other area you should take note of is the entry point for the axle tubes in the center section. In a stock 12-bolt, this spot is rather fragile. It has been seriously beefed up in the Mark Williams casting to handle much larger loads than a stock GM 12-bolt.

When it comes to dimensions, Mark Williams can pretty much build the housing for any width you require. Several types of housing ends are available from Mark Williams. The featured housing incorporates 45-mm housing ends that accept a sealed bearing and do not use "C-clips" (in fact, none of the Mark Williams housings are constructed for troublesome C-clips). In this example, the car was constructed with drum brakes on the back half,

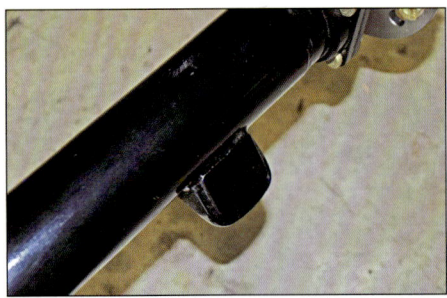

This 12-bolt was built from the beginning to work with CalTracs bars. The preferred spring perch with CalTracs is this Mopar-style setup. Look closely and you can see how Mark Williams boxed the perch for additional strength.

This photo gives you a good idea how the custom perch built by Mark Williams works with a CalTracs bar. It's a clean and simple arrangement.

and this system is a direct bolt-on for early-style Nova four-bolt brake backing plates.

Subtle differences exist in axle perch layout between these housings and an OEM piece. The brackets are usually fully welded (which isn't the case with the factory arrangement), and the housing shown in the photos uses a Chrysler (or Ford) style of spring perch. What's up with that? Simple. The Nova that it's going under is set up with CalTracs bars. Those bars are best suited to a Chrysler perch (rather than a GM perch). Equally important, Mark Williams can install the perches to your pinion angle specs.

In case you're wondering, I double-checked the dimensions between the custom Mark Williams leaf spring housing in the photos and a stock OEM housing. The locations for all brackets are exactly the same as stock. This means the piece will physically bolt into a specific car with zero modifications.

On the nose of their complete 12-bolt setup, Mark Williams incorporates a forged 4340 steel pinion yoke. The pinion yoke is often a potential weak link in the rear-end chain. Most OEM and replacement yokes for the 12-bolt are fragile cast-iron pieces, and for the most part, they can't accept a large-diameter, 1350 Spicer universal joint. That's why Mark Williams includes a 4340 forged steel yoke on its extreme-duty custom 12-bolt. Following forging, the yokes are CNC-machined to exact tolerances; in addition, they're heat-treated to 200,000 psi. Each yoke is symmetrical for balance and alignment. Special snap ring grooves also allow for easy U-joint installation. As mentioned above, they're designed to accept a massive, almost indestructible Spicer 1350 universal joint.

A close look shows the double-drilled axles. Both are for a Chevy 5-on-4-3/4 pattern. One set of holes is for a 1/2-inch stud (shown) while the second set is for a 5/8-inch Mark Williams drive stud.

On the outside, the axle flange includes dual patterns. In the case of the 12-bolt in our photos, both patterns are GM 5 on 4¾, but one is drilled to accept a conventional 1/2-inch stud while the other pattern is drilled to accept a set of Mark Williams' huge drive studs. The wheel studs shown in the photos are short 1/2-inch jobs, which the Williams crew designed to fit under a stock Chevy dog dish hubcap (think "sleeper"). I dig deeper into axles later in this chapter.

All sorts of details are inside; some you can't see and some you

On the backside of the housing bearing flange you can see how Mark Williams trims the bearing retainer studs so that they clear the huge bearing. The retainer is horseshoe shaped to allow for easy axle removal.

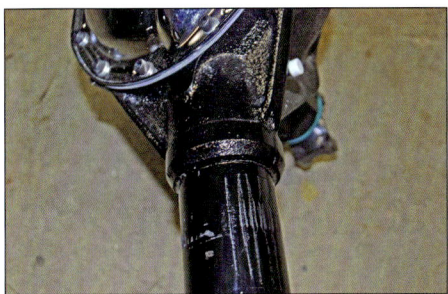

Believe it or not, this is a weak spot on all original 12-bolt housings. General Motors used plug welds to attach the axle tube to the housing. Mark Williams welds the axle tubes directly to the (much stronger) custom iron case.

The bearing retainer looks like this when it's off the housing. To use this setup (large 45-mm bearing), minor machining is required on the brake backing plate.

This view shows the modified backing plate. Here, the center bore size on the backing place has been increased to 3.152/3.155 inches to go over the 3.150-inch OD bearing and seal from Mark Williams.

Mark Williams' custom case has a lot more meat in it than a production line Chevrolet piece. The area behind the main caps is solid (instead of hollow) and the caps are massive. A billet cap or a rear cover girdle is not needed.

This is another view of the cap. It's massive, and note how the pair of caps are held in place by way of strong internal socket cap screws.

can. If you check out the photos, you see that each ring gear bolt is safety wired. Each of those bolts is a high-quality piece from ARP. In fact, many of the fasteners used during the build are either ARP or high-strength socket head Allen jobs. The same applies to bearings. You might think it's easy to nail down bearings for a 12-bolt. But you'd be wrong. Today, many offshore parts are available, and it's often difficult to locate quality pieces. That's why Williams makes use of Timken bearings in its rear-end assemblies, and that includes the custom 12-bolt in this series.

On the outside, all the little details (which often go forgotten) are taken care of: The housing includes a correct vent. The rear cover is chrome steel, and it's even fitted with Allen-head fasteners. The studs for the axle bearing retainers (and the brake backing plates) are milled on the backside to clear the huge wheel bearings, and each stud is zinc dichromate plated. The CNC-machined bearing retainers are horseshoe shaped, which allows installation or removal from the axle without having to remove the axle bearings. Timken manufactures the actual axle bearings. In the end, a 12-bolt such as this could very well be the best street/strip rear end available for a Nova, and that includes the two setups that follow.

Ford 9-Inch

Ford's 9-inch rear end is the darling of both drag racing and hot rodding. And for good reason. The rear end allows for easy center section changes (you can remove the pumpkin and service it on your workbench, which sure beats lying under a car getting drenched in rear axle lube). It also offers considerable choice when it comes to gear ratios and hardware. To be quite honest, it's incredibly strong in modified form (likely the strongest by far of any passenger car– and light truck–based rear-end assemblies used in drag racing).

But in stock form, the Ford isn't so hot. The newest junkyard housing you come across is at least 20 years old, so finding a used one isn't easy. Aside from age, the 9-inch is hampered by three major drawbacks from the high-performance perspective: First, the housing axle tubes are not round; they taper from 3½ to 3 inches. Second, all the tubes have

On the nose, the custom Mark Williams 12-bolt makes use of a forged 4340 steel pinion yoke. The CNC-machined yoke is designed to accept a large Spicer 1350 universal joint. This is the same size universal joint found in medium-duty truck applications.

Note how each of the ring gear bolts is safety wired following installation. ARP builds the fasteners especially for Mark Williams.

REAR AXLE

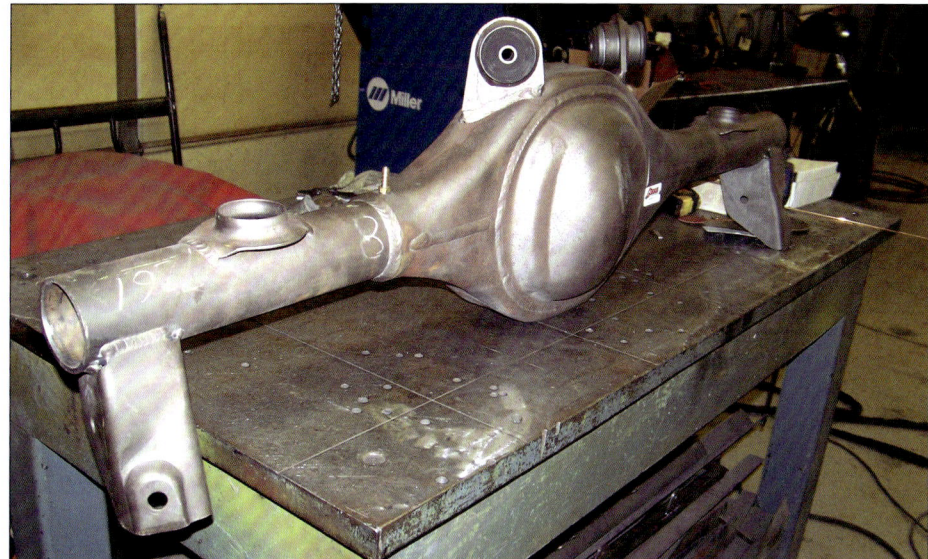

Here's a basic 9-inch Ford housing. This one on the bench is for a GM G-Body, but leaf spring examples are quite similar.

Ford housings usually mandate some sort of brace when you mix them with big power and sticky tires. The reason for bracing a Ford housing is to curb its tendency to move fore and aft (flex on the ends).

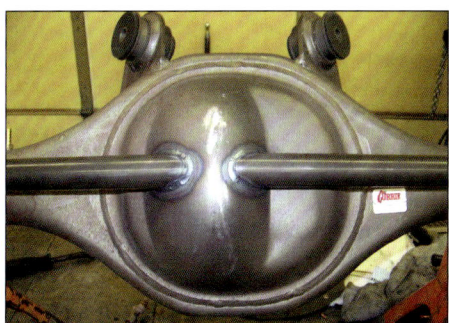

Box braces are common in drag racing, but a simple tubular brace such as this works equally well and it's a bit cleaner. Here you can see how the center section is tied to the tube structure.

On the outboard sides, the back brace ties directly to the axle tubes. Here, they're adjacent to the suspension mount points.

"flats" that are somewhat squashed onto the tubes. These two factors force a chassis builder to custom build every bracket, because they aren't symmetrical. There's more, too: The factory Ford housing face is approximately 24 inches wide. Because of this, you must weld brackets to the face in some cars. This means you lose adjustment holes for items such as the four-link.

Much of the detail work that goes into a good 9-inch is hidden; therefore, many of these housings look more stock than they actually are. Even many of the new aftermarket 9-inch housings mandate a ton of work. Case in point: The 9-inch Ford housing shown in the accompanying photos took the better part of a week to rework, but on the outside, it doesn't look much different from other setups. While space precludes a full-blown step-by-step investigation of the methods used to fortify a Ford, I can give you a bit of insight into some of the techniques.

For high-powered cars, it's standard practice to add a brace to the rear of a Ford 9-inch. This brace essentially ties the ends of the axle tubes to one another, and at the same time, anchors the back of the housing. This addition greatly increases the strength of the housing, eliminating the trend for the housing to physically move forward and aft. Fair enough, but there's a catch to the back-brace scenario, one that some chassis builders forget, ignore, or simply don't know about: When the back brace is added, the housing does not deflect forward and back. Instead, it deflects downward under power. The solution? A tube affixed between the four-link brackets (see the accompanying photos for a closer look). Of course, most

CHEVY NOVA 1968–1974: HOW TO BUILD AND MODIFY

CHAPTER 3

This is a custom sheet-metal 9-inch housing I had built for another project. As you can see, it incorporates a similar tubular back brace along with a bottom brace that serves to keep the housing from bending downward.

This is another look at the bottom brace. This type of brace is typically used on cars with four-link. The bar ties the lower four-link brackets together.

builders use custom-built 360-degree four-link brackets (that wrap completely around the respective axle tubes), but there's still more to the 9-inch prep.

Almost all 9-inch housing "banjos" are formed by stamping. When loaded by way of sticky tires, extra weight, and a strong engine, the construction really doesn't work. What ends up happening is the housing flexes at the carrier. In turn, the life cycle of the ring and pinion is shortened. A big issue is the rear "cover" found on the housing. The back of a 9-inch isn't one piece; it consists of a stamped cover pressed into the housing. The hypoid action of the third member attempts to force the carrier out the back of the housing. Welding the cover to the back of the housing doesn't fix the problem.

The fix is to weld the stamped pieces of the housing together and then add an internal housing "cage." This cage is, in essence, a series of tubes that tie the front face of the housing to the rear. What it does is improve ring gear life.

Ford Center Section

What about the center section? Ford center sections were typically manufactured with a separate bolt-in support for the pinion. Cars with nodular center sections were regularly fitted with what was called a "Daytona" pinion support. These supports make use of the same size outer bearing as the more pedestrian supports; however, the inner bearing is much larger, and the inner webbing is much more robust. Most nodular-iron 31-spline muscle-Fords came with Ford's clutch pack–equipped Traction Lok differential (which is a conventional limited-slip arrangement). Then, with the dawn of the 1970 model year, a positive locking (gear-driven) differential manufactured by a company called Detroit Automotive Products

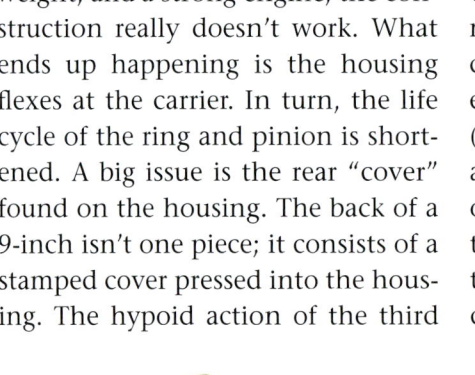

The hypoid action of the ring gear causes a tendency for the Ford to flex fore and aft at the center section. To stop this, the inside of the housing is "caged." Two of the cage braces can be seen at the bottom of the housing.

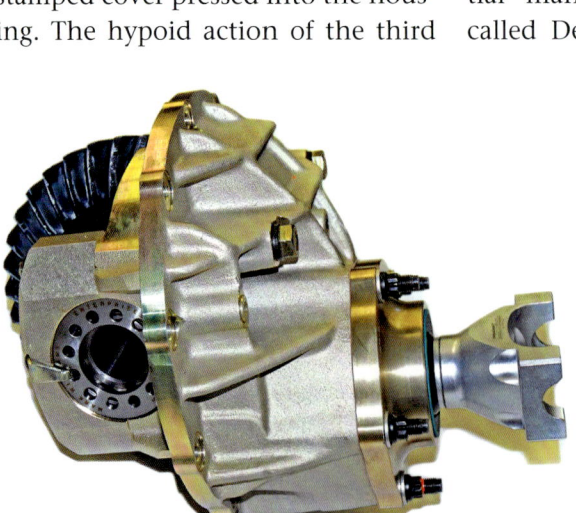

If you need the ultimate in 9-inch Ford center sections for a street/strip Nova, this is it. It's a Mark Williams through-bolt-configuration aluminum center section, complete with a pinion support, billet carrier adjusters, 1350 universal joint yoke, billet 35-spline Detroit Locker, and in this case, a 3.89:1 ring and pinion.

36 CHEVY NOVA 1968–1974: HOW TO BUILD AND MODIFY

Detroit Locker

The muscle-car era was filled with interesting and often memorable hardware. The Detroit Locker, found under big-power Fords with a Drag Pack, was one of them. As it turns out, the Detroit Locker was likely the toughest, meanest, gnarliest differential that ever turned a tire on the street. But what does this have to do with Novas? In all honesty, the Detroit Locker is still the most durable and dependable locking differential available. It is certainly not limited to 9-inch Ford applications either. Way back when, the Locker had some decidedly naughty manners (which didn't hurt the bad-boy reputation one bit). The Detroit Locker functions as an automatic locking differential designed to lock both wheels of the axle together automatically with power input when forward or reverse torque is applied. This means that both driving wheels deliver 100 percent of the power to the ground. When "locked," it's like a spool that solidly connects both axles (and consequently connects both wheels). When torque isn't applied, the Detroit Locker "unlocks." The locking and unlocking wasn't exactly invisible (you could hear and feel clunking and banging). Sure, it was a bit naughty, but the Locker also had a reputation for brute strength.

Today, Eaton owns Detroit Locker and most of the bad manners have been banished. The latest "soft lockers" still let you know when they lock and unlock, but not quite with the same ferocity of the older models. They're rather civilized.

Born as a "Thornton Drive" the Locker was first manufactured by Detroit Automotive Product Corporation. Through the 1940s and into the 1950s and 1960s, the Thornton Drive became available as original equipment under all sorts of light- and medium-duty trucks. Over time, Detroit Automotive Product Corporation transformed into Tractech (the name changed in 1979). By the 1960s, the Thornton Drive came to be known as the Detroit Locker.

In 2005, Eaton Corporation purchased Tractech Holdings, Inc. With the purchase came the Detroit Locker. Eaton Corporation offers Detroit Lockers for a wide array of rear-end applications, including Dana 60, Ford 9-inch, Dana 44, Chrysler 8¾, GM 10 (various configurations), and 12-bolts (standard and aftermarket 33- or 35-spline) and others.

The bottom line here is, the Detroit Locker was and still is the toughest limited-slip setup available anywhere. If you need brute strength from the differential in your Nova, your first stop should be a Detroit Locker. ■

Because Detroit Lockers have "backlash" or "slack" between the drive and driven teeth, they are audible in everyday use going through corners and when going from drive mode to coast mode. Eaton notes that with the Nova on the ground and the transmission in neutral you have 1/4 to 1/3 turn of lash in the driveshaft; this is completely normal.

The case found on a Detroit Locker is extremely beefy. No special setup is required with this limited slip. In many examples, you can use stock replacement bearings. In the unlikely event you break a Locker, it is possible to repair it. Eaton offers a full range of replacement pieces and service parts.

You can see the carrier splines from this angle. This example is engineered for use with 35-spline axles. As far as lubricant for the Locker is concerned, you can use any quality petroleum/mineral-based rear axle lube. Friction additives/modifiers are not required. Eaton does not recommend synthetic lube for the Locker.

Detroit Lockers are available for 3- and 4-series gear sets. The Locker locks up 100 percent when operating in a straight line or if the Nova is spinning, which means power is transmitted to both wheels. In a turn, the unit unlocks for the wheel turning the fastest.

Corporation was made available in high-horsepower cars with gear ratios of 4.30:1. These are the legendary "Detroit Lockers."

Ford did something good with the design and layout of the 9-inch. No secret. It's pretty much the standard go-to rear end for drag racing. If you're so inclined, it is possible to track down most of the stock hardware to piece together a factory-style nodular-iron 31-spline 9-inch, complete with a Daytona pinion support and even a Detroit Locker. However, the truth is that what you find is old, used-up hardware. You should be prepared to drop some serious coin to whip the old stuff into shape. Not good. And not race effective either. What is good is the selection out there (in the racing aftermarket) for updated, brute force Ford center sections. The setups I show you are head and shoulders above the original parts.

Ford 9-Inch Case

Several companies manufacture and sell nodular-iron cases. Nodular iron is a type of cast iron that first saw the light of day in 1943. While most varieties of cast iron prove to be brittle, nodular iron is much more ductile because of its "nodular graphite" inclusions. When you consider aftermarket products, think about the availability of upgrades. Mark Williams has a reinforced nodular-iron case that is stronger than stock but comparable in weight to a stock Ford assembly. These 9-inch cases come complete with billet steel rear-end caps that have been precision alignment bored. They also include special billet-steel adjusters and studs to secure the pinion assembly. They're available with 3.062- or 3.250-inch bore sizes (the larger the bore, the

This is a through-bolt design. Instead of a bolt (for the main caps) threading into the body of the center section, a high-strength Grade-9 bolt goes completely through the center section.

larger the axle diameter/spline you can use, the larger the axle diameter and spline, the stronger the axle).

Another option is the "through bolt" aluminum case manufactured by Mark Williams. Isn't aluminum weaker than nodular iron? Not necessarily. This is a highly refined, extreme-duty component that has become pretty much the standard in NHRA Pro Stock. It's also used with regularity in slower-class drag race cars, "pro/street" cars, and any number of seriously quick street machines. It weighs 11 pounds less than Williams' comparable nodular-iron carrier or a stock Ford carrier. Cast from an ultra-strong aircraft alloy (30 percent stronger than 6061T6), the case is engineered with special "through bolts" that go completely through the center section to secure the main caps.

The actual main caps are machined from 7075 aluminum and include billet-steel carrier adjusters. The pinion pilot-bearing bore incorporates an extra-length bearing that is completely captive and retained by fasteners. Meanwhile, the pinion support is held in place by way of large-diameter 7/16-inch studs. The case is manufactured in three bore sizes (3.062, 3.250, and 3.812 inches,

With a through-bolt case, no threads engage the center section, which means no chance of stripped fasteners. It also means the strength is increased many times.

although for anything short of an all-out drag car, the 3.812-inch piece isn't necessary). All through-bolt case configurations have clearance for 9½-inch gears (9¼-inch actual diameters). Fluid passage ports for external lubrication systems are pre-drilled. In addition, the case is set up so that you can add a load bolt if necessary. What is a load bolt? Essentially, a load bolt is a bolt positioned close to the backside of the ring gear, but not in contact with it. It only contacts the ring gear if there is deflection under severe load. Load bolts were originally used on heavy-duty truck differentials. They prevented chipped teeth if the driver's foot slipped off the clutch when backing up. The bottom line here is, it might be necessary in *extreme* power applications, but for we mere mortals, it's not required.

Ford 9-Inch Carrier

When it comes to the carrier (differential) for a 9-inch Ford, three basic options are available: Spool, Posi-Traction, and Locker, and of course, a series of variants in each. You can also get an open carrier, but honestly, this isn't really a performance choice, at least for anyone

REAR AXLE

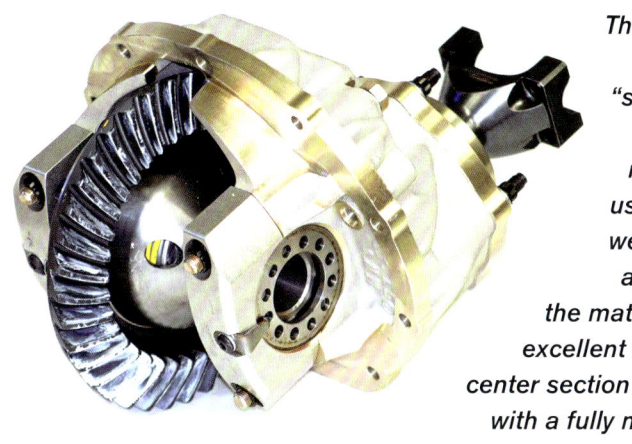

This center section is based around "standard" or "street" gears (in this case, a 3.89:1 ratio from Richmond Gear). The material used is 8620 steel. It works well in oval track and street applications. Furthermore, the material was heat-treated for excellent wear and service life. The center section includes a Detroit Locker with a fully machined billet-steel case (designed for huge 35-spline axles).

contemplating a drag race situation. Mark Williams notes, "An open carrier uses a set of gears to allow slip. The thing to remember with an open carrier is that torque is always equal between both wheels. This means that if one wheel is slipping, the other is only able to apply as much torque as the slipping wheel.

"A spool is a single piece carrier and does not offer any compensation for different rotating speeds in the wheels. Because of additional stresses created by a spool, it is not a good idea to run stock-spline axles with a spool. Spools should be run in race only–type applications and are not intended for use on the street.

"Lockers use a ratcheting technique in combination with a cam to ensure that both wheels are locked together. The locker does not allow the wheels to spin at different speeds as long as there is forward torque on both wheels. The unit allows the outer tire to ratchet while turning a large radius such as cornering.

"Torque Sensing differentials use mechanical means to control slip. They are rated with a bias, such as 5:1, that rates the amount of torque the unit is capable of applying to the non-slipping wheel. For instance, if you are spinning with 20 ft-lbs of torque, the non-spinning wheel is able to receive 100 ft-lbs in a 5:1 ratio. In a case where there is no torque on the loose wheel, the differential does not apply torque (this is why they recommend off-roaders apply the brakes when they slip). With an adjustable bias, you can tune the differential to your needs.

"Posi-Traction is similar to an open carrier and uses a set of clutches to apply torque to both axles. The clutches are pre-loaded by springs and the separating action of the spider gears increases the pressure on the clutch discs. Different clutch materials can be used as well as different static preloads to change the amount of torque needed to make the wheels slip."

For a street/strip Nova, it's difficult to beat a Detroit Locker. I dig deep inside the Locker elsewhere, but for a strip-only Nova, your best bet is a spool. Spools are available in both steel and aluminum. On the steel spool side, Williams' spools begin as 4140 steel forgings that are CNC-machined, and heat-treated using the same austemper process as axles. During the machining process, the ring gear register and the bearing diameters are precision ground to ensure zero run out on the ring-gear mount surface. The cross section beneath the ring gear register is increased to prevent ring gear deflection. Lightweight steel spools incorporate lightening holes drilled through the hub of the spool, as well as a profile-milled ring gear flange. This reduces weight by as much as 25 percent over the standard steel spool, and it doesn't sacrifice strength.

Standard steel spools for 9-inch Fords are available in 28-, 31-, 35-, or 40-spline axle configurations. Lightweight steel spools are available only in 35- or 40-spline configurations. The 35-spline spools require a stock 2.893-inch case or a 3.062-inch case. The 40-spline spools require a 3.250-inch-bore case, 45-mm wheel bearings, and matching housing ends.

Aluminum spools are manufactured from 7075-T6 alloy forgings (they're gold coated following

In the Ford rear, after the pattern and backlash have been established, you must set the preload on the differential bearings. This is accomplished using these adjusters. In practice, the adjusters are first snugged by hand only (both sides). Typically, each adjuster must be moved anywhere from .004 to .006 inch (depending on the bearings used). The holes in the adjusters are a guide. Rotating the adjuster from one hole to the next provides changes in preload. A spanner wrench is used to set the adjuster, and then it's locked in place.

machining). An aluminum spool is approximately half the weight of a profile-milled steel spool. They're available for 28-, 31-, 35-, and 40-spline axle combinations (keep in mind that the guidelines for case and wheel bearing sizes mentioned above still apply).

The 9-inch Ford pinion support assemblies are available for a number of applications, Novas included. The support housings for the Mark Williams components are CNC-machined from aircraft-quality aluminum and use either oversized tapered roller bearings or low-friction angular contact ball bearings. All pinion supports come preassembled. The bearing pre-load is set through the use of a solid, hardened pre-load spacer rather than a crush sleeve or stack of thin shims. The spacer is factory machined to the required pre-load for each assembly. Pinion seals are included. Housings are drilled to accommodate the 7/16-inch studs used in all MW cases. That doesn't preclude the use of these custom pinion supports in a stock Ford case. By using special reducer bushings from Williams and accompanying studs the housing can also be used with stock-style 9-inch Ford cases equipped with 3/8-inch threads.

Dana 60

If you want a big brute of a rear end under your Nova, look no further than a Dana 60. Even in the heyday of the muscle car, Dana 60s were renowned for their strength, along with being difficult to locate. Today they're incredibly easy to track down. For example, Strange Engineering and DTS offer a full range of heavy-duty, bolt-in rear-end assemblies for many popular applications, including our favorite, the 1968–1974 Nova. The truth is, in modified form, you can now build a better rear than a Dana (an example is the 12-bolt that I discussed earlier), but for street-driven cars it's a decent choice.

Dana 60s are equipped with a huge, 9¾-inch-diameter ring gear, and when fitted with a contemporary Posi-Traction setup (there are several, including Detroit Lockers), the axle splines increase to a hefty 35. The pinion is a large, 1⅝-inch-diameter affair (29-spline) that can be set up to accept massive Spicer 1350-series universal joints. Gear ratio choices prove to be plentiful too, ranging from 3.31:1 to 7.17:1. As you can

For a street-driven Nova, a tapered-bearing pinion support such as this Mark Williams version is what you need. This piece is engineered to work with OEM-style 1.313-inch-diameter 28-spline pinion gears. The aftermarket also offers Ford 9-inch pinion gears in 35-spline derivatives (1.875-inch diameter). Don't confuse the pinion spline with the axle spline. Large pinion gear sets are only available in 9310 alloys, which are specifically designed for the shock loads drag racing places upon them.

Mark Williams includes a special billet yoke machined from 4340 steel in its pro/street center section (in this case, "pro" doesn't necessarily mean fat back tires). They use special tooling to ensure that the yoke is machined concentric to the pinion spline (not always the case with pinion yokes). These yokes are engineered to accept a huge Spicer-style 1350 universal joint.

Strange Engineering came up with the idea of improving upon the vintage Dana 60. Its version is dubbed the "S-60," and it's full of neat tricks and rear-end innovation. As pointed out elsewhere, it's available in any number of configurations from a bare housing without ends and brackets to a bolt-in Nova housing (as shown here) all the way up to a complete rear axle assembly.

REAR AXLE

The Strange S60 center section is cast from premium nodular iron, and so are the large bearing caps. Like the 12-bolt shown earlier, this is one beefy rear end.

Check out the material under the main caps. In a conventional Dana 60 this large support doesn't exist. Strange added this material where it counted and shaved bulk off the exterior of the case. Overall, the S60 case is thicker than a standard Dana 60.

In a conventional Dana 60, it's not uncommon to replace the caps with billet-steel models because they add strength. When stressed (big power, big tires, sticky pavement), the car attempts to force the carrier right out of the back. The fix isn't required here. The extra material within the case prevents the carrier from migrating. Note the hefty Allen-head cap screws included in the mix.

Production line Dana 60s have the axle tubes pressed into place and plug welded. The Strange S60, on the other hand, has the tubes cleanly rosette-welded and then each tube is totally welded to the case. Welding the axle tubes to the case prevents them from rotating under hard use.

The housing ends are similarly welded to the axle tubes. This is what a proper weld on a housing end looks like. For this Nova application, a small-bearing GM housing end is used. This allows the use of a stock GM drum brake backing plate.

For a Nova application, Strange equips the S60 with OEM-style leaf spring perches. You can order any type of perch, including mono-leaf, multi-leaf, and Mopar style for Cal-Tracs bars. Each side is fully welded (wherever accessible).

Strange includes these internal adjusters as standard equipment in the S60 case. This allows for easy backlash setup.

see, the Dana 60 has always been the bully of the boulevard when it comes to rear-end housings.

But that's not the end of it. Strange Engineering's Dana 60 (dubbed the "S60") isn't exactly a piece-by-piece clone of the original. Instead, it's jam packed with interesting technology, much of it garnered from lessons learned in the drag racing trade. Essentially, the Strange Engineering team took the stock Dana 60 and filled it with a full complement of modern features.

Gear Sets

You can specify ring and pinion assemblies in at least two materials. They're most often referred to as a street gear or a pro gear. What's the difference? Mark Williams elaborates: "Pro gears are made from 9310 and then heat treated. It is a softer alloy than the 8620 street gears. The softer 9310 alloy allows the gear to absorb higher-impact loads that are generated in drag racing without developing cracks. A harder 8620 street gear could shatter under the same loads. As a side effect, the pro gears are not the best choice for street use because they wear faster. Also available in the pro gears is a large pinion with a 35-spline shaft for high-powered applications. This requires a bearing change in the pinion support as well as a 35-spline pinion yoke. Gears termed 9½-inchers are also available for the 9-inch third member. They offer a slight strength advantage over a standard 9-inch gear."

Axles

If you see a Nova that just pitched a wheel (most often with a chunk of the axle attached), you'll get a far better understanding of why axles are critical. It's also the reason why most race sanctioning bodies have rules that lay out what you can and cannot have when it comes to axles (case in point: some sort of positive axle retention device, which translates to *no C-clips*).

But let's start from the beginning. Original equipment automotive axles are most often manufactured from 1055 or 1541 steel, usually on the borderline between a medium- and a high-carbon steel with a relatively large manganese content. The 1055 steel has a carbon content between .50 and .60 percent, while 1541 has between .36 and .44 percent. The carbon content allows the shaft to be induction hardened. It's also easy to work with. These original equipment axles are induction hardened up to the bearing mount surface (next to the flange, induction hardening is used to selectively harden areas of a part or assembly without affecting the properties of the entire component).

With induction hardening, the axle shaft passes through an electromagnetic coil. Eddy currents are generated within the metal, which in turn heats the shaft. The shaft is then quenched. This hardening process leaves the shaft with a surface hardness of 55–58 Rockwell, penetrating to a depth of approximately .150 to .300 inch. The core of the axle remains relatively soft, but the surface is very hard, almost brittle. So far so good, but an axle with a soft flange is better suited for folks smacking curbs than it is to handle the shock loads of something such as a drag race car.

Curbs and potholes aren't the biggest concern for a dedicated Nova race car or, for that matter, a street/strip combination. More relevant factors for these applications include the load that will be placed on the axles at launch, the overall weight of the various drivetrain pieces, and of course, budget.

Calculating the amount of torque applied to an axle is easy. Take the engine torque output and multiply it by both the transmission first gear and rear-end gear ratios. If it's an automatic, the multiplication factor from the torque converter should also be added in the mix. In total, it's not unusual to see figures of more than 10,000 ft-lbs of torque transmitted to the axles. That's a bunch.

With these kinds of loads there's more to it than simply the tensile strength of the material. The ductility of the axle shaft itself plays an important role. The torsional load presented to the axle is so large that it must be able to twist and rebound like a torsion bar instead of being too stiff and ultimately snapping.

Rewind a couple of paragraphs. Recall that induction hardening used on OEM axles? While it might be great to combat impacts from curbs and potholes, something else is needed for race car and super-high-performance pieces. I turned to Mark Williams Enterprises for information on axle performance and, especially, ductility.

To achieve the kind of ductility necessary for racing purposes, Mark Williams Enterprises employs an austempering process on its nickel-chromium-molybdenum alloy Hi-Torque axles. This heat-treating process involves submerging the axle in a molten solution at more than 1,500 degrees F and then quenching the components in a molten brine solution. This results in a material structure known as

This is what a quality axle looks like after it is forged, machined, heat-treated, and assembled with bearings and wheel studs. Mark Williams Enterprises uses quality high manganese steel for its MasterLine series of axles and a more durable nickel-chromium-molybdenum alloy for the Hi-Torque series. A 300M alloy is also offered for extreme-duty use. This is a Hi-Torque pro/street axle.

Determine Axle Housing Width

Poll all of the chassis shops and they will quickly tell you that a car should be built around the wheels and tires (particularly the back ones). A good number of home-built cars are constructed that way too, but plenty aren't. If the business end of the car isn't built around the rear rolling stock, the wheel fit along with the ride height may never be right. Get the ride height wrong and you're asking for suspension grief. Ditto with the wheel fit. The bottom line here is to measure everything multiple times before ordering parts.

Fair enough, but where do you begin? The place to start is the rear-end housing. Each car is different. That shouldn't be a surprise. But if you have the back wheels and tires in hand (mounted), that's the only piece of the puzzle, aside from the car, that you need. In a few cases it's simply a matter of jamming the wheel and tire combination up inside the existing wheelwell, squaring the works up in the chassis, and measuring between the respective wheel mount flanges. You're pretty much done.

However, that's the easy route. What if you have to chop the floor, cut out the wheel tubs, or narrow or fab the frame before anything fits? And what if you don't want to cut anything up before you have a new frame or frame segment to slide under the car? After all, for some cars the floor is one of the few structural pieces that hold the body together. If you drag out the Sawzall too soon, you'll have to deal with a flexing, flopping carcass. That can make a simple job like moving the body around the shop rather difficult.

To figure out the rear width, you need some simple tools. Included in the mix are a couple of plumb bobs, a tape measure, a carpenter's square, and a straight edge. A wee bit of tape, a Sharpie marker, and a hand calculator come in handy too. Housing calculus isn't difficult. ■

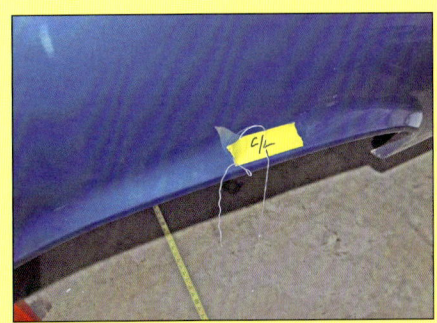

First things first: See the scribbles on the tape? First, the centerline of the rear axle in relation to the body is determined. In some cars, the back axle isn't centered in the wheelwell. Assuming everything is square, just measure between the leading and trailing edges of the lower fender and split the difference. That's the "C/L," or "center line," mark on the fender.

Overall, this Nova measures 72.40 inches wide. If you're wondering why I didn't measure from the inside wheel lip on each side, it's because I take clearance measurements into account later.

Drop a plumb bob down from the axle centerline on the outside edge of each fender. You can use an inexpensive carpenter's plumb or you simply use a heavy nut strung through some string. Run a tape measure from one plumb line to the other (on each side of the car).

The rolling stock is critical in determining the width of the rear-end housing. You really can't determine anything unless you have the exact wheel and tire combination in your hands. Here is a set of 16 x 10 wheels wrapped with a set of P285/60R16 tires. This setup is relatively wide and definitely tall. And no, the package doesn't fit inside a stock Nova wheelwell.

CHAPTER 3

Determine Axle Housing Width *CONTINUED*

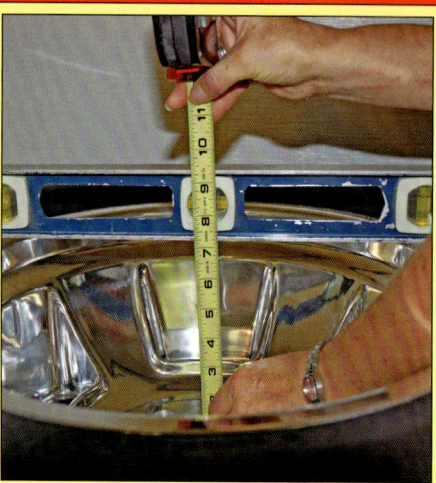

Next get the dimension from the wheel-mounting surface to the tire bulge on the curb, or outboard, side of the wheel/tire. You can use one of two methods to check the wheel face dimension. The first photo shows the tape measure stretched from the wheel mount flange (the part where the brake drum or the disc brake hat meets the wheel) to the bulge using a carpenter's square. The second photo shows another way to do it. Simply place a straight edge over the tire bulge and measure down to the wheel mount flange. Write down the number (in this case it's 7 3/16 inches).

It's a good idea to hang a square over the tire to determine overall width. It's easy on a square-shouldered radial such as this. The mounted tire is just over 12 inches in width (sidewall bulge dimension). When this figure is compared to the tire company dimensional data, the numbers prove to be a long ways off (they claim 11.4 inches for the section width). The catch: The tire specs assume the tire is mounted on an 8.5-inch-wide wheel. These wheels are 10 inches wide. The extra 1.5 inches in wheel width stretch the tire out a bit more. The point is, you really can't use printed tire dimensional data when it comes to rear-end housing measurements. Instead, measure the rolling stock you intend to use.

Several elements affect the clearance between the curbside of the tire and the inner fender, not the least being the thickness of the wheel at the mount flange. Case in point: the wheel studs (first photo). They're actually "drive studs," where the stud drives the wheel, not the shank of the lug nut. The drive studs in this photo measure 1.250 inches in length. Meanwhile, the wheel has a center flange thickness of 1.00 inch (second photo). That means there must be 2.250 inches of clearance between the curbside of the wheel and the inner fender to allow for wheel removal. The trimmed wheelwell lip in the back quarter measures .500 inch per side. I therefore have a minimum clearance figure of 2.75 inches per side. I add an extra quarter inch for a fudge factor. With the wheel installed, this also provides room to clear the curvature of the back fender.

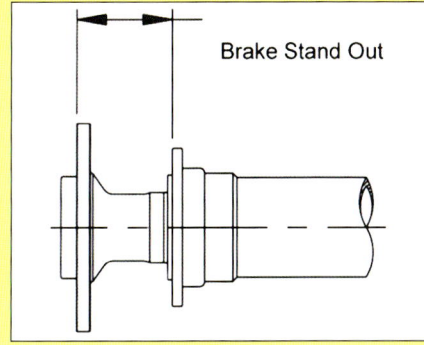

The next thing you need to figure out is the brake "stand out" dimension for disc brakes, or the drum thickness for drum brakes. Mark Williams offers several standout dimensions for its line of aftermarket discs based upon the housing end you select.

GM 10- to 12-bolt ends, 2.812 inches
Symmetrical ends, 2.834 inches
Olds ends, 2.834 inches
Mopar ends, 2.500 inches
Ford ends, 2.500 inches

Double-check these dimensions with your brake supplier. If the plan is to use a drum setup out back, take into account the drum width along with the thickness dimensions of the backing plate. (Illustration Courtesy Mark Williams Enterprises)

When measuring for a rear end, consider the thickness of the drum or the disc brake hat. A typical iron drum measures in the .100- to .125-inch range while disc brake hats such as those manufactured by Mark Williams have a hat thickness of .250 inch. Measure yours and write down the number.

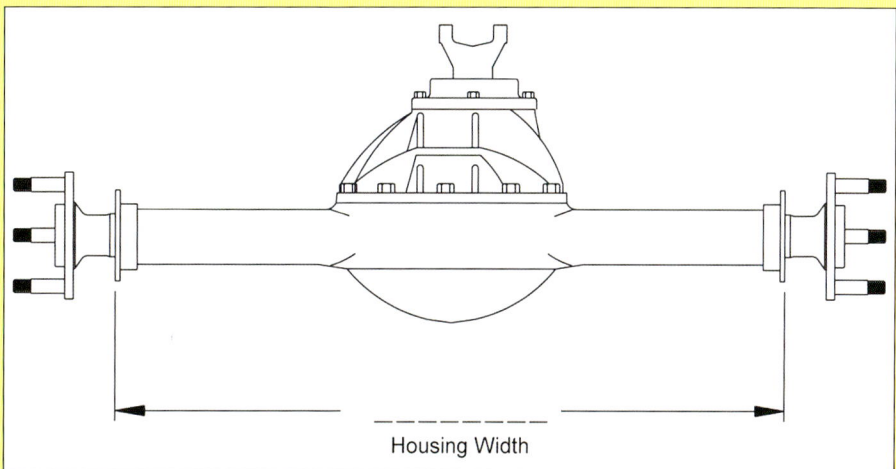

At this point, you can use your dimensions to figure out exactly what you have and what you need. (Illustration Courtesy Mark Williams Enterprises)

Bainite; it proves to be far superior to the Martinsite structure that comes with the ordinary heat treating and oil-quench processes that are commonly employed (that results in a more brittle axle). Other important benefits of austempering include higher impact and fatigue strengths, resistance to hydrogen embrittlement, a more uniform hardness, and increased wear resistance. In the end, the choice of materials coupled with the austempering process provide an axle with an ultimate tensile strength of 225,000 to 253,000 psi along with exceptional ductility (the ability to change shape or form without breaking). The shaft surface hardness is approximately 50 Rockwell, which proves to be far less brittle than an induction-hardened carbon steel axle.

If all of that is necessary to build good axles, why do you see "alloy axles" advertised so cheaply? The reality is, those components are produced by an OEM axle forging company. The main business of that company is to manufacture axles for the heavy truck and construction industries. And yes, the material used is carbon steel, common to original equipment axles. In this case, the manufacturer produces an axle blank. The companies selling those inexpensive alloy components cut the axle to length and then spline it. These axles are made from the same material as stock axles and receive the same heat treatment. The only real difference is that they are available in shorter lengths and with different splines. Now you know why they're cheap; you get what you pay for.

CHAPTER 3

When you examine a set of axle splines, the outer edge of the spline defines the major diameter. The lowest portion of the groove within the spline defines the minor diameter. The minor diameter is what determines the strength of the axle shaft. The included angle of the spline (commonly called the "pressure angle") is important as well. Some pressure angles measure 30 degrees (which works out to a 60-degree included angle). But for racing applications, a 45-degree pressure angle (90-degree included angle) is superior. The reason is, the spline depth is shorter, which allows for a *larger* minor axle diameter (on a specific axle outside diameter).

Most modern axles are manufactured with a 24-pitch. If an axle has a 1-inch circular pitch diameter (the midpoint between the major and minor diameters), it has exactly 24 splines (or teeth). The distance between the centerline of adjacent splines remains constant, so as the diameter of the shaft increases, so does the number of splines. As an example, a 35-spline axle has a major diameter of 1.500 inches while a 40-spline axle measures 1.708 inches in diameter.

The actual shape of the spline is important too. Original equipment axles are manufactured with what is called an "involute spline." This means the face of each spline is slightly curved. This type of spline provides for an optimum contact patch along with even pressure while engaged. But there's a hiccup: You can't re-create an involute spline by way of fly cutting (re-splining). That results in a straight-cut spline. To manufacture an involute spline, you must hobb the spline. Hobbing is a machining process that incorporates a special type of mill. The teeth, or splines, are progressively machined into the component by a series of cuts made by a cutting tool, which is called a hob. It is possible to fit (and use) a fly-cut flat-axle spline into a spool or differential designed for an involute spline. But what happens is the spline on the axle(s) is stressed, often considerably. Reliability diminishes. That's why it's not a good idea to mix and match splines.

But can't axles with similar spline counts be interchanged? No! For example, if you compare an original equipment 35-spline Dana axle with something such as a special MW 35-spline axle, you find they are not interchangeable because the MW spline features a 45-degree pressure angle, which (obviously) differs from the stock Dana 30-degree pressure angle configuration. Mark Williams does, however, offer Hi-Torque forged-steel axles with OEM-type splines. Because of this, be sure to get the right axle spline for the right spool or differential assembly in your Nova.

Why do some axles have a reduced diameter after the spline? For a splined shaft to carry its maximum torsional load it is necessary to have a working shaft diameter smaller than the major spline diameter. The reduced section after the spline works like a torsion bar, allowing the rotational wind up to occur over a longer area. This prevents the axle from experiencing permanent set. Axles that are not undercut twist at the end of the spline engagement and eventually fail at this point.

The actual shape of a given axle has a major influence upon ductility. For example, the MW Hi-Torque axle(s) shown in the accompanying photos taper from the axle bearing shoulder (1.774 inches) down to the minor diameter of the spline. This effectively creates a profile in the shape of a triangle. In turn, this triangulation provides the axle with more resistance to bowing (it's not uncommon for the rear end in high-horsepower cars to bow, which creates an axle toe-in situation; obviously, this has an effect upon performance). Approximately one-third of the axle remains in the minor diameter to allow for torsion bar–like twisting. The triangulated profile of the axle prevents it from permanently changing shape.

You sometimes see axles with shorter spline areas. The reason is, many axle builders gang-run axles

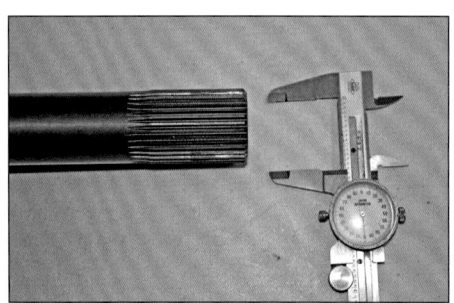

Here's the spline end (35 spline) of a Mark Williams Hi-Torque axle for a 9-inch Ford. This is actually a pro/street setup. As you can see, this 35-spline axle measures a full 1.50 inches on the OD. The axle tapers down slightly after the spline.

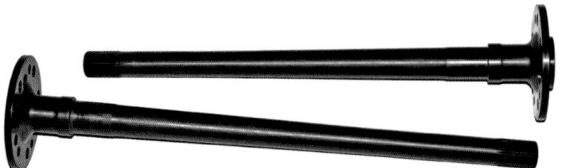

If you view the profile of the Hi-Torque axle, you see that the entire axle is tapered. There's good reason for this triangulation (which, as most know, is the strongest of geometric shapes). Williams builds axles that are designed to work like a torsion bar.

Measure for Custom Axles

In this chapter I discuss the intricacies of high-quality aftermarket axles for your Nova. It's a lot to digest, but when you're done reading and you need new (quality) axles, how do you measure for them? While that sounds simple enough, more than one person has made a critical error in axle dimensions. It's important to get it right, though, because once you have them, you have them.

Fortunately, a foolproof method exists to measure for axles. Before going any further, keep in mind that many housings make use of an offset pinion. Because of this, each axle is a slightly different length (sometimes considerably). The following method might take a bit more time to calculate than some of the quick and dirty means, but after the dimensions are established, there's no need to worry about axles being too long or too short.

This is a list of dimensions you need on a bare housing:

- A   Housing flange to flange
- B   Driver-side housing flange to pinion center
- C   Passenger-side housing flange to pinion center
- D   Wheel-to-wheel width
- E   Axle flange (driver side) to pinion center
- F   Axle flange (passenger side) to pinion center

The photos provide an easy measuring system. ■

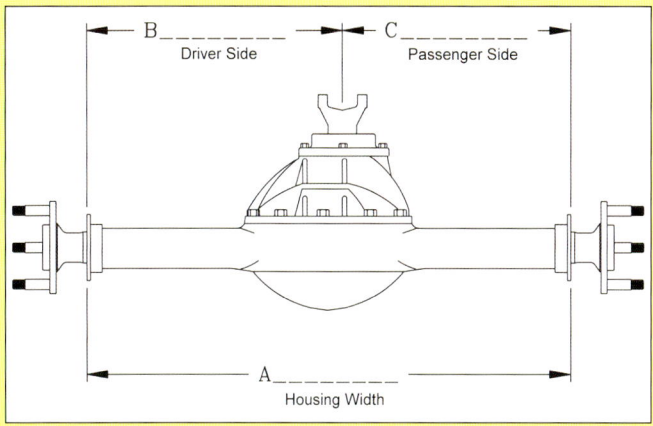

Many production cars do not have centered engines. They're often offset toward the passenger's side of the vehicle. To compensate, the pinion in some applications is also offset (for example, in some later-model Fords, the offset is just under 1.00 inch). Consequently, the passenger-side axle is shorter than the driver-side axle. By the way, Mark Williams points out that an offset to the passenger's side is normal, but a pinion offset to the driver's side is abnormal. In a race car application or one in which the driveshaft is very short, the pinion should be centered. The housing must then be constructed with the offset taken into consideration. (Illustration Courtesy Mark Williams Enterprises)

With the housing out of the car, I simply set it up on a set of axle stands with the pinion rotated to face upward.

The first step is to measure the width of the housing, flange to flange. Simply run a tape measure through the bare housing to get the number. Here, I'm first measuring for offset; the total housing measures 52.75 inches wide.

CHAPTER 3

Measure for Custom Axles CONTINUED

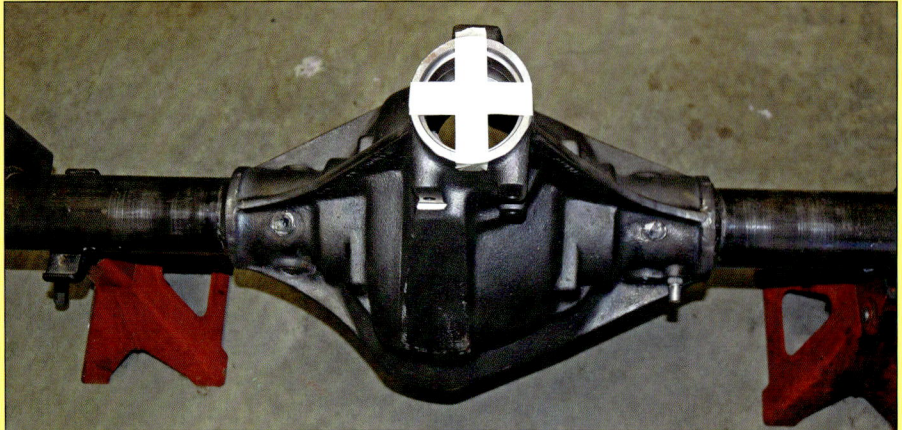

I found the centerline of the pinion and taped it over as shown here.

A plumb line was dropped from the pinion centerline out the back of the S60 housing. I measured from the axle-housing flange back toward the plumb line. The passenger's side measured 25.875 inches while the driver's side checked out at 26.875 inches. Even though the axle tubes welded to the center section are the same width, there's an inch difference in actual axles. The reason is the pinion offset. To double-check the numbers, add the pair of measurements together (25.875 inches + 26.875 inches = 52.750 inches). They should be the same as the axle flange–to–axle flange figure.

in batches in a few specific lengths. They manufacture those axles with very long splines. When the company receives an order, they simply cut off the excess spline. On the other hand, those companies with shorter splines build the axle to the correct length, which allows for 100-percent engagement in the spool or differential. If you have excess (unused) spline, the torsional capability of the axle is reduced.

On a similar note, some axles are shorter than others for a given application. The reason is, the spline location in some spools is located farther outboard. This allows for a larger (stronger) spline, but at the same time, the axles can be built shorter. This means the axles are lighter, and that's a bonus.

Finally, the shoulder of the axle bearing is another area to ponder. Standard 12-bolt Chevy axles typically

The basic axle following all machining is manufactured with a step on the flange. This is to secure the bearing.

This is a pair of axles for the same car. There's quite a difference in axle length because of the pinion offset in a Ford housing.

48 CHEVY NOVA 1968–1974: HOW TO BUILD AND MODIFY

REAR AXLE

These are the basic components used to secure the axle to the housing (obviously, no C-clip is used). Below the axle and from the left are bearing lock ring, bearing, seal, and axle retainer. All are from Mark Williams.

Viewed from the spline end, you can see how the bearing is pressed in place and secured. This setup uses a drag race–style wheel seal (the bearing incorporates an O-ring rather than a separate seal).

This is the flange side of the pro/street axle. Different applications mandate different flanges. A pro/street piece is thicker (heavier) than a dedicated drag race axle (for example, no worries about curbs on the strip).

have a 1.400-inch bearing (ID); a small Ford housing has a 1.378-inch ID. Most mid-range performance axles make use of a 1.562-inch ID bearing whereas a race axle such as the MW Hi-Torque is designed for a 1.774-inch ID bearing. That's a huge difference, especially when you consider that the larger the bearing, the greater the surface area to both carry weight and transfer the load.

The flange on an original equipment axle typically measures .375 inches in thickness. Wheel studs are of the press-in variety (with a knurled shank) and usually measure 7/16 inch (small GM vehicles such as the Nova and select early Mopars) or 1/2 inch (the rest). Later-model cars are usually fitted with metric studs, but again, they're of the press-in variety. Most aftermarket axles have a thicker flange. It is (most often) drilled and tapped to accept 1/2-inch-diameter screw-in studs. Quality race axles are set up for 5/8-inch-diameter drive studs.

What type of axle retention is required? Most race-sanctioning bodies require some form of positive axle retention. The original equipment C-clip (which fastens the axle on the inboard side at the very end of the spline) does not meet these requirements. Accordingly, MW offers a special bolt-in C-clip eliminator kit that provides the necessary retention. If, on the other hand, you plan on narrowing the housing, it's a good idea to change the housing ends. Weld-on aftermarket housing ends provide for a much larger (stronger) bearing and provide for positive retention by way of a hefty retainer. They can be mated to most popular brake applications (ranging from OEM drums to aftermarket disc brakes).

If you're a dedicated Nova drag racer, a big consideration should be weight. A set of lightened axles can reduce weight by at least 9½ pounds (depending upon the length of the axles and the type of rear end they're going into). As an example, one standard Mark Williams axle for a typical S/S car weighs 17.3 pounds. The same axle in a Mark Williams Super-Light configuration weighs 12.4 pounds. How is axle weight reduced? With a "gun" drilled axle. Using Mark Williams' pieces as an example, the core of the axle shaft is bored 11/16 inch to resemble a gun barrel. As you can well imagine, this requires special machine tools, but Mark Williams takes an extra step in the process (which is seldom, if ever, done by other companies): It precision hones the gun drill bore to remove tooling marks on axles produced from 300M steel. The gun drill found on the 4340 axles is actually smooth. This might seem like a small step, but the honing process improves the strength of a gun-drilled axle. Whenever Mark Williams gun drills an axle, it also includes round lightening holes in the axle flange. These two steps reduce axle weight by 17 percent over a standard axle.

This is the standard axle flange found on Mark Williams' Hi Torque axles. It's double drilled for conventional 1/2-inch studs and drag race–style drive studs.

CHAPTER 4

REAR SUSPENSION

Something many grizzled old Nova racers remember is the saying "hooks hard; goes straight." It was used everywhere, and was often attached to cars advertised for sale. It wasn't just a passing statement either. There were plenty of squirrelly cars out there (including Novas), and the truth is, there still are! Getting a car to hook properly isn't quite as easy as it looks, even with back-to-basics leaf springs out back.

All Novas used leaf springs on the rear. That makes bolting on rear traction devices quite simple. Unfortunately, simple doesn't necessarily mean adjustable. Simple doesn't always work that well either, especially if your car has serious horsepower under the hood. Furthermore, some of the traction bar information gleaned in years gone by has little or nothing to do with the way cars are set up today.

Bolt-On Bars

Ask anyone in the know about bolt-on traction bars and the first thing he (or she) will tell you is to forget the rest and go straight for CalTracs. Calvert Racing Suspensions manufactures a complete bolt-on system for 1968–1974 Novas that includes CalTracs traction bars, unique split mono-leaf springs, dedicated shock absorbers designed specifically for the CalTracs, and several tuning bits.

I look at the CalTracs springs in Chapter 5, but here's the scoop on the CalTracs bars: John Calvert and Larry Kieser designed them many years ago. Together, they developed a traction bar that hooks a (limited tire) NHRA Stock Eliminator car. The design is "tunable," easy to install and set up, and works far better than the "slapper bars" of old. It also had to fit the NHRA Stock regulations, which mandated a bolt-on bar only. For Nova applications, the CalTracs bar bolts to the front spring eye mount location and the bottom. It replaces the OEM spring seat.

Compared to a slapper bar, which pushes up on the spring when loaded, the CalTracs bar basically reverses the "pushing forces" on the car. For all intents and purposes, a slapper bar is engineered to prevent spring wrap-up. On the other hand, a CalTracs bar is much

One of the best and most successful traction devices available for 1968–1974 Novas has to be the CalTracs bar. These traction bars have set the standard for most small-tire applications. Cars have run deep into the 8-second zone with CalTracs.

REAR SUSPENSION

This pivot arrangement mounts at the front of the CalTracs traction bar. When installed, it mounts over the top of the leaf spring pack. In operation, it forces down on the leaf. A conventional slapper bar primarily stops leaf wrap-up. To install the bar, the front leaf spring mount must be removed (note that in this photo, the pieces are upside down).

Here's another look at the front pivot; this time from the side, as installed inside the stock Nova forward leaf spring mount. Installation is simple, but keep in mind that the three OEM bolts that hold the production spring mount might be difficult to remove. If you break the captured nuts, Classic Industries has replacements in stock.

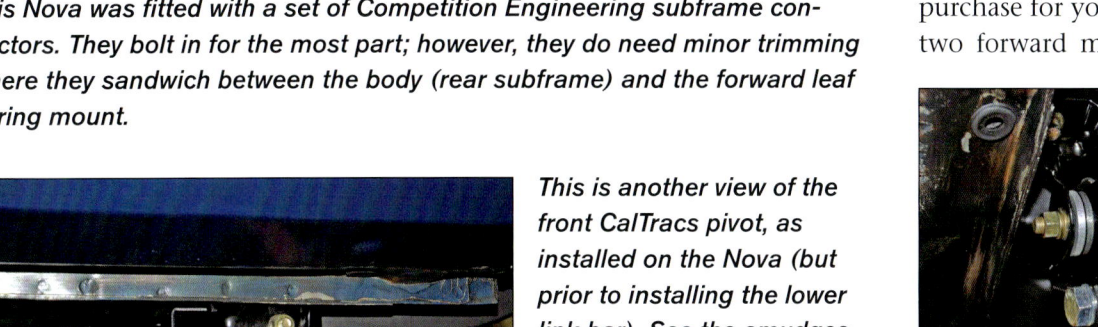

This Nova was fitted with a set of Competition Engineering subframe connectors. They bolt in for the most part; however, they do need minor trimming where they sandwich between the body (rear subframe) and the forward leaf spring mount.

This is another view of the front CalTracs pivot, as installed on the Nova (but prior to installing the lower link bar). See the smudges on the side plate on the bar? That's anti-seize. Use it on the threads every time you install a rod end; otherwise, you run the risk of galling threads (which is bad news from an adjustment point of view).

like the lower half of a four-link. The chassis instant center (IC) location is moved forward. This allows the car to pick up weight in a location near the front end of the Nova and transfer it to the drive wheels. In operation, the front pivot applies force to the front spring eye and loads with a down-force on the forward segment of the Nova leaf spring. As the rear end of the car rotates, the CalTracs bar creates a forward motion. This motion drives forward on the pivot and forward on the body. This is the opposite of a slapper bar, which drives motion upward. As a result of the forces manipulated by the CalTracs bar system, pinion angle is maintained and the Nova hooks. The Nova exhibits less body separation than with a slapper bar combination, but more weight transfer (effectively, this means serious hook). As pointed out previously, the bars feature multiple adjustment points, and it is possible to preload them as necessary. I'll get to tuning them in a moment.

Adjustment is easy, likely easier than a ladder bar or even a four-link. The bars can be moved for more preload, and depending upon the set you purchase for your Nova, they include two forward mount holes (you can

In operation (bar attached), as you load the tire with power, the link bar moves forward, which, in turn, loads the spring.

CHEVY NOVA 1968–1974: HOW TO BUILD AND MODIFY

CHAPTER 4

The back end of the CalTracs bar is easy to work with too. It bolts in at the lower shock mount perch. This is much the same rear mount arrangement that's used with a good slapper bar. As you can see, the OEM factory mount location is maintained. You don't need the rubber spring seat that is sometimes sandwiched between the spring and the shock mount bracket. Obviously, the rear end isn't installed here.

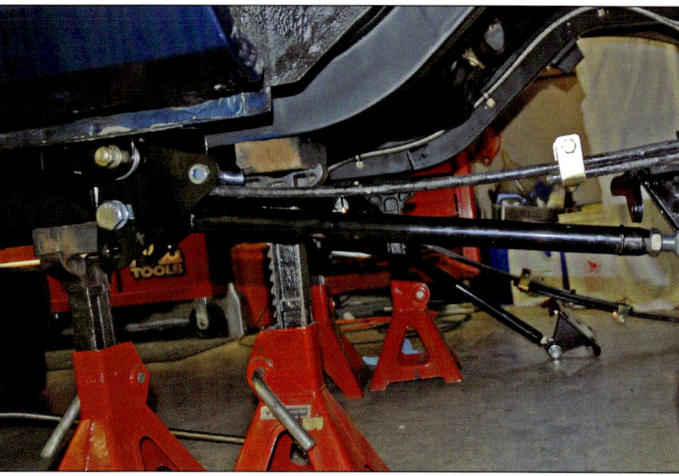

Under the front pivot is the chrome-moly lower link. A rod end is incorporated at this location, along with "wrenching flats" on the lower link for ease of adjustment. Left- and right-hand rod ends are used at both the front and rear.

purchase CalTracs bars with a single forward mount location, but that restricts tuning capability). When the force link bar is moved to the lower mount location, the IC moves farther forward. This allows nose-heavy applications (for example, an all-steel iron-head big-block such as an NHRA-legal B/Stock Nova) to transfer weight to the rear (and hook).

I'll tell you right now that a well-set-up Nova with CalTracs has outstanding traction capability without any extra fabrication. The bottom line here is, you simply bolt them on and tune the bars for the track or road surface and the horsepower conditions. Lots of folks run them on the track and, yes, an equally large number is run on the street (although they can be a bit noisy when the leaf spring is loaded under power).

Tuning CalTracs

Unlike a four-link Nova, which can be adjusted by way of the suspension links, shock, and strut settings, a stock Nova–style leaf spring suspension system is adjusted in a slightly different manner. The big change is the way you deal with the back end. As mentioned earlier, with CalTracs, changing instant center comes from the link attaching point (upper or lower hole). Preload settings have an effect upon the action in the back of the Nova, and preload on one side or the other helps steer the car while the front wheels are in the air, much the same as an upper bar in a four-link or an anti-roll adjustment.

For the setup, try this: Starting at the front of the Nova, ensure that the front end is not binding. "Stiction" in a bushing (for example, a poly bushing) tends to induce front-end binding. With a dedicated drag car or a street/strip Nova, what you really need is either a bearing or rod end, or a Delrin bushing in the control arm. Front springs should be "soft," which is achieved with either a special drag race spring or something like a 6-cylinder spring with a small-block or a small-block spring with a big-block (engine). You need something in the range of 5 to 6 inches of travel. This is a case where more is better. You need a "loose" shock. The CalTracs shocks for Novas are 90/10 jobs and they're perfect for the application. If you use adjustable shocks, set them full loose for the baseline. You can adjust them from this point.

At the back of the Nova, again check for binding. The most likely spots for suspension bind are at the rear spring shackle and/or the front mount bolt (the one that passes through the spring eye). In many

You can sometimes use a slider instead of a shackle, but for a street-driven car, it's best to stick with the tried and true rear shackle arrangement. Be sure the shackle and spring bolts are not over-tightened. That causes them to bind.

REAR SUSPENSION

Adjusting the length of the lower bar determines how much space you have between the load bolt and the spring. Shortening the bar increases the space; lengthening the bar decreases it.

This is the load bolt mentioned in the previous photo. When you set up the CalTracs bar, the consensus is to run a gap with the thickness of a dime as the baseline.

The upper front hole (where the bar is currently attached) makes for a more violent hook than the lower hole (where I'm pointing). If the car flattens the tire on the hook (squashes the tire to a flat shape), move the bar to the lower hole.

cases, the shackle bolts and spring eyebolts are over-tightened. Lube the bushings too. Without the shocks and the CalTracs bars in place, you should be able to easily push the rear of the car down several inches by hand. If the car doesn't move, the suspension is most likely binding.

Begin with the upper adjustment hole in the CalTracs bars. Set the preload on the CalTracs at 1/16 inch. Rather than use the 1/16-inch preload, some folks use a dime and set up the bars so that the dime just slides out from between the spring and the load bolt.

For now, set the rear shocks at full tight (extension). At this point, you're ready to test the car. What follows are several scenarios you're likely to encounter.

- The Nova works perfectly!
- The Nova hooks and wheelstands. If the wheelstand is huge, tighten down the front end. You can do this with the shock and/or a suspension travel limiter.
- The Nova hooks, but starts spinning the tires when it's past the Christmas tree. Loosen the extension on the rear shock absorb-

If your Nova hooks and then wheelstands violently, you need to reduce front-end travel. See that long Grade-8 bolt on the top of the front control arm? To tie down the front end, the bolt must be tightened.

If the Nova hooks hard but then turns (spins) the tires, try loosening the back shocks. This is easy enough with an externally adjustable shock, as shown here (Calvert Racing single adjustable). Chapter 5 has more information on shock settings.

ers. Try loosening them by one adjustment "click" until it hooks without blowing off the tire.
- The Nova hooks but it pulls to the right or to the left. Add a small amount of preload to the

side the car pulls toward.
- If the Nova hooks too hard and wads up the tires (hits the tires too hard), move the bar into the lower front mount position and re-tune using the above steps.

CHEVY NOVA 1968–1974: HOW TO BUILD AND MODIFY

CHAPTER 4

The most common mistake a tuner makes with a CalTracs setup is to tune it like a big-tire car. For example, if you leave the starting line using a transbrake, don't leave with the RPM too high. That (obviously) turns the tires. If you leave the starting line off the foot brake, use a two-step. It adds consistency to the launch. With a stick shift combination, too much clutch air gap, too much clutch base pressure, and too much RPM (basically a violent clutch setup) make the tires spin.

Four-Links and Ladder Bars

If you've decided that bolt-on bars aren't for you, the logical options include a ladder bar setup or a four-link. Let's start at the beginning. When a Nova launches at the dragstrip the rear end wraps up. No news to anyone. The purpose of a traction device (ladder bar or four-link) is to turn that wrap-up into forward motion. Consider the case of a ladder bar. This is a simple device constructed in a triangle-like shape that connects the rear-end housing to a point on the frame. Excessive suspension wrap-up is prevented by pushing up on the frame at the point of forward connection on the frame rail (basically the point where the upper and lower bars of the ladder bar intersect). This intersection point is where the car is "picked up." A ladder bar car has two "pickup points," one on each side of the Nova.

Consider what happens when the ladder bars push up on the chassis at the pickup point. The respective bar on each side of the car also pushes down on the tires and wheels. This effectively "plants" the tires, which in turn make the car hook.

That all makes sense, but over time it didn't take long for racers and hot rodders to figure out that changes in that pickup point location can have a sizeable influence upon the way the car reacts. If, for example the pickup points were situated rather high and short (closer to the back axle), the car would launch violently. This regularly resulted in the tire wadding up at the launch. Following this hit to the tire, load transfer usually wasn't sufficient to maintain traction. The car would start to turn the tires again. The excessive initial hit to the tire coupled with the inability to maintain load transfer, caused the ET of the car to suffer. That wasn't the end of it either. A ladder bar with a short, high pickup point usually creates major body separation during the launch. With body separation, the rear of the body drastically rises above the wheels and tires. It looks wild, but it also can result is horrendous driveshaft alignment, and that can spell serious grief for universal joints, driveshafts, tail shaft housings, and even third members.

What if, instead of a short, high pickup point, you had a long, low pickup point? This arrangement tends to hit the tires with less violence, but it can still generate more total load transfer to the rear tires. For most Novas, this is generally an acceptable situation, but if you go too far, the chassis may squat markedly (again, not good for universal joint angles) or, worse, shake the tires.

If there is a downside to ladder bars and four-links, it is that ladder bars allow less body roll than a four-link and a four-link has less body roll than a bone-stock leaf spring suspension system. Neither a ladder bar nor a four-link is perfect on the street. To be perfect, the suspension must be capable of rolling independent of the body (for example, when one wheel hits a pothole). Basically, both setups allow for some of this roll, but less than a stock rear suspension system. Does that make them a bad choice? Not really, because there's a catch: The majority of street/strip cars (Novas included) equipped with a ladder bar or four-link suspension setup are tubbed and fitted with tall and wide tires. Those big tires actually add suspension to the car.

Tuning

The big question with a ladder bar setup is this: Is it possible to make the ladder bar adjustable so that you can tune it from a range of short, high pickup point to long, low pickup point? It's not that easy. It can be accomplished with several ladder bars along with several forward ladder bar mounting positions. If you begin with a four-link, pro chassis builder Jerry Bickel notes, it is entirely possible to create both pickup point extremes (short and high versus long and low). That's

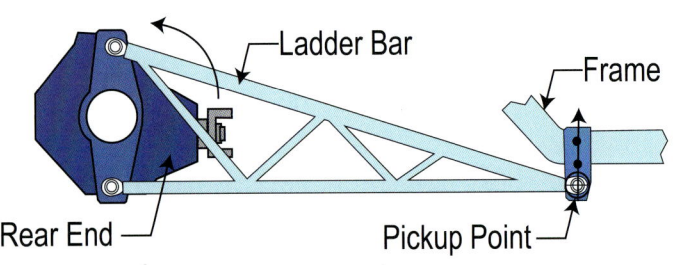

With a ladder bar, pickup points are limited. You can move them up or down. If you want to shorten or lengthen them, you need another ladder bar (shorter or longer). (Illustration Courtesy Jerry Bickel Race Cars)

54 CHEVY NOVA 1968–1974: HOW TO BUILD AND MODIFY

REAR SUSPENSION

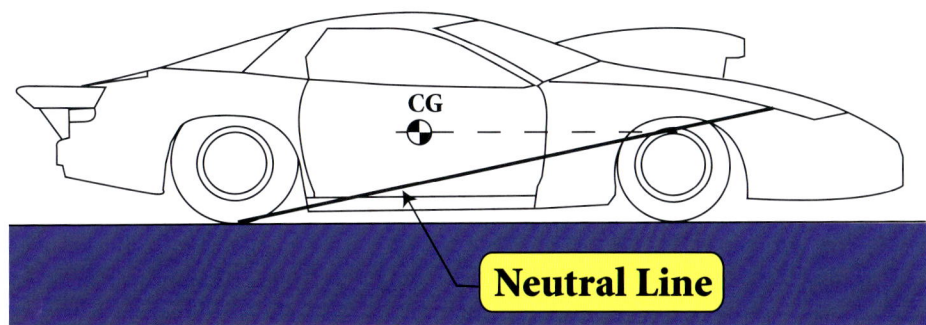

The neutral line in the chassis is where the car's body neither squats nor separates on the suspension. (Illustration Courtesy Jerry Bickel Race Cars)

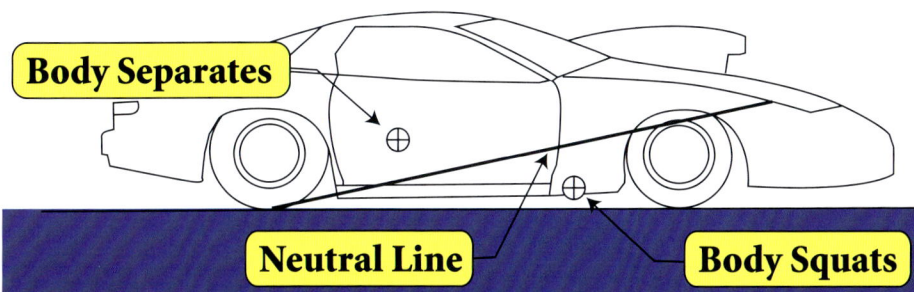

When it comes to "imaginary" pickup points, the ideal location would be somewhere close to the neutral line, as shown here. (Illustration Courtesy Jerry Bickel Race Cars)

why four-link suspension systems are more versatile on the track.

What is the ideal pickup point location? It depends on multiple factors; however, there is one constant. All cars have a neutral line that determines how the chassis behaves. If the pickup point is located about this line, the body separates upon acceleration. If the pickup point is located below this neutral line, the body squats.

In a perfect situation, the front pickup point should be located near the neutral line. This setup ultimately works well and proves to be very stable. The Nova neither shows squat nor encounters excess body separation. The question is, how do you figure out the neutral line location? Most pros feel that the neutral line of a drag car can be determined by extending a line level with the height of the CG (Center of Gravity) until it crosses a vertical line through the front spindle. The neutral line can be represented as a diagonal that intersects this location as well as the center of the rear tire–to–pavement contact point.

So far so good, but according to chassis wizard Jerry Bickel, there are several difficulties with this method, "It is difficult to measure the height of the CG accurately. Most racers use the camshaft centerline as the CG height, but without an accurate measurement, it is impossible to locate the neutral line with precision.

"Another problem with this traditional neutral line location theory is that many drag race cars wheelstand through low gear. After the front tires are in the air, I do not believe that they have an effect upon neutral line location. Experience has shown that the pickup point distance from the rear axles is at least as important as its height.

"In practice, I find that pickup point location must be changed, depending upon racetrack conditions and vehicle performance. You should rely on conventional neutral line theory only as a starting point for rear suspension setup."

Chassis Instant Center

Fair enough, but what you need is an idea of something called the "instant center." What's that? The instant center, or "IC," is an imaginary point about which the chassis

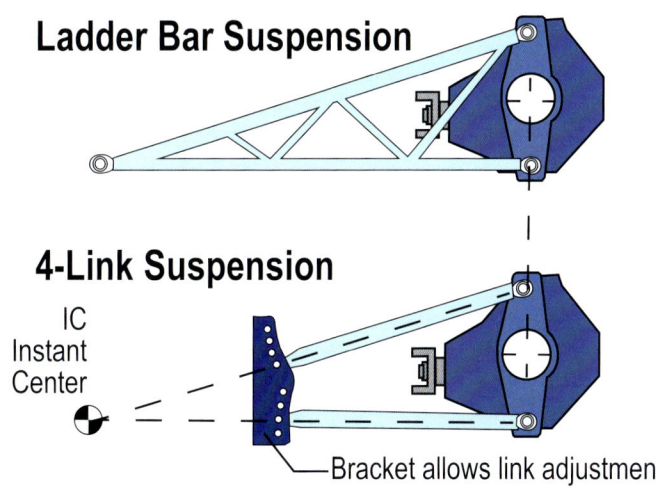

A ladder bar is very limited when it comes to setting up the instant center (pickup point), but a four-link offers many possibilities. (Illustration Courtesy Jerry Bickel Race Cars)

or a suspension member rotates (in a given or "instant" position) with power applied to it. You can find it by simply projecting lines along suspension members to a point of intersection. This is easy enough on a ladder bar. The intersection point is regularly the front rod end. However, it can move to any number of locations with a four-link. If you examine Jerry Bickel's drawing carefully, you can see that the four-link instant center is invisible, and that invisible point is the actual "pickup point" for the rear suspension.

Because the respective brackets found on something such as a four-link are under load during acceleration and braking, they must be robust. When the Nova accelerates, the rear end wraps up, placing the upper bars in tension while the lower bars are held in compression. As you brake, the forces are reversed. But I digress.

Establishing Four-Link IC Location

When you or your chassis builder install the rear end in your Nova with a four-link setup, that's the time to decide exactly which bracket holes you use for the links. The location where the four-link (front mount bracket) is installed determines the length and height of the instant center. That in turn determines how the car works. Bickel says that if the tire is driven down too hard by way of the IC location, it tends to fold up the sidewalls, which in turn makes for poor surface contact. If the four-link doesn't apply sufficient force to the tire, it spins. If you look closely at Jerry's illustration, it's easy to see the many possible IC locations in a four-link. Pick the one that works best for your car, but it's not cut and dry.

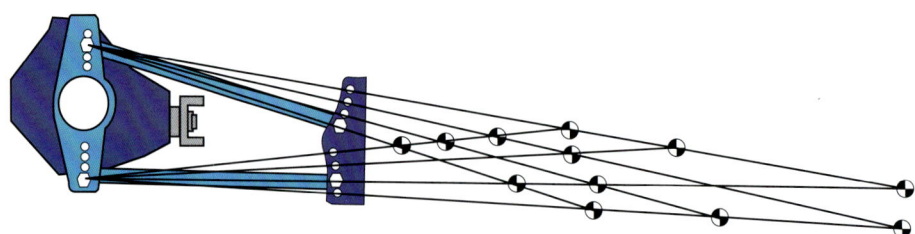

This is a look at the many possible combinations you can come up with for tuning the instant center on your Nova. (Illustration Courtesy Jerry Bickel Race Cars)

So where do you begin? Jerry offers a very simple explanation to choose the IC pickup points, "Long, low-intersect points create traction for the longest time, but react slowly. Short, high-intersect points create traction for the least time, but react fast."

Figuring Instant Center Length

IC can affect the overall vehicle reaction time (this includes the Nova and you). If you have good reactions to a light, a long IC point (50 to 60 inches) works better than a short one (50 inches or less). The long IC plants the tires smoothly and tends to keep them planted for a considerable length of time. Earlier, I noted that if you lay down too much initial power coupled with a long IC point, you will likely end up with tire shake. Tires "shake" when they become oval shaped and consequently become unbalanced under power.

That brings me to the torque output of the engine in your Nova. Bickel has an example, and although the first one probably doesn't apply to a four-link Nova, it does offer a lot of insight into how this all works. "Racers of high-powered Pro Mod cars often use tires that were initially designed for solid suspension Funny Cars and Top Fuel dragsters. The sidewalls of these tires are tall and very flexible, acting like a sort of spongy suspension system. They work best when you limit the rear movement to as little as possible with an IC point on or near the neutral line of the car.

"Further to this, I like to run a long, low IC point in an application such as a high-RPM low-horsepower

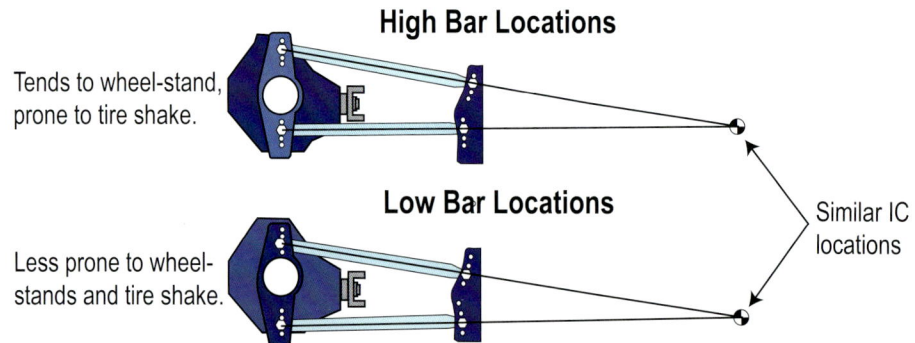

This is where four-link tuning gets interesting! As you can see, there are several ways to come up with the same instant center (or at least instant centers that are close). One tends to wheelstand and/or rattle the tires. The other does not. (Illustration Courtesy Jerry Bickel Race Cars)

small-block clutch car. This combination seems to help overcome the impact from the high-RPM launch and the engine usually doesn't have enough power to shake the tires."

Remember when I initially discussed location of the bars in the four-link? If you have a side view of a four-link, the location of the bars in relation to the centerline of the rear axle makes a difference in performance, even if the IC point remains the same. The closer to the housing the upper bar is, therefore, the less the car tends to wheelstand. When the bottom four-link bar is located lower in the car the suspension maintains better traction control, and at the same time, is less prone to tire shake.

Figuring Instant Center Height

The neutral line (examined previously) slopes within the car from the front to the rear. Bickel states that, should you decide to change the length of the IC, you must also change the height to maintain the same anti-squat characteristics.

When it comes to IC height settings in your Nova chassis, the farther forward you move the Instant Center, the lower it must be. The farther back you move the IC, the higher it must be.

Some other food for thought is this (again, taken from Jerry's tuning bag of tricks): Automatic-transmission cars along with lower-torque stick-shift cars work best when the IC point is from 1 to 2 inches above the racing surface. Big-power stick-shift cars typically need to stay 3 to 7 inches above the racing surface.

The bottom line here is, you must take your time setting up a four-link for your Nova. Jerry recommends you follow the above methodology and make only one change at a time.

It's very important to keep notes of the changes too.

Before moving on, there's something you should consider if you chose to use a ladder bar or four-link in your Nova and you want to retain the factory leaf springs: With this arrangement, the suspension is placed in a bind as it travels up and down. If it binds it bends the ladder bars (or four-link) or the leaf springs. Or both. There are a couple of solutions: You can use ladder bars with slotted front mount points or a housing floater. With either of these setups (and leaf springs), the ladder bars (or four-link) control suspension movement and front to rear, rear axle placement. However, they do not control side-to-side motion, at least not very well. You still need some form of lateral link (more on this later). In the end, though, using leaf springs and ladder bars (or a four-link) isn't much fun; it's a noisy, bulky setup, and if you've gone this far you're far better off with coil-over springs out back.

Pinion Angle

The rear suspension in a Nova under power experiences "wrap up," and with it the pinion is driven upward (out of whack). Rear axle and driveshaft manufacturer Mark Williams notes that the optimal angle for any driveshaft to run at is 1/2 degree, where many vibration and friction problems are non-existent. To minimize power loss and vibration in an offset configuration, the pinion centerline and the transmission centerline need to be parallel. In general, the largest angle for high-performance applications should be 2 degrees, and the centerlines should be parallel within a few tenths of a degree.

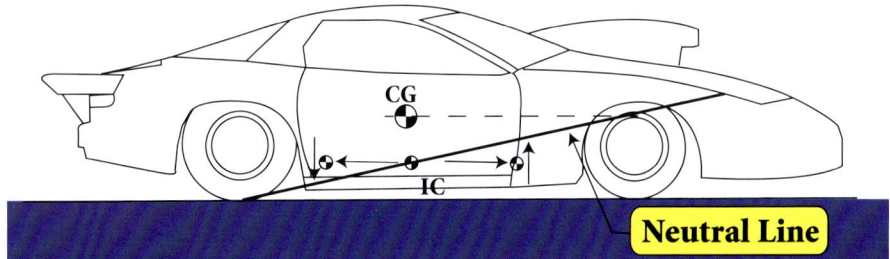

This drawing shows why changes in the instant center length must be accompanied with a change in instant center height. (Illustration Courtesy Jerry Bickel Race Cars)

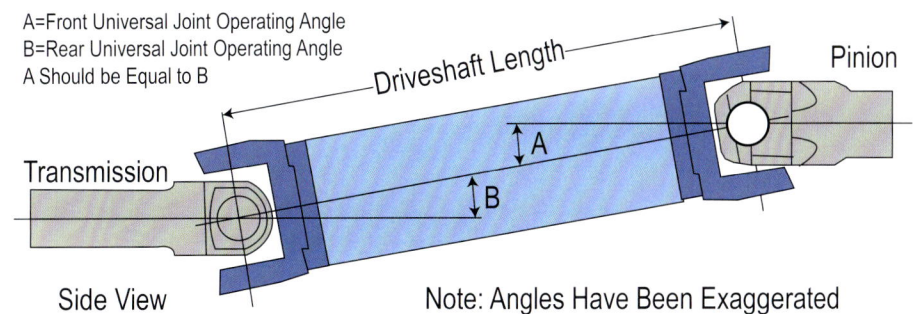

Pinion angle is critical in any car, and your Nova is no different. If you don't get the pinion angles sorted out, you'll be chasing trouble (which usually translates into broken parts) for a long time. (Illustration Courtesy Mark Williams Enterprises)

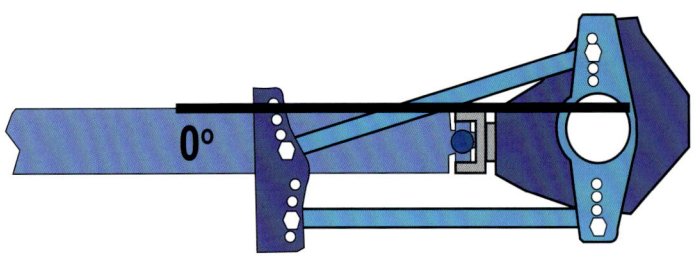

Under power, the pinion angle should be zero.

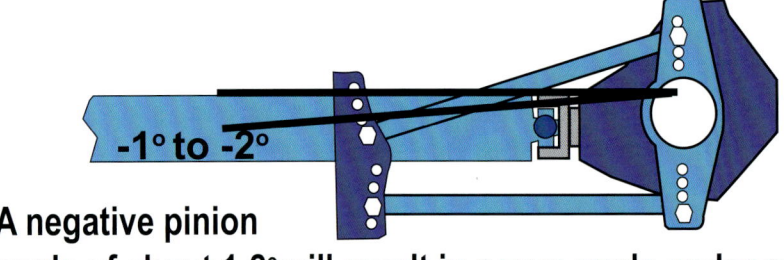

A negative pinion angle of about 1-2° will result in a zero angle under power.

Jerry Bickel is quick to point out that under power, you must ensure that the pinion angle is zero. (Illustration Courtesy Jerry Bickel Race Cars)

Bickel goes on to show that with a race-style four-link, you most likely need a pinion angle nosed downward of 1 to 2 degrees to obtain a pinion angle of zero while under power. (Illustration Courtesy Jerry Bickel Race Cars)

If the chassis has some type of a parallel traction bars system, the angles should remain parallel throughout the suspension travel.

Drag race chassis builder Jerry Bickel adds, "There should be no pinion angle (0 degrees) on acceleration, or vibrations, power loss, and universal joint breakage can result."

Keep in mind that with suspension movement the operating angle increases but should not exceed a few degrees. If the parallelism of the centerlines changes, the U-joints travel at uneven operating velocities, causing vibration (this is the same problem induced by poorly phased end yokes). This vibration is hard to distinguish from an unbalanced driveshaft.

To ensure that the pinion is in the correct location under power, it is typically set nose down static. Mark Williams notes that some of the most common information (or perhaps misinformation) on setup was derived from the very early years of Mopar racing. The very early Chrysler cars had a thick spring that was subject to wind up. To try to make allowances for this wind up the pinion was dropped down a few degrees in an effort to have the centerlines running close to parallel when under power. If the car has OEM-style rubber suspension bushings, a pinion angle of -3 to -4 degrees is likely more appropriate. Williams notes that this nose-down attitude was originally done to compensate for the compression of the rubber bushings.

To set the pinion angle on a four-link car with adjustment capability (for example, a Nova with a four-link), you lengthen or shorten one or both of the upper bars to move down or up. If the Nova has stock leaf springs, you can use wedge plates (wedge-shaped aluminum shims) to move the pinion up or down. The wedge plates effectively rotate the pinion upward or downward depending on which way the wedge is facing. The wedge plates are designed to sandwich between the rear-end housing perches and the leaf springs.

Pinion angle should be checked and adjusted any time there are changes in the chassis that affect the ride height or the length and location of the suspension link bars. Prior to setting up the pinion angle, you should have the four-link instant center set, the rear end aligned, the chassis at correct ride height, the weight distribution set, the tire rollout checked, and the tire pressure set.

So far so good, but the other thing to keep in mind about the

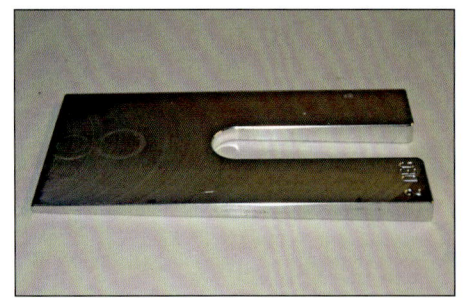

Classic Industries offers several offset wedges for leaf spring Nova applications. This particular example is a 2-degree aluminum job for a split mono-leaf (Cal-Tracs) spring. It can be used to move the pinion down (or up) 2 degrees.

The upper bars in a four-link typically are used to set the pinion angle. If you look closely, you'll see wrenching "flats" on the left-hand side of the bar. After the jamb nuts are loosened (on both sides), you can turn the bar out.

driveshaft is critical speed. Critical speed is the speed at which a spinning shaft becomes unstable. This is one of the single largest factors in driveshaft selection. When the whirling frequency and the natural frequency coincide, any vibration is multiplied, so much that the shaft may self-destruct. Another way to think of this is that if a shaft naturally vibrates at 130 times a second, and one point on the shaft passes through 0 degrees 130 times per second (7,800 rpm) then the shaft has hit a critical speed. The critical speed of a driveshaft can be raised by several means. You can make it lighter, stiffer, or increase diameter without increasing weight. This is the reason carbon fiber makes a good driveshaft; it is stiff and light and can be made to any diameter or wall thickness. Aluminum, while it has a higher critical speed than steel (same diameter and length shaft) is not quite as strong as steel. Steel, with good strength characteristics, has a lower critical speed. Because of this, it's important to check with a driveshaft manufacturer before you decide upon a specific driveshaft for a specific application.

Laterally Linked

If you've installed a four-link or ladder bar in your Nova, you must ponder a way to control the side-to-side movement of the axle housing. The only exception is if the Nova car is equipped with conventional leaf springs fitted without a housing floater. All other suspension arrangements encompass some form of coil-over spring and, as a result, a means of positively locating the rear axle laterally is required. You must be able to control this motion as the rear suspension moves completely through its travel.

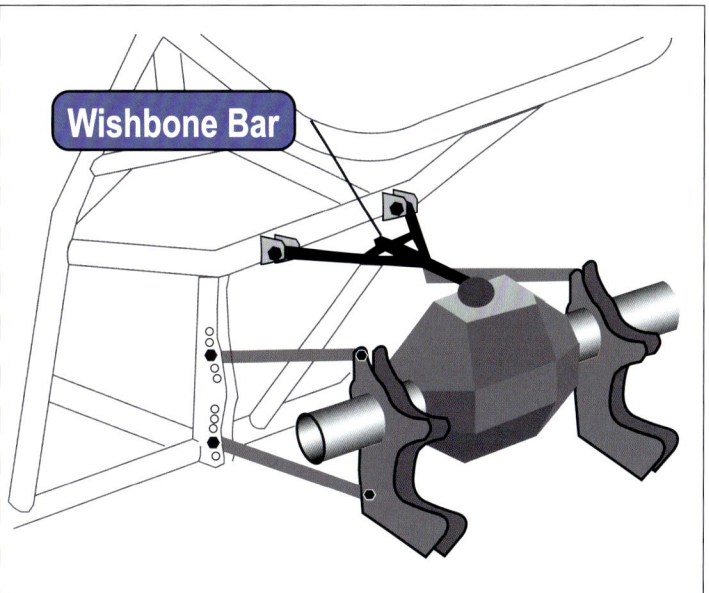

Bickel likes to mount the wishbone above the rear housing. This location provides for much easier access to the third member. It also gets the wishbone away from the road surface. (Illustration Courtesy Jerry Bickel Race Cars)

The control of lateral movement is imperative. Take, for example, a four-link setup coupled with coil-over springs (obviously, a very common arrangement); there is absolutely nothing to hold the rear axle housing from moving side to side. Without some form of lateral control to keep the housing in check, it can shift itself right out of the car. You can't drive the Nova without controlling the lateral motion.

So, what are the options for controlling this motion? Several designs are in use today. Included in the mix are diagonal bars (often called a "track locator"), Panhard bars, wishbone track locators, Watt's linkage systems, and angled trailing arms. What's best?

Before I begin, one form of suspension (the triangulated four-link) doesn't need a lateral link of any sort, but fitting one to a Nova is rare, and if you do, fabrication is a real chore.

Panhard Bar

A Panhard bar is designed to link the axle housing to the frame. Panhard bars are simple devices. They're effective too. They can be light in weight, but beefy mounting brackets usually offset that. The brackets must be large and strong and that usually translates to heavy. In operation, the arc the Panhard bar travels in must be kept as small as possible. Accordingly, the Panhard bar must be built as long as possible. The travel arc is created during suspension travel. It produces a slight side-to-side movement of the axle housing (typically you see movement of between 1/16 and 1/8 inch). If your Nova has large amounts of wheel travel and you run a Panhard bar, it's a very good idea to increase the length of the Panhard bar. There's a catch: When you build a long Panhard bar, it must clear the

Panhard bars are a good way to maintain side-to-side motion (between the car and the housing). This big, curved job is designed so that it can clear the "bump" on a rear-end housing.

CHAPTER 4

differential. This can be troublesome if the housing is back braced. The most important factor when installing a Panhard bar is to ensure that the bar is parallel to the rear-end housing at ride height. For a closer look at a great Panhard bar setup, take a look at the setup used in a 1982–2002 Firebird or Camaro. The size and heft of the associated bracketry is considerable, but the geometry is spot on.

Watt's Linkage

The Watt's linkage system eliminates the small side-to-side movement that occurs when you use a Panhard bar. The downside to a Watt's link is that it is often difficult to package at the appropriate height for many chassis setups (Novas included). You need to get it set up at the Nova ride height, plus it's difficult to mount on the nose of the rear axle assembly (although it is possible). Why? A Watt's link requires a bell crank system to work. If you choose to mount the Watt's link behind the axle, the brackets must be extremely robust to handle loads that may be very high. Factor in the need for third member access and/or a back brace on the rear and you can see why there aren't many Watt's linkage systems in use today.

Diagonal Bar

Compared to a Watt's linkage, a diagonal bar is an extremely simple component that connects between the respective lower links of the suspension (most often the lower two bars in a four-link). By connecting the bars diagonally (and, of course, by using rod ends on either side of the diagonal bar), the housing cannot move from side to side, but it's free to move up and down. In some applications with considerable travel, there is some side-to-side deflection. With a diagonal bar installed in the car, at least one end must be removed to service the third member in something like a 9-inch. It's also important to note that in any application that sees cornering forces, you should not use a diagonal bar. As you go around a corner with a car using a diagonal link, the loads placed upon the front of the bar are incredible. Diagonal links sometimes bend when used in a street-driven application. For any Nova that sees any amount of street use, a Panhard bar (or even a wishbone) is a far better option.

Wishbone Bar

A wishbone bar typically connects to one bracket on the rear-end housing along with a pair of brackets on the chassis. Rod ends allow the wishbone bar to pivot as the rear-end housing moves up and down during suspension travel. The single rear rod telescopes to prevent binding, but it cannot move laterally. Wishbones are really the best choice for applications where the frame is narrow (for example, a Nova with big tubs). A point to consider with a wishbone is the clearance in the slip joint. The joint must be machined to keep clearances tight. If the joint is sloppy, you're assured some amount of side-to-side movement. Access to the third member is difficult when conventionally mounted under the housing. Equally important, a bottom-mounted wishbone is susceptible to damage on the telescope rod from debris. That's why the top-mount setup championed by Jerry Bickel is a good idea. However, with the wishbone mounted upstairs, exhaust clearance is an issue.

Controlling the Roll

If your Nova has coil-over springs on the back, it needs an anti-roll bar. If it doesn't have coil-overs (let's say it's equipped with factory leaf springs), there's a good chance it could still use one. Why is it so important? First, let's look at why you need an anti-sway device on the back of a car that mainly sees straight-line use (and keep in mind that the anti-sway bar does a far different job than a track locating device). The first thing to do is to consider the torque loads placed upon the rear housing. If you haven't considered these factors, you should, along with torque loads.

The torque produced by your Nova engine is not constant. It varies with the RPM of the engine. Basically, the engine produces a torque curve, and that curve might peak with 500 ft-lbs at 5,000 rpm. Easy enough but remember, too, that as engine speed increases or decreases from this peak in the curve, the torque produced is lower. Furthermore, if the Nova in question is equipped with an automatic (as shown in our mathematical example below), the true amount of torque delivered to the drive wheels (and, of course, through the chassis setup) is huge.

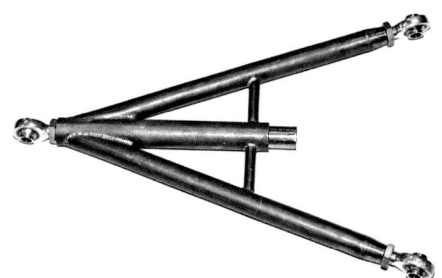

One of the best choices for rear-end control is a wishbone. The center tube contains a machined rod that telescopes as the suspension in the Nova goes through its travel. You must keep it lubed and, obviously, free of debris.

REAR SUSPENSION

Calculating Maximum Torque Load

Here's a hypothetical set of relatively mild (and easily attainable) Nova specifications.

A	Engine Torque	450 ft-lbs
B	Torque Converter Multiplication Factor	2.2:1
C	Transmission First Gear Ratio	2.52:1
D	Rear Axle Ratio	3.73:1

Plug these numbers into the following formula:

Rear Axle Torque Load = A x B x C x D
That's 9,305 ft-lbs (450 x 2.2 x 2.52 x 3.73).

Gulp. The loads working through the rear axle assembly (and, ultimately, attempting to twist it right out of the car) prove to be considerable, and that's with a mild combination. If the car dead-hooks, you could easily encounter breakage, or at least bending forces somewhere.

The maximum torque load passed through the rear axle is very easy to calculate.

I should point out that stick-shift cars do not have the benefit of torque multiplication; however, they tend to leave the starting line at a higher RPM (when compared to their automatic-equipped counterparts) and they tend to have much smaller driveline parasitic power losses. That's the reason automatics and sticks sometimes have similar performances.

Torque Rotation

Let's back up a bit and see exactly how physics forces things to happen inside a car. When you dump the clutch or leave the line with an automatic (foot brake or transbrake), something happens in the Nova. A huge amount of engine flywheel torque reaction is transferred to the chassis. And as our friend Jerry Bickel is quick to note, Sir Isaac Newton's Third Law of Motion states that for every action, there is an equal and opposite reaction.

When the engine in your Nova is running, the pistons and, eventually, the connecting rods apply torque to the crank. When you view this from the front of the car, the crankshaft rotates clockwise. Taking Newton's Third Law of Motion into account, something opposite to this must happen. That opposite thing is the engine block in your Nova. It's applying torque in the opposite direction of the crankshaft. In other words, the engine is rolling (twisting) counterclockwise.

Inertial Torque

The inertia forces created by spinning power train components should not be overlooked. Inertia is the force that causes an object to resist changes in motion. If your Nova is equipped with a manual gearbox, the engine, crankshaft, flywheel, and clutch could be spinning at 5,000 rpm or more as you sidestep the clutch at the starting line. Combined, the spinning mass of these components might weigh more than 140 pounds, storing a considerable amount of inertial energy. When you dump the clutch at the starting line (or even if you take off gradually at a stoplight), this added inertia tends to boost chassis roll.

The same applies to an automatic transmission. If you deliver too much power (and, consequently, too much inertial energy) too quickly into the drivetrain, the tires spin (no secret). That's why clutch setup and adjustment along with torque converter selection play an important role in chassis setup. The bottom line here

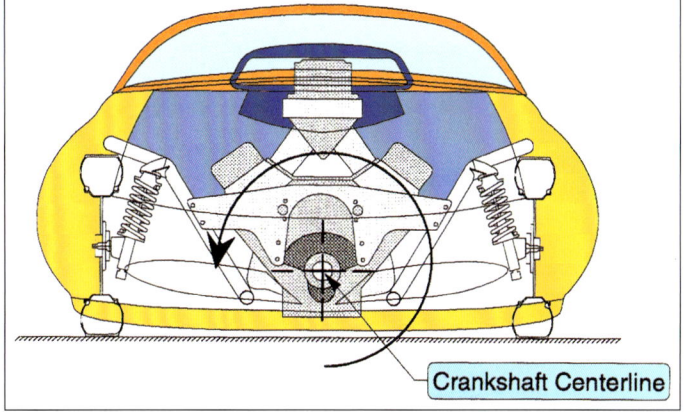

As each cylinder in the Nova engine fires, the pistons (and consequently the connecting rods) apply a force to the crankshaft. The crank rotates and applies a clockwise twisting force (when you view it from the front). Fair enough, but then our pal Mr. Newton's Third Law of Motion enters the equation. As the crank spins, an equal amount of torque is applied in the opposite direction. That occurs within the cylinder block. Obviously, that upsets the chassis. (Illustration Courtesy Jerry Bickel Race Cars)

is, with today's cheap and readily available horsepower, it's not hard to overpower the chassis with too much torque.

Rear-End Torque

The gears inside the rear end in your Nova turn the driveline power 90 degrees to the axles. This in turn produces rear-end torque rotation. What happens is that a certain amount of inertia in the chassis resists the rotation of the wheels, axles, differential (or spool), and ring gear. The resistance causes the pinion gear to convey rotational force or "torque rotation" to the rear-end housing.

This causes a car to have more traction on the left rear wheel and less traction on the right rear wheel. Rear-end torque rotation is also the reason most cars want to move right when you accelerate.

Remember Newton's Third Law of Motion? The roll in the chassis caused by engine torque should be equal and opposite that of rear-end torque reaction. A Nova constructed with a completely rigid chassis should, in theory, allow these two forces to counteract each another. As a result, the Nova could rocket straight and true down the racetrack. Unfortunately, it's not a perfect world, and you almost always end up with a certain amount of flex in the chassis. That's not to say you should build a "flexi-flier." They simply do not work and they're almost impossible to tune. What you should strive for is a chassis constructed as rigid as possible to harness the opposing twisting forces created by the torque. With a rigid platform for your Nova, spring and shock rates can be set and tuned so that you're able to compensate for weather and track conditions as well as racetrack irregularities.

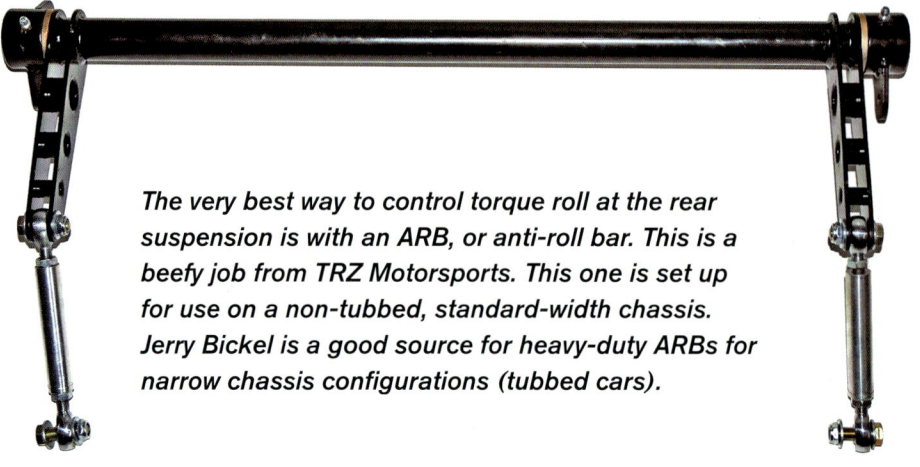

The very best way to control torque roll at the rear suspension is with an ARB, or anti-roll bar. This is a beefy job from TRZ Motorsports. This one is set up for use on a non-tubbed, standard-width chassis. Jerry Bickel is a good source for heavy-duty ARBs for narrow chassis configurations (tubbed cars).

How to Control Torque Factors

Just how can one control chassis roll? One approach is to install extremely stiff springs. Another approach used in the past and still rather common today is to install an air bag or two in or over the back springs (stock spring applications). This approach may limit roll, but it creates a very rigid suspension system that cannot comply with racetrack irregularities. If you have a big-power Nova with a ladder bar or four-link suspension and it has coil-over rear springs, you should use a rear stabilizer bar (sway bar). The bar provides significant resistance to roll, but at the same time, doesn't really affect the normal travel of the rear suspension system.

Solutions

What if you have a small-tire, stock mounting point suspension arrangement Nova and you're trying to make it hook? Or what if you have a Nova with a four-link or ladder bar setup? Several years ago I built a high-horsepower coil-spring street-driven car. It certainly wasn't a Pro Stock car, but it sure did have plenty of rotation out back. Enter TRZ Motorsports. They had (and still have) a very nice weld-in ARB (anti-roll bar) kit. FYI: Our pal Jerry Bickel also offers a wide range of ARBs designed for narrow-chassis, large-tire cars.

The anti-roll bar shown in the accompanying photos is a chrome-moly tube that pivots on bronze bushings captured within the end brackets. As with other configurations, it connects to the rear end through attaching levers and links fitted with rod ends. The stabilizer bar itself is bolted to a tubular chrome-moly cross brace that welds between the respective frame rails. On straight up and down suspension travel (no chassis roll), the attaching levers move together. The stabilizer bar simply rotates on the bushings and suspension movement is unaffected. Chassis roll, on the other hand, causes the links to pull the attaching levers into different angles,

TRZ's ARB is engineered with a bronze bushing on each end, and as you can see, it comes with grease fittings (zerks) installed.

REAR SUSPENSION

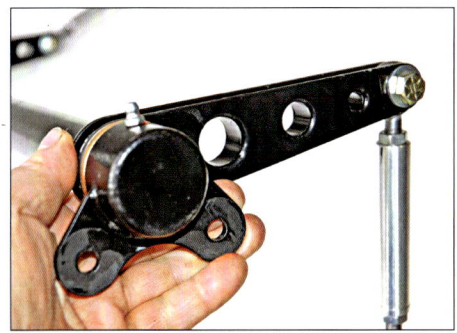

The mount pad below the bushing bolts to a tubular crossmember, which in turn is welded between the frame (or subframe) rails. TRZ supplies the mount crossmember and components with its kit.

Each of the ARB arms incorporates two rod ends. A pair of rod ends bolts to a set of tabs (supplied) that are welded to the rear-end housing. One rod end per side is right-hand while the other is left-hand. You can therefore adjust the ARB by loosening the lock nuts and turning the respective links in or out.

The Basics of Rod-End Construction

What makes up a quality rod end? Basically, a rod end consists of a spherical ball engineered to rotate inside a housing. This ball does the bearing "work" while the housing wrapped around becomes the race. The rod-end ball has a machined flat on each side, and it is bored with a hole right through the center. That, of course, is the basics of rod-end construction, but as you might expect, quite a bit more goes into the equation. When scouring the marketplace for rod ends, you regularly find "economy" or "commercial" examples. Many economy rod ends are available, but the only type you should even think about are the fully "swaged" two-piece examples. When these rod ends are manufactured, the body is swaged around the ball so that the race that the ball rides on is part of the body. When it comes to the cheaper rod ends, you will find that two-piece swaged-construction rod ends are the only examples that can provide good axial strength along with decent radial or pull strength. What is "axial strength"? It's the resistance of the ball being pushed out of the side of the body.

Top-of-the-line rod ends are manufactured in a precision three-piece

Although not a Nova, this G-Body, I built several years ago shows how the ARB is installed. Adjusting the ARB links allows you to preload the chassis (which is all dependent upon how your car reacts). It works fabulously.

which, in effect, twists the stabilizer bar. The bar resists this twist and chassis-rolling force is delivered directly into the rear-end housing.

What about the installation? Is a weld-on bar difficult to install? It's not difficult, and in the photo that follows you see how a system was mounted in a real-world application. Keep in mind, this was done on a GM G-Body, but the process is exactly the same with a Nova.

Rod Ends

Inside any modern high-performance Nova, one thing is certain: You're going to find more than a couple of rod ends or spherical bearings. All rear suspension components I discuss in this chapter make use of rod ends. And they're incredibly important. Rod ends are regularly used in places where they must absorb considerable loads. Basically, it comes down to the strength of the rod end versus the demands of the load. Should a rod end break in your Nova, you can appreciate the trouble this can cause. Given the potential ramifications, each and every rod end tends to become a critical component.

This is a three-piece, or "aircraft," rod end. That means it is constructed with three separate primary components. There are all sorts of ways and combinations to put this together.

format. In these cases, the race is formed around the ball. Next, the race insert is staked into the body. What makes this so vital? That's easy. This manufacturing process provides for a much closer fit as well as a much higher degree of precision between the ball and the race. Essentially, the three-piece design is what is commonly called an "aircraft" rod end. Because three pieces are used in the manufacture, the rod end can be built with different materials. For example, races can be built of mild, alloy, or stainless steel. Don't bother with brass or aluminum bronze races; they don't have the strength necessary for any race application. Similarly, the rod-end body can be manufactured from mild steel, alloy steel, stainless steel, aluminum, or even titanium.

More Material Types

Rod-end balls are most often heat-treated steel (most often chrome-moly steel, stainless steel, or 52100 bearing steel). So that they remain round, the balls must be tremendously hard (it is common for the rod balls to be chrome plated to provide a smooth bearing surface).

Given the heat treatment along with the overall hardness of the

How to Clock Rod Ends

When a pair of rod ends is used in a single component (using that four-link bar as an example), the orientation of the rod ends on either end is important. This is what chassis builders refer to as "clocking" the rod end. Stop right here for one second. When you make very small adjustments in a suspension link that sees preload, it turns out you can make a huge difference in the way the car works or handles. According to pro chassis builder Jerry Bickel, one-sixth of a turn at a time is all that is required to see a change in the way the car works. Keeping this in mind, counting the number of "flats" (the flat side of the rod-end jamb nut) you turn on a link is critical.

Included are a couple of illustrations. The first one shows how a typical link is configured. One side of the link is fitted with right-hand threads while the other end of the link is fitted with left-hand threads. By simply loosening the jam nuts, you can lengthen or shorten the entire four-link bar.

What about clocking? It's easy. When the rod ends are properly "clocked," then they are aligned. When aligned you don't encounter binding in the suspension. At the same time, a link with clocked rod ends makes it easy to determine if the link is under tension. Simply grab the link by hand and rotate it back and forth. You can tell if the link is neutral or under load. ■

Rod ends used in conjunction with four-link bars (as shown here) should be "clocked." That means you should align them after adjusting (or otherwise changing) the link length.

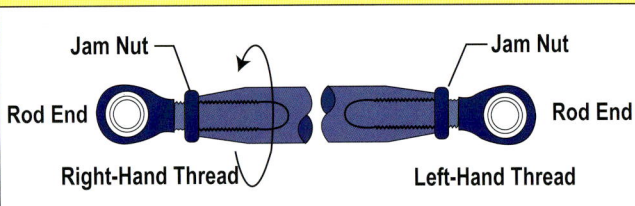

When you adjust something such as a four-link bar, you loosen the jamb nuts on each end and turn the link (bar). That moves the link in or out. It can also change the orientation of the rod end after you re-tighten the jamb nuts. Each rod end can become "cocked," or twisted sideways. (Illustration Courtesy Jerry Bickel Race Cars)

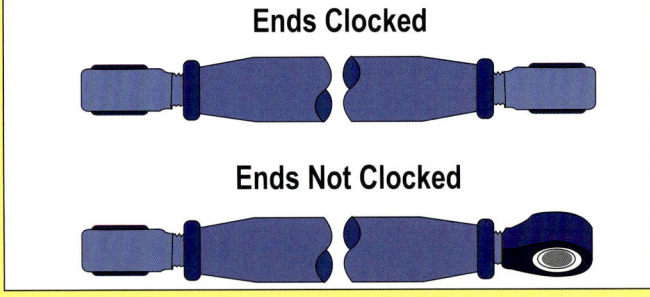

You must "clock" the rod ends when you've completed the length adjustment on the link. This drawing compares a clocked rod end to one that is not clocked. Properly clocked rod ends on a given link allow the rod end to function without binding. (Illustration Courtesy Jerry Bickel Race Cars)

ball, the race must also be hard, but it can't be as hard as the ball. It is common to find three-piece rod ends manufactured with a race built from through-hardened steel alloy or a stainless steel. In either case, the outer race is heat treated for strength and wear resistance.

Is there such a thing as less expensive rod ends? Certainly, but as you see, there are limits. Economy rod ends are usually built with bodies manufactured from low-carbon grades of mild steel. It is not possible to through-harden this material (through-hardening, or quench and temper, is a process used to increase the hardness and tensile strength of a given material). While this less costly material works reasonably well under lightly loaded applications, a rod-end body built from chrome-moly or heat-treated stainless steel is far superior in racing applications. When the manufacturer builds the rod-end body from chrome-moly or stainless steel, the physical size of the rod end can be reduced because the material is stronger. Some rod-end bodies are built from 7075-T6 aluminum. This is a beefy grade of aluminum with a tensile strength that is actually slightly greater than mild steel. But when carefully analyzed, aluminum is not as forgiving as mild steel. It does not stretch or bend as much before breaking. Compare the strength of an aluminum rod end with a heat-treated chrome-moly or stainless component; the steel jobs have almost double the strength.

Teflon Liners

A common (and good) option for rod ends is the Teflon liner. The liner allows the rod end to be self-lubricating. This feature is important because it eliminates the need to grease a rod end after it is installed on your race car. What about a rod end with a grease fitting? Stay away! They're not a good concept, because drilling a hole in the rod end for a grease fitting weakens it (much the same as a driveshaft universal joint with a grease fitting). Besides, grease or oil on the rod-end ball attracts dirt, which in turn promotes wear on the ball/race.

Use a Teflon liner and the need for lube is pretty much history. Please note that Teflon is a DuPont product. DuPont invented it, and Teflon is its name brand. DuPont is not the only company that manufactures polytetrafluoroethylene (PTFE) products. A Teflon liner consists of a carrier component, often a fabric that provides compressive strength, a Teflon component for lubricity, and various bonding resins. The Teflon liner is bonded to the race, which means the rod-end ball physically rotates on the liner. As the ball moves, Teflon rubs on the ball. That, of course, provides lubrication. Rod ends with Teflon liners are manufactured in

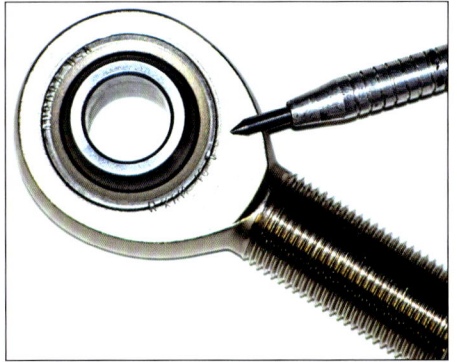

What you're looking at is a very-high-quality, extreme-strength, made-in-the-USA Teflon-lined rod end. Aurora Bearing is the manufacturer. Teflon provides the lubricant necessary to maintain free movement. By the way, you can't go wrong with Aurora Bearing when it comes to rod ends.

two- or three-piece configurations, but watch out for cheap rod ends assembled with virgin Teflon. Virgin Teflon is comparatively soft. It has a compressive strength of (+ or –) 10,000 pounds psi. Compare that to a high-quality composite Teflon liner, which usually has a compressive strength of somewhere between 40,000 and 60,000 psi, and you can see there's a huge difference. A quality Teflon liner provides another bonus as well: It eliminates extra clearance between the ball and race. This means the ball and race have a much tighter fit.

Here is something else to consider: If a manufacturer adds a Teflon liner to a rod end, it doesn't always mean that it's a precise piece. In addition, it doesn't mean that it's a high-performance piece. When you shop for rod ends, you'll probably come across a phrase that includes the words "beating out." Beating out usually refers to the deformation of low-strength "self-lubricating" liners. Some cheap rod ends are built with races constructed from molded plastic (sometimes they're mixed with a fiberglass filler). They can also add a small amount of Teflon for increased lubrication. Sounds fair enough, but cheap rod ends such as this might look and sound like trick, but they usually have a compressive strength of 15,000 psi or less. Under a given load, the race can deform, and you might not see it because the body can be undamaged.

Rod-End Alignment

The misalignment of a rod end is important. A bolt, stud, or other form of fastener goes through the hole bored through the center of the rod end. That means the ball inside the rod end has limited rotation (a

CHAPTER 4

full 360-degree rotation is obviously out of the question). Accordingly, all rod ends have definite limitations on how far they can be "misaligned" before the sphere becomes bound up in the housing. What you're dealing with is the "angle of misalignment" and it's important when selecting a rod end for a given task. As it turns out, not all rod ends are designed to accept the same degree of misalignment. That's why misalignment angles are published in the specifications of most high-quality rod ends. What, then, is the consequence of exceeding the manufacturer's recommended maximum misalignment angle? At the least, you end up with early rod-end wear. At worst, you bind and break the rod end.

That's not good, so how on earth do you figure out the misalignment angles? It's not difficult. Remember that grade school protractor you had? You can use it to check the geometry. Compare that to the "angles of misalignment" laid out in the manufacturer catalog. By the way, you can attempt to shortcut the job by simply using a big honking rod end, but in truth, that won't fix the problem. That's why manufacturers build high-misalignment rod ends.

Two Aurora Bearing rod ends. Two identical shanks. The rod end on the right has a small bore size; however, it also has a much larger body and is therefore much stronger than the rod end on the left. Quite often, these are referred to as "racing rod ends."

Is Bigger Better?

Is a bigger rod end better? From a size point of view, a rod end can be constructed two ways. The first example incorporates a shank (the threaded segment) that is the same diameter as the hole in the ball (as an example, a 1/2-inch bore coupled with a 1/2-inch shank). The next setup is built with shank one size larger than the bore (a common example here is a 1/2-inch bore mated to a 5/8-inch shank). The second configuration (small bore, large shank) comes with benefits, particularly when the rod end encounters bending loads. You don't have to look too far to find this in a custom-built Nova. Think four-link. Here I have a four-link that acts as levers. They transfer (often) huge forces from the chassis to the rolling stock, transmitting considerable forces from the chassis to the tires (and vice versa). Because of this, the larger-than-normal shank gives the rod end more ultimate strength, but it also adds a large margin of additional reserve strength to the respective four-link bar.

The oversize shank rod end is most often built by installing an insert one size smaller in the body of a rod end. A 1/2 x 5/8–inch rod end always demonstrates higher load capacities than a 5/8 x 5/8–inch rod end, assuming both are built with similar materials and specifications, because of the amount of body material found around the insert. Rod ends of this configuration give you added wrench access too. The reason is, the fastener that goes through the bore of the rod-end ball is smaller. An asymmetrical rod end can be built by adding a larger shank to a smaller body. It serves the same purpose, but you end up with less material surrounding the ball, which in turn, makes it less desirable.

It should be no surprise that you get what you pay for. Quality rod ends, such the pieces we're showing in the accompanying photos, aren't cheap. What you're paying for is an extensive engineering background, arduous research, development, and equally demanding testing agendas. The bottom line here is, when you buy into a manufacturer's product, you trust them to keep you safe.

This is what the "alignment angle" mentioned in the text looks like. Essentially, it shows just how far a rod end can go before it is misaligned. FYI: This is actually a special high-misalignment bearing manufactured by Aurora. It is engineered to operate successfully at angles such as this.

You get what you pay for when it comes to rod ends. When a component such as this is charged with holding major suspension and steering components in check on a modified Nova, don't even think about getting cheap here!

CHAPTER 5

Springs and Shock Absorbers

Springs and shock absorbers do more than hold the car up and keep it from bouncing uncontrollably. Springs can be used to your advantage to determine ride height, help launch the car down the quarter-mile, and help with lateral acceleration. Shock absorbers (or perhaps better, "dampeners") are capable tuning devices that can be used to control the motion of the suspension. I delve into the why's and how's in this chapter.

Springs

Springs? What's so important about the front coil springs on your Nova? Quite a bit actually. Springs tend to be one of the most important and often the most misunderstood components on a modified Nova, whether it is a street or race application. A lot of issues can arise with springs, many in the "out of sight, out of mind" category. For example, springs tend to settle with age. How old are the springs on your car? Equally important, far too many Novas operate with springs that have been improperly modified (coils cut by way of a torch, springs that are coil bound, sagged springs, and so on).

Crude modifications to springs can do more harm than good, obviously. A drag Nova with a stock-style front suspension system is an example. It's common to install a set of race front coils, but sometimes the ride height is too tall. The quick "fix" is to cut the springs. A month or two later, the car sags. Instead of buying correct springs, the next "fix" is to slip in a set of black plastic spacer donuts on the spring to restore the ride height. Not a good idea. This stiffens the spring rate to the point where the car is seriously over-sprung. The spring rate has been messed up by shortening it. More often than not, the ETs change and the Nova develops quirky handling characteristics. The real fix is to use a quality spring that isn't cut (even if it means having a set of springs custom wound).

Coil-overs aren't exempt from this either. It's just as easy to install springs with the wrong rate when using coil-overs. Springs of all configurations are correctly picked by way of calculations based upon the geometry of the car (short-long control arms, MacPherson strut, etc.), the corner weight of the car, the dimensions of the spring, and a series of component measurements. There is no magic one-size-fits-all when it comes to springs. Each car requires a different spring and spring rate. Spring rate refers to the amount of weight needed to compress a spring 1 inch.

Coil springs are not all created equal. And they're not as simple as "they look okay; they fit." This chapter lays out how to select springs correctly.

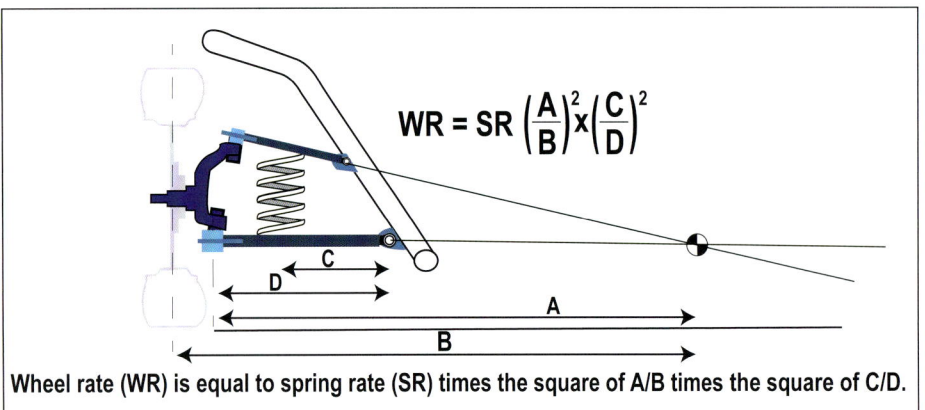

Here's an easy-to-use formula for approximating front wheel rate (WR) versus spring rate (SR). (Illustration Courtesy Jerry Bickel Race Cars)

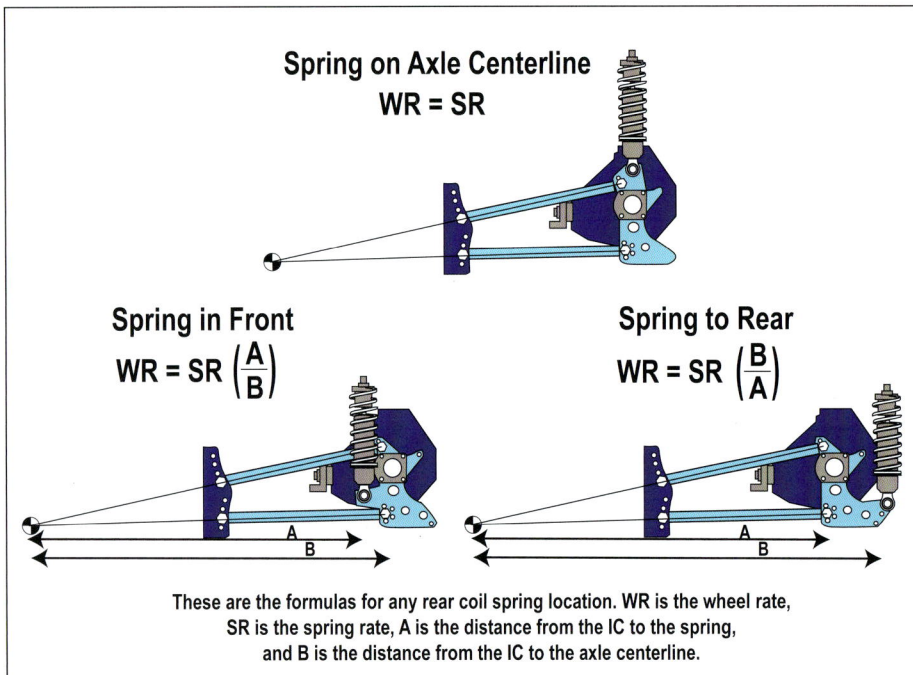

These are the formulas to determine rear wheel rate for a drag race car. (Illustration Courtesy Jerry Bickel Race Cars)

the spring increases, the spring rate decreases. A spring with a closed end has a coil that is "squashed" into the next coil in the stack.

To figure out spring rates, the first thing you should do is determine the exact corner weights of your Nova (left front, right front, left rear, right rear) with the car at running weight or race weight (including the driver weight, fuel, oil, etc.). Spring rates are determined by the amount the spring deflects versus the weight placed upon it. The actual suspension geometry can influence how much the spring deflects. You must compensate for the geometry when determining the correct spring rate for your race car. Here's an important quote from Jerry Bickel on the topic: "When you buy front springs, the listed spring rate (in-lbs) is not the same as the rate at the wheel. Front control arms are lever systems that alter the motion and applied forces between the coil springs and the wheels. The front wheels gain a mechanical advantage against the coil springs, so the wheel rate is always less than the spring rate."

Jerry points out: "If the car has MacPherson struts, the top line should be drawn from the top strut mount at 90 degrees to the strut. Actual wheel rate is extremely difficult to calculate with accuracy. This is because the angles of suspension members change continuously though the normal range of travel and the front coil springs are not perpendicular with the pavement.

"Fortunately, front spring rates are not quite as critical in drag cars as they are for road race or stock cars. If your spring and wheel weights are within the correct range, little or no performance gain should be expected from changing them. Remember this

(For example, a 250-pound-per-inch spring with 250 pounds resting upon it compresses 1 inch). Three factors influence spring rate.

Wire Diameter: This affects rate since a greater wire diameter is stronger than a smaller-diameter wire. When the wire diameter of the spring is increased, the spring rate increases.

Mean Spring Diameter: This refers to the overall outside diameter of the spring, less one wire diameter. When the mean spring diameter increases, the spring rate decreases.

Active Coils: Determining the number of active coils varies with the configuration of the spring. For springs where both ends are closed, count the total coils minus two. For springs with one end closed and one end open, count the total coils minus one. As the number of active coils in

SPRINGS AND SHOCK ABSORBERS

Front Spring Selection

Here is a handy front spring selection chart for drag race cars equipped with MacPherson struts. Remember, this is only a rough guide for spring rates. The correct rate for your car may be somewhat higher or lower than those listed below.

Gross Vehicle Weight (lbs)	Front Spring Rate (in-lbs approx.)	Rear Spring Rate (in-lbs approx.)
2,000	185	85
2,350	200	95
2,500	215	120 to 140
3,000 to 3,500	250 to 350	150 to 200

rule when selecting spring rates: *The farther the spring is from the tire, the lower the wheel rate will be. The closer the spring is to the tire, the higher the wheel rate will be.*

"All of our Pro cars are equipped with MacPherson struts in front, with the springs very close to the tires. This is why the front spring rates I use are low compared to those used on cars with unequal-length control arms.

"Rear suspension members may also create leverage against the rear coil springs and affect wheel rate. This depends on the type of rear suspension system and the location of the coil-over-shocks.

"Depending on the builder, the rear coil springs may be located in front, on, or behind the rear axle centerline.

"The same formula can be used for ladder bar suspension systems. Simply use the front pivot as the IC reference point. I prefer to mount the coil-over shock behind the axle centerline. This keeps it from interfering with the four-link bars and lowers the top mounting location."

As it turns out, the approximate spring rates provided by Jerry Bickel are similar to those required in many drag race Novas, even those without MacPherson strut front suspension systems. Many companies out there can build you a trick drag race spring (Moroso being one of them). Typically, springs of this sort are manufactured with a small wire diameter. They're also built rather long. As a result of these two factors, the spring helps promote front-end lift, which makes for better weight transfer. Moroso says that many factors, including wheel offset, influence the front-end height of a car. A front wheel offset to the outside tends to increase leverage of the lower A-arm against the coil spring. The result is a lower ride height. Disc brake spacers do the same thing. Of course, moving weight around on your car can do the same thing too. Replacing a steel hood with a lift-off fiberglass job, moving the battery to the trunk, replacing the water pump with an aluminum job, swapping to aluminum heads, and so on can radically change the front corner weights, allowing the nose of your Nova to sit higher. Believe it or not, in some cars, taking out as little as 50 pounds can affect ride height.

All sorts of custom springs with all sorts of different spring rates are available for Novas. The front-end weight is the ultimate decision maker when the time comes to select front springs. This is something you should consider for all Novas (drag race, street/strip, pro-touring, and so on). A good chassis builder nails down the exact corner weights on a car during the setup phase.

In the end, it's easy enough to see that there are many front suspension arrangements (modified MacPherson strut, short-long control arm, etc.) and that the geometry of each design differs considerably. Because of this, spring rates can differ dramatically too, even when overall front-end weights are similar. So, what can you do to get it right? Get the corner weights of your Nova right and take the time to do the math.

Split Mono-Leaf Springs

What's the story with "split" leaf springs? According to the folks at

The spring might look "bowed" in this photo, but it's not. What worked for this Nova was a stock small-block spring for a car with power steering and a few other options. The car will eventually receive a big-block.

CHAPTER 5

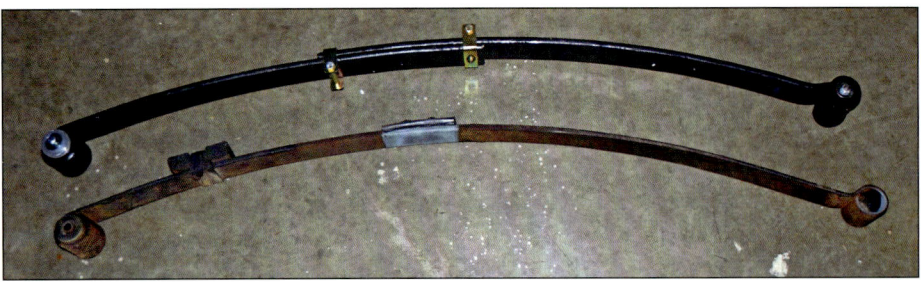

At the rear of a Nova, it's easy enough to run stock mono-leaf springs or stock multi-leaf springs (or custom versions of each). Or you can opt for what is likely the best bet: a split mono-leaf.

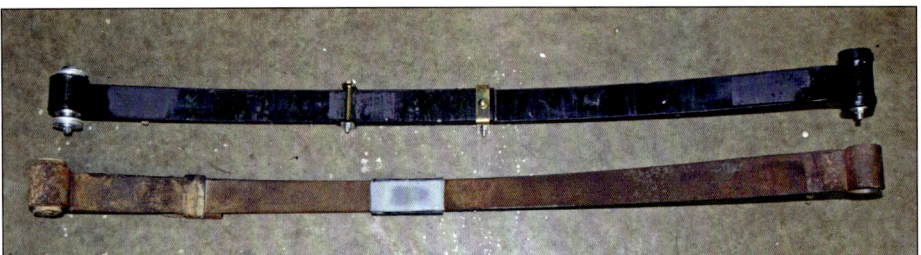

From the top (or the bottom), the split mono-leaf follows the same shape and size as a stock mono-leaf. The split segments are the difference (and what make it work).

Here's a look at the side of the spring. Not only does the split mono-leaf spring work better (when it comes to hook), it's also easy to change ride height. It's a simple matter of exchanging spring segments.

Calvert Racing (the folks who brought the design into popularity), split mono-leaf springs are considerably lighter than factory leaf springs (especially multi-leaf jobs). This reduces unsprung weight, and at the same time, the new spring package allows you to select the ride height you need for your car. In addition, split mono-leafs are designed to work with the CalTracs traction bars. Calvert also points out that it has tested countless different leaf spring configurations over the years. Included are stock mono-leaf, multi-leaf, multi-leaf with a single added thick leaf, multi-leaf with very heavy leafs, biased multi-leafs (such as an old Chrysler SS spring), parabolic mono-leafs, and finally, split mono-leafs. Overall, cars have performed the best (in drag racing or street/strip applications) with the split mono-leaf springs. A big reason for this is the fact the front segment of the spring can be manufactured super-stiff. Coupled with the way the CalTracs works, it allows the suspension to mimic a four-link.

Split mono-leaf springs can be built for a wide range of combinations, including a number of ride heights: stock, +1, and -1 are the basics (special orders are possible). You can also get the springs tailor-made with regard to spring rate (the rate ranges from approximately 200 to 225 pounds).

Now, if you're wondering, these springs are at home on the street. That's one of the basic tenets of the CalTracs "system." Many Calvert customers with leaf spring vehicles still use them as double-duty machines (street and strip). If those cars were converted to something such as a ladder bar or a four-link, the suspension hardware required to get the job done (panhard bar, anti-roll bar, Watts linkage components, and so on) could limit their usefulness on the street. The complete CalTracs setup doesn't have those issues.

Those split mono-leaf springs we're talking about do look quite a bit different than the setups you're used to.

Shock Absorbers

The truth about making a quick Nova work on the street or on the strip is that the shock absorber is a key ingredient. The reason is simple: If you can control wheel motion, you can control the dynamics of the car. The better the control of the wheel motion, the better the control of the dynamics of the entire car. Interpretation? In the world of acceleration this boils down to hook. It also means your tuning capabilities are amplified manifold.

What really is a shock and what does it do? A shock is a hydraulic device that resists chassis movement by passing oil through a set of orifices and valved passages. Manipulating the fluid movement through the valving of an adjustable shock changes its dampening characteristics.

SPRINGS AND SHOCK ABSORBERS

All sorts of shock absorbers are built for third-gen Novas. This is a complete set from Strange Engineering. The fronts are single adjustable (right) while the rears (left) are double adjustable.

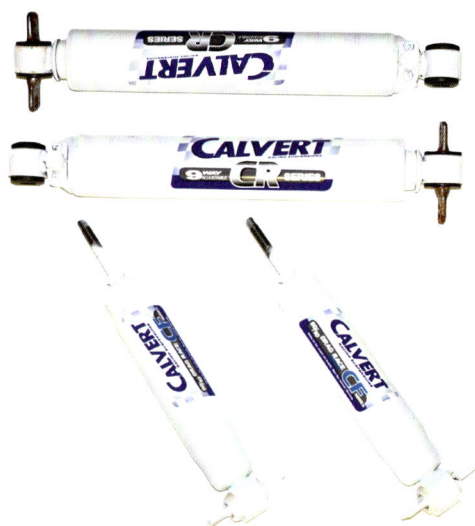

Calvert Racing offers a pretty neat (well-tested) set of shocks for Novas. These are an inexpensive option. The fronts are non-adjustable (bottom) while the rears are single adjustable (top).

Rebound (extension) is the shock's resistance to being pulled apart. It can be used to control chassis separation, the point at which the axle housing is pushed away from the chassis and the tires are applied to the track. During separation, many things occur. Forces push the Nova up and forward and the axle housing sees the opposite force (don't forget the tire sidewalls are also wrapping up). While the car moves forward, torque is created as the tires generate traction to start this movement. Too much body separation can lead to undesirable side effects. Wheel hop can occur as the tire tries to return to its original form (the tire unwraps). Stiffening the rebound can control wheel hop. Tire shake is similar to wheel hop and can be addressed similarly. For the most part, something such as a "bald" starting line or unprepared surface mandates a softer rebound setting to apply the tires with more force. On the track, a good starting line can use a stiffer setting. A stiffer rebound setting on a well-prepped track can provide quicker vehicle reaction times. Essentially, too much separation is an ET and energy waster.

Bump (compression) is the shock's resistance to the chassis moving down or the axle housing moving up or into the chassis. The bump adjustment is important since it determines how long the tires are held down on the track after chassis separation. When you use a soft rebound setting on a double adjustable, try using a slightly stiffer compression setting.

"Bump-Rebound-Compression-Extension." Whew. It all gets a little confusing. Let's take a closer look at the terms used by the shock manufacturers. Different shock companies use different lingo. Quite often the words "bump," "rebound," "compression," and "extension" are used interchangeably. A shock absorber travels in two directions: It gets shorter (compresses) and it gets longer (extends). Some shock absorber manufacturers call this "bump" and "rebound," but that can get confusing. To get a grasp of what this is all about, pretend you drive your car over a good old-fashioned speed bump. The speed bump "bumps" the shock that in turn compresses it. After you drive over the speed bump, the shock rebounds and extends. That's where you get the term "bump" and "rebound."

In the old days, a loose front shock (worn out stocker or a special 90/10 valving shock) was used to allow the nose to rise quickly. That transferred as much weight as possible to the back wheels. It was simple because there were virtually no rebound forces at work (the "10" in the 90/10) coupled with a whole bunch of bump at work (the "90" in the 90/10). With the 90/10 up front, the nose remained in the air. You can imagine how this messed with the race car aerodynamics. But that was then. Today, Calvert Racing has a new 90/10 designed specifically for maximum weight transfer. Internally, it comes equipped with modern dual-stage valving on the compression side that allows the nose of the car to settle on the top

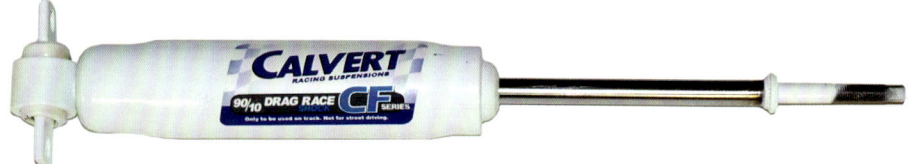

Calvert Racing front shocks have a traditional 90-10 valving arrangement. These differ from the old-school 90-10 valving packages in that they settle down quickly at speed.

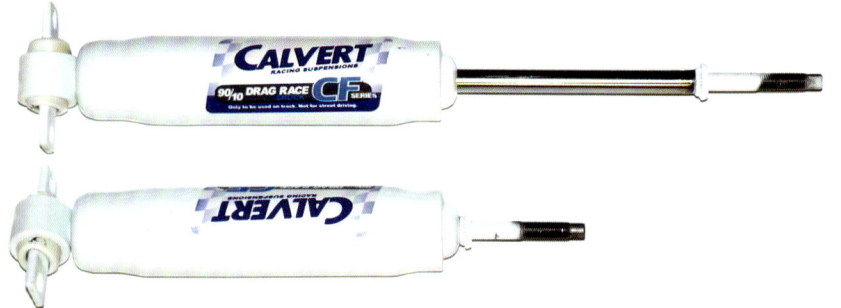

90-10 means the shock extends quickly. It compresses slowly (but again, with dual-stage valving, the nose of your Nova settles down much faster than the old 90-10).

end. They work well (they're very well-proven) and you don't have to fiddle with them.

On the other end of the spectrum are shocks such as those manufactured by Afco, Strange Engineering, Penske, Calvert Racing, and others that are available as single-adjustable and double-adjustable assemblies. A single-adjustable shock with external adjustment allows adjustment of the rebound while the shock assembly is still mounted in the car. A double-adjustable shock with external adjustment allows adjustment of the compression valving and rebound valving. Because of the increased sophistication of the internal valving, the double-adjustable shocks cost more than their single-adjustable counterparts.

With a Strange double-adjustable shock, the compression is adjusted by turning the knob from 1 (softest) to 12 (firmest). Because of the precision of the adjuster, only a click or two change is necessary to make a noticeable change in tuning the chassis. On a Calvert Racing single-adjustable shock, the range of adjustment is from 1 (softest) to 9 (firmest). There's more on setting up Strange and Calvert shocks later.

With an adjustable shock, where do you begin? It all depends upon how sophisticated the Nova is and how deep your pockets are. Many adjustable shocks are similar when it comes to adjustment. The shock absorber doesn't have to be removed for adjustment. After it's installed in the car, all changes are handled externally by way of the adjustment knob. After installation, the knob is accessible through the side of the spring (on typical front applications).

Using the Strange Engineering shocks as the example, setup works like this: Turn the knob fully counterclockwise. The "end" of the adjustment (where it does not turn or click any farther) is the softest setting, position 1. By turning the knob clockwise, each click increases the shock resistance. The full stop counterclockwise (front shock baseline) has valving like that of a 90/10. As you can see, this offers a

Single-adjustable front shocks such as these examples from Strange Engineering allow for external rebound adjustment.

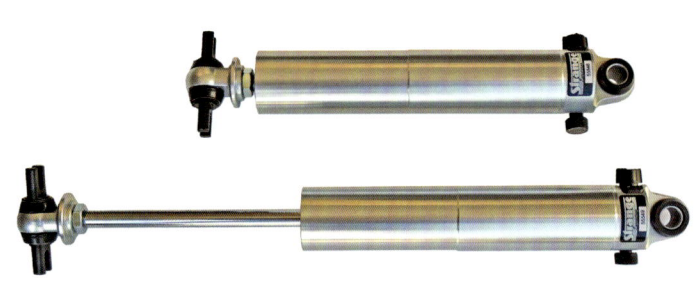

Double-adjustable shock absorbers such as these rear models from Strange Engineering allow for external rebound and bump adjustment. The shock has a separate adjustment knob for each.

SPRINGS AND SHOCK ABSORBERS

This is a good look at the adjustment knob on a single-adjustable shock absorber. While adjustments between shock manufacturers are often similar, each has its own take on where and how adjustments begin.

Single-Adjustable Front Shock

Strange provides the starting point for adjustment on a single-adjustable front shock as follows:

Drag Race
- Turn to position 2 or 3 (position 1 is full counterclockwise).
- To increase weight transfer (front-end travel) rotate counterclockwise.

Street
- Turn to position 4 or 5 (position 1 is full counterclockwise).
- For a firmer ride, rotate clockwise.

Calvert Racing offers the following setup advice for its single-adjustable shock:

Drag Race
- Foot Brake: Firmer settings are typical, usually between 6 and 9.
- Trans Brake: Softer settings are typical, usually between 1 and 3.

Street
- Adjust your Calvert Racing shocks to settings from 2 to 5.

very large range of adjustment. On the single-adjustable models, after you go past 6 clicks clockwise, the adjuster works primarily on extension (rebound). Moving all the way to the right (clockwise) makes the shock stiff.

On a single-adjustable Calvert Racing shock (available for rear applications only), the adjustment sequence goes like this: Begin the shock adjustment process by turning the adjustment knob fully counterclockwise until it reaches the 1/9 setting on the indicator. This is (obviously) setting number 1. Turn the dial clockwise until you achieve designated adjustment. The firmest setting is one revolution from the softest setting.

What about back double-adjustable shocks? A double-adjustable shock allows adjustment of the compression valving and rebound valving. In a Strange Engineering double adjustable, the compression is adjusted by turning the marked knob from 1 (full counterclockwise) to 12 (full clockwise). The rebound adjuster is extremely sensitive to change. Just 1 click makes a significant change in tuning the chassis.

Here are the double-adjustment knobs up close on the Strange shock. When installing these shocks, it's a good idea to plan the orientation on your Nova. As you can see, one adjuster is larger than the other. With some suspension arrangements, it could be better to have the small adjuster inboard.

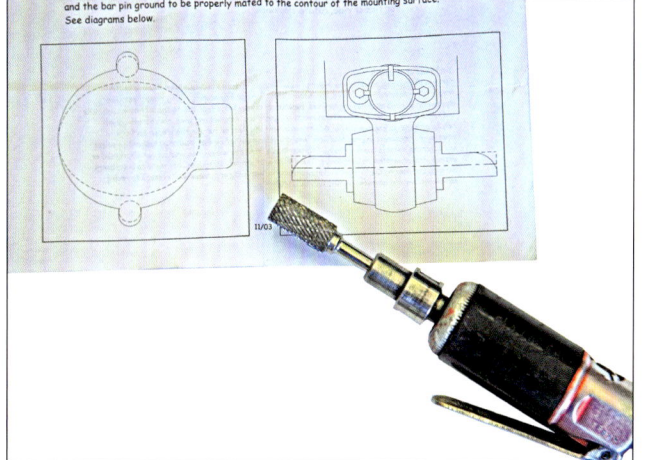

Fit up front is another issue when the shock absorber has a large adjuster knob. Strange Engineering includes a diagram showing how and where the lower front A-arm must be clearanced for shock fit.

Each car requires a different setting when it comes to sophisticated double-adjustable shocks. Chassis builder Jerry Bickel notes, "A good starting point for rear shock adjustment is to set the rebound adjustment tight and the bump adjuster loose. Remember that the final

Some aftermarket lower control arms come pre-notched for a shock absorber with an external adjuster. This is a TRZ Motorsports A-arm for a Nova.

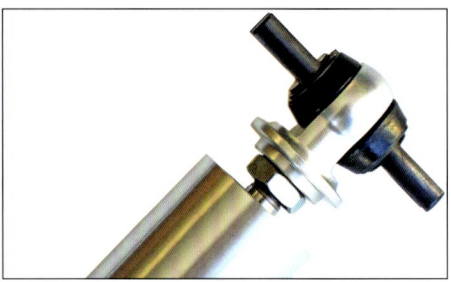

Tie bars are used on both the front and the back shocks on a third-gen Nova (bottom on the front and top on the rear). These Strange Engineering shocks use a hard durometer to keep the tie bar in place (note the snap rings on either end too).

This is a good look at how a rear shock fits a stock Nova. These Calvert Racing shock absorbers are a bolt-in. Note the use of Grade-8 bolts too. While not necessary, the zinc plate fights corrosion.

This Nova has obviously been mocked up without the rear end in place. Notice how the adjuster on this Calvert Racing shock is on the wheel side. And yes, it's a good fit.

On a single-adjustable Strange Engineering shock absorber, it's best to start the adjustment process by turning the adjuster to full counterclockwise first. That's position number 1.

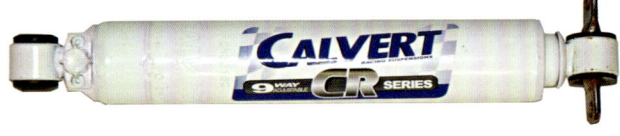

This is Calvert Racing's single-adjustable rear shock.

Double-Adjustable Rear Shock

For a double-adjustable rear shock, Strange offers the following basic setup information:

Drag Race
- Turn to position 5 (position 1 is full counterclockwise).
- To plant the tires harder, rotate counterclockwise.
- To decrease wheel hop, rotate clockwise.

Street
- Turn to position 4 or 5 (position 1 is full counterclockwise).
- For a firmer ride, rotate clockwise.

SPRINGS AND SHOCK ABSORBERS

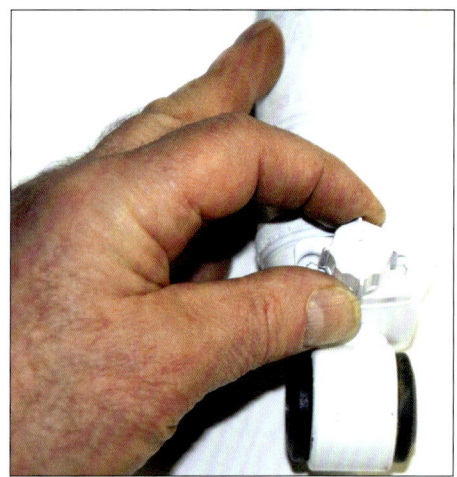

Calvert Racing shocks are numbered on the dial. Softer settings are lower numbers, and as the number of clicks increase, so does the stiffness.

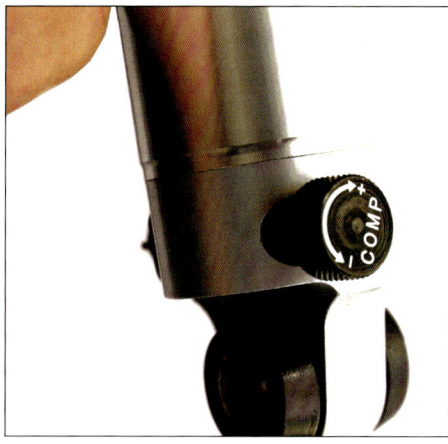

This is the compression (or bump) adjuster for the Strange double-adjustable shock absorber. Turn to full counterclockwise for the softest (lowest) setting and work your way up.

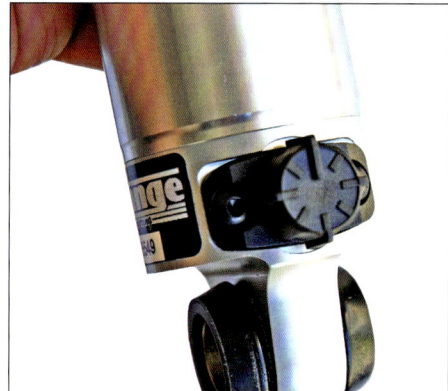

The rebound or (extension) adjuster on the Strange double-adjustable shock is on the opposite side of the lower body. It's best to start the adjustment process in the full clockwise (stiffest) position and tune from there.

setting that is best for your car must be found with some thoughtful trial and error and may change with track conditions."

Which End Do You Adjust First?

You have the shocks, you know how to adjust them, and you know how to install them on your Nova. Now what? Try the following steps.

If the Nova wheelstands excessively or bounces on the gear change (more likely), adjust the front shocks first. If the car rattles the rear tires, wheel hops, or has way too much body separation, adjust the rear shock absorbers first.

The idea is to get a smooth transition in the front-end movement as the car launches right through the first gear change. Bouncing and jerking motions do not help the launch, or the ET for that matter. If the car is violent on the launch and physically jerks the front wheels off the ground, the shock setting is too soft or loose. If the car bounces on the gear change the shock needs to be stiffer. When the car bounces on the gear change, it's coming down on the front suspen-

sion travel limiter, and then bouncing back up again. Obviously, if the shock is set too tight (stiff), the front doesn't move sufficiently to transfer weight. On a similar note, a too-stiff setting on the front shock bounces the car on the tire after the launch. Don't get this confused with bouncing off the front suspension limiter.

When it comes to the back shock absorber, the idea is to hit the tire as hard as possible (track conditions permitting). Keep in mind that it's the shock that controls how much force or "hit" you're applying to the

slick. If the shock is too loose on the extension (rebound), you might get way too much rear body separation. If the shock is too tight, the car flattens the tire excessively or simply causes the car to spin. Generally speaking, start soft on the rear and keep tightening up the valving until the car slows down.

Shackles and Bushings

The stock rear leaf springs in your Nova were fitted with rubber bushings front and rear. For any

On the bench and on the floor, these photos provide a good look at the complete package of solid bushing, spring pocket mount, and Caltracs bracket for a third-gen Nova. Even if you don't have a set of Caltracs traction bars on your car, a solid front bushing is a good idea.

CHAPTER 5

Calvert Racing manufactures solid aluminum front spring eye bushings. Others, such as Competition Engineering, make them too. The Calvert bushings are three-piece jobs with large spacers designed for use with its traction bars.

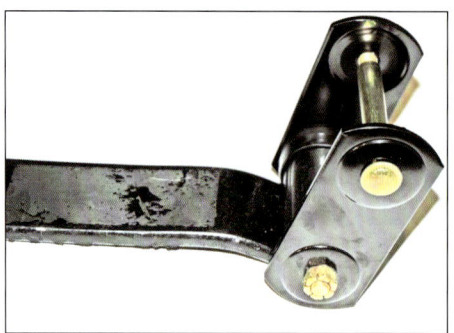

On the backside you don't need a special bushing or a special shackle. Good old-fashioned stock (length) shackles work perfectly. Never use a shackle to increase ride height. That's the job of the spring arch.

Stock bushings or urethane bushings as shown here work perfectly in the rear leaf spring segment. Obviously, a urethane bushing is more rigid than a stock or replacement rubber job.

performance work, it's advisable to replace the front bushing with a solid aluminum job. The reason is, when you're working the car hard (with decent power under the hood and particularly with a good traction device), the front bushing deflects. That's why quality springs, such as a Calvert split mono-leaf, come with aluminum bushings pre-installed. Even if you're not using a split mono-leaf, it's a good idea to replace the front spring eye bushings with solid bushings. Calvert Racing, Competition Engineering, and others offer direct replacement solid aluminum bushings.

At the rear segment of the leaf spring you should simply replace the stock upper bushings with new rubber ones. Companies such as Classic Industries offer exact reproduction bushings. Urethane bushings work well on the bottom end. Why not use solid bushings at the back end? Simple. That part of the leaf is along for the ride. There simply isn't a significant load (from the traction bar point of view) placed upon the rear of the spring.

What about shackles? Two schools of thought exist about the rear of the leaf spring in Novas: use stock shackles or go with a spring slider. What's a slider? Your local round-track store more than likely has a set hanging on the wall. They have been used in circle track for years. With a slider, the rear of the leaf connects to a box with a roller bearing that slides fore/aft. The box assembly bolts or welds to the rear subframe and the spring can then move with the roller. They need to be lubricated regularly, and they tend to be noisy. The idea is that sliders maintain a consistent load on the spring while going down the track. Do they work? You get a mixed bag of answers, but most confess, unless you're building stratospheric horsepower, you're better off with a standard shackle and fresh (OEM-style) rubber bushings.

Upstairs, the spring can be installed by way of stock rubber bushings. With this car, the stock bolts have been zinc-plated. The shackles were cleaned and powder coated.

CHAPTER 6

BRAKES

If you're into Nova drag cars or Pro Touring, you know that specialized brakes are nothing new. They've been around for all sorts of applications for decades. However, all of those systems had one thing in common: They were designed from the beginning for purpose-built cars. For drag cars, that meant that the rotors were usually thin, non-vented designs; calipers were usually built as small as practical (many were tiny two-piston affairs). The idea was to keep the weight down and to rely upon the back brakes and perhaps the drag chute to do most of the stopping. Those systems work great for stripped down race machines, but not so great for dual-purpose Novas.

In the case of Pro Touring Novas, the brakes are just the opposite: They're built with massive vented rotors and equally huge calipers. They'd probably bring the old space shuttle down from warp speed to a grinding halt safely. But there's a wee problem here too. Those big honking brakes mandate equally huge wheels to clear the works. In a nutshell, you can't fit them on a car with 15- or even 16-inch wheels (many are so large you need 18-inch-or-larger-diameter wheels).

When it comes to street/strip Novas, they're often much heavier (nose heavier too) than a dedicated drag race–only counterpart. How much heavier? Where the common drag car might weigh 2,400 to 2,800 pounds, today's trend has street/strip cars tipping the Toledos at 3,500 or more pounds. That's not the end of it either. Plenty of these heavy street cars run elapsed times and MPH figures that would embarrass a decade-old legal NHRA Pro Stocker. Using brakes designed for lightweight cars on something portly certainly doesn't allow you to make the first turn-off road at the strip, and in most cases, the thin rotors crack or warp because of the excess heat. Calipers are stressed to the max and often flex at the mounts due to the strain. The bottom line is, these new-angle street/strip Novas usually have a wide range of street equipment on

There's no question disc brakes are the answer when it comes to bringing your Nova down from speed. Today, there are all sorts of disc brake kits out there. One of the best for street/strip cars is the package from Baer Brakes.

CHEVY NOVA 1968–1974: HOW TO BUILD AND MODIFY

CHAPTER 6

This is the complete Deep Stage Brake kit. As you can see, it's a comprehensive kit. Baer follows the old-school principle of "made-in-the-USA," which is important.

board, they're portly, and they really do mandate a different type of brake arrangement.

What's needed for these Nova fat flyers (that's not an insult; those new-wave machines are very cool) is some form of brake that fits inside a skinny drag race wheel, but with a larger vented rotor; something that reliably dissipates the heat with sufficient capability for hot laps at the dragstrip yet functions as a street car.

Stop for one minute before I move on. Believe it or not, plenty of brake packages (race, Pro Touring, and otherwise) are manufactured in China. Worse, some are repackaged, so you might not even know the source. I can assure you that the quality of some of those pieces is rather suspect. It's buyer beware.

Back to Nova brakes. What if you have a car with old-school 15-inch rolling stock? Baer Brakes offers a high-quality, affordable, made-in-the-USA brake systems (the Deep Stage Brake lineup) designed specifically for high-power, fast street/strip cars.

When the folks from Baer took note of what was happening on the racetrack, they sat down and engineered a new brake system that fit the application. For the front (where I concentrate now) Baer began with its tried and true SS4+ package and reworked it with an eye to drag racing. Keep in mind, they had to make everything fit inside drag race–style skinny 15-inch front wheels too.

The rotors are a very important part of the equation. Here, Baer's system features an 11-inch-diameter

Multiple options exist when it comes to rotors. This set has been zinc-plated and includes milled slots and drilled holes.

78 CHEVY NOVA 1968–1974: HOW TO BUILD AND MODIFY

two-piece rotor. The actual rotors are 1-inch thick, cast from high-silicone cast iron, and follow the directional vane configuration. Rick Elam of Baer Brakes contends that this setup is superior to a straight vane or solid rotor in that it cools the brake while rotating. Something most don't consider is that a directional vane is actually longer (when compared to a straight vane). This effectively adds to the stability of the rotor. Depending upon the options you tick off on the order sheet, the Baer Deep Stage Brake rotors can be drilled, slotted, and zinc-plated. You can specify the whole works (slotted, drilled, and plated) or slot only with no zinc plate, or plain (no slots, no holes, no zinc).

Because the rotors are directionally vaned, they must rotate in the correct direction to obtain proper airflow. When you open the boxes containing the brake kit, you find the rotors are clearly marked "left" and "right." If you miss that, just remember that the internal vanes curve toward the back (not the front of the car). That provides the proper

Here's a good look at Baer's reverse slot and hole layout, which prevents carbon build-up inside the slots.

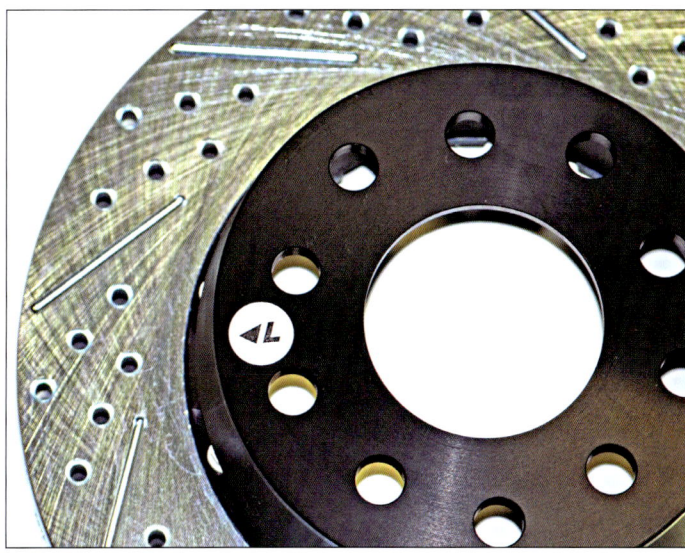

These rotors are directional. That means they are "sided" to the car. They're labeled for the respective side of the car.

Look carefully at the rotor and notice that the internal vanes are curved. Curved directional vanes improve the cooling and, at the same time, strengthen the rotor.

These two photos show the front side and the backside of the rotor and hat assembly. This is a two-piece arrangement. That means the rotor can be serviced (and replaced as necessary) separate from the hat.

CHAPTER 6

The rotor is affixed to the hat with 10 NAS fasteners and mechanical lock nuts. With this system, no fasteners thread into the aluminum hat.

The hubs are machined from billet aluminum, and after anodizing, they're fit with U.S.–sourced bearings and races. There's no need to pack bearings or add grease. Baer does that for you. It's ready to go.

orientation. The rotors have what is called a "reverse slot" or a "reverse slot and drill" pattern. While it looks "backward" to the uninitiated, it's actually correct. Baer Brake's Rick Elam says this is current race car practice, and it lowers the potential for "carbon smearing," or transfer from the pad material to the trailing side of the slots on the rotor. This is rather important since carbon smearing affects the rotational balance of the rotor. That imbalance can cause shake you can feel while braking.

Since the Baer Deep Stage Brake package is based upon a two-piece rotor (rotor "ring" and a hat), it's easy to replace the rotors when necessary. Baer has them in stock and they sell for under $200 each.

The rotor hats are machined from 6061-T billet aluminum and then anodized black. Baer never screws hardware directly into the aluminum hats. Instead, it incorporates 10 NAS (National Aerospace Standard) stainless-steel bolts and mechanical lock nuts to affix the rotor to the hat. Baer notes that in theory, NAS hardware is reusable multiple times, but if you're replacing rotors, it's best to be on the safe side and replace the lock nuts every second time a rotor is changed (which, from experience, isn't often). Keep in mind that rotor replacement isn't something you have to do on a regular basis, but it's nice to know it's possible and easy to accomplish.

A step is machined into the rotor to allow the hat to recess flat. This lowers the weight of the iron rotor/aluminum hat configuration without compromising strength. Typically, a fully assembled rotor and hat combination weigh no more than 12.4 pounds (that's the heaviest combination with the deepest hat).

The hub is CNC-machined from 6061-T6 billet aluminum and is then hard anodized black. The hubs come pre-fit and preassembled with American-sourced races, bearings, and seals (typically Timken or SKF hardware). If you look closely at the hub, you see the cap is an O-ring-sealed billet job that simply snaps into place. The hubs come double drilled with a 5-on-4.5–inch (Ford and Mopar) pattern as well as a 5-on-4.75–inch (GM) bolt pattern. The wheel studs are press-in, and in the case of a Nova kit, they're high-end ARP 1/2 20-inch jobs with a quick start nose.

The folks from Baer pre-pack the bearings with synthetic grease. You do not have to add more grease to the bearings! However, during the install, it's a good idea to add grease to the hub seal surface prior to installation. Simply use a tiny amount of synthetic grease for the job.

Another consideration is the actual caliper mount. Mounts must be robust, because if the caliper is cocked or flexes, stopping power is eliminated or, at the very best,

Baer's hubs are double drilled for Ford- or GM-pattern wheels. This set is complete with press-in ARP wheel studs of the long variety.

The cap in this brake package is a billet-aluminum snap-in design complete with an O-ring seal.

80 CHEVY NOVA 1968–1974: HOW TO BUILD AND MODIFY

reduced. Baer Brake's front mount setup for a 1968–1974 Nova incorporates a base bracket machined from billet aluminum and black anodized. It's a beefy piece, measuring .550 inch in thickness, and is held in place by two 1/2 20-inch Grade-8 bolts. FYI: In this application, the bracket mounts using the same holes in the spindle as the steering arm (but on the wheel side). Where some brake caliper mounts for some applications require machining to install, the Baer setup for Novas is a basic bolt-on (instructions are clear and virtually all of the hardware is included). The caliper is designed to mount to the rear of the spindle.

Added to the base bracket is what Baer terms an "intermediate" bracket. This too is a heavy-duty, black-anodized, billet-aluminum component. It's a honking .650-inch thick and it's held in place by way of a pair of 1.5-inch-long 9/16-inch Grade-8 bolts. Essentially, this piece mounts the caliper to the base bracket. The reason for using a two-piece caliper bracket is to allow for caliper shimming. Why the need to shim the caliper? To ensure the caliper sits centered atop the rotor. The shimming practice (which is spelled out in Baer's instruction sheets) compensates for variances in the factory spindle due to vehicle production line machining tolerances.

Baer Deep Stage calipers aren't converted race pieces; instead, they're heavy-duty, four-piston, purpose-built designs. These calipers are deeper than many you find because they include road-going dust shields that are recessed in the bore. They're sufficiently deep so that they never contact the backside of the brake pad. The seals are square-shoulder configurations (in contrast to the O-ring style used by many manufacturers). The reason for using this type of seal is to produce the maximum amount of retraction. This provides the least amount of brake drag and simultaneously eliminates the need for a pair of inline residual pressure valves. By the way, the seals are both dust/weather and pressure sealed. They meet DOT specifications.

Part of the benefit of a deeper-than-normal caliper is that it allows for deeper (longer) pistons. A longer piston is far less prone to cocking in the bore. In fact, when the pads are completely removed, the piston remains in the bore. With many race calipers, the piston tends to fall out of the bore when the pad is removed. Each of the four pistons within the calipers is hard-anodized aluminum. In addition, each caliper half is fastened by way of four 10-mm cross bolts. This provides maximum caliper stiffness.

The fluid crossover design of this caliper incorporates internal fluid passages. There are no external fluid lines from each half of the caliper. Typical of an original equipment manufactured caliper design, the Baer S4 caliper accepts a banjo fitting with a crush washer on the inlet side. The thread is a 10-mm affair that is compatible with any number of late-model brake hoses (no pipe threads are used on the components). In addition, Baer includes a 10-mm to -3AN conversion fitting with the brakes. That means you can also use a very common high-performance AN brake hose. Baer even includes a special hardline adapter for Novas (with factory disc brakes). In any case, it's a super-clean plumbing arrangement with these calipers.

Pads for Baer's S4 configuration caliper are loaded from the bottom of the caliper. The design is such that the pad cannot exit through the top. Baer uses stainless-steel abutment plates to eliminate wear on the aluminum caliper body. These plates minimize pad migration and, as a side benefit, eliminate excess pad noise. Pads used on these calipers are easy to source (common) four-piston jobs. Good replacement examples include Hawks no. HB100 or a no. DR1 pad.

Two brackets are used to mount the Baer caliper: a large base bracket followed by an intermediate bracket. This allows you to shim the caliper. The shimming process places the caliper square in relation to the rotor.

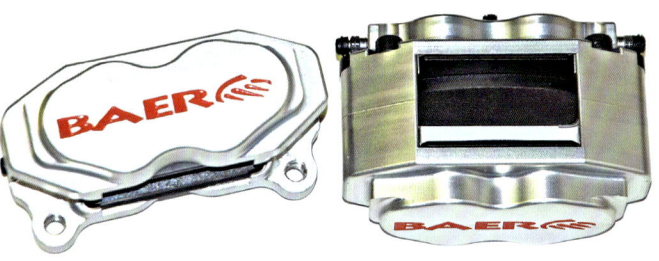

The caliper used in the Deep Stage kit is Baer's S4 (four-piston) job. The calipers are machined from 6061-T6 billet aluminum. This example has been clear anodized, although Baer provides a wide range of color options.

CHAPTER 6

The brake pads are common four-piston examples (for example, Hawk Brake pads). They are installed through the bottom (only).

Each caliper is engineered for a specific rotor thickness. The standard rotor thickness is 1 inch in the Deep Stage Brake systems.

Caliper halves are held together with four 10-mm cross bolts (two are tucked behind the respective bleeders).

The brake fluid ports measure 10 mm. This allows you to use a common banjo-style brake hose with a copper washer, or you can use the supplied 10-mm to -3AN adapter fitting included with the kit.

Each caliper for the Deep Stage series is engineered to a specific rotor thickness. Baer notes that it does not use spacers between the caliper halves to make up for a thicker rotor. Most Deep Stage kits are designed for use with 1.00-inch-thick rotors. For specialized applications, however, the Baer S4 caliper can be supplied for rotor thicknesses as small as .400 to 1.375 inches. Each of the front calipers for the standard 1.00-inch-thick Deep Stage rotor weighs 4.10 pounds. Rear set calipers are slightly lighter at 3.78 pounds. Yes, they're heavier than common drag race calipers, but they're obviously more robust too!

When it comes time to order a Deep Stage Brake kit, you have several caliper options (I covered the rotor options previously) in more than a dozen color choices. If that's not enough, Baer can provide you with a wide range of custom colors. The calipers shown in the accompanying photos are clear anodized with a red Baer logo.

How to Build Drum Brakes

Drum brakes are a common commodity on Novas. All of them had drums on at least one axle. Plenty had drums all the way around too. Sure, drums are old-school tech and, yes, they get a bad knock. They can fade. They're definitely affected by water. Some require periodic adjustment. Moreover, there's no question that a set of disc brakes not only hauls the car down from warp speed in a more efficient manner, but they also use far few pieces. A typical pair of drums for a Nova might contain more than six dozen (!) individual parts you have to deal with.

What can you do about it? Throw away a set of correct drums and switch to four-wheel discs? Get someone else to assemble them? Buy the backing plates already "loaded"? Likely none of the above. Building up a set of drum brakes really isn't difficult. Certainly, plenty of parts are involved, and some of the many pieces are on the fussy side. Several special tools are required, but they're inexpensive and easy to source. In the end, after the drums are turned (by a brake shop, and when necessary), the job isn't really all that difficult. You can do it in an evening or two. In the photos that accompany this chapter, you can see just how it's done.

Drum brakes are common in Novas. They all had them on at least one axle. They still work perfectly in many combinations when coupled with discs on the nose.

BRAKES

When working on Nova drum brakes, you need a pair of brake pliers (the silver pliers on the right are KD PN 298), a coil-spring shoe retainer tool (the red handled tool is KD PN 285; new examples do not have the external levers), along with a small packet of synthetic brake grease. Not shown is a spray can of brake cleaner.

The place to start is with a set of undamaged, clean backing plates. This set of GM backing plates was powder coated semi-gloss black prior to assembly.

If you remove the anchors from the backing plates, you need to re-torque them during assembly. The torque spec is 80 ft-lbs for the anchor nuts.

Drum brake backing plates are "sided," meaning the plate is designed to mount on a specific side of the car. The opening for the e-brake cable faces forward. Keep in mind that many of the small parts are sided within the assembly too.

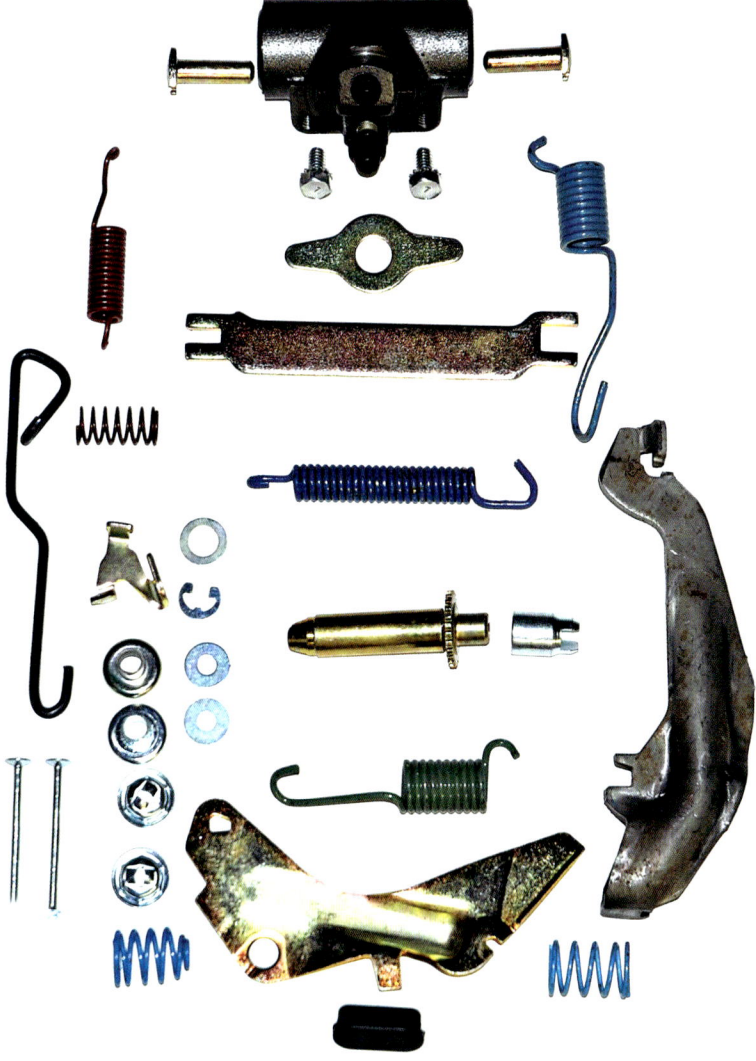

This is most of the small parts required to assemble (and thoroughly rebuild) one rear drum brake. Everything shown here, from the wheel cylinder (at the top) down to the drum brake adjuster plug, is available from Classic Industries, Inline Tube, and other sources.

  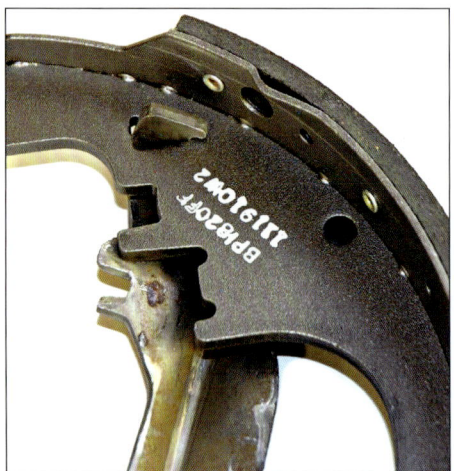

When rebuilding drum brakes, begin with the wheel cylinder(s). They're installed as shown here. Basically, they can only go in one way. Classic Industries catalogs the wheel cylinders along with the impossible-to-find mount pushrods for each wheel cylinder.

It's a good idea to lubricate the backing plates before going any further. Each backing plate has a raised surface complete with dimples. That's where the lube goes. Apply a small amount to each lubrication point. Lube should not contact the brake shoe surface (if it does, clean it with brake cleaner).

The park brake lever fits into the trailing (longer) shoe. It is hooked in from behind. It's a good idea to install it before the shoe is assembled onto the backing plate.

The easiest way to install the adjuster mechanism is to hook up the spring first with the shoes off the backing plate. Next, hook one end of the adjuster into one shoe. With a little bit of finesse, you can install the second side of the adjuster in place on the opposite shoe. Note that the adjuster wheel is close to the park brake lever. Each backing plate is different. The spring can only be installed one way (as shown here) so that it clears the adjuster wheel.

Both shoes (leading and trailing) are held in place by a coil spring. The leading shoe incorporates a beehive-style spring. The KD installation tool is used to compress the spring while you hold the nail (which passes through the back end of the backing plate) in place. A quick turn of the tool seats the nail in the spring retainer recess.

The self-adjuster actuator lever is located on the face of the trailing (back) shoe. The lever is two pieces (a small secondary hook slipped into the top). The hook, or "pawl," is for the return spring; it must be installed now. The coil attachment spring differs from the leading shoe job. Here it's a flat-bottom affair that works in conjunction with a spring seat. The spring seat installs in the actuator lever and is followed by the spring and retainer. Use the same spring tool to compress the spring as you hold the nail in place. Seat the nail correctly in the retainer. The secondary shoe is now in place.

BRAKES

Note the small flange on the actuator. This is where the small bumper spring resides. It slips into place. When it is fully assembled, the other springs in the assembly keep the bumper spring under tension.

Install the park brake strut next. The spring at one end only fits on the leading shoe side. Slide the strut into the trailing shoe. The slot in the strut also engages the park brake lever. Spread the shoes apart slightly and install the sprung end of the strut into the primary shoe.

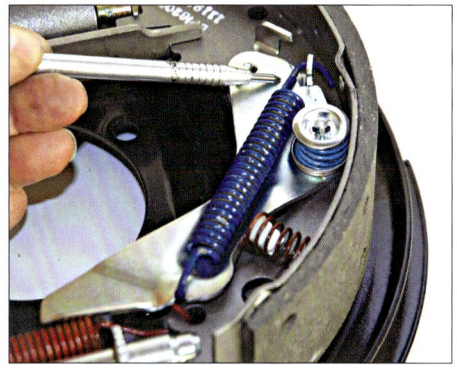

The actuator pull back spring is installed at this point. Install the lower hooked end first, and then with one end of the brake pliers handle inserted through the spring eye, stretch the spring out and over the tab on the pawl. The actuator lever body is dished for the spring body. This ensures the spring can only be installed one way.

Install the actuator link next. Place the anchor guide (the flat plate with a hole in the center) over the anchor pin and then hook the actuator link to the pawl.

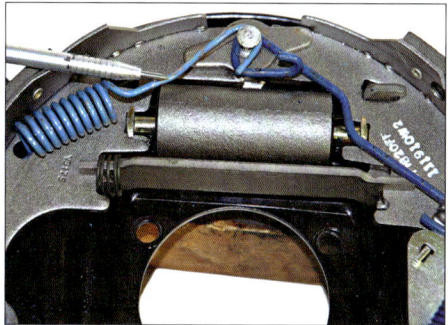

The leading shoe spring can now be installed. Hook the shoe end in first, and with the help of brake pliers, work the spring over the anchor pin.

The spring for the trailing shoe is the last piece to be installed on the backing plate (aside from the park brake cables, and of course, the drums). The spring is first attached to the shoe, but instead of hooking directly to the anchor pin, the opposite end attaches to the open end of the actuator link.

Here's the finished product. Assembling drum brakes just takes time. It's something anyone can do at home with the right tools. (Note that this assembly is on the passenger's side of the car, and the front of the car is on the right-hand side of this photo.)

CHEVY NOVA 1968–1974: HOW TO BUILD AND MODIFY

Master Cylinder and Proportioning Valves

Master cylinder choices are too numerous to be able to zoom in on all of them in this book. The pick of the litter (at least at this writing) is Baer's Remaster cylinder. This is a fully machined, billet-aluminum job, and unlike some other master cylinders available that are "universal" (with left- and right-hand outlet port fittings), the Remaster is built for the application. You can specify which side of the master the outlets are located and you'll get a cleaner look for the brake lines. For a Nova, the outlet ports are on the driver's side.

The Remaster is a short, compact design that fits both power booster and manual brake applications. The master is shorter than most. The 15/16-bore job for a Nova has an overall length (to the firewall) of 6.050 inches. It's just under 5 inches tall to the filler cap and it's 3 inches wide. The 1-inch-bore Remasters are the same overall size; however, the 1 1/8-inch-bore jobs are slightly larger. In any case, it's a tightly wrapped package.

The actual mount pattern is such that General Motors and Ford applications can make use of the

The master cylinder filler caps are knurled billet aluminum and they simply screw on.

same master cylinder. The firewall mount is engineered to fit both. For long-pushrod applications, Baer includes a special insert adapter (bullet adapter). Another neat feature is the two-piece mount arrangement. Baer designed the master with a removable-mount block. If you change configuration (or even cars), you can take the master with you. All you need to change is the mount block.

The filler cap is a screw-on assembly. Each billet cap is engineered with a knurled edge. You don't need any special tools to check or add fluid. Simply unscrew the caps to gain access to the respective fluid chambers.

All Baer Remasters accept bolting a proportioning valve block to the bottom of the master cylinder. You don't need a special bracket to mount the prop valve, plus it really simplifies brake line routing on a Nova application. In addition, if you already have a Baer proportioning valve, it's a simple matter of specifying your master to accept it.

Speaking of prop valves, you need one for your Nova. Baer recommends it on any disc brake conversion (with rear discs or with rear drums). Keep in mind that some Novas have had the original factory distribution

Look closely at the mount. It bolts on and can be replaced. This means the master can be re-purposed if necessary.

and proportioning valves eliminated. These OEM valves were often called "combination valves." They included a brake pressure warning light sender along with a fixed rear brake-proportioning valve. Although I don't have room to go into all of it here, with a front disc/rear drum setup, too much brake pressure is applied to the drums without a prop valve. Adding taller tires on the rear (for example, slicks or tall DOT tires) also upsets the brake balance, simply because the taller tire provides more leverage when you hit the brakes. With these variables on cars without a prop valve installed (and adjusted), what you regularly encounter is back brakes locking up way before the front, and with a really fast Nova, that's no fun. The solution is to reduce the brake line pressure to the back wheels.

This is Baer's Remaster master cylinder. It's a compact unit, measuring just more than 6 inches from the firewall forward.

This master has ports on the left side (correct for a Nova). Baer also offers it with right-hand ports.

BRAKES

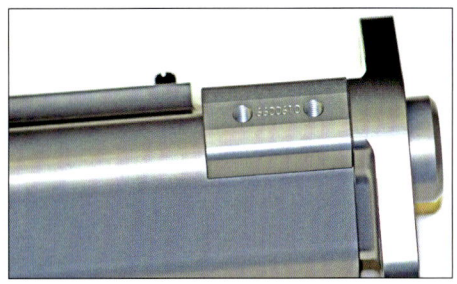

On the bottom side, Baer has included a special built-in mount bracket for the proportioning valve. There is no need for an extra bracket.

This is the proportioning valve Baer Brakes has available for its Deep Stage Brake package. It's adjustable.

Adjustment of the proportioning valve is accomplished by simply turning the knob. It's all very simple.

And that's where the adjustable proportioning valve comes in. According to Baer, "Our prop valve has approximately nine turns, lock to lock. Turning the valve all the way counterclockwise will make the outlet pressure approximately 57 percent of the inlet pressure. With the valve in the full clockwise position, the outlet pressure will be approximately 90 percent of the inlet pressure.

"Starting with the valve set approximately 4½ turns, test the brakes. When set properly, the rear brakes should lock up just *after* the front brakes. If the system is not set properly, readjust the valve and test the vehicle again. Continue adjusting until you are satisfied with the front/rear brake bias for your vehicle."

One last thing: Just like with the calipers, Baer can color coordinate your Remaster to your calipers or to match the underhood accessories in your Nova. Baer does all its coloring in-house, so custom mixes are possible.

Roll Control

Performing a burnout in a Nova isn't that difficult with an automatic. We've all done it; one foot on the brake and the other on the gas. Sure, it raises havoc with the back brakes, but it still cooks the tires nicely. Doing the same thing with a stick is another matter. It's next to impossible, unless you have a line lock, or roll control. It's basically the piece of the puzzle that allows you to perform a burnout seamlessly.

In terms of layout, the roll control consists of an electric valve plumbed into the brake line(s), a micro switch to operate the system, and a red "On" warning lamp. When drag racing the roll control is used during burnouts and staging (you never do a burn out on the street, right?). To set up the operation, the brake pedal is pumped a couple of times to ensure line pressure to the front brakes, and with the brake pedal depressed, the roll control switch is engaged. At this point, the foot brake pedal is released. Pressure to the front brakes is maintained, but pressure to the rear brakes is released. This means the front brakes are locked (the warning lamp glows after the roll control is engaged). You can put the Nova in gear, and if it's a stick, hit the gas and release the clutch. Or, with an automatic, simply nail the gas pedal. Obviously, you're now performing a burnout.

Installation is simple, but given the fact it involves the brakes, take the installation seriously! Brakes are critical components!

The first step is to mount the "valve" in the engine compartment.

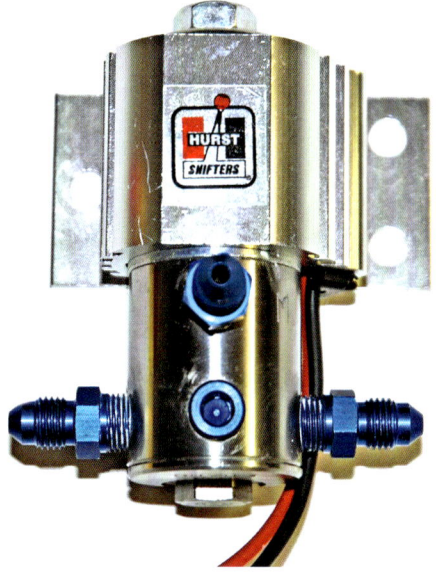

A roll control (or "line lock") is a pretty simple device. When a switch engages it, the solenoid maintains brake fluid pressure at the front wheels on your Nova. In turn, the back brakes have no pressure, allowing you to perform an effortless burnout.

CHAPTER 6

The Nova offers a lot of potential roll-control mounting locations, but this spot on the inner fender is one of the best (and easiest). Three bolts hold it in place.

Plumbing is a bit more complex. Each brake combination can differ, but with the Baer setup, this is how it's laid out. The front brake line runs to the roll control, and from there it splits to each of the front wheels.

It's a good idea to pick a mount location that's relatively close to the master cylinder. This makes for easier plumbing. For a Nova, the most obvious spot is on the driver-side inner fender well. If it's a Hurst roll control you'll need three mounting fasteners.

As far as plumbing is concerned, there isn't one accepted method of hooking up the system. An aftermarket brake system with a prop valve will certainly result in different plumbing than something such as a 1968 Nova with drum brakes on all four corners. Hurst provides a series of diagrams showing the plumbing requirements for most common master cylinder arrangements. Because several lines require fabrication, you need a flaring tool along with a tubing bender. When hand building your own line, be sure to use seamless steel or seamless stainless tubing designed specifically for brake use. The preferred size is 3/16-inch line.

When plumbing a roll control, keep in mind that most of the solenoid valves have the respective ports machined in pipe thread. If you're using AN fittings (as shown in the accompanying photos), you need AN-to-pipe thread adapters. When installing any pipe thread fitting (including adapter fittings), the pipe-thread side requires Teflon tape or Teflon-based thread sealant. You must also ensure that none of the sealant gets inside and contaminates the lines or the roll control valve.

The electrical hookup isn't difficult, but it takes time to route the wires. Electrical wiring obviously must start and end somewhere. The place to begin is the switch. Hurst roll control assemblies have a pair of wires that originate in the micro switch. It doesn't matter which wire is "hot" (routed to the fuse panel) or which one goes to the roll control valve. The switch works in either case. Nova fuse panels already have provisions for such accessory instal-

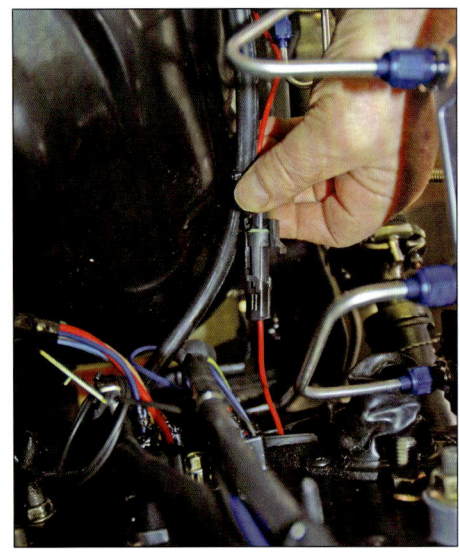

If you use the steel inner fender as the mount, you can ground the roll control solenoid to the fender. Then you need to route a power line to the car. Shown here is a quick connector. This is used to allow for easier servicing down the road.

lations. Virtually all 1960s, 1970s, and later fuse panels have a readily marked spare "LPS" terminal, a spare "BATT" terminal, and a spare "ACC"

88 CHEVY NOVA 1968–1974: HOW TO BUILD AND MODIFY

BRAKES

Inside the car, the roll control switch is routed to the shifter tunnel (and in this case, eventually installed on the shifter handle).

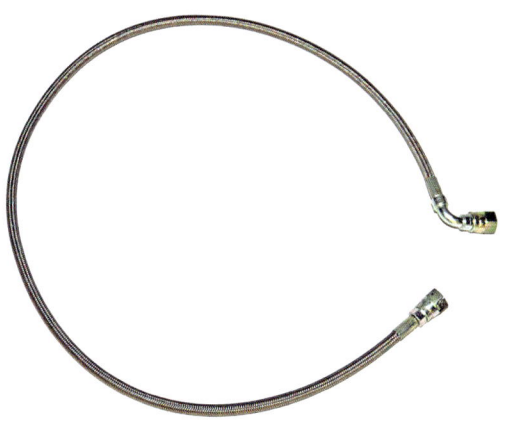

Hurst's roll control includes a red warning lamp. This tells you the system is armed. It's important to include it in the installation. This Nova has the lamp installed right over the accessory gauges.

terminal. Use the spare spade terminal on the ACC side. ACC stands for accessory. It's hot when the ignition switch is clicked to ACC or ON, or when the vehicle is running.

Hurst includes a red "On" indicator lamp with the system. Use it! The last thing you need is to accidentally engage the roll control when you're on the brakes. Lamp wiring is basic. The lamp is spliced between the wire leading from the solenoid valve and the activation switch. After it's wired, whenever the system is engaged, the roll control light comes on. Finally, you should be certain that the ground is adequate. In most Nova applications, the roll control valve is mounted to a metal inner fender. If that's the case, the system is simply grounded directly to the fender using one of the roll control mounting bolts. One way or another, be sure the ground connection is sound and clean. You're done.

Brake Flex Hoses

Here's a scary thought: You stand on the brake pedal of your Nova at the end of a quick pass down the street or the quarter-mile. The fluid pressure exceeds 1,000 psi. Then the pedal goes to the floor. There's no need to explain what happens next (let your imagination be your guide), but the cause of the grief could very well have been a fitting that was blown off the end of a braided brake hose.

Sound impossible? Not so. One of the most perplexing scenes you may ever see is someone building AN (braided stainless-steel reinforced) brake hoses. More often than not, the hose is assembled incorrectly. The sad truth is, it's not hard to assemble the hose correctly or incorrectly. When planning (and building) brake flex hoses, you have only a few choices: OEM rubber flex hose, home-assembled -3 AN Teflon core hose, and preassembled -3 AN Teflon core hose (with and without a DOT-approved label).

Of those options, the best bet is a preassembled -3 AN Teflon core hose

If you're going to use braided-steel brake hoses, this is what you need: a Teflon-core braided-stainless hose. Never use neoprene-lined AN hose for brakes. Under brake system pressure, a neoprene-lined hose expands, which increases brake pedal travel.

Rather than building your own hoses (and taking the chance you assembled them incorrectly), consider using factory assembled brake hose. The hose ends are installed by one of two methods by the manufacturer. The end is either crimped or swaged in place. That means the hose end attachment is permanent.

assembly. Here's why: You *cannot* use neoprene-lined AN hose for brakes. Under brake system pressure, a neoprene-lined hose expands, which in turn soaks up brake pedal travel. Instead of forcing the brake piston (inside the caliper) against the brake rotor, the hydraulic forces take the path of least resistance and expand the hose. In the mid-1960s, Earl's Performance Products pioneered the use of armored flex hose with an extruded Teflon core to solve the problem. The stiffness of the Teflon liner combined

---

CHEVY NOVA 1968–1974: HOW TO BUILD AND MODIFY

with the tightly woven high-tensile stainless-steel outer braid fixed the dilemma of brake pedal travel, but it also offered another advantage. By eliminating hose swell (which is still present in OEM brake hoses to some degree), pedal firmness and feel improve significantly. Of course, the stainless-steel outer braid improves the abrasion resistance, and the design of this hose increases the temperature capacity as well.

Before you run out and buy some bargain basement Teflon hose, remember that there are two types of Teflon-lined braided stainless-steel hose on the market: commercial specification and aircraft specification. The difference is in the wall thicknesses of the Teflon. Commercial hose has a .030-inch thickness while the aircraft specification hose has a .040-inch thickness. Furthermore, some hose is manufactured with a stainless braid that is loose on the Teflon liner. This type of hose offers good pressure capacity, but it's limited in its resistance to expansion. For our purposes, we're dealing only with aircraft specification hose that is bonded tightly to the stainless-steel braid.

So far so good. Given the benefits of the -3 AN hose for brake applications, it seems like the way to go. And it is, unless you mess up the hose end

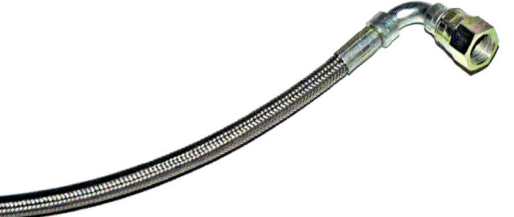

You can purchase stainless-steel braided brake hoses with any number of end fitting combinations. As you can see in this photo, each end of the hose has a conventional -3 female end.

installation. Although there's nothing complicated about the hose end installation (and no special tools are required), improper hose end installation can result in a catastrophe of the worst kind. During the assembly, the problem usually occurs when installing the sleeve (sometimes called an "olive") between the stainless-steel outer braid and the Teflon core. A small tool is available for this job (Earl's sells one under PN 007), but a small screwdriver or scribe can be used. Unfortunately, separating the braid from the liner is more difficult than it sounds. This can become a tedious job and you must be careful not to mark the Teflon. You also must be absolutely positive that none of the braid is trapped between the Teflon core and the sleeve. When you've reached that point, you then must be sure that the Teflon core is completely bottomed against the inside of the sleeve. Finally, you must be sure that the sleeve is square in relation to the Teflon core.

Part and parcel of the operation is usually a succession of holes punctured in your fingertips. It's inevitable. The stainless-steel outer braid is sharp. And the more you handle the cut hose, the better the chances of wounding yourself. To complicate matters even more, if you don't follow the instructions carefully, there's a very good chance that the hose end will back out under pressure. Unfortunately, folks often become frustrated with the process and the bleeding fingers that go along with it. Most of the time, the "that's good enough" attitude prevails, even if the internal sleeve isn't installed correctly. Then the hose is assembled and Lady Luck is your only friend. Evidence of an improperly assembled hose end on -3 Teflon hose is the final

gap between the face of the socket and the hex of the nipple. According to Earl's, it should be between .023 and .046 inch (a feeler gauge must be used to check this measurement). If you've been around the block, you see plenty of assemblies that exceed these dimensions significantly.

Given the above, it's easy to see why preassembled, crimped Teflon brake hose is the best bet. Aeroquip, Earl's, Russell, and others have offered it as a service for years. With this type of brake hose, the hose ends are installed by one of two methods: The end is either swaged in place or it's crimped. In either case, the hose end attachment is permanent. After the manufacturer attaches the ends, *each hose* is pressure checked. They typically use a hydrostatic pressure test that goes to 4,000 psi on each hose. Obviously, this far exceeds the pressures of a brake system, and for the home-based Nova mechanic, there's no way to test the hose to this pressure.

What types of hose end combinations are available? Typically each hose manufacturer offers racing brake hose packages in countless configurations. You can specify -3 straight female swivel ends, -3 90-degree female swivel ends, 10-mm 3/8-inch banjo (.425-inch-thick) ends, 7/16-inch banjo (.425-inch-thick) ends, 3/16-inch tube inverted flare (3/8-24 thread) female ends, 3/16-inch inverted flare (3/8-24) male ends, 10-mm x 1 female ends, 10-mm x 1 male ends, and several -4 AN configurations (for pressure gauge and hydraulic clutch applications). You can also mix and match each of these end configurations; in each hose configuration, you can also specify the length. If that's not enough, the manufacturers can build a custom hose in any configuration and in any length. Bottom line? Whatever the type of brake hose end and length required, it's readily available.

After installation, the hose must be kept clean and free flowing. There must not be any possibility that the installed hose assemblies can stretch, crimp, or kink under any conditions of wheel travel and steering angle. It's also a good idea to inspect all brake hoses periodically for condition (this is a good idea for any form of brake hose).

Brake Hard Lines

When it comes to replacing brake hard lines on a Nova, you have two choices: Fit reproduction lines on the car or build them. Reproduction brake lines more or less fit, depending upon the manufacturer and how they're packaged. Expect some aggravation. Enough said.

The other option is to build lines. If your Nova has custom features (for example, aftermarket brakes and aftermarket master cylinder, or a roll control), you need to fabricate at least some of the lines. Nothing beats the look of a carefully fabricated hard line. Done right, it's drop dead gorgeous. Done wrong, it can be a dangerous mess. So how do you do it right and where do you begin?

When building brake lines, .020- to .025-inch-wall stainless steel works well (although the thicker tubing is quite a bit harder to flare). The next thing is very important: Only use hard line with an ISO certification. This is usually of United States, Canada, Japan, German, or other European origin.

When it comes to fabbing hard lines, there are no tricks. It's just a matter of trial and error coupled with time. The key is, keep safety in mind. Your lines must be functional and leak proof. At the same time, you can make them look good too. Mistakes can and do happen with regularity when forming hard line, but that's part of the process.

First you must determine where each line is routed. Because every Nova application differs, there really isn't one way to do the job. When figuring out where the lines go, keep the scrub line in mind. The "scrub line" is the imaginary intersection point where a part of the chassis or a piece of suspension hardware might contact the pavement in the event of a mishap (for example, a blown tire).

Another concern is potential damage in the event a piece of the driveline or the engine decides to take a vacation. What you need to do here is ensure the brake lines aren't routed near the bellhousing or close to the driveshaft.

Two other things to consider are maintenance and excess heat. You want to be sure your brake lines aren't compromised whenever you jack up the car. It's just common sense to keep the lines away from a high heat source such as headers or exhaust pipes.

General Motors typically routed brake lines on the inner side of the front subframe, and then they ran on the inside of the rocker panel lip until they reached the rear subframe. From that point they again went on the inner side. Given the routing, the lines are well protected from potential on-road damage. Moreover, the factory routing tends to keep the brake line as far away as possible from the exhaust system and rotating driveline parts. The bottom line here is, you have several hours tied up in just the planning phase of brake line construction.

As far as material is concerned, you can build lines from .028-inch wall thickness, or .020-inch-wall-thickness 3/16-inch OD seamless tubing (some better auto supply stores sell it and so do aircraft parts houses). It's available in a number of lengths; however, you need something in the range of 30 feet for a complete car (this takes mistakes into consideration). When working

Getting Away with Single Flares

Automotive brake line fittings have a 45-degree double flare. AN fittings have a 37-degree single flare. Aircraft, various military applications, and race cars typically incorporate 37-degree AN fittings for brakes.

For the most part, stainless brake hard lines need to be flared at 37 degrees (which requires a special flaring tool) and not 45 degrees. One reason is that stainless-steel hard line is too hard to double flare, and it will most likely split if you attempt it. A single flare at 37 degrees, on the other hand, can easily be formed in stainless steel, provided you have the correct tools. But how does it seal? Simple. The 37-degree AN flare is designed to seal with a special tube nut and ferrule assembly. You cannot interchange 37- and 45-degree fittings. If you use a 37-degree flare where a 45-degree fitting is incorporated (and vise versa), it does not seal properly.

CHAPTER 6

These are the tools you need to fabricate brake line: A Rigid single flaring tool (top), a Mac Tools tubing cutter (right), and a dedicated 3/16-inch-line Imperial Eastman bender (bottom).

with the tubing you discover that .020-inch-wall stainless forms far easier than the thicker stuff. You also need a supply of AN tube nuts and sleeves. Earl's and other hose manufacturers sell them.

When it comes to tools, you need several specialized items. Included in the mix are a tubing cutter, a 37-degree flaring tool, and a tubing bender. It's easy enough to find tools that work great on soft materials (for example, aluminum), but when dealing with stainless, the tools must be robust. Good options include a Rigid tubing cutter, a Rigid flaring tool, and Imperial Eastman benders (a dedicated bender for 3/16-inch line works far better than the universal options out there).

Hard lines, like wiring, must begin and end somewhere. Begin at the source and work from there. That means starting at the master cylinder. What you need to do is to convert all fittings (master cylinder, prop valve, roll control, and calipers) to AN. For example, a common replacement master cylinder for high-performance applications is the aluminum/plastic Mopar setup. It has two outlet ports (one for the front brakes and one for the back brakes) that happen to be different sizes. The leading port is 9/16-20 inverted flare while the rear port is 1/2-20 inverted flare. Wilwood can supply you with inverted flare fittings for this combination, but you should try to keep everything in a single configuration. In this case, Lamb Components machines a -3 AN adapter fitting just for the job. On a similar note, Hurst roll controls are built with 1/8-inch female pipe thread ports. This means you need an adapter to convert over to -3 AN. Every setup is slightly different, but all the major AN hose companies have adapters to fit almost anything.

Finally, you need some way to figure out how much line you need for a specific spot in your Nova. The easiest way to measure line is to fab up a pattern with easy-to-bend mechanic's wire. After you make the appropriate bends in the mechanic's wire, straighten it and measure it, or use a piece of string on the pattern and measure the string. That way, the mechanic's wire pattern can be used to fab up the stainless line.

In the accompanying photos, you can see how the line is formed.

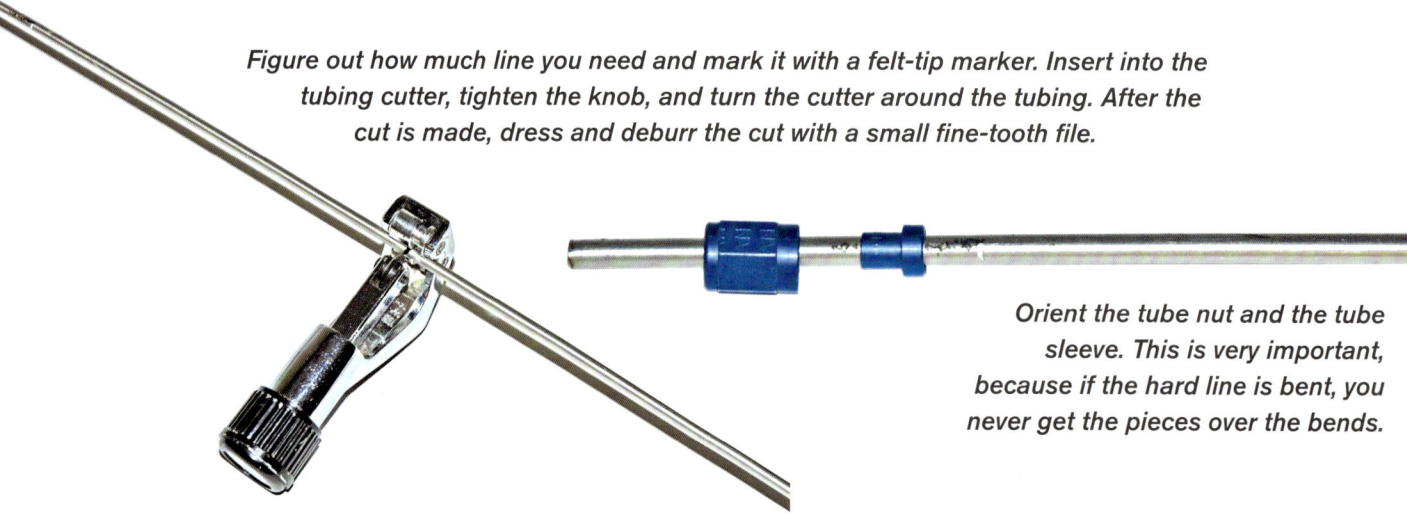

Figure out how much line you need and mark it with a felt-tip marker. Insert into the tubing cutter, tighten the knob, and turn the cutter around the tubing. After the cut is made, dress and deburr the cut with a small fine-tooth file.

Orient the tube nut and the tube sleeve. This is very important, because if the hard line is bent, you never get the pieces over the bends.

BRAKES

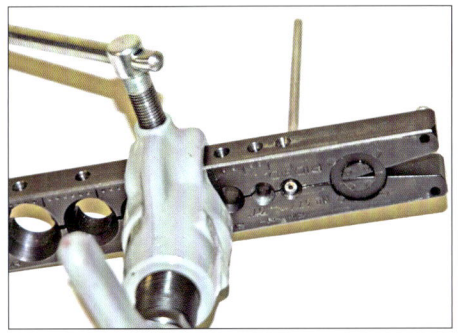

Place the tubing inside the flaring tool in the opening marked "3/16-inch." Roughly .100 inch of tubing must overhang from the flush surface of the tool.

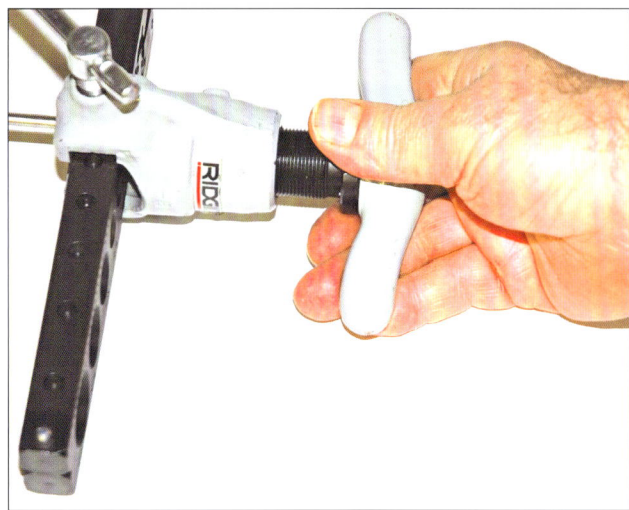

With the tubing locked into the tool (see the text for details), turn the large top handle until the internal cam releases.

Here's the finished flare. It's a good idea to lightly dress the flare with a small fine-tooth file. The idea here is to deburr it.

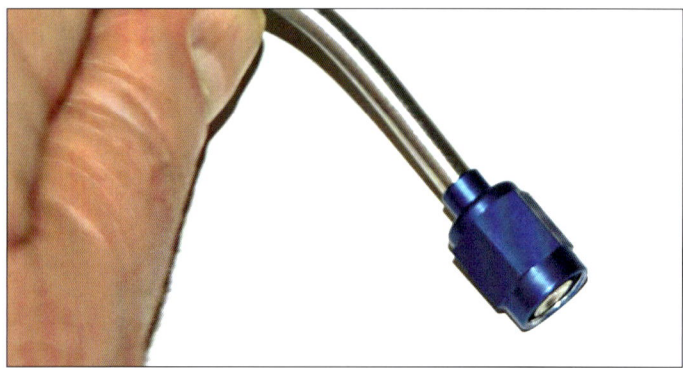

This is the finished flare with the tube nut and sleeve installed. It's ready to accept a male AN fitting (which in turn mates to a hose end).

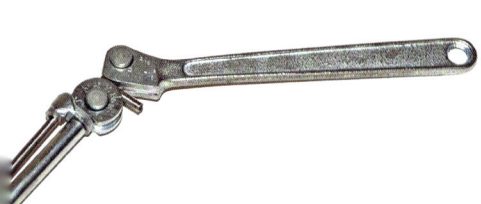

When making a bend, examine the tubing bender closely. You find it's indexed from 0 to 180 degrees (in 45-degree increments). These numbers indicate the number of degrees for each respective bend. Making a 90-degree bend is easy. Insert the tubing between the respective dies in the tool and flip the clamp on the handle over. Simply bend the tubing with the handle so that the index marks read 90 degrees. Done.

This is a look at several completed custom bends on a Nova roll control assembly. If you take your time, you get fabulous, high-quality results; but remember that you will make mistakes. They come hand-in-hand with fabricating tubing.

CHEVY NOVA 1968–1974: HOW TO BUILD AND MODIFY

CHAPTER 7

ENGINE SWAPS

The cackle of a thundering Chevy V-8 loping at idle is hard to ignore. It's addictive. Whack the gas pedal a time or two and chances are you'll be forever hooked. Chevy's V-8 engines personify Detroit-built muscle. And that's good news, because Novas from 1968 to 1974 are absolutely ripe for engine swaps. Generally, swapping an engine into a Nova is pretty simple, and the reality is, various engines can be installed without changing much. Still, though, the details make a huge difference.

A series of frame mount–engine mount combinations were used over the years, alternator locations varied with engines and model years, decidedly different transmission crossmembers were fitted, and so on. Include an LS engine in the mix and everything changes, but fortunately, the aftermarket is filled to the brim with swap hardware. In short, vintage Novas are easy enough to build in the backyard, but you have to know what fits where and how. What follows is a guide to swapping Chevy power and transmissions into your Nova. Check it out. It sure beats dragging out the torch.

Swaps such as this LS transplant into a third-gen Nova are becoming more and more common. This is a clean swap; it looks production, right down to the twin snorkel air cleaner on the EFI throttle body.

Frame Mounts

During the muscle-car era, three frame mounts were used in Nova applications: a 6-cylinder mount, a small-block mount, and a big-block mount. 1967 Camaro as well as 1968 Camaro and Nova mounts differ from 1969 mounts. Any of the engines physically fit any of the mounts, but the location and "angle" of the engine with respect to the frame is affected. Big-block frame mounts incorporate a distinct difference in height between left- and right-hand sides. The factory mounts typically place the engine farther forward in the engine compartment.

On the other hand, this doesn't mean that a fat block can't fit on small-block frame mounts. It works, but the engine sits farther to the rear of the compartment and the driver's side of the engine sits slightly lower than normal. As expected, this can create some header fit problems and makes for tight clearances between the engine and the firewall. Of course, if you want to gain some immediate engine setback (and therefore more rear-weight bias), you can use this system, or if you want to get radical, use a set of 6-cylinder frame mounts.

ENGINE SWAPS

When performing a traditional swap (for example, swapping in a big-block), the frame mounts must be exchanged. A rat motor in a Nova is moved (slightly) to the passenger's side with factory parts.

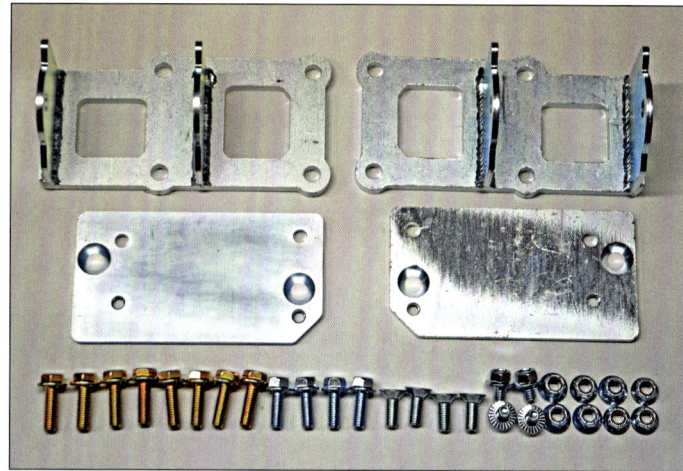

Hooker manufactures this mount package for LS swaps into Novas. The flat plates on the bottom are used to mount OEM clamshell mounts, while the top brackets bolt to the engine.

They provide even more setback. Unfortunately, with this setup the firewall often requires hammer surgery for distributor clearance. With a bunch of engine setback, the bellhousing bolts become almost impossible to reach.

Finally, I should point out that General Motors probably cataloged hundreds of frame mounts. Most of them don't exist anymore. Companies such as Classic Industries offer a good selection of quality reproduction mounts.

What about the LS engine? It's incredibly popular today, but it has a wee hitch: The mount arrangement is different than in Chevys of old. Plenty of solutions out there can get you past this, however. One that is really good is Hooker Headers' arrangement. The Hooker mounts are specifically designed for bolt-in compatibility with the Hooker transmission swap components. Essentially, it's a complete swap "system." The LS is designed to use a four-bolt motor mount. It's also situated farther back than traditional small-block or big-block mount locations (it's closer to the bellhousing on the LS). Hooker's engine mount brackets are designed to adapt the 1972–up (later model) GM clamshell engine mounts. The OEM-style clamshell mounts bolt to the subframe by way of a set of Hooker adapter plates (see the accompanying photos). Then the engine, fitted with Hooker's mounts, drops in over the top. What the Hooker system does is provide you

Frame Mount Part Numbers

The big-block part numbers that follow are correct.

Application Engine	Location	Part Number
1967–1968 Camaro, 1968 Nova V-8-BB	Left and Right	K702
1969–1970 Nova V-8-BB	Left and Right	K701

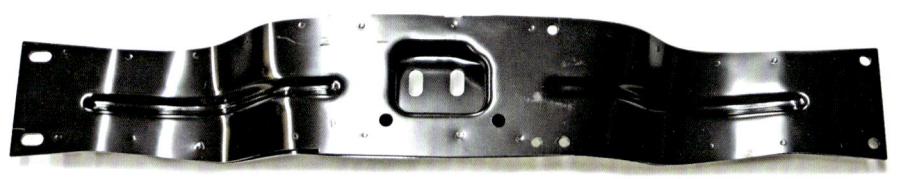

Chevrolet used a specific transmission crossmember for specific applications. This is a big-block, stick shift crossmember. It's positioned upside down in this photo, but you can see the offset.

Hooker Engine Swap Bracket

Manufacturer	Engine	Location	Part Number
Hooker	LS	Left and Right	12618HKR

CHAPTER 7

Motor Mount Part Numbers			
Manufacturer	Engine	Location	Part Number
Classic Industries	V-8-BB	Left and Right	T82283
Lakewood Industries	V-8-BB	Left and Right	24087
Anchor	LS	Left and Right	2292

with the right geometry (driveline angles) when the engine is installed. It also ensures the headers fit correctly.

Motor Mounts

The original Chevy rubber/steel composite mounts had a bad habit of self-destructing. Factor in years of use, oil soaking, and considerable heat cycles, and the need for new mounts soon becomes apparent. Both Classic Industries and Lakewood build mounts for big-block applications. The parts from Classic Industries are reproductions. Lakewood's components are from the "muscle mount" series. They incorporate a heavy-gauge steel frame and both pieces (frame mount side and engine mount side) are vulcanized to a hard durometer rubber. They also incorporate a safety interlock design where applicable, eliminating the need for torque straps or cables.

As far as the LS swap is concerned, Hooker recommends you use an Anchor brand clamshell mount for the application.

Transmission Crossmembers

Novas were built for a wide array of buyers. Because of this, an equally wide cross section of transmissions was available. Everything from two-speed Powerglides to Muncie 4-speeds occupied the territory under the floorboards. Given this situation, many non-stock combinations are possible. Examples include Powerglides behind rat motors, Muncies behind straight-6s, and so on. In factory form the big-block either had a Turbo 400 or a Muncie.

What about an LS Swap? Hooker's mounting brackets coupled with its transmission swap crossmembers allow you to use a GM Powerglide, TH350, TH400, 700R4, 2004R, or 4L60/4L65/4L70/4L75 automatic in any 1968–1974 Nova without cutting or hammering the transmission tunnel. The use of a 6-speed manual mandates some tunnel work because the Tremacs are huge.

Transmission Mount

The actual transmission mount (known as the "mounting" in GM parts catalogs) is similar for all models.

This cool girder structure is Hooker's LS swap crossmember for T56 and automatic transmissions. Hooker used high-tech FEA (Finite Element Analysis) in the design.

Transmission Crossmember Part Numbers		
The following are available (I use Classic Industries part numbers here for reference).		
Application	Transmission	Crossmember
1968–1974 Nova	THM400 big-block	3912573
1968–1974 Nova	4-speed manual, HD 3-speed manual big-block	HC109
1968–1974 Nova	THM400 small-block	C148561
1968–1974 Nova	4-speed manual, 3-speed manual, Powerglide, TH350	E374

Hooker Crossmembers		
Application	Transmission	Part Number
1968–1974 Nova	T56 manual	12626HKR
1968–1974 Nova	4L60-4L65-4L70-4L75 automatic	12625HKR
1968–1974 Nova	4L80-4L85 automatic	12627HKR
1968–1974 Nova	Adapter – THM400 and 2004R to fit 12626HKR	12650HKR

ENGINE SWAPS

Transmission Crossmember Mount Part Numbers

Classic Industries Part Numbers

Application	Part Number
3-speed, 4-speed manual, TH 350, Powerglide	T82224
Turbo-Hydramatic 400	T82268

Hooker LS Swap Crossmember Mount

Application	Part Number
T56, 4L60 series, 4Ll80 series Prothane	7-1604

Aftermarket solid jobs are available, but when coupled with solid motor mounts, these parts tend to tie the powertrain together too tightly. This often results in broken mount ears on 4-speed cases or fractured cases on automatics. Stick with the rubber stuff.

Flywheels, Flexplates and Starters

LS engines use their own dedicated flywheels, flexplates, and starters. With an original small-block or big-block engine, the crankshaft flange extends .400 inch farther rearward than in an LS application. That means for LS swaps where you're using an early non-LS automatic, you need a flexplate spacer kit (Chevrolet PN 12563532K). It spaces the converter outward on the flexplate so that it can engage the crank flange. With stick shifts the LS makes use of a distinct crankshaft mounting flange, which necessitates use of an LS flywheel. If you use an LS flywheel and an early manual transmission, you'll also need a swap bellhousing (QuickTime has a wide range of swap bellhousings for LS applications).

When you get into early engines, things aren't exactly straightforward either. Two systems of balance have been used on vintage Chevy V-8s: internal balance and external

When it comes to flywheels, lots of differences are seen between various engines in the Chevrolet family. For example, some engines were externally balanced; some came with 153-tooth ring gears; some came with 168-tooth ring gears; LS engines have a different bellhousing spacing; and so on. This is a 168-tooth aluminum/steel flywheel for a conventional small- or big-block.

Flywheels and Flexplates

I use these part numbers as reference only.

Flywheels

Description	Part Number
12¾-inch nodular iron, 10.4-inch clutch, neutral balance	14085720
12¾-inch nodular iron, 10.4-inch clutch, counterweighted for 454	3963537
12¾-inch nodular iron, 10.4- and 11-inch clutch, lightweight, 1-piece seal	14088646
12¾-inch iron, 10.4-inch clutch, 1-piece seal	14088650
14-inch iron, 11- and 11.85-inch clutch, 1-piece seal	10105832
14-inch iron, 11-inch clutch, counterweighted for 400	3986394
14-inch iron, 11-inch clutch, counterweighted for 454	3993827
14-inch iron, 10.4- and 11-inch clutch, neutral balance	3991469

Flexplates

Description	Part Number
14-inch neutral balance, 168-tooth, small-block	471598
14-inch neutral balance, 168-tooth, big-block	471597
14-inch counterweighted for 400, 168-tooth	471578
14-inch counterweighted for 454, 168-tooth	14001992
12¾-inch neutral balance, 153-tooth, small-block	471529
12¾-inch, 1-piece seal	10128412
14-inch heavy-duty, 1-piece seal	10128413
14-inch, 1-piece seal	10128414

Note: Flywheels and automatic transmission flexplates are interchangeable between V-6-90 and small-block V-8 engines.

CHAPTER 7

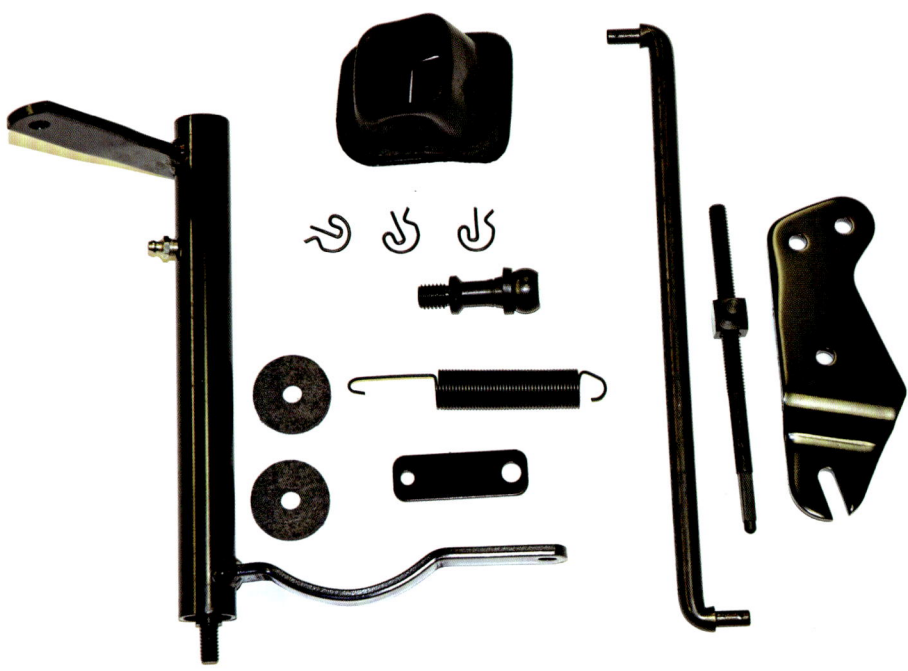

The mechanical clutch linkage systems used on Novas all pretty much look the same. This example is a big-block reproduction package from Classic Industries.

large-diameter flywheels incorporate 168 teeth on the ring gear while the 12¾-inch models have 153 teeth. The following chart shows most of the flywheel and flexplate combinations (keeping in mind that the 14-inch jobs are the most common for big-blocks).

Because two diameters of flywheels and flexplates have been used in small- and big-block applications, a couple of starter combinations are available. Large-diameter flywheels and flexplates require a starter with offset bolt holes in the nosepiece, while small-diameter models use a starter with bolt holes that are parallel. The majority of Chevrolet blocks are drilled for both types of starters.

Clutch Linkage

When it comes to clutch linkages, differences between big-block, small-block, and 6-cylinder cross-shaft applications preclude interchange. The added width of the big-block causes the trouble. You need an appropriate clutch bell

balance. The 400-ci small-blocks and 454-ci big-blocks are externally balanced (or "counterweighted") and use special flywheels and harmonic dampeners. Late-model engines make use of one-piece rear main seals, whereas early engines have two-piece rear seals. One-piece rear-seal engines feature a smaller 3.00-inch crank flange bolt circle whereas earlier examples incorporate a 3.58-inch pattern. The right mix of flywheels and flexplates must be used for each family of engines.

Chevrolet offered flywheels in two sizes: 12¾ and 14 inches. The

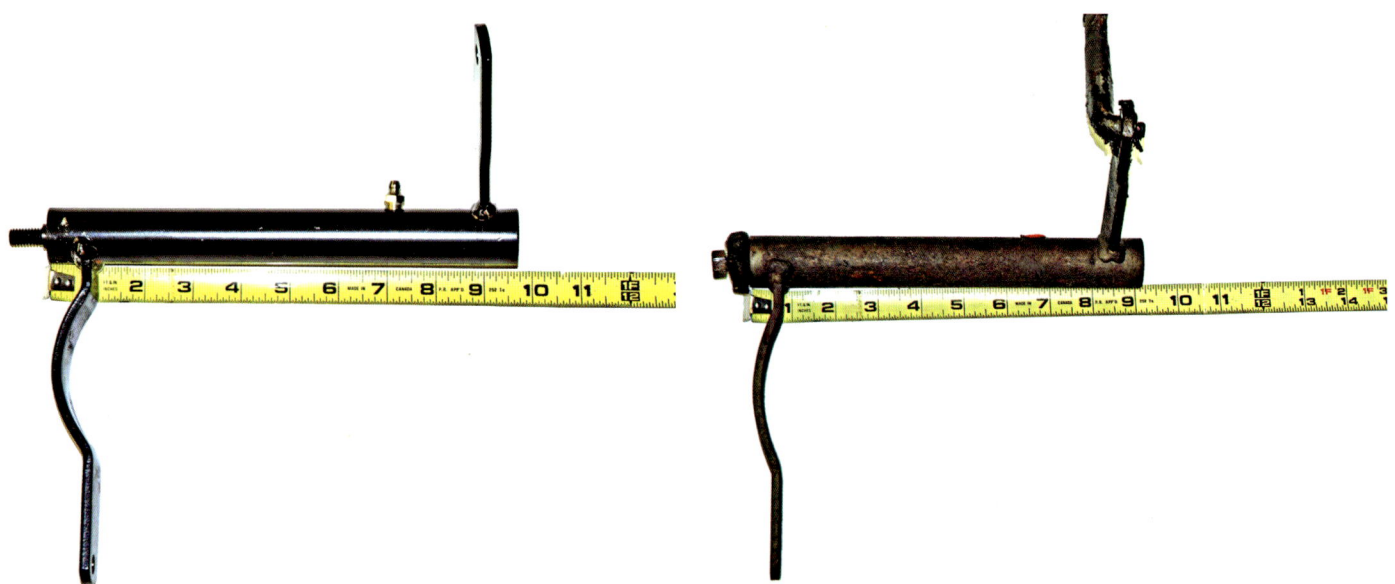

Recall when I mentioned the engine offset with a big-block? The first photo shows a clutch Z-bar (cross shaft) for a big-block application. The second photo shows a Z-bar for a small-block. Note the difference in length.

ENGINE SWAPS

Clutch Linkage Part Numbers

Application	Description	Part Number
1968–1974 Nova	Big-block bell crank	3912602
1968–1974 Nova	Big-block clutch conversion	K510

crank. Using Classic Industries as the basis, here's the basic bell crank part number along with a part number for a complete big-block clutch conversion kit (includes everything except the pedals to install a clutch setup in a vintage Nova).

What if you want to run a stock mechanical clutch linkage with an LS engine? If the transmission is mounted in the stock location, you can use a Scoggin Dickey or Jegs adapter bracket (originally designed for the Gen V/VI factory big-blocks without a provision for the clutch ball stud). These brackets bolt to the lower two bellhousing bolts on the driver's side and place the ball stud in exactly the right position for a stock small-block Z-bar. Fair enough, but most full-length LS swap headers aren't designed to fit a mechanical clutch linkage. So, if you choose to run a clutch in an LS-swapped Nova, you're best off looking at a hydraulic setup. McLeod Racing has a setup that's almost a bolt-in for this application (PN 1434002).

Building A Bulletproof Mechanical Clutch Linkage

The standard clutch linkage setup found in a Nova consists of a fork at the bellhousing (for the release bearing) along with a couple of shafts and a bell crank (Z-bar) linkage. It was simple. It worked great. But time can take its toll. Ditto with big clutch pressures. In the 1960s and 1970s (and even later) plenty of folks regularly experienced clutch linkages that bent and buckled. The reason was massive pressure plate spring pressure. Today, clutch assemblies don't use those massive, leg-breaking pressures, but the big problem is wear. If you look closely at the clutch linkage in a well-used Nova, you'll most likely discover that the linkage rods are equally well-worn at the pin ends, and most (if not all) of the mounting holes in the Z-bar and the pedal are oval. Now what?

You can replace the parts. That's a no-brainer. Most reproduction parts houses offer a wide array of replacement hardware (and, in fact, a reproduction Z-bar is used in our example). However, if you want a slick action clutch linkage, a better option is to build a heavy-duty linkage setup incorporating rod ends and chrome-moly tubing.

Many of you are thinking, "Old news." You're right. Several magazine articles have appeared on this topic over the years, but every last one missed important details along with important pieces in the puzzle. For example, the pinholes in a typical Chevy (or other GM) measure 5/16 inch in diameter. Over time (and as pointed out above), that hole diameter becomes oval. Building a clutch linkage with 5/16-inch rod ends doesn't help much because the holes the bolts pass through (in the pedal as well as the Z-bar) are sloppy.

You're pretty much forced to move up a size in rod ends. That means you should use a 3/8-inch-diameter rod end (not a 5/16-inch one). Drilling out the respective holes in a Z-bar or a clutch pedal to 3/8 inch takes out the ovaling. Furthermore, if you do your homework, you find that the tubing you need is definitely 5/8-inch OD (the same as you'd use for a 5/16-inch rod end). As an example, the folks from Mark Williams offer chrome-moly tubing in this OD with a .058-inch wall. You can use a 3/8-24 to 5/8 x .058–inch tubing adapter (weld spud) to build the linkage. This allows the use of a 3/8-inch rod end on the same-diameter tubing you'd use with smaller 5/16-inch rod ends.

Why not make it easy for yourself and build a linkage that can also be used to adjust the clutch? Use a left- and a right-hand-thread tubing adapter on each side of the respective linkage pieces instead of using all standard right-hand rod ends. With this setup, to adjust the clutch you simply back off the jam nuts on the rod ends and turn the linkage rod one way or another to lengthen or loosen the respective link. That's how race car shops such as Jerry Bickel Race Cars set up their linkage systems, and it works the same on a street-driven Nova. If the thing has all right-hand threads, you have to go through the mess of removing the bolts, holding the rod ends in place, turning the linkage in or out, buttoning it back up, and checking the gap. If you're wrong, you have to start all over again. That's way too much trouble.

So what's it like to build the linkage properly? It's not much harder than the alternative. ■

CHAPTER 7

Building A Bulletproof Mechanical Clutch Linkage CONTINUED

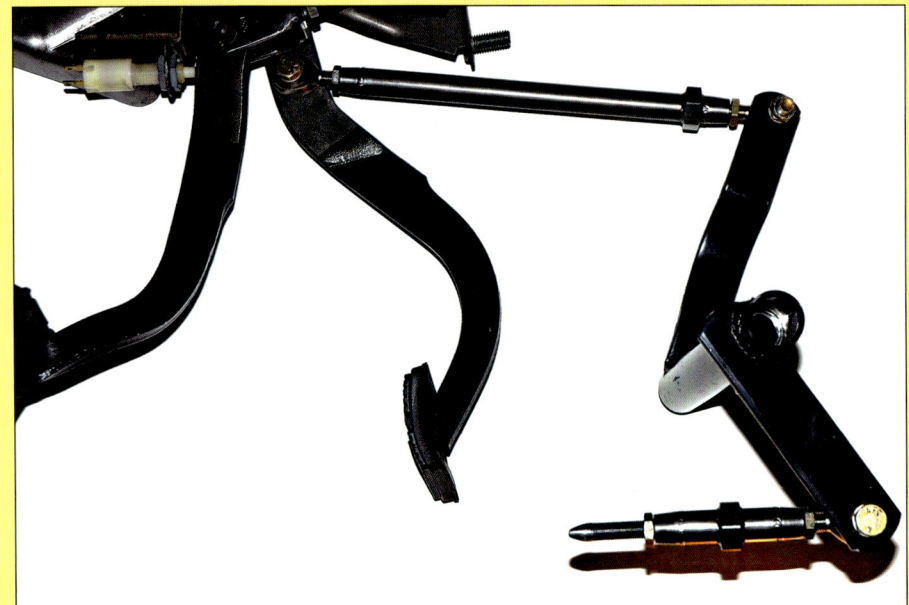

This is a modified clutch linkage for a Nova. It features spherical bearing rod ends on the upper and lower pushrods, AN hardware, and complete adjustability.

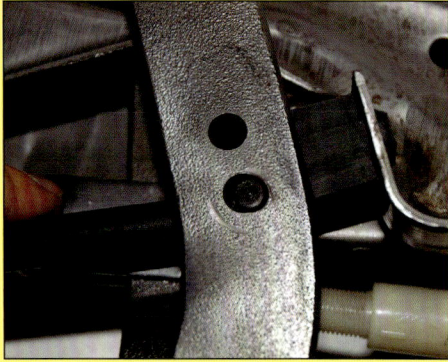

If you need proof of how the holes in a linkage oval over time, have a look at this photo. This guarantees a sloppy linkage.

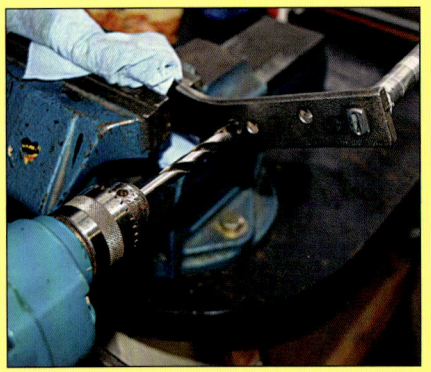

The fix for the ovaling isn't that difficult. First, drill out the hole to 3/8 inch using a sharp drill bit.

Next, drill out the pair of holes in the clutch linkage Z-bar. What you're looking at is a 3/8-inch fine-thread AN bolt that passes through a high-quality 3/8-inch rod end.

The clutch pushrod setups found in a Nova have a pointed or semi-ball end at the clutch fork side. First cut the head off a 3/8-inch fine-thread bolt. You have to "turn" it by chucking the bolt into an electric drill motor. This allows you to "turn" the piece on both a stone as well as a piece of coarse sand paper. In the end this provides for a nice, clean radius.

Measure each of the stock pushrods. Take the length of each tubing adapter (weld spud) into account, along with approximately one-half of the threads of a rod end for each side. FYI: Many tube adapters measure just under 7/8 inch (each) when pressed into the tube; JBRC adapters are slightly shorter.

To cut a piece of 5/8-inch .058-inch-wall chrome-moly to size, you have a couple of options: Use a hacksaw butted up against a hose clamp or use a big tubing cutter. Either works.

CHEVY NOVA 1968–1974: HOW TO BUILD AND MODIFY

ENGINE SWAPS

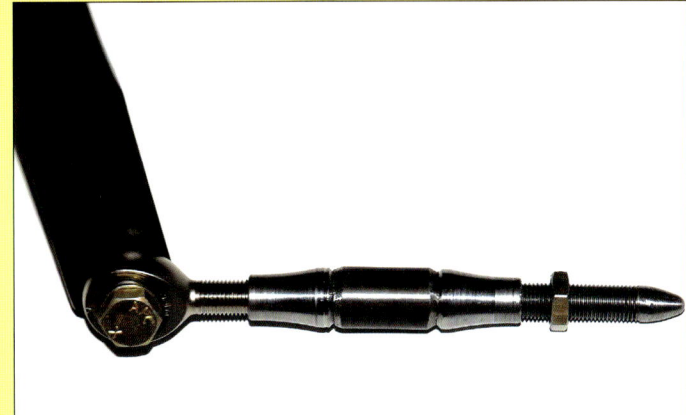

These are custom linkage rods built by Jerry Bickel Race Cars. They're the same general setup as shown in the previous photos. In addition, they are also fabricated from chrome-moly. JBRC added an adjuster nut on each of the rods. It's a great idea.

The ends of the tubing should be filed to remove flash, then a pair of weld spuds (tubing ends) are pressed into place. One side has left-hand threads while the other has right-hand threads. Repeat on the longer pushrod and weld the tubing adapters in place.

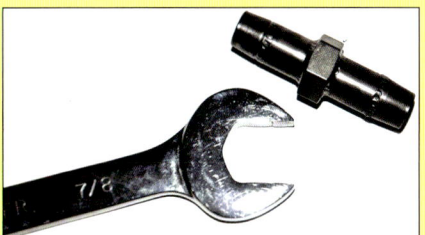

With the left- and right-hand threads on each tubing adapter, the nut allows you to turn the linkage "in" or "out" after backing off the jam nuts on the rod ends. That's a lot easier than dropping the linkage to adjust the clutch.

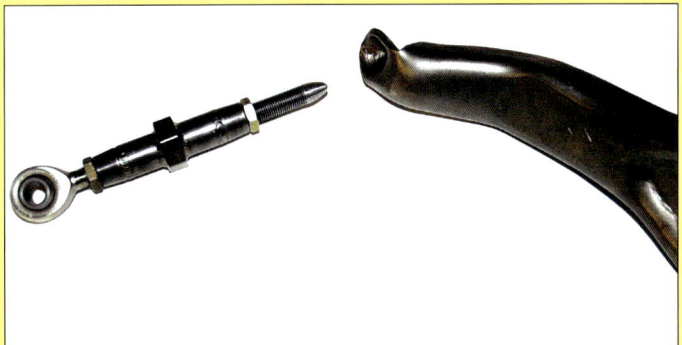

Here's a look at the lower custom linkage next to a GM clutch fork. You can see how the modified 3/8-inch (fine RH thread) fastener works. After cutting the head off the bolt, be sure to chase the threads (with a die).

These are the high-quality 3/8-inch rod ends used in this build. You can probably get away with cheaper quality pieces, but these three-piece aircraft jobs are top of the heap.

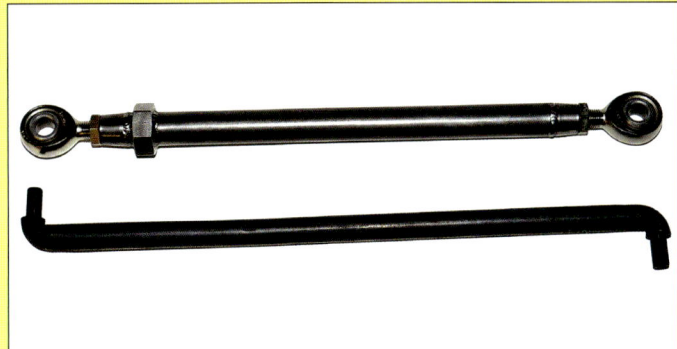

This is a direct comparison of a stock linkage (stock at the bottom in both photos) and a custom rod end setup. There's no comparison when it comes to adjustability or beef.

CHAPTER 7

Building A Bulletproof Mechanical Clutch Linkage CONTINUED

Installed in both the Z-bar and the clutch pedal, this is what each piece of linkage looks like. In the end, this setup provides you with a linkage that is smooth, easy to adjust, has no slop, and doesn't bend!

Alternators, Water Pumps and Pulleys

Vintage Chevrolet alternators are generally similar in external size and layout, but 1968-and-earlier models were mounted on the driver's side of the engine whereas 1969-and-later alternators mounted to the passenger's side. This coincides with the introduction of the "long"-style water pumps (which are slightly more than 1 inch longer than the earlier models). Because of the pump length, there is no interchange between the brackets, most pulleys, and hardware. Obviously, it's better to use the appropriate hardware for either long or short model years. The big reason is wiring. There's a hefty alternator harness lead on the driver's side for 1968-and-earlier cars whereas on later models the wiring harness is on the passenger's side.

Chevrolet's Corvette was not converted to the long water pump design in 1969; it remained as a "shorty" setup for many years. This could also be a source (particularly at resto supply houses) for complete bits and pieces, especially if you are changing over to a short configuration.

LS Drives

When it comes to accessory drive assemblies, water pumps, and associated hardware, the LS engine is a completely different animal. An LS power plant has three basic accessory drive systems: shallow, mid-length, and long. All are based off specific harmonic dampener (balancer) dimensions. The Corvette dampener arrangement is the shallowest, followed by the early Camaro/GTO systems, followed by the truck setup. With the factory Corvette drive system, the alternator is above the water pump. The factory Camaro and GTO setup mounts the power steering pump over the alternator. The factory truck mounts are bulky and take up a

Alternator Brackets

Although alternator brackets for big-blocks look like those found on small-block cars, they're not the same. Here's a rundown on the pieces you need for a swap (Classic Industries part numbers).

Application	Description	Part Number
1968	Standard water pump	58133
1968	High-performance water pump	58133P
1969–1970	All big-block water pumps	58135
All 1969 and later	Alternator bracket kit, complete	E329
All big-block	396/375 HP deep groove alternator pulley	KW609
1969 and later	Crank pulley, without AC	KW396
1969–1970	Crank pulley, with AC	14542
1970 and later	Crank pulley, with AC	G2122
1969 and later	Water pump pulley, single groove, high performance	KW394
1970	Water pump pulley, single groove	14546

ENGINE SWAPS

Holley Kits	
Holley offers so many options that I can't list them all, but here is a list of comprehensive kits.	
Description	*Part Number*
Complete drive, SD7 A/C pump, alternator, P/S pump, tensioner, belt, pulleys	20-138
Complete drive, SD508 A/C pump, alternator, P/S pump, tensioner, belt, pulleys	20-137
Complete drive, R4 A/C pump, alternator, P/S pump, tensioner, belt, pulleys	20-136
Passenger-side A/C drive, SD508 A/C pump, tensioner, pulleys	20-141
Passenger-side A/C drive, SD7 A/C pump, tensioner, pulleys	20-142
Passenger-side A/C drive, R4 A/C pump, tensioner, pulleys	20-140
Driver-side alternator and P/S pump, pulleys	20-143

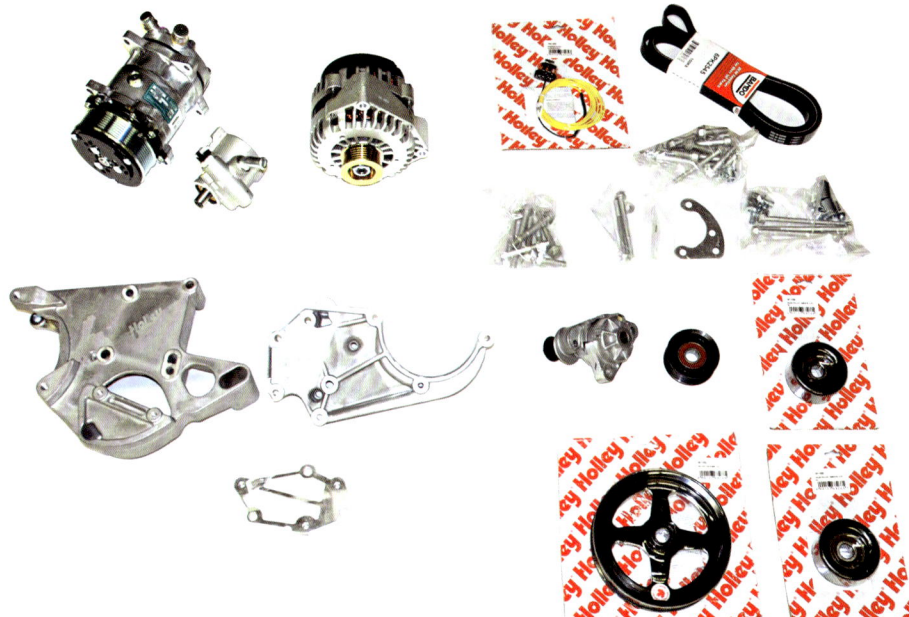

The accessory drive system you use on your Nova depends upon the engine you select. This Holley drive setup is for an LS with power steering and air conditioning.

lot of real estate under the hood. Obviously, there are a bunch of variations to the above, but the big challenge is finding the desirable drives (Corvette and to some degree Camaro-GTO). The problem is, anything that relates to a Corvette in a wrecking yard seems to double or triple the price.

Enter Holley's drive system. Holley based all of its drive packages off the short Corvette harmonic dampener (balancer) dimension. Then it uses a spacer package to make up the difference for the dampener you have on your engine. It's a simple solution that means you don't have to buy an expensive new harmonic dampener to fit the drive system.

In terms of systems, Holley offers a wide range of packages, beginning with comprehensive kits complete with an A/C pump, power steering pump, and an alternator, down to simple brackets that allow the install of an alternator only. Holley's kits are designed to accept the most common (and least costly) factory truck or early F-car alternator. Suffice it to say, it has you covered when it comes to LS drives and accessories.

Throttle Linkage

Early Novas used a mechanical throttle linkage. In other words, no cable setups but a simple lever and rod arrangement instead. While most of the Holley pieces for a big-block and

With traditional (non-LS) engines, the throttle linkage varies from engine to engine, and carburetor type to carburetor type. This is a big-block Holley carburetor throttle linkage setup from Classic Industries.

Reproduction Linkage	
The following are part numbers for a Classic Industries reproduction linkage.	
Description	*Part Number*
Big-block throttle linkage	3923549
Small-block throttle linkage	3923539

CHAPTER 7

When you install a big-block where a small-block or 6-cylinder once lived in a Nova, you should also change the heater. Big-block heaters had their cores "reversed." That meant the hoses were closer to the fender. The setup shown here is a complete big-block heater setup from Classic Industries.

If you don't need a heater, it's possible to delete it with this plate setup, again from Classic Industries. This is a reproduction C-48 Heater Delete. It certainly cleans up the firewall area.

a small-block do interchange (even though they feature different bends and have different part numbers), the other parts do not. The simple solution is to procure the right parts the first time out rather than trying to cobble up a linkage from scratch.

Heater

When the first rat motor was shoehorned into a 1967 Camaro engine bay, one of the first changes was the relocation of the heater hoses. This change applies to Novas too. In essence, a new heater core was designed: one with reversed inlet/outlet fittings. Rather than exiting near the cylinder head, the fittings were placed near the inner fender. Reproduction heater cores are readily available and by simply cutting new holes in the heater core cover, you can re-position your heater hoses.

Ignition Controls

Conventional small- and big-block Chevrolets can use any number of ignition systems. The LS engine family was born "distributorless," and while technically simpler, it does complicate things. If you have an LS swap planned, first determine if it's going to be a carbureted example or fuel injected. If injected and the power plant is close to stock, you can use an OEM production line Chevy wiring harness and Engine Control Module. Chevrolet Performance sells ECUs and harnesses, but most are very specific (and calibrated) to a given crate engine.

If your car is heavily modified, something such as a Holley (or other aftermarket) ECU is likely the best choice. If the engine is carbureted, you can use a GM Controller Kit or a similar example from MSD. Controllers for carbureted LS engines provide the ignition component. When selecting a controller of some sort for any LS swap, consider if the engine has a 24X reluctor wheel or a 58X reluctor wheel. Essentially, a reluctor wheel is what generates the firing sequence signal to the ECU. Pre-2006 LS engines have a 24X reluctor setup. The 2006 and newer LS engines have a 58X reluctor wheel.

For further insight into LS swaps, pick up a copy of SA Design's *LS Swaps: How to Swap GM LS Engines into Almost Anything*. Another good option is SA Design's *Swap LS Engines into Camaros and Firebirds: 1967–1981*. Follow the 1967–1969 Camaro recommendations. Just keep in mind, many Nova radiators are different from Camaro examples.

Headers

While it's possible to use cast-iron factory manifolds in most swaps, the difference in both performance and

Heater Core Part Numbers	
Here are the non-A/C big-block heater component part numbers from Classic Industries.	
Description	**Part Number**
Big-block heater core	3018864
Big-block heater core cover	AL303
Big-block heater core seal kit	K933

ENGINE SWAPS

There are a lot of header configurations out there, but this is a look at some of the best. Both of these big-block header sets are from Hooker. The black ones are Super Competition street headers, and the ceramic-coated ones are Hooker Race headers.

cost when compared to headers does not justify their use. Most Chevrolet exhaust manifolds were designed for the chassis. In other words, a set of streamlined big-block Corvette manifolds don't work in your Nova engine compartment.

When it comes to headers for Novas, keep this in mind: The type of motor mount you use in the swap dictates the headers you select. In other words, if you try to fit headers to something such as a big-block positioned on small-block or 6-cylinder mounts, you're asking for trouble. Use the right mount combination and you won't have grief!

Race headers are adjustable; you can change the length of both the primary tubes and the collectors. This is Hooker Headers' complete kit for a big-block application.

Hooker also makes a very nice swap header for use with an LS installed in a Nova chassis. These ceramic-coated examples are designed for use with Hooker's motor mounts.

The primary tubes on the LS swap headers measure 1⅞ inches in diameter. Meanwhile, the collector is 3 inches in diameter (second photo).

CHAPTER 7

Finally, the number of headers out there is mind boggling, too many to list all the available part numbers. Here is a look a Hooker's swap headers along with two big-block combinations. By the way, American Racing Headers (ARH) offers several clean LS swap header options. Check them out. They're all great examples. When buying LS headers, it's a good idea to be sure you have the correct engine mounts (mounts used when the header manufacturer built the headers). Otherwise fit can become an issue.

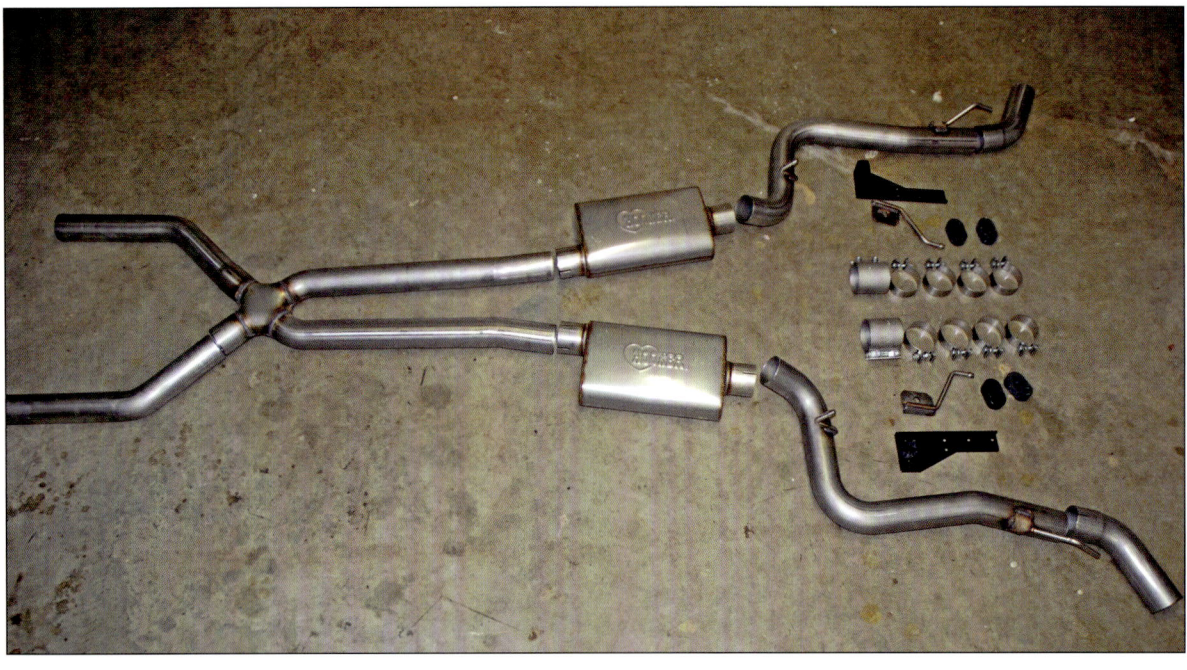

No matter what engine you choose, you need an exhaust system. When it comes to exhaust, bigger is better. This is a 3-inch Hooker setup designed to fit its LS headers.

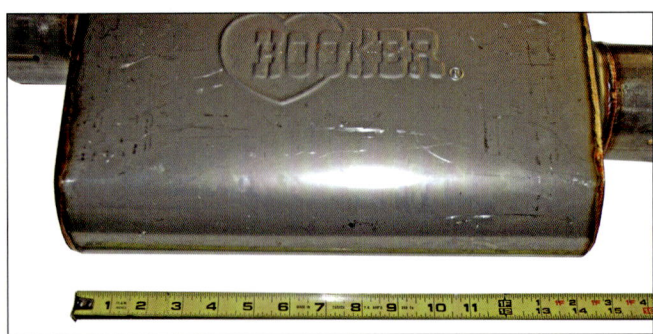

Hooker's mufflers are big. They can be used with a healthy big-block. Note that the case measures about 14 inches in length.

Inlet and outlet on the mufflers is 3 inches in diameter. If you have a conventional small- or big-block, you can use this system with one change: The head pipes from the muffler to the header collector need to be fabricated.

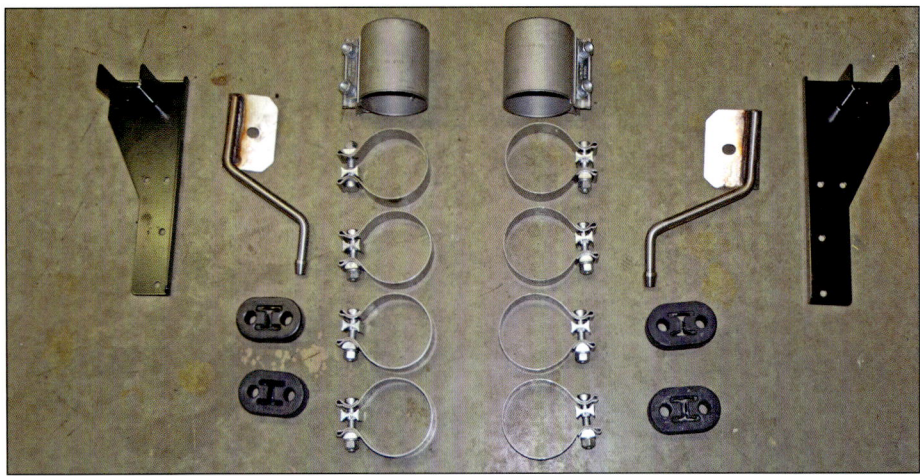

The Hooker exhaust system kit includes all the necessary hangers and mounts. It's designed so that the tailpipes exit just past the rear-wheel opening on a Nova.

CHAPTER 8

WHEELS AND TIRES

The power of a vintage, bone-stock V-8 Nova can pretty much annihilate a set of E70 x 14 Polyglass tires mounted on a set of 14 x 7–inch wheels. No secret. That's reason enough to consider adding fat tires to your Nova. In the accompanying photos, you see many wheels and tires. Not all are mounted on Novas, but that's not the point. You see, no matter what the construction methods or style, all wheels share a number of characteristics. They are, after all, automotive wheels. Before I go much further, let's look at what makes up a wheel.

Critical Parts of a Wheel

Wheel backspace is a critical dimension, particularly if you're fitting larger-than-stock wheels and tires on your Nova. This figure tells you how far the wheel is "inset," or in other terms, how much of the backside of the wheel hangs over the brake drum (or disc). The measurement is easy. Place a straight edge over the backside of the wheel lip and then measure down to the wheel-mounting surface in the wheel center. The thickness of the wheel lip affects the backspace figure. For true backspace dimensions, you should subtract the lip figure. Another term you come across is "offset." Offset is based upon backspace, but it's not quite the same. Wheel offset is the distance from the hub-mounting surface to the centerline of the wheel.

At first glance, this steel wheel–dog dish hubcap combination looks benign. Think again! That's a custom 8-inch-wide wheel stuffed into a stock, unmodified Nova wheelwell. And it's wrapped with a P275-60R15 Nitto drag radial.

Initially, everyone is swayed by the looks of the front side of a wheel. Big mistake. The business end of the wheel is the backside. It's the dimension here that determines how the wheel and tire fit your Nova.

CHEVY NOVA 1968–1974: HOW TO BUILD AND MODIFY

> ## Offset Types
>
> There are three types of offset.
>
> - Zero offset: The wheel hub-mounting surface is centered.
> - Negative offset: The wheel's hub-mounting surface is offset toward the brake side. "Reverse" wheels are typically a negative offset (and for anyone who was involved with cars in the 1960s, who can forget "chrome reverse" wheels?). The backspace dimension on these wheels is smaller than that found on a zero-offset wheel.
> - Positive offset: The wheel's hub-mounting surface is offset toward the curbside. Positive-offset wheels are used on many late-model cars such as Corvettes. Backspace dimension on these wheels is larger than that found on a zero-offset wheel. This is the type of wheel that works best on the rear of a Nova.

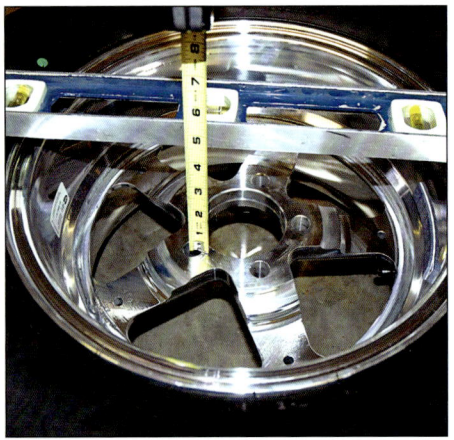

To determine backspace, measure the distance from the wheel center to the wheel bead (not the outside flange).

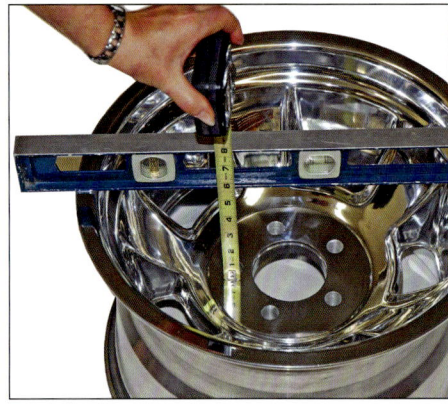

Wheel face, or curbside, dimension settings are much the same. Getting measurements is much easier without the tire mounted.

This is a 10-inch-wide wheel. What's up with the width? The rim flange is not included in the measured wheel width.

Measured from inside the wheel lip, or rim flange to rim flange, you can see that the wheel measures 10 inches. Keep this in mind when measuring any wheel, aluminum, or steel.

"Wheel face," or curbside dimension, is measured the same way as backspace. When measuring wheel face dimensions, remember that the thickness of the lip, or "wheel flange," is a factor (the same as it is when determining backspace). Take it into consideration when determining the face dimension. The face dimension plus the backspace dimension plus the thickness of the wheel mount flange (hub center) less the wheel flange (lip) dimension equal the width of the wheel. This dimension becomes critical when figuring out how much wheel and tire can fit on a given axle in a specific Nova without having the tire hang out in the breeze (a practice from the 1960s that most folks would like to forget!).

Register bore, or the wheel center bore, is the part where the hub passes through the wheel (at the mount flange). It's also where the center cap snaps in or bolts on. For some applications, this opening is machined to exactly match the hub. It is designed this way to precisely position and center the wheel while the lug nuts are torqued to spec. This centering method eliminates the chance of vibration from a wheel that isn't centered. In cases where the wheels use precision-bored registers (typically late models), the wheels are vehicle model specific. The wheel manufacturer machines the register to the precise size specified by the car manufacturer, or a series of plastic or metal "adapters" (for lack of a better word) are used to fit the wheel to the hub.

The Novas I deal with are engineered with non-hubcentric wheel register bores (the correct terminology is a "lug-centric" wheel). With some of these wheels it's a good idea to torque the lug hardware with the vehicle off the ground (for example,

WHEELS AND TIRES

This is the wheel center bore, or "register bore," I mentioned in the text. On later-model cars, the wheel and hub register center the wheel. On a Nova, the lug nuts center the wheel.

You can determine wheel bolt's circle dimensions by measuring from one lug nut to the next in the pattern. Here, the center-to-center is approximately 2¾ inches. Consulting the chart, you can see this is a Chevy 5-on-4¾–inch pattern.

on axle stands). This practice allows the nuts or bolts to center the wheel and then be torqued into place without the car weight pushing them off center.

Virtually all third-gen Novas incorporate a five-bolt wheel pattern. Bigger usually means stronger when it comes to bolt patterns. If you don't know the bolt circle dimensions of a given wheel, try this tip from Mark Williams Enterprises: Measure between the center (B.C.) of two adjacent wheel studs.

Occasionally, you hear the term "drop center." What's that? Basically, this means the center of the wheel is built with a smaller diameter than the outside segments. This allows for easier tire installation and removal. After the tire is deflated, one of the beads can fall into the drop center. In addition, wheels are equipped with small raised "lips" or "safety beads" outboard of the drop center. The purpose of the safety beads is to keep the tire on the wheel if the car experiences a blowout or a flat.

Valve stems are more important than you might think. Two sizes of valves are commonly used today: .453 and .625 inch. Several types of high-quality valves are available from companies such as Schrader-Bridgeport including snap-in (rubber), snap-in with chrome sleeve (rubber), clamp-in nickel (metal), high-performance clamp-in chrome (metal), and high-pressure snap-in (for applications up to 100 psi). So far so good, but when shopping for valve stems be cautious. Plenty of foreign made stems are constructed from natural rubber instead of EPDM (a robust synthetic rubber used in the construction of most quality valve stems). Schrader notes that EPDM has a much broader temperature range than natural rubber and remains flexible in the coldest weather. Ozone and chemical attack can deteriorate natural rubber, but not EPDM. A concern with offshore stems is the fact that natural rubber dries out, and following a couple of years of service, they become brittle. The result? Leaks.

Torqueing lug nuts to spec is important, and even more important when you've installed fresh wheels on your Nova. The reason is, new wheels tend to move around because of thermal stresses along with compression and elongation. In case the clamping loads have changed following the initial installation, wait for the wheels to cool to ambient temperature before the re-torque (never torque a hot wheel, because the values change as the wheel temperature changes). Loosen and retighten to the torque value, in sequence on each wheel. If your Nova has stock-style wheels, you can simply use the specifications found in the shop manual. In addition, many wheel manufacturers provide their own specs for torque.

For example, a set of aftermarket cast-aluminum wheels I've used in the past mandated a maximum torque of 60 ft-lbs for 1/2-inch wheel studs and 50 ft-lbs for 7/16-inch studs; otherwise, use the figures from the following chart. In either case, the lug nuts should be torqued dry, and you should use a conventional "star" or crisscross pattern.

Five-Bolt Wheel Pattern

- 2.645 inches = 4½-inch B.C. (normal later Ford or Mopar pattern)
- 2.792 inches = 4¾-inch B.C. (normal Chevrolet or small GM passenger car pattern)
- 2.939 inches = 5-inch B.C. (normal older Olds-Pontiac or large GM passenger car)
- 3.233 inches = 5½-inch B.C. (normal early Ford or Ford truck)

CHAPTER 8

Wheel Lug Torque	
Wheel Stud Size (inch)	Typical Torque (ft-lbs)
7/16	70 to 80
1/2	75 to 85

It's good practice to torque the lug nuts on your Nova and then re-torque them after they've seen miles. You might be surprised to find that aluminum wheels can move around quite a bit (lose torque) after a few miles.

Stuffing Fenders

The 1968–1972 Novas don't have a lot of room for big back tires. No secret, and in fact, tire room (or lack of it) is a concern for all Novas, no matter the model year. Certainly, you can stuff big rubber under a third-gen Nova if the wheelwells were carved out, but the truth is, it is actually possible to get some good-sized tires under the back without any real drama. You just have to determine how much "tire" can actually fit within the existing wheelwell without creating interference on the inside or the lip.

As you're well aware, wheels are available in a staggering array of dimensions. For example, you might be able to purchase a 15 x 8–inch wheel with backspaces that range from 2 inches to more than 5 inches. This means that the tire can either be tucked up inside the stock wheelwell of your car (which is good) or you must jack the Nova up and let it hang out in the draft (which is not so good).

There are likely dozens of ways to determine rear wheel dimensions. Some rely upon hit and miss tactics. The following three steps make it an easy way to figure it out using common hand tools.

Step 1

Clamp a straightedge (in this case, a carpenter's level) on the brake drum and take measurements from the brake drum mount surface to various locations on the inner wheelwell. At the same time, take measurements from the brake drum to the outer body (most likely, the wheelwell lip).

Step 2

Never clamp over the axle register in the drum; the raised lip found on the register (obviously) skews the dimensions.

As you can see, the Chevy brake drum register bore is raised. If you clamp over it, the dimensions you come up with will be wrong.

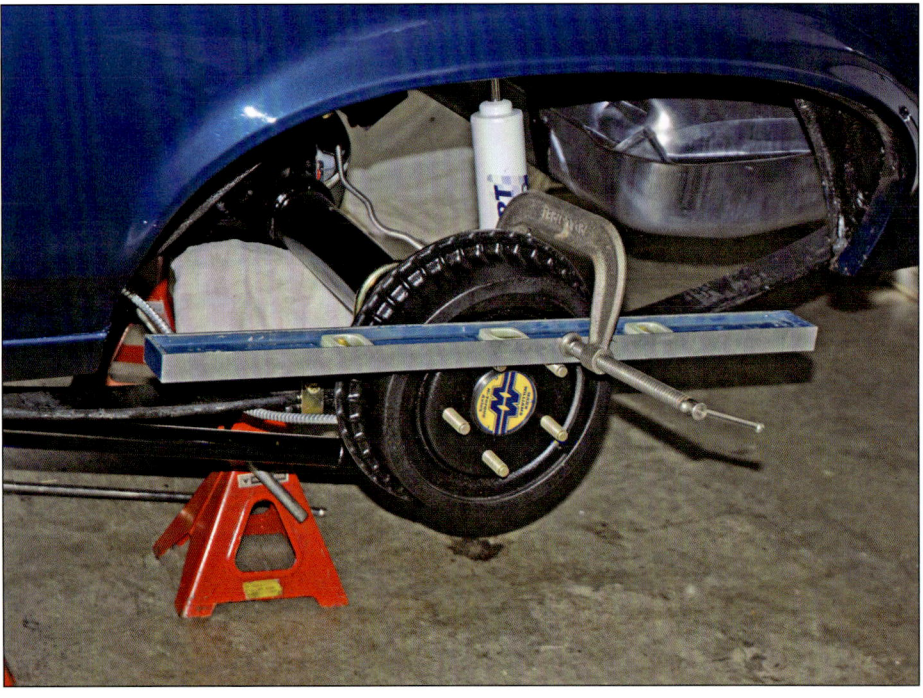

When figuring out what kind of room you have for tires on your Nova, you need a few simple tools: A known straight edge and a big C-clamp. Here's how it hooks up.

WHEELS AND TIRES

Clamp the straight edge and measure vertically to get the distance from the inside of the straight edge to the inner wheelwell and/or shock absorber. At the same time, you can also obtain measurements from the straight edge to the wheelwell's lip area.

Repeat the process with the straight edge at 45 degrees. You should do this at 45 degrees the other way and horizontal too. That way, you can't miss any potential clearance spots.

Step 3

Repeat the process with the inside and outside measurements at horizontal, 90 degrees, and 45 degrees front and back of center. Move to the other side of the car and start all over again. Why? Simple. Most cars vary dimensionally from side to side. It could be manufacturing tolerance stack up, where the spring perches were welded to the housing, and so on. The bottom line is, you absolutely must measure both sides.

It's a whole bunch easier if you have a visual to work with when you're keeping track of the dimensions and eventually figuring out what works on your Nova. You certainly don't have to be an artist to draw up some rough sketches of the wheelwell. It's best to make drawings of both sides of the car, and have one drawing for the inside (brake drum mount surface to the inner wheelwell) and another for the outside (brake drum mount surface to the outer wheelwell lip).

As the drawings show, I took the time to add the rear shock. With a Nova, the shock absorber in the stock location is potentially the first point of interference inside the wheelwell. Measure the distance from the shock to the drum mount surface in two locations. The lower of the two aren't that significant. And the reason is, it's "low" in relation to the wheel. Where clearance gets tight is

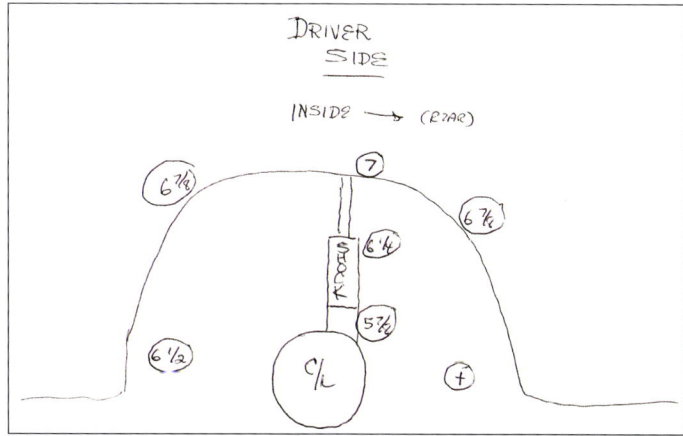

On the sample Nova, the inside clearance dimensions have been mapped out. As you can see, the illustration can be kept simple.

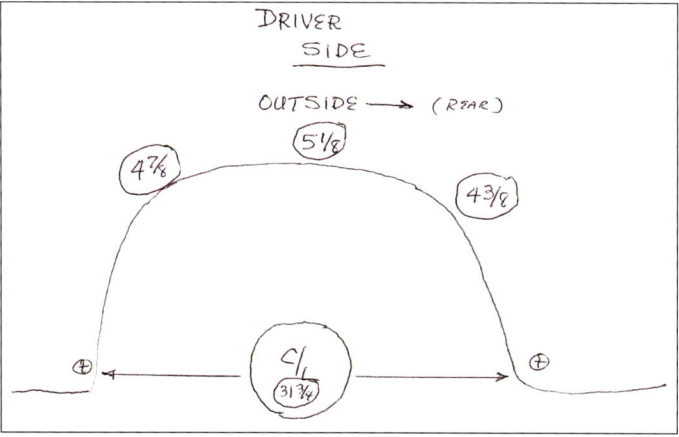

Repeat on the same side, but with outside (brake drum to wheelwell lip) dimensions.

CHEVY NOVA 1968–1974: HOW TO BUILD AND MODIFY

CHAPTER 8

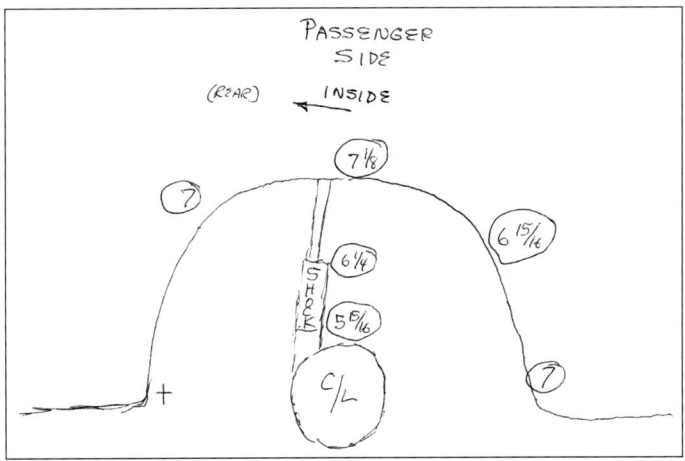

main reason for this is that the car had a very well constructed rear end with precisely located spring perches.

When you go over to the other side of the car, you find that the dimensions differ. That's because no two Novas are the same. No two rear-end assemblies are the same either. This example is rather close, but the

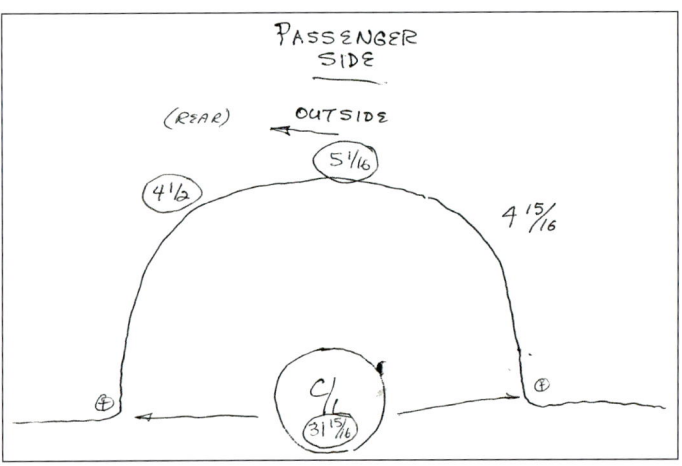

The same applies to the outside dimensions. They differ from the driver's to the passenger's side of the car. This is the why you absolutely must measure both sides of the car before you buy wheels and tires.

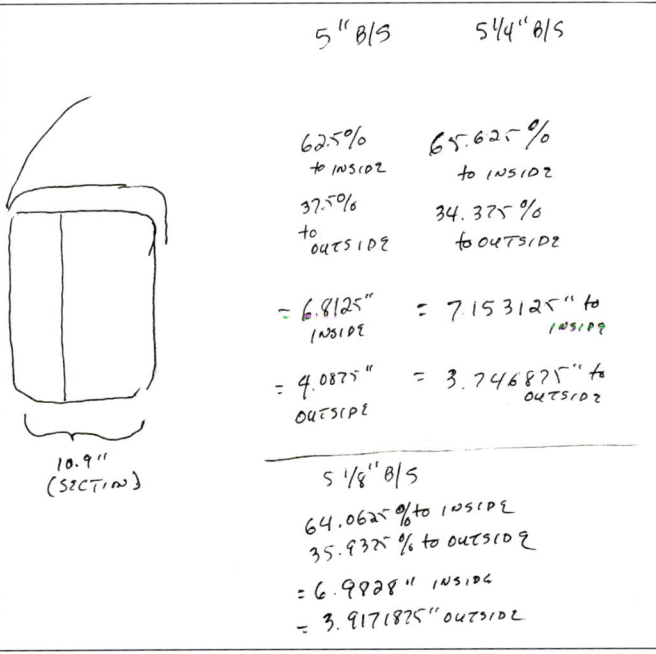

Once you have the dimensions, you can calculate the actual tire fit, based upon the section width of a given tire. The text offers more details.

where the tire bulge comes into play. I also took the time to measure the distance between the leading and trailing edges of the wheelwells. On some cars, if the tire diameter is too large, that marks the first point of interference. On this Nova, the distance is rather large; the shock body isn't huge and, as a result, it's of no consequence for a street/strip tire.

Recall that tire bulge mentioned previously? It's a critical component of measuring for wheels and tires. Each manufacturer prints a maximum tire cross section measurement for every tire sold. For example, something such as a Nitto P275-60R-15

If you need to measure tire bulge (section width), the best way is to drape a carpenter's square over the tire and nail down the section width exactly.

112 CHEVY NOVA 1968–1974: HOW TO BUILD AND MODIFY

WHEELS AND TIRES

drag radial has a cross section dimension of 11.10 inches when mounted on a recommended 15 x 8–inch wheel. Using a 5-inch backspace wheel as an example, that means 62.5 percent of the tire is on the backside. It's simple math: 5 inches (backspace) divided by 8 inches (wheel width) times 100 works out to 62.5 percent. Take 62.5 percent of the 11.10-inch cross section, and you come up with 6.9375 inches of tire bulge on the inside when mounted on a 5-inch backspace 8-inch-wide wheel. That leaves 37.5 percent of the total on the outside, which works out to 4.1625 inches. You can then use these dimensions to figure out where the tire may or may not contact the wheelwell in your car.

For this combination, the car could use a 5-inch backspace and a 5-1/8-inch backspace wheel. Ultimately, the 5-inch backspace wheel option was selected. If there is a point of interference, the first point of contact is here.

If it does interfere the solution is to swap out this Grade-8 bolt on the lower shock mount for a shock stud. The shock stud can be bent a few degrees, and that effectively rotates the shock away from the wheel. You can't go too far because cars such as a Nova use a double bolt tie bar for the upper shock mount, which can lead to shock bind.

As you can see, stuffing your back fenders with big rubber isn't that difficult a job. Just be sure to measure twice before you order the wheels and tires.

Wheel Studs

Wheel studs and lug nuts are pieces of hardware many people simply take for granted. If a wheel doesn't fall off when you're on the loud pedal, you've found bliss. Unfortunately, these pieces regularly fall into the "who cares" domain of the car. Why worry about parts if they work? Safety is primary among the many reasons to give these components extra thought. Not only are these parts much more important than you might think, picking the proper rear wheel studs, nuts, and washers might not be as easy as you think either.

Bigger is better. The stock GM wheel stud size of 7/16 inch (or equivalent metric size) is simply inadequate on the drive axle for any vehicle destined for competition (even mild competition) or other high-performance use, and that includes Novas. All high-horsepower applications with aftermarket axles should have their drive axle studs set up with a minimum 1/2-inch fasteners. For example, axle builder

If the shock presents itself as a point of interference (not common, but can occur with a large body shock absorber), swap the bolt for a shock stud. You can bend a shock stud in a vise if necessary. This rotates the shock out of the way.

There's much more to wheel studs and lug nuts than first meets the eye. This is a mix of common and not-so-common components. The big bits are drive studs.

This is a Moroso wheel stud with a quick start nose. This stud has a knurled shank and presses into the axle or wheel hub. This stud measures 7/16-20 x 2⅞ inches with a knurl measurement of .560-inch.

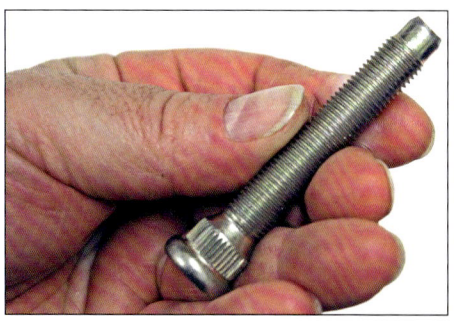

Drag race studs are typically longer than stock, but otherwise they're similar to what a production car uses. The idea with the quick start, or "bullet" nose, is to facilitate lug nut installation. FYI: This 7/16-inch stud is destined for the front only! You should use a larger stud on the back if you have aftermarket axles.

CHAPTER 8

Mark Williams sells this 1/2-20 x 3½–inch stud for use on the rear of a race car. This stud (or probably more correct, "bolt") screws in on the backside of the axle and is held in place with a lock washer. When using studs such as this, it's a good idea to use Loctite or an equivalent thread cleaner along with a "most severe service" thread locking compound (use red Loctite on the bolt/flange only, not on the actual lug segment of the stud!) The bolt head on the backside of a Mark Williams stud must be torqued to 65 ft-lbs.

extraordinaire Mark Williams does not offer axles in the 7/16-inch stud format and, as a result, supplies all axles drilled and tapped to accept 1/2-inch-or-larger studs. Proper replacement studs are fashioned from high-strength materials (often chrome-moly steel) and are threaded all the way to the head. Because of this, the stud can be fully engaged in the backside of the axle.

By the way, while it is entirely possible to have a machine shop re-drill and tap OEM axles to 1/2 inch, it's not really a great idea. You're still stuck with C-clips for axle retention, plus the original axles are now getting pretty long in the tooth. If you're using a stock (or stock-type) wheel there's a good chance you have to enlarge the wheel stud hole very slightly. A quality step drill that goes from 7/16 to 1/2 inch works perfectly for this job. Aftermarket wheels aren't much of a problem. You simply swap the supplied 7/16-inch lug nuts for 1/2-inch examples.

Keep in mind the stud is the element that transfers the load to the wheel, and the wheel and tire are what transfer the load to the pavement. Some of these loads at the axle might be much larger than you think. Just look at the basic math (and it is basic; there's nothing here that takes the tire "hook," track conditions, or overall tire dimensions into consideration).

Engine Torque x Torque Converter Multiplication x Transmission 1st Gear Ratio x Rear Axle Ratio = Load

With a typical small-block Nova hot rod, the loads can exceed 10,000 ft-lbs of torque at the axles. Arguably, there are two axles and ten studs to distribute this load over, but it's still a bunch. Because of this, really serious big-power Novas can benefit from the use of "drive studs." These are huge studs that measure up to a full 11/16-inch diameter (on the drive shoulder). Designed to fit the holes in

Here's another stud type you might come across. Basically, it's a Mark Williams piece that was initially designed for NASCAR competition. This stud has a "quick start" segment machined on the nose. As you've probably gathered, this allows the lug nut to be installed rapidly without cross threading. Again, this is more of a bolt than a stud, and it too is installed from the backside of the axle, using a lock washer for retention. This stud should only be used with the GN-style quick start nuts, or "acorn"-type, nuts.

aluminum race wheels (e.g., Centerline, Cragar, Weld, Bogart, etc.), the studs make use of an equally huge 5/8-18–inch axle thread (the portion of the stud that screws into the axle). Consider these components overkill if you like, but if bent or broken axle studs are plaguing your Nova, you need them.

A good example of a quality drive stud is the MW piece shown in the accompanying photos. These studs have 11/16-inch-diameter shoulders for use with racing wheels. The drive stud is threaded into a 5/8-18–inch thread in the axle flange and secured with a jam nut. Wheels are held on with an open-end flanged lug nut with an aluminum washer. The drive studs incorporate a smooth shoulder (see the photos) that physically drives the wheel. In comparison, a street lug nut for aftermarket wheels has a built-in shoulder that drives

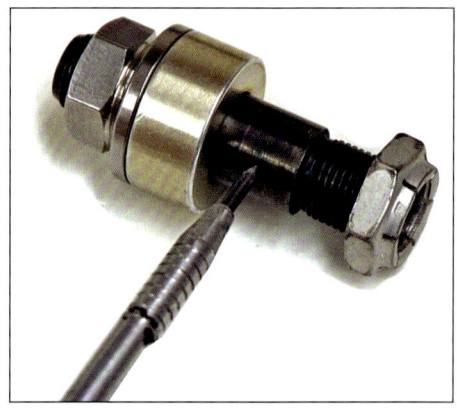

A drive stud (such as this Mark Williams version) is designed with a 5/8-18-inch thread on each end with an 11/16-inch shoulder in between. Obviously, the shorter threaded segment is installed in the axle and secured with a jam nut. Meanwhile, the shoulder (see the pointer) is the same OD as the lughole ID in common aluminum wheels. This ensures that the stud actually does the driving of the wheel, not the lug nut.

the wheel. These street-oriented lug nuts are designed for use with small-diameter studs (1/2 inch being the largest). In simple terms, the street models use much-smaller-diameter studs and the actual lug nut serves to drive the wheel.

What gets confusing for a lot of folks (even Pro racers have been baffled by the combinations) is the number of combinations of stud lengths and washer thickness available. Mark Williams offers several washer sizes and stud lengths (the drive shoulder length of the stud differs). The reason for the multitude of combinations is the range of wheel center thickness on the market, coupled with the actual thickness of the brake drum or disc brake hat and wheel spacer (if one is used). According to Williams, the most important factor when choosing the proper stud is that the driving portion of the stud is fully engaged into the wheel. The smooth "drive" segment dimension of the stud needs to be slightly greater than the combined thickness of the brake adapter/drum and the thickness of the wheel. Meanwhile, the washer thickness should be greater than the shoulder extending past the wheel. When ordering a set of drive studs, you must specify the wheel center and brake hat (or brake drum) thickness.

As you can see, lug nuts and wheel studs are components that should not be taken lightly. More than one car has been mortally wounded simply because the owner turned into Scrooge on elementary hardware such as this. In the photos that follow, you find a selection of stud and nut combinations along with information on how to determine the right wheel stud/lug nut mix for your Nova.

Drag Radials

When it comes to tires for your Nova, you have all sorts of options. Much has been written about the various types of tires available, and I won't go there. What I will do is look at something you don't read that much about, and that's a drag radial.

This big-boy P325 drag radial doesn't fit under a Nova, but it gives you a good point of reference when it comes to tread layout. Some examples (certain M/T and Hoosier drag radials) have even less tread. They're pretty much slicks with a couple of grooves in them.

In conjunction with the drive studs, Mark Williams also manufactures a series of lug nuts, including the standard flanged model on the left and a series of reduced hex nuts. These nuts have a hex head size of 7/8 inch and are designed for use with special Mark Williams washers.

Getting a third-gen Nova to hook has its challenges, primarily due to the limited amount of wheelwell room. Two keys to making them "work" are the rear suspension components coupled with the back tires. Drag radials are a great choice out back.

CHAPTER 8

Drag radials might look tame at first glance, but plenty of cars have seen almost insane levels of performance with seemingly little street-legal tires. Some 6-second (quarter-mile) cars use drag radials.

Two things to note here, other than the size: The tire meets DOT standards and it's directional. Note the arrow pointing out the direction of rotation.

The sidewall information lays out the tire construction. These MandH tires are built with two plies of polyester, two plies of aramid, and 1 ply of nylon. In case you're wondering, aramid is a synthetic fiber that is used in things such as body armor. It also sees use in everything from bicycle tires to aerospace components. Note the maximum load (per tire) on the sidewall.

In truth, these are fair weather sticky tires that are perfect for big-power cars with limited wheelwell room (which includes many Novas out there). They wear quickly, but ask yourself just how many miles you put on your car in a given year.

It's no secret that plenty of street cars (Novas included) out there today are capable of running 8-second quarter mile ETs. Some have even dipped into the 6-second zone on relatively small DOT legal rubber.

What really brought this incredible small tire performance into focus is simple. The rules for many categories of street car drag racing mandate a tire that has Department of Transportation (DOT) approval. Many of the more popular categories mandate radial tires. DOT drag radials were born to meet both needs. The DOT requirement places a considerable burden on the tire manufacturer. The company must develop a tire that can effectively cope with an almost obscene amount of horsepower, but at the same time, it must pass a rigid set of requirements laid out by the DOT. Keep in mind that these specialized DOT-approved tires aren't for everyone. They wear quickly. They're not that happy in the rain. Nevertheless, they do hook, and that's what this is all about.

Given the mix of mandates (DOT and great hook), the "street" tires used in street car drag racing might at first glance look like slicks with a couple of grooves sliced in them, but they have a number of subtle and not-so-subtle differences. Weight of the car is a huge issue. One has to remember that a typical fastest street Nova is quite portly in comparison to a dragstrip-only car.

It's not uncommon for an "Outlaw" P275-60 drag radial racer to tip the scales at more than 3,000 pounds. That same car can have an ultimate performance well below 7-seconds in the quarter-mile. Think about that for a minute. It wasn't that long ago that high-6-second ET slips were rare in a Pro Stock racer; and those things tip the scales at 2,350 pounds and have far more substantial rubber. Building a tire to support a 3,000-pound car that runs 6-second laps is impressive, but it's not the final word in design.

It should be no surprise to anyone that drag slicks for unlimited applications are regularly constructed as light as possible. Lower wheel and tire mass almost always equates to lower ETs. But when a tire is forced to pass a DOT requirement, peeling out pounds isn't so easy. A DOT tire must have a load range (and it must have that load range cast into the side of the tire).

WHEELS AND TIRES

Grizzled old drag racers are the first to tell you that performance improves as tire weight decreases. Test a light tire against a heavy one and you most likely find that the Nova is quicker with the lighter tire.

Using a MandH Racemaster P325-50R15 as an example, the overall tire weight is about 25 pounds (at least on a bathroom scale). I've observed another similarly sized drag radial that tipped the scales at 29 pounds, while another one weighed a whopping 37 pounds (that's definitely big-boned). In comparison, a similarly sized conventional drag slick tips the scales at approximately 23 pounds.

Where does the weight loss come from? MandH was careful in the design of its tire. That's why the weight of its drag radial isn't over the top; however, it notes that a bit more belt material is required in the drag radial tire. This makes for a more rigid sidewall and, of course, a heavier tire. To some extent, the tire manufacturer is forced to build a more robust tire if it must conform to heavier cars and DOT requirements.

Sizing

What size ranges of drag radials are available? You might be surprised at the choices, but again, for a Nova with a stock wheelwell, the biggest you can possibly fit is a P275-60R15. When you think about sizing, it's important to keep this in mind: Don't directly compare tires based upon the size shown on the sidewall. Compare them by dimensions.

Tubes or Tubeless?

Some DOT street car "drag tires" are designed as tube-type tires (primarily bias ply jobs). There are a number of reasons for this, but safety is a primary concern. In addition, a tube helps to maintain air pressure. It's not uncommon for a tubeless bias ply fastest street car tire to deflate quickly (that even includes several of the more streetable types with a full complement of tread). That isn't the case with a drag radial. They're definitely tubeless. Besides, adding a tube effectively increases the weight of the tire.

Compounds

When it comes to sticky tires that comply with DOT specifications, compounding is a huge issue addressed by tire manufacturers. The various companies who have entered the street car drag racing arena have gone down a couple of different

P275-60R15 Tire Dimensions			
	MandH	M/T	Nitto
Tread Width	9.5 inches	9.3 inches	n/a
Section Width	10.9 inches	11.1 inches	11.10 inches
Diameter	28.0 inches	28.2 inches	27.76 inches
Circumference	88.0 inches	88.6 inches	87.21 inches
Measured Rim Size	8.0 inches	8.0 inches	8.0 inches

Without a mini-tub (and moved spring), this tire will not fit into your Nova. But you can fit a P275-60R15 in the wheelwell, as indicated earlier.

The way the tire is constructed (belt layout, belt materials) determines how much the tire weighs and how it works. Factor in the compound (which is equally important) and you can appreciate why certain tires "work" better than others. On a related note, modern drag radials work well tubeless. That might not be the case with sticky bias plies (some can leak).

CHEVY NOVA 1968–1974: HOW TO BUILD AND MODIFY

avenues in response. For example, MandH Racemaster has developed an entire new line of compounds just for its newest "HB" series of street car drag race tires.

M/T incorporates its relatively soft "R2" compound in the tire, which provides for superior traction on the strip. Meanwhile, the radial construction provides for excellent ride control on the street. To make the tires "work," they use a special proprietary sidewall construction. M/T uses a combination polyester and steel belt construction, which it claims adds to the tire life. Tread patterns are directional with low voids. That provides the maximum amount of rubber on the road, but at the same time, still meets DOT requirements.

Air Pressure

How much air pressure is required for these tires? According to MandH Racemaster, proper air pressure is critical in its DOT drag radial tire, especially from a performance perspective. The folks from MandH note that recommending air pressure isn't easy, since many variables are involved; for example, the weight distribution of the car, transmission type, chassis set up, wheel size, and other factors. The truth is, in drag racing, many racers feel that "less is better" with regard to air pressure. This is not always the case. While there are exceptions to every rule, higher pressures (than you might expect) generally work best with drag radial tires. Not only do the higher pressures lead to quicker times, but they also contribute to a safer, more stable ride at the finish stripe.

MandH notes that the actual optimum air pressure may vary significantly, depending, of course, on the variables noted above.

Tire pressure is critical. There's good advice on the topic in the text, but the quick story is, start at about 75 percent of the maximum pressure and test lower. Every car might require a different tire psi.

M/T states that no tire in this series (DOT drag radial) should be operated below 11 psi. For tire sizes of P275 and smaller, it suggests that you set pressures between 12 and 16 psi at the strip. Larger tires (P295 and bigger) should have pressures set between 11 and 14 psi.

For use on the street, Mickey Thompson of Mickey Thompson Tires suggests you check the sidewall for maximum pressure and start at approximately 75 percent of that figure. As an example, the P275-60R15 Nittos shown in the accompanying photos have a maximum pressure of 44 pounds. 75 percent of that figure is 33 pounds.

Burnout

The type of burnout you perform is related to the tire compound. For a car equipped with HB11 compound tires, MandH offers this advice: "A hard burnout is not necessary. For the first pass of the day, make a light to moderate burnout. After that, a light burnout should suffice. Continue the burnout until the engine starts to pull down. A dry hop after the burnout isn't recommended. For a stick-shift car, perform a light burnout, haze the tires, and stage immediately. Generally speaking, drag radials work better with a light burnout rather than a hard burnout. Drag radial tires may require a fairly hard burnout on the first and second pass to break them in."

Mickey Thompson advises the tread compound used in the ET Street Radials is designed to heat quickly and does not require a heavy burnout. (A dry hop is where you dump the clutch or hit the gas with the converter stalled after the initial water box burnout.)

When it comes to tire life, these new-generation fast street car tires are similar to slicks. Drag slick life can vary from car to car. Inconsistent 60-foot and 330-foot times are often caused by tread wear or carcass breakdown. Take that as an indicator to change tires. While slicks have wear holes on the tread face, street car tires don't. When the grooves in a street car drag tire vanish, it's time to buy new rubber (common sense, obviously). Keep in mind that a hard-hooking Nova can cause the tire carcass material to break down. Inspect your tires carefully after 30 passes and even more often if the car is really quick.

Dragstrip Tire Pressure	
The recommended baseline pressures for dragstrip use are as follows.	
Tire Size	Air Pressure
Under 30 inches in diameter	12 to 16 psi and up
Over 30 inches in diameter	11 to 14 psi and up

CHAPTER 9

FUEL SYSTEM

The fuel system in your Nova is comprised of several key components: the gas tank (or fuel cell), the fuel pickup, a mechanical or electric fuel pump, a fuel filter, fuel line and/or hose, and sometimes a fuel pressure regulator. The performance of the engine and the entire car dictate whether you need to upgrade to something such as an electric pump with a fuel pressure regulator. Of course, if your Nova has an EFI setup, you definitely need an electric system of some sort. I discuss the fuel requirements later, but where do you really begin? The best place to start is at the source: gas tank or fuel cell.

Gas Tanks and Fuel Cells

There's no question that today's crop of "fast" street cars (Novas included) have stretched the performance envelope. It wasn't that long ago that an 11- or 12-second "lap" easily got the job done. Not so today.

As you might have guessed, it takes more than pure horsepower to run super quick ET numbers. Virtually every inch of the car has to be poked and prodded to wring out the last drop of performance. What does this have to do with you, the little-guy owner of a street-driven Nova that might be raced on occasion? More than you might imagine.

Today, NHRA Pro Stock cars are fuel injected. Prior to 2016, a legal NHRA Pro Stock car had two carburetors with a total of four needle and seat assemblies and four (or as many as eight) fuel lines leading to the fuel bowl. Your Nova likely has one carburetor and, at the most, only a pair of needle and seat assemblies

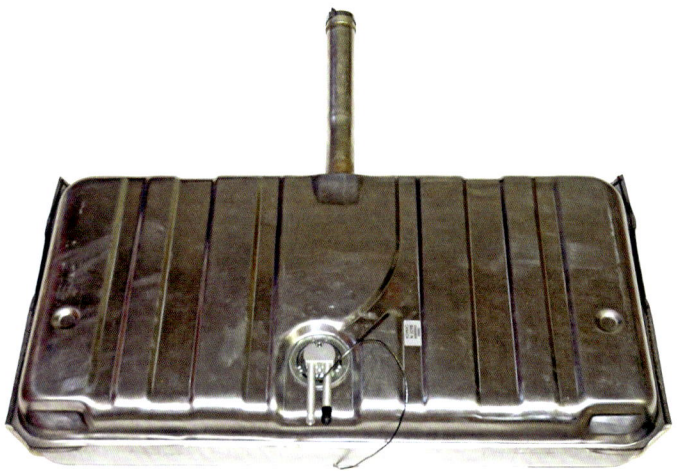

This is likely the best-quality stock replacement gas tank you'll find for a Nova. A company named Spectra Premium manufactures it. That fuel sending unit is definitely not stock, however.

Fuel cells come in all different shapes, capacities, and styles. Small drag race cells such as this don't get you very far on the street.

CHEVY NOVA 1968–1974: HOW TO BUILD AND MODIFY

CHAPTER 9

Building an AN Hose Fuel Line

Assembling AN hose for fuel line is straightforward, but get it wrong and you have a leaking fitting. Get it right and you have a good-looking and equally functional component. In between, you can mar the fittings, leave unsightly (and potentially faulty) gaps, and generally make a mess of the fittings and your fingers (cut braided hose is sharp).

The market offers several types of quality hose ends in tapered and cutter styles. The cutter style (such as the Earl's Swivel Seal fitting shown in the accompanying photos) is assembled in a slightly different manner than the tapered style. The cutter-style hose end is considered by many in the racing biz to be more secure than the tapered style. Both work well, but misconceptions about assembling cutter-style hose ends sometimes discourage their use. After those are out of the way, cutter hose ends become almost as easy to assemble as the tapered style. By the way, the process shown in the accompanying photos works for both styles of hose ends.

If you lock the hose with the socket (tube nut) end in a vise and try to assemble it, you'll encounter grief. Instead, lock the cutter end of the fitting into the vise and as you push the hose on, engage the threads. This way, there's far less chance of the hose backing out. Another bonus seems to be less chance of getting a wayward rubber "flapper" (loose piece of hose) in the line.

Another issue is tools. You should use a proper set of AN fitting vise jaws (Earl's Performance has a nice one, PN 1004ERL). This tool locks the fitting in place without damage, allowing you to properly engage the fitting threads. Another must-have tool is the Koul Tool. This is a unique tool that's easy to use; just insert the socket into the tool, twist in the hose, and socket assembly is complete in less than 10 seconds. If you'd like to eliminate the hard struggle of assembling hose ends, these kits get the job done.

The final issue is getting a clean cut on the hose before you attempt to assemble it. Years ago, it was common practice to tightly wrap the hose with duct (racer) tape, clamp it in a vise, and cut it with a fine-tooth blade hacksaw. It works, but you still end up with frayed edges. Instead, try using an angle grinder fitted with a cut-off wheel. It's way faster, it's way cleaner (fewer stray stainless braids), and it makes for a nice, straight cut. If you do have a crooked cut or if you encounter some wayward braids, don't bother trying to trim them with hand tools. Instead, simply dress the hose end(s) on a bench grinder. Easy, and painless too.

So how does all this stuff go together? Check out the following:

Earl's hose end, at the top, is engineered with a "cutter" and the other without. On the outside, both types of hose end look pretty much the same. Take them apart, though, and you can easily spot the differences.

An Earl's Swivel Seal hose end built with a cutter is designed to physically slice into the inner hose liner. This makes for a more secure engagement into the hose. They're more difficult to work with, however, and anytime you have to remove the fitting, the hose must be shortened because the cutter requires fresh hose to slice in securely.

FUEL SYSTEM

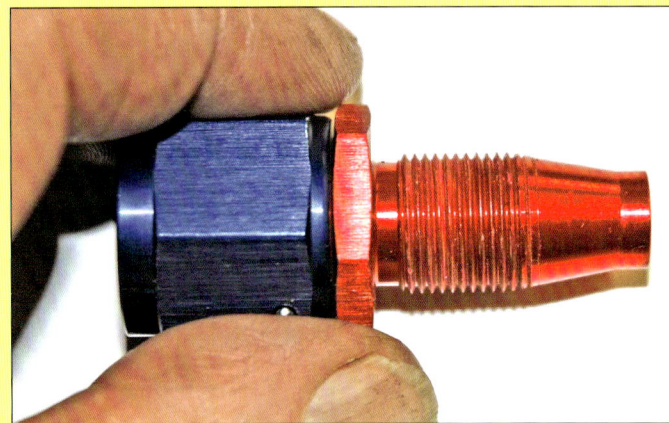

In comparison is a hose end with a taper. Up close, you can see that in this sort of configuration, the hose slides over the nipple and is held in place by the compression of the threads. These hose ends are not as strong a connection (ultimately) as a cutter.

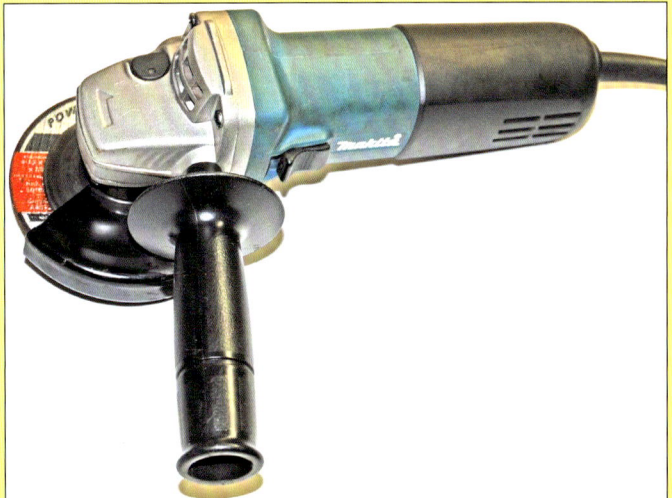

This is the best tool for cleanly cutting AN hose. It's a simple 4½-inch angle grinder fitted with a cut-off wheel. It slices through hose like a hot knife through butter.

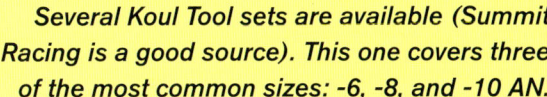

Several Koul Tool sets are available (Summit Racing is a good source). This one covers three of the most common sizes: -6, -8, and -10 AN.

Before you cut the hose, wrap it tightly with duct tape and clamp it in your vise.

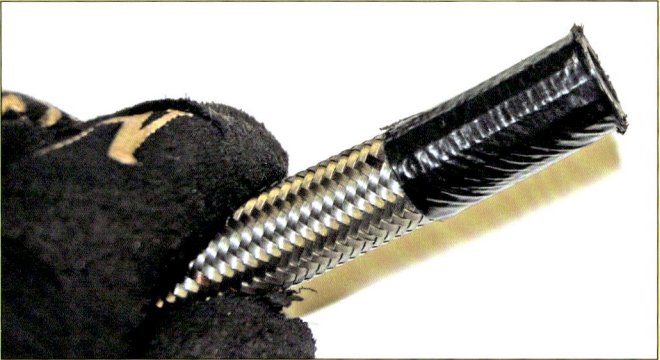

This is typical of the type of cut you get with a cut-off wheel. If there are any extra stainless strands, simply dress the hose on a bench grinder.

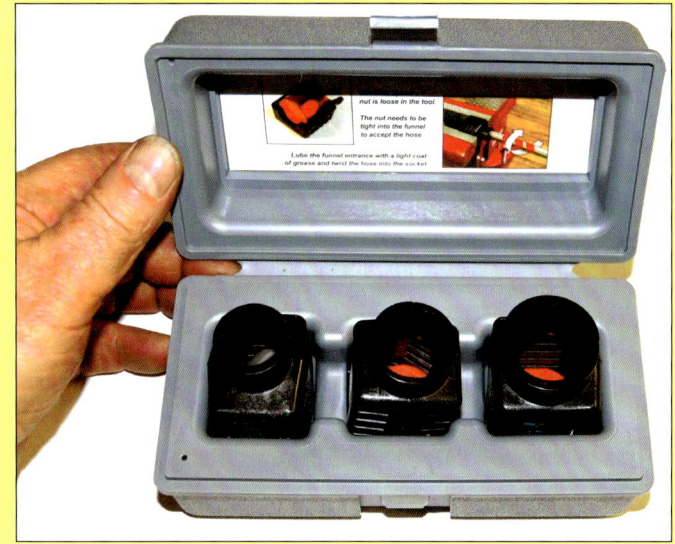

CHEVY NOVA 1968–1974: HOW TO BUILD AND MODIFY

Building an AN Hose Fuel Line CONTINUED

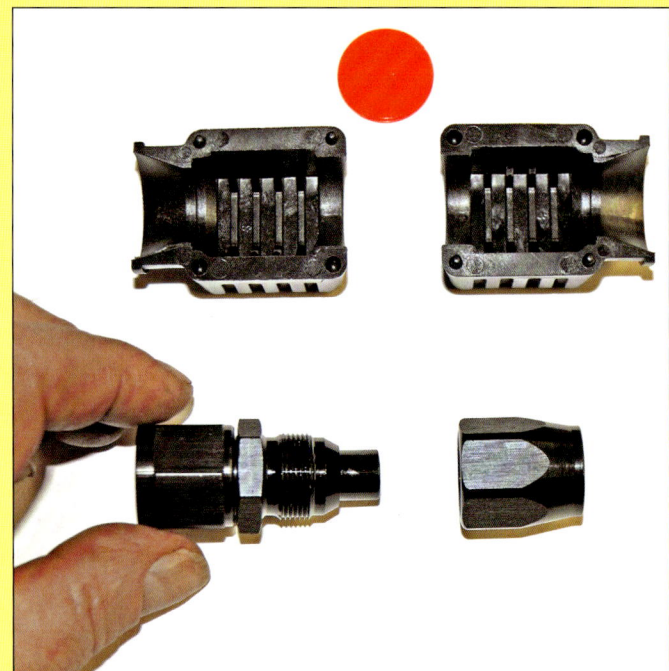

To use the Koul Tool, disassemble the hose end. See the red circle? That's a spacer that might be needed for hose ends with short sockets. It's not required for the Earl's hose ends.

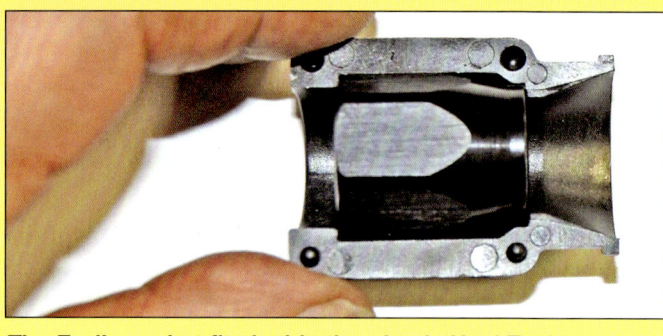

The Earl's socket fits inside the plastic Koul Tool as shown.

Close the Koul Tool. Add a small amount of grease to the taper in the tool (where the hose enters the tool).

Here the Koul Tool is clamped into the Earl's aluminum vise jaw set. At this point, you simply twist the hose into the hose end socket. It goes easier than you think, plus there's no chance of stabbing yourself.

Mark the end of the hose (behind the socket) and then simply add a wrap of duct tape to this spot. The idea here is to watch for hose back out.

Push the hose into the socket until it reaches the threads.

FUEL SYSTEM

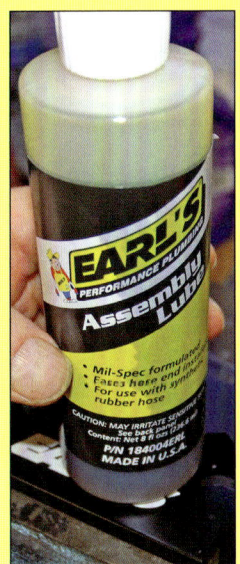

Lightly lube the ID of the hose and the threads on both the socket and the cutter. Earl's Assembly Lube (PN 184004ERL) is engineered for this job and it works better than any other lube. Period.

Clamp the cutter portion of the hose end into the vise jaws. Oil the threads and the cutter with Earl's Assembly Lube. Now you can easily push the hose and the socket onto the cutter and simultaneously engage the threads.

Using an appropriately sized open-end wrench (these Mac Tools' "knuckle savers" fit tightly), complete the tightening process. Believe it or not, a tight fitting open-end wrench is the best tool for the job. Be careful not to damage either the nipple end or the socket when tightening.

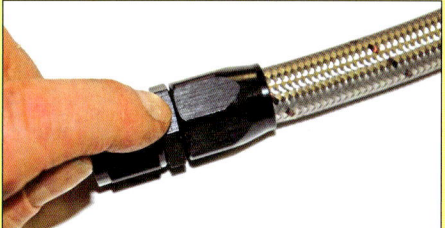

Tighten the nipple end into the socket until there is a gap of approximately .031 inch between the socket and the shoulder of the nipple. A good rule of thumb (pun intended) is your thumbnail; it's close to .031 inch. Double-check the mark for push-out. If the hose has backed out by more than 1/16 inch, go back to square one and start all over again. This often means you must re-cut the hose (back to clean, undamaged "rubber"). Also, carefully clean the hose end so that the threads aren't filled with rubber.

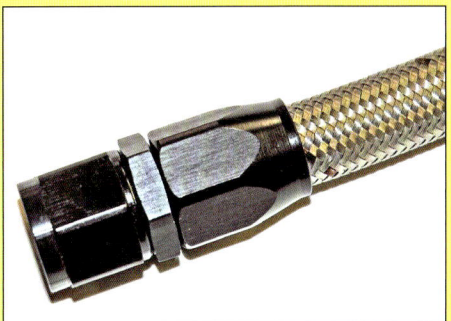

Clean the hose and hose end (good old-fashioned solvent works). Wipe clean.

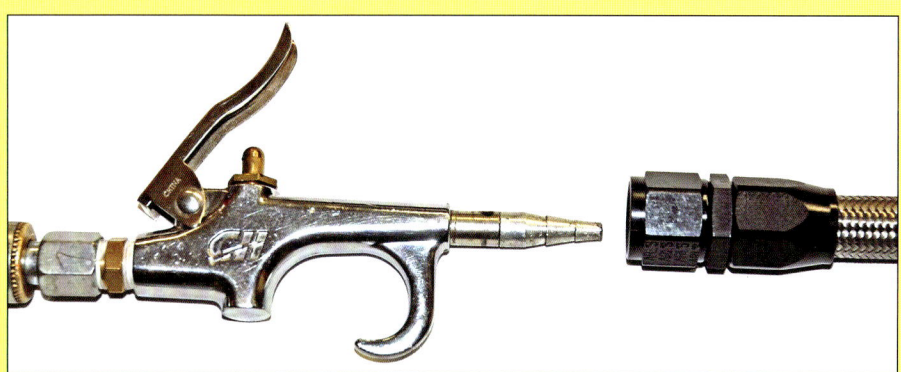

Blow out the hose assembly. A couple of blasts of high-pressure air clean it out perfectly.

CHEVY NOVA 1968–1974: HOW TO BUILD AND MODIFY

Building an AN Hose Fuel Line CONTINUED

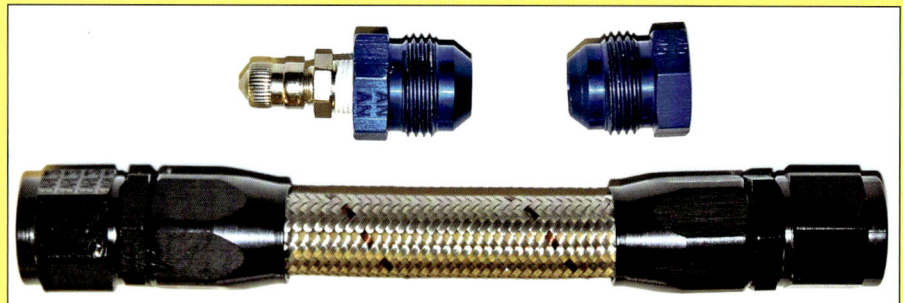

Before use, the hose should be tested. These special test fittings from Earl's Performance (PN D016ERL) are designed for the job.

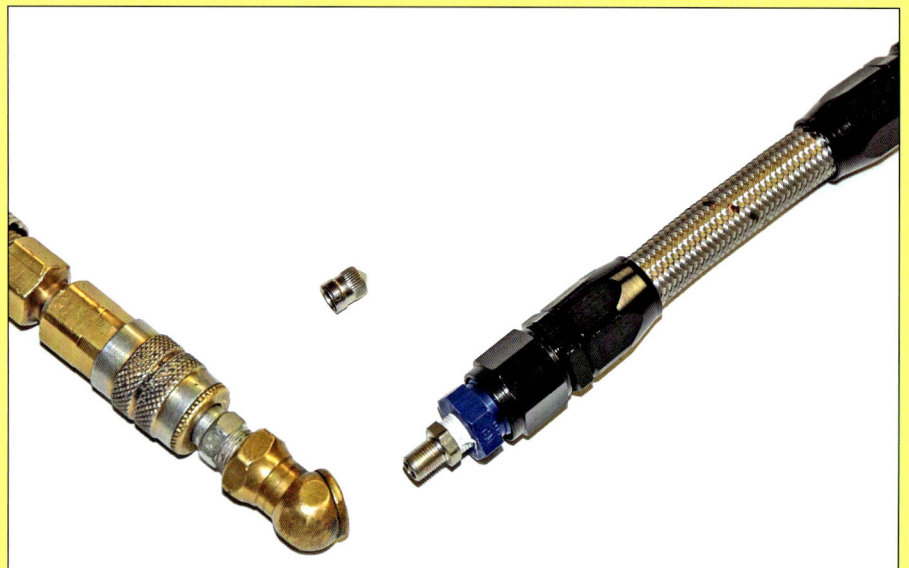

Using an aluminum hose end wrench, assemble the test fittings into your hose. Tighten so that the adapters seat. Be sure to double-check the Shrader valve to ensure it's tight. Air it up. It's a good idea to test the hose at twice the maximum operating pressure. Simply air it up with an air compressor, and then check the pressure with a common tire gauge.

Place the hose under water and check for leaks. No bubbles. No leaks. The hose assembly passed.

This is the finished top-of-the-line Earl's hose package.

(along with a maximum of two fuel lines leading to the respective bowls). Plenty of Novas have only one needle and seat assembly coupled with a single (small) OEM fuel bowl (for example, the stock setup with a Rochester QJ). Yesterday's Pro Stock car had a bit of fuel capacity "reserve" in the fuel bowls and fuel lines.

On the track, a "little-guy" Nova just might have a harder initial launch than some Pro Stock cars (if only for a millisecond). Because of this, it can run out of fuel quicker. How can that be? It's simple torque multiplication math. If you have an engine with 500 ft-lbs of torque multiplied by a torque converter (assume a torque multiplication factor of 2), which in turn operates through a 2.52:1 low-gear transmission multiplied by a 5.14:1 gear set, the axles see a torque output of approximately 12,950 ft-lbs. The math also shows a Pro Stock car might only have 10,000 ft-lbs of starting line torque production. What this means is the fuel cell or tank in a relatively low-horsepower car is more important than you might think.

Should you use a tank or a cell? Not all fuel cells are the same. A dedicated drag race car can get away with a 3- or 5-gallon fuel cell. With a true street-driven Nova, 3 or even 5 gallons of gas don't go far. Race cars mandate big amounts of fuel in a short period of time. Street cars and dual-duty street/strip cars demand this on occasion too, but they also have to deliver fuel over the long haul. There are quite a few similarities, but plenty of differences.

What constitutes a fuel cell? It must accomplish at least two chores: provide a margin of safety and improve performance. Unfortunately, not all fuel cells are created equal. Some inferior fuel "cells" are nothing more than plastic gas tanks. A proper fuel cell maintains integrity even when involved in a heavy crash. That's a strong statement, but what it really means is the cell doesn't leak. Fuel does not spill out of the assembly, and it resists punctures. To resist punctures, manufacturers of plastic-bodied fuel cells incorporate a type of "deformable plastic" for the outer body. That material is most often a special cross-linked polyethylene.

Cross-linking is a process that is used to strengthen plastics. Plastics such as polyethylene contain molecules that are narrow and long. They tend to be weak. To strengthen these molecules during the manufacturing process (using a system called "rotational molding"), a series of vertical supports, or braces, are added to the molecules. These vertical supports are called "cross links." A fuel cell container that has been produced with the cross-linked construction resists bursting or rupture upon impact.

Many fuel cells contain an internal foam bladder. The purpose is to prevent fuel from sloshing within the cell and, simultaneously, minimize the possibility of a fuel explosion due to impact in a crash. Some of those foam bladders can be eaten by today's pump gas. If you're using a fuel cell on the street, you should contact the manufacturer to determine if it is safe to use the cell with pump gas (if the gasoline is laced with alcohol, be double careful).

What about a gas tank for your Nova? Of the many sources, Spectra Premium builds the best. Its line of high-quality tanks is manufactured in Canada, and they're absolutely dead ringers for an OEM Nova tank. That includes everything from the construction to the materials to the appearance. They're often private labeled, but you can usually find them from better retailers throughout North America.

What about EFI applications? There are plenty of ways to sort through the EFI puzzle. One item you absolutely need is an electric fuel pump out back along with a fuel pressure regulator at the front of the car. Some form of return line system goes back to the tank. Because of this, the tank or the cell must either be able to accept an in-tank pump or it must have the capability of accepting plumbing for an external pump. It also must have a provision for a return line.

Back to the tanks and cells: Believe it or not, the proper venting of a fuel cell or fuel tank is critical. Unlike gas tanks, fuel cells don't incorporate conventional "vented" gas caps. Instead, a cell features some form of vent system. Why is this so important? A fuel cell (or any gas tank) must breathe in *and* out.

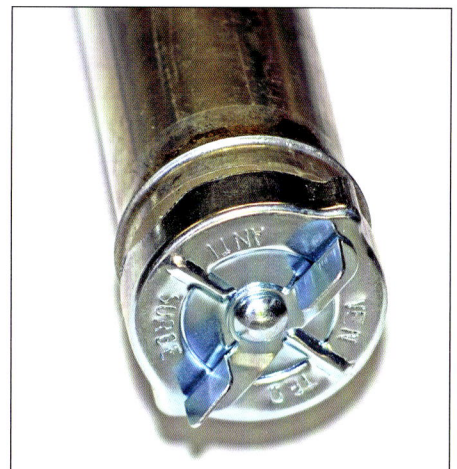

Venting a gas tank or a fuel cell is very important (a vented Nova gas cap is shown here). As the fuel pump draws the fuel out of the tank, it also displaces air. Without proper venting the tank can actually collapse.

As a fuel pump draws the gasoline, it naturally draws in air that is inside the cell. If the fuel cell or tank is completely sealed, the walls eventually collapse from the pulling action of the pump. With the advent of the colossal fuel pumps, an ordinary vent line simply isn't sufficient. The pulling action of the large electric pumps (they can actually draw a vacuum) can outstrip the capacity of a lone 3/8-inch vent line. In answer to this problem, today's race-only fuel cells incorporate a large number-8 AN (1/2 inch) vent system. Street systems usually carry a number-6 AN vent arrangement. Some fuel cells also include a special "roll-over" valve in the vent line. In most cases, these rollover valves are based upon a check-ball. In operation, a moveable ball closes the vent line if the tank is turned upside down. This prevents fuel from escaping through the vent should the car overturn.

Something a true street-driven car needs that isn't seen on pro/street or other race cars is a fuel (level) gauge. They incorporate specialized senders designed to work with the safety foam used in a modern fuel cell.

A typical "professional class" fuel cell has 12-AN pickups. Street car cells or tanks can get by with 8-AN pickups. Mounted low on the cell (in the sump area), the pickup is situated in a location that virtually force-feeds the pump. For a Nova tank, you can either modify it to accept a special AN pickup (which requires welding) or you can use one of the neat fuel pickups shown here.

High-Flow Pickups for Stock Nova Tanks

Getting the fuel from the Nova gas tank to the carb is rather important. If you don't have sufficient fuel, the ET slip will certainly reflect it. A big part of the puzzle for any Nova is to supply a sufficient volume of gasoline. You might think this is all very simple. The reality is, it's not, especially if you want to get it done with a lone stock-style mechanical fuel pump. Ponder this: You're kicking back a milkshake. Instead of using that big fat straw the shake normally comes with, substitute it for the itsy-bitsy straw you'd normally use with a soda pop. You soon discover that sucking that mouthful of shake isn't exactly easy. Replace that soda pop straw with a big milk shake straw and it's pretty comfortable. The same applies to a fuel system. That's why L78 Novas were factory-fitted with a 3/8-inch line instead of a more common 5/16-inch line.

A big restriction in a production line fuel delivery system is the fuel tank pickup/sending unit combination. If you're building a high-flow system you have two choices: Try to find a 3/8-inch replacement pickup and sending unit or replace the factory sender/pickup with a custom billet job from RobbMc Performance Products. The RobbMc setup is based upon a huge 1/2-inch-diameter pickup and it does away with the troublesome sock filter. The dilemma with the sock is that it can become plugged and you won't know it. The custom pickup requires an external fuel filter but otherwise bolts into place as stock. It's a slick piece, and

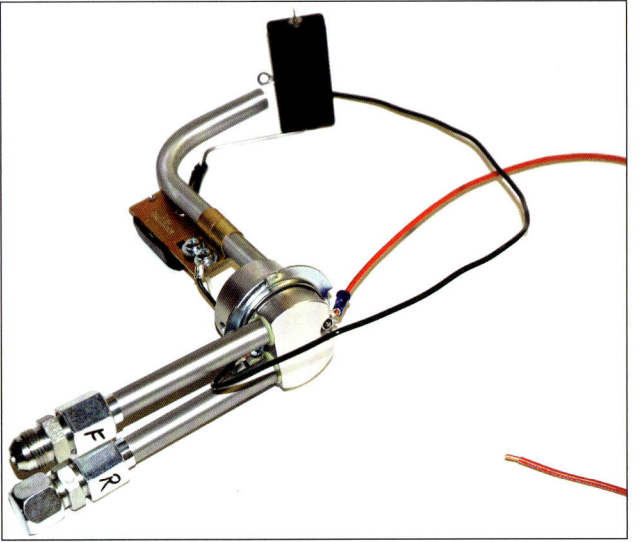

One of the slickest fuel pickup assemblies/gas tank senders available today is this billet piece manufactured by RobbMC. This Nova example has AN fittings for the supply and return lines.

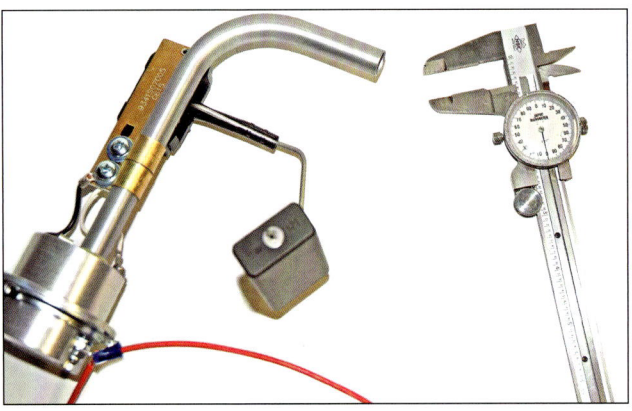

The RobbMC -8 AN pickup for a Nova measures 1/2 inch in diameter. Note there is no problematic sock filter. This means an inline filter of some sort is mandatory.

FUEL SYSTEM

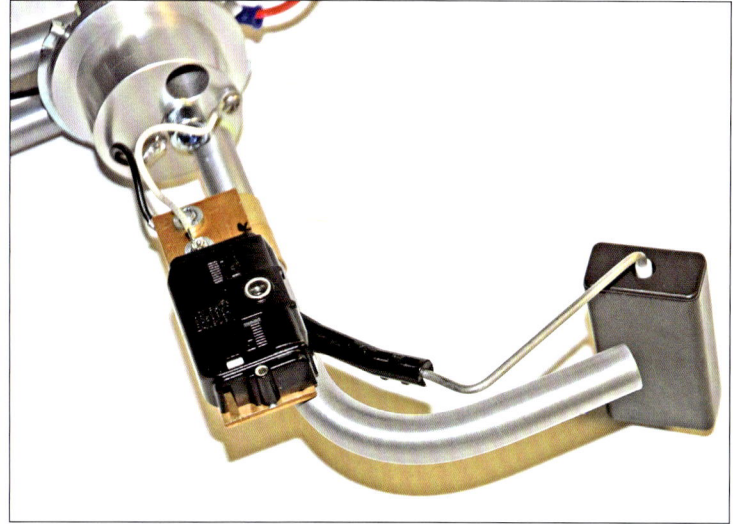

The float assembly is engineered to work with the stock Nova gas gauge. You have to splice into one OEM sender electrical wire, but that's the extent of the mods. Otherwise, it's a bolt-in.

This is a good look at the AN lines supplied with the sender. For this Nova application, there's no need for a return, so it's capped off. The fittings are -8 AN.

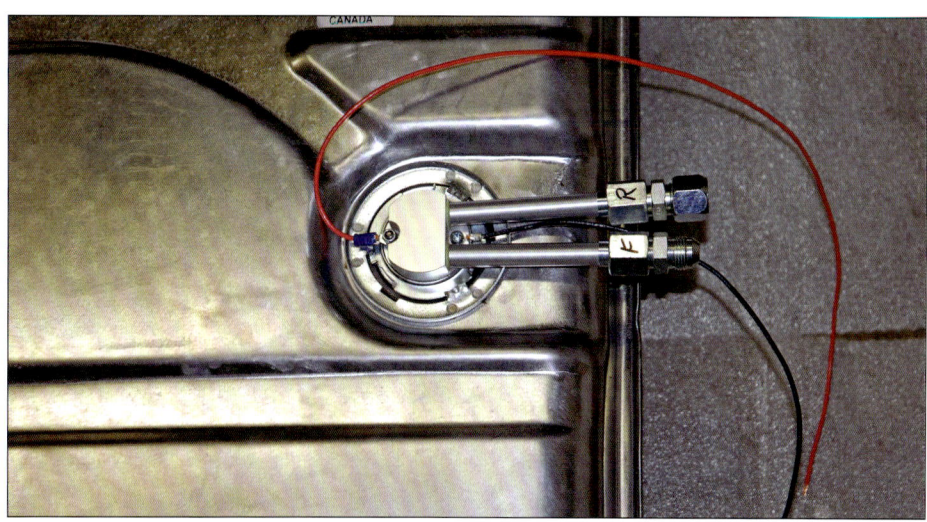

The pickup mounts easily in a stock replacement Nova tank. The lesson here is, for most high-performance applications, a large-diameter -8 or 1/2-inch feed line keeps most big-horsepower street-driven Novas happy.

if you're searching for maximum fuel flow from a stock gas tank this is the place to begin.

RobbMc has several versions for a Nova. You can order it with a conventional 1/2-inch tube outlet/return or you can specify -8 AN or even -10 AN outlet and return lines. The setup shown in the accompanying photos is designed for a Nova and comes equipped with -8 AN male fittings on both the feed and return lines. If you don't need the return, simply cap it. It's extremely well built.

These trick senders/fuel pickups end fuel starvation right at the source. They're not even that expensive. The RobbMc piece shown here costs $149 plus an additional $20 for the -8 AN package.

Mechanical Fuel Pumps

Chevy mechanical fuel pumps are driven off the camshaft by way of a pushrod. That is probably not news. With a mechanical fuel pump, as engine speed increases, so does the speed of the fuel pump. It's a good setup for a street/strip Nova.

But how much fuel do you need? According to Holley Engineering "Typically, at wide open throttle, full power, an engine requires .5 pound of fuel per horsepower every hour. A gallon of gasoline weighs approximately 6 pounds. Therefore, an engine rated at 350 hp requires about 175 pounds (29 gallons) of fuel every hour."

350 hp x .5 lbs = 175 lbs of fuel
175 lbs ÷ 6 lbs = 29 gallons per hour

"The relationship of pressure to volume is inversely proportional," states Holley. "That is, as pressure increases, volume decreases, everything else being equal. A certain amount of fuel pressure is always required to maintain engine performance by assuring that fuel is available on demand. Also, other factors and conditions must be taken into account, such as acceleration G-forces and friction within the fuel system itself. At the same time, an

CHAPTER 9

adequate fuel volume is needed to ensure that the proper amount of fuel can always flow to the engine, especially during peak demand situations. A basic understanding of this critical pressure/volume relationship is needed when designing the proper fuel supply system for your vehicle."

Some of today's mechanical pumps are perfect for high-flow applications. Plenty are not. Some good examples include Holley's High Output pumps (with or without external fuel pressure regulator), along with Holley's HP series pump. The basic High Output pump has a gallon per hour (GPH) rating of 110. The High Output pump with the external regulator has a rating of 130. The HP pump carries a rating of a whopping 170 gph, while the billet models flow 170 and 200 gph respectively.

Holley 170 GPH

This pump has a flow rating of 170 gph at 8 psi. It incorporates a cast body with a lower housing that can be rotated. This allows for any number of plumbing situations. The inlet and outlet ports are machined for -8 AN fittings (O-ring configuration). The pump features heavy-duty construction and is designed for continuous high-RPM operation. Internally, the high-flow valving has been redesigned to ensure adequate fuel delivery. Because of the 8-psi setting, a fuel pressure regulator is required. This pump is for gasoline-fueled applications only.

Holley 170 GPH (Billet)

This is one of Holley's HP billet-aluminum body mechanical fuel pumps. It too has a free flow rating of 170 gallons per hour. This pump features a pre-set idle psi rating of 7.5, which means it can operate without an additional external fuel pressure regulator. The inlet and outlet are both pre-plumbed with -8 AN male fittings. Like the pump above, the lower body of the pump can be rotated for various plumbing situations. The pump is designed for gasoline only. Holley offers rebuild (service) components for these pumps so that you can rebuild them at home, if necessary.

Holley 200 GPH

This is a black-anodized billet-aluminum body Ultra HP job with a flow rating of a whopping 200 gallons per hour. The body is machined from 6061-T6 aluminum and is hard coat–anodized for corrosion protection. The inlet and outlet ports are machined for 1/2-inch pipe thread, but fittings are not included. Like the other pumps, the base can be rotated, but there's a difference here: The lower base (inlet) can be rotated independent of the upper base (outlet). Basically, the lower pump body is a two-piece affair, which (obviously) adds to the versatility. The pump is designed for use with gasoline (although a similar alky job with a 225-gph rating [!] is available). This gasoline fuel pump is designed for use with an auxiliary fuel pressure regulator.

All sorts of mechanical fuel pumps are available. This cast (tumbled finish) Holley pump delivers 170 gph at 8 psi. You need an auxiliary fuel pressure regulator for this pump.

Here's another Holley mechanical fuel pump for a big-block, manufactured from billet aluminum. This pump also delivers 170 gph, but it's pre-set at 7.5 psi, so no regulator is needed.

Need a monster mechanical pump? Holley offers billet-body mechanical pumps that can produce a whopping 200 gallons per hour. An auxiliary fuel pressure regulator is mandatory with this big boy.

FUEL SYSTEM

The Ultra HP pumps are also fully serviceable. In fact, Holley has a maintenance schedule for Ultra HP fuel pumps such as this. The diaphragm assembly should be replaced every 750 to 1,000 hours. During the rebuild, the gaskets should be replaced (kit number 12-757). The fuel pump lever arm should be examined for excess wear, and replaced as necessary. Finally, when the pump is apart, Holley recommends you inspect the valve body for damage to the rubber diaphragms, and replace as necessary.

Electric Fuel Pumps

When it comes to delivering fuel, consider what's hot on the quarter-mile–only cars. "Big" is pretty much the operative word when it comes to drag race pumps. Big works perfectly. When a drag race system must operate perfectly for a few minutes at a time, a street system has to function flawlessly any time, every time, and it has to work over the long haul. If you have a Nova that does double duty (street and strip), fuel injected or carbureted, you face a fuel delivery conundrum. If you have a big-cubic-inch engine between the fenders, or if you have a power-adder or two (blower, turbo, nitrous, or even a combination of the three), fuel delivery becomes critical. Here's the hitch: Those honking fuel pumps that feed an all-out race car don't particularly like to run for extended periods of time. They were not designed for that purpose. They consume plenty of electricity (amps), and before long heat becomes an issue. There are some solutions, but before I get to them, ponder the following.

There are essentially two very different types of fuel delivery systems in use today: one for carbureted vehicles (low pressure) and one for fuel-injected vehicles (high pressure). Carbureted cars were almost always originally fitted with a mechanical pump. Late models with EFI have an electric system. EFI cars can use an internal or an external pump. The most common you find today is an internal pump, which is basically an electric pump submerged inside the fuel tank. Some systems and many high-volume aftermarket electric fuel pumps for late-model fuel-injected vehicles are externally mounted (with fuel pickup lines mounted to the tank).

There are all sorts of pumps out there. The following are several electric pump examples that work for most high-performance Nova applications.

Holley 97 GPH

This is one of the original Holley electric pumps that have been available for decades (although it has had periodic updates). At one time, it was the standard of all fuel pumps for carbureted applications (it doesn't have the pressure necessary to operate an electronic fuel injection system). The pump operates by way of a rotor vane assembly (at the base), and it's easily serviced. It is rather tolerant of fuel contamination (something to consider with a street-driven car), but it is not compatible with alcohol or methanol fuels. The pump produces 97 gallons per hour (free flow) and 71 gallons per hour when regulated to 4 psi. The pump is fitted with an external pressure relief valve that can be set for a maximum of 7 psi. The pump draws 2 amps of current and weighs 2.88 pounds.

Holley 140 GPH

Holley's pump with the black logo is an upgraded version of the 97-gph pump. The lower casting has been modified for enhanced flow. This pump has a free-flow rating of 140 gallons per hour, while the flow at 9 psi is still 120 gallons per hour. The pump has a maximum pressure

Holley's 97-gph "Red" electric fuel pump has been available for decades. Tens of thousands have likely been sold, and it's always been regarded as a reliable workhorse.

Holley's "Black" electric fuel pump is a step up from the red model. It produces a higher line pressure (140 gph) and, as mentioned in the text, mandates an external fuel pressure regulator.

rating of 14 psi (set by way of the external pressure relief valve). This fuel pump does not have the pressure capability to operate an EFI system. This example is safe for use with gasoline, alcohol, or methanol. An external regulator is required. Holley recommends PN 12-704 for gasoline and PN 12-707 for alcohol/methanol. The pump draws 4 amps of current and weighs 3 pounds.

Holley 150 GPH

The 150-gph pump is a newer design with a gerotor setup instead of a vane- (blade-) style impeller. This configuration has less noise than vane impeller pumps. It has a free-flow rating of 150 gph, and at 7 psi it still flows 140 gph. The pump is compatible with gasoline along with E85 as well as other alcohol and methanol fuels. It is designed for use in carbureted applications only (there isn't sufficient pressure for fuel injection). The pump is internally regulated to 16 psi and it includes an adjustable fuel pressure regulator (4½ to 9 psi), PN 12-803. At maximum pressure (16 psi), the pump draws 10 amps of current. The pump is slightly larger in size than the vane-style jobs (it measures 6.25 inches tall). It has 3/8-inch NPT inlet and outlet ports (the same as the previous two pumps).

Holley 160 GPH

A big step up in streetable fuel electric pumps is the Dominator "shotgun-style" dual pump setup from Holley. This pump is a twin design that allows you to use one pump for cruising and both pumps when you get on the power. You can also use the second stage of the pump when you activate the nitrous switch or, in the case of a blown or turbo engine, when it begins to build boost. The pump's layout (staging the second pump) eliminates unnecessary recirculating and heating of extra fuel. This pump is also engineered so that it can be fully submersed within a fuel tank. In terms of size, the pump is 7.66 inches long by 5 inches wide by 2.5 inches tall. It weighs 5.1 pounds and draws 28 amps of current at maximum performance. At a "mere" 43 psi and 13.5 volts DC the current draw is 17.2 amps. The pump has a free-flow rating of 160 gallons per hour. It can be used for either carbureted or EFI applications (the regulator choice dictates the application). Inlet and outlet ports are -10 AN (huge!). Holley has other examples that work with E85, methanol, alcohol, or diesel (!).

Fuel Pressure Regulators

Before fuel enters the fuel line or fuel rail(s) in your Nova, and ultimately, before it reaches the fuel bowls or the fuel injectors, some sort of device is often necessary to harness the flow and pressure of the fuel. That job belongs to a fuel pressure regulator. For EFI applications, a regulator is mandatory. For carbureted applications with fuel pump pressures higher than approximately 7.5 psi, a regulator is required too. For these carbureted applications, too much fuel pressure for a given needle and seat assembly can overload the needle and seat and may cause flooding or drivability problems. In the case of Holley examples, each fuel pressure regulator is fully adjustable, so regulating the fuel pressure to your engine requirements is a simple task. These regulators are pre-set at the factory, typically, so there is no guesswork when first installing the regulator.

On the EFI front, some companies build fixed regulators (most common in OEM applications), but others (particularly aftermarket vendors) offer adjustable regulators. What's the advantage? An adjustable regulator allows an engine tuner to

Moving to the HP 150 electric fuel pump from Holley is a big step up. Instead of a vane (which is standard in the smaller pumps), this one makes use of a more efficient gerotor.

This is a very good fuel delivery concept for an ultimate Nova. Basically, Holley siamesed a pair of pumps in one body to create the shotgun-style Dominator pump. Each side of the pump can be separately switched, which means you can add the second stage when necessary.

FUEL SYSTEM

test varying levels of fuel pressure to find the exact level the engine is most "happy" with. You want a regulator that doesn't "creep." Creeping means the regulator has difficulty maintaining a set level of pressure. Most high-quality (more costly) regulators meet these criteria.

Some high-flow EFI systems also bypass the fuel. What that means is they take in more fuel than is necessary and return the balance to the gas tank. This is done to eliminate fuel aeration and efficiently pump fuel, not a frothy mix of air and fuel. When equipped with a bypass system, a valve of sorts controls the amount of fuel that actually bypasses and is returned to the fuel tank. The following are some good examples of readily available regulators.

Holley 12-803

This is the standard fuel pressure regulator that has been used for what seems like forever. At one time, they were painted blue (and that was the identifier for most speed shops). Today, they're shiny with a tumbled exterior. This regular has a .220-inch restriction and 3/8-inch NPT ports: one inlet and two outlets (non-return style). The range of adjustment is between 4.5 to 9 psi.

Holley 12-704

Holley's 12-704 fuel pressure regulator looks a lot like the standard 12-803 model until you place them side by side. The 12-704 is much larger, as are the inlet and dual outlet ports. For this regulator, use the large 1/2-inch NPTs. This regulator also has a much larger restriction size (.437 inch). It is not a bypass (return-style) regulator; however, it's suitable for use with gasoline or alcohol fuels. The range of adjustment is from 4.5 to 9 psi.

Holley 12-843

Next up is a huge-by-large billet-aluminum regulator. This is a non-return regulator with a range of 4.5 to 9 psi. It's obviously for carbureted applications. The big billet regulator features a huge -10 AN inlet port along with a pair of -8 AN outlet ports. Both ports mandate an O-ring for sealing. This big, high-volume regulator can be used with electric or mechanical fuel pumps.

Holley 12-848

The last regulator in our selection is a billet bypass unit that is designed for use in electronic

A newer regulator from Holley is this PN 12-843 model. It's manufactured from billet aluminum and fitted with a massive -10 AN inlet and a pair of -8 AN outlet ports.

With many pumps (electric or mechanical), there may be a need to regulate the pressure. This is the standard of fuel pressure regulators (Holley PN 12-803). Holley has produced this for what seems like forever and it has been used in myriad applications.

Next up is Holley's PN 12-704 pressure regulator. This piece is much larger than the PN 12-803, and it's fitted with larger inlet and outlet ports (1/2 versus 3/8 inch).

If you run EFI on your Nova and you have a high-horsepower combination, consider this regulator. It's billet aluminum with a bypass circuit. It also has a vacuum reference port (brass fitting on the right of the body).

fuel injection applications. The billet-aluminum regulator has a range of 40 to 70 psi and is equipped with a -10 AN O-ring inlet; a -10 AN O-ring outlet, and an -8 AN O-ring return port (that should be plumbed back to the fuel tank). Near the top of the regulator is a vacuum reference port. This port can be connected to full manifold vacuum to slightly decrease fuel pressure at idle and cruise. Holley notes this is a requirement on forced induction engines, so that the differential fuel pressure stays constant under boost.

Fuel Filters

Fuel is filthy. That's no secret, and pump gas is regularly worse than race gas. That's why a fuel filter is especially important. It's a good idea to use a high-capacity in-line filter, or even a pair of them, one before the pump (pre-filter) and one after. Of course, there are a lot of fuel filters available today. You can even track down ones that are pure vintage in the looks department. Unfortunately, from a flow perspective, some of those vintage fuel filters don't do so well. A good option is Holley's latest line of billet in-line filters. They're huge-capacity jobs machined for -8 AN–and–larger fittings. Holley's filter easily disassembles, allowing you to access the internal wire mesh filter. Typically, these filters have a GPH flow rating of 260 or so gallons per hour. Obviously, for the majority of situations, these filters do not act as a restriction in the system.

Where do you locate the filter? The arguments regarding filter location will probably never end (before the fuel pump or after the fuel pump), but in the interest of saving any electric pump from carnage, the best location is *before* the fuel enters the pump. Unfortunately, this sometimes places the filter in an awkward location, and in some cases, the large aftermarket filters are difficult to mount and even more difficult to service in a street-vehicle application.

So, what can you do about the problem? That's where the Holley filters come into the equation. They're big in capacity, but in terms of size, they're quite compact. The body diameter is 2 inches while the

The Holley filter is easily serviced too. If you remove the end cap, this is what you'll see inside. The wire mesh filter can be cleaned, which means replacement isn't necessary.

These two billet clamps are available from Holley. They're designed specifically for Hooker's big in-line filter. Obviously, this addresses the question about how you mount a round filter on a Nova.

Forget plastic fuel filters. They're restrictive and dangerous. Use something such as this in-line filter. Holley manufactures it, and it's available in several formats (varying micron capacities).

If you look under a third-gen Nova, you'll find a good spot to mount a filter on the passenger's side, just below the door. This location keeps the filter out of the way and it's protected somewhat by the rocker panel (and, of course, the frame connector if you have them).

FUEL SYSTEM

When planning fuel line routing it's best to start at the tank. Here's a Nova with a stock tank fitted with a RobbMC pickup/sending unit. The feed line is open and the return is capped for this application.

This is a good look at routing fuel line. The -8 AN hose is held in place by way of Adel (aircraft) cushioned clamps. Careful routing keeps the hose away form any suspension components, and it's well above the scrub line.

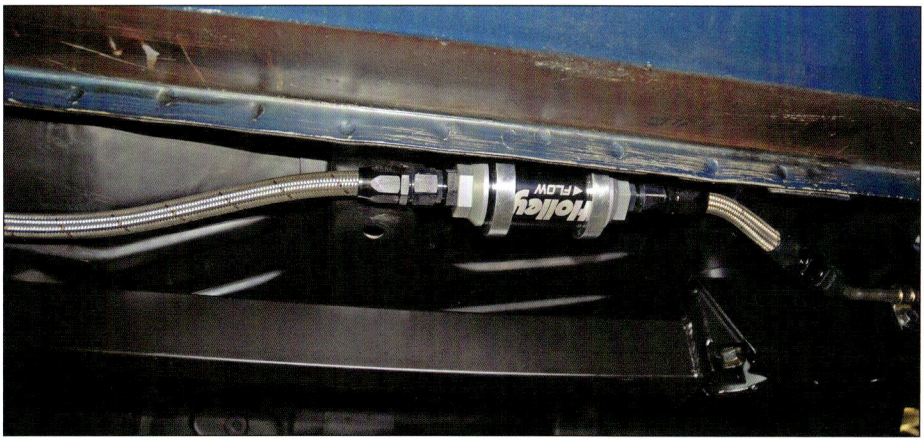

The line runs from the tank to the filter as shown here, and then forward in the car. This is a nice, clean arrangement and it keeps the fuel line tucked away from possible damage.

length is 5½ inches overall. Other readily available aluminum body assemblies do a decent job of filtration on stock combinations, but many are just too small and cannot handle the volume of fuel required for a healthy engine. They can therefore constitute a restriction in the fuel delivery system, even if they aren't plugged.

What about the disposable plastic filters? When you look at them from a performance perspective, they're a waste of time and dollars. To make matters worse, they can be dangerous. Cheap plastic filters constitute a rather large fuel system restriction; they plug easily; and on almost all examples the inlet/outlet port is too small for high-performance use.

Dirt is the real enemy of any fuel delivery system. It can spell immediate grief and possible engine damage. In the accompanying photos (and captions) are several filter options, along with a mounting solution that's perfect for third-gen Novas.

CHAPTER 10

RADIATORS AND ELECTRIC FANS

Most folks leave the cooling system to the end of their projects. I'm probably just as guilty (after all, it's near the end of this book), but that certainly doesn't mean that the cooling system isn't important. Far from it. Without it, you won't be driving far. In this chapter, I dig deep into radiators, cooling fans, and accessories. There's a lot more to keeping your Nova cool than first meets the eye.

Radiator

When the dog days of August roll around, you'll be quick to think of the radiator in the nose of your Nova. If you've added horsepower over the winter, there's added pressure, because more horsepower equals more heat. And with that comes the need for cooling system attention. One trip to a local car show in the heat of the summer with an inadequate cooling system will make you wish you had paid more attention to that heat producer under the hood.

Fair enough. Everyone knows that a high-performance engine produces heat, and a bunch of it. Roughly one-half of the total heat energy produced by the engine is transferred back to the cooling system. In a conventional liquid cooled application (your typical Chevy), the heat energy moves into the radiator and is then "radiated" back into the atmosphere. Taking this one step further, the liquid cooling system in your Nova operates very simply. As the coolant (to keep things simple, let's use plain water as an example) temperature approaches 212 degrees F, air pressure begins to build. Since the radiator is closed (with a cap), pressure builds from within without any opportunity to escape. This air pressure actually expands, which in turn allows the water to reach a temperature higher than 212 degrees F before boiling. As the air pressure increases, so does the boiling point of the water. Basically, this is an efficient system that works well in passenger car applications, but if the coolant temperature continues to increase (without leveling

There's a lot of choice out there for Nova radiators. Here's a great example built by Ron Davis Racing Radiators. During the radiator build, CNC-cutting results in precision to .005-inch, which in turn results in a perfect fit and a high degree of repeatability. Davis is one of the few, if not the only, aluminum radiator manufacturer that can manufacture to the high tolerance needed in military and aerospace applications.

off), the internal pressure will be too great for the radiator cap to handle. What happens next is predictable. Your Nova boils over.

The radiator in such a system is a huge tank that allows large amounts of hot coolant to contact an equally large amount of cool (it is hoped) air. The coolant is first forced into the radiator side tank (upper tank if you're thinking of the old-fashioned non–cross flow system). From this point, the coolant makes its way through rows of very small copper or aluminum tubes, finally returning to the adjoining side tank where it is returned to the engine. While the coolant marches through the tiny tubes, it is cooled by air flowing over and alongside the tubes. The primary purpose of the "fins" contained within the core (and surrounding the little tubes) is to direct airflow into the proper area of the radiator; however, there are secondary reasons for the fins, as you soon see. (The most common core construction is the tube-fin or the ribbon-cellular design.)

Fin count plays an important role in cooling. As a rule, a radiator has between 8 and 14 fins per inch. When the fin count number is increased, the radiator can "radiate" more heat to both the surface airflow and the surrounding air. Unfortunately, as fin count increases, so does the opportunity for plugging, especially by bugs, dirt, and other foreign road junk.

Copper or Aluminum?

When it comes to radiator construction material, what's the better choice for your Nova, copper or aluminum? That's a good question. Most recently Detroit has embraced aluminum as the radiator material of choice. The reason for this, aside from considerable vehicle mass reduction

Cores for a Davis radiator are of proprietary design. They're Nocolok furnace brazed and, whereas most companies offer one fin count, Ron Davis Racing Radiators sizes the fin count and thickness to the application. Davis incorporates quality Spal fans in the package. Note the way the fans are completely sealed to the rad by way of the aluminum shroud.

This is likely the best OEM-style radiator available for a 1968–1972 Nova. It's an exact reproduction of the stock copper-brass "gooseneck" radiators fitted to COPO Camaros and a select few 396 Novas. Classic Industries offers these radiators as special orders.

(aluminum radiators, on average, can be as much as 1/3 lighter than an equivalent copper-brass radiator), is cooling capability.

Certainly, the choice of copper is a good one for radiators. It has better heat dissipating properties than aluminum. But there's a caveat: Tubes are the primary source of cooling in any radiator. Heat dissipates from the coolant through the tube walls. This heat is then transferred to the fins that are in contact with the tubes. In turn, this provides a secondary source of cooling. As air passes through the fins, the heat is carried away. Radiator manufacturers know that wider tubes are more efficient because there is more tube-to-fin contact (in a typical modern aluminum radiator, the tube-to-fin contact surface area is increased by 20 percent over an identically sized copper/brass unit). This isn't possible with a copper-brass design because of tube wall thickness limitations. Today's radiator technology, which uses wider tubes inside aluminum rads coupled with multi-louvered fins, has allowed the aluminum radiator to cool efficiently. Just as important, aluminum rads are now as strong as, if not stronger, than their older copper-brass relatives.

The truth is, today, an aluminum radiator in your Nova cools better. Tests from various sources document a 28-percent increase in performance over a brass-copper equivalent, provided both radiators are identical in size. The reality is, the use of aluminum in radiator construction can lower engine temperature by 30 degrees. Any vehicle, including your Nova, benefits from an aluminum radiator.

But what if you want something really close to stock, something built in the traditional copper-brass format? Today, original Harrison radiators are next to impossible to find. Moreover, to score something such as a super-rare new or mint gooseneck heavy-duty radiator, well, you should invest in lottery tickets. Those old gooseneck radiators were the very best pieces available for a Nova (they also showed up on 427-powered COPO Camaros). In the 1960s and early 1970s, if you had to pick a go-to radiator for a stubborn cooling problem, that's the piece you'd select. Unfortunately, originals aren't available, but the good news is you can buy a perfect made-in-the-USA reproduction from the folks at Classic Industries; for example, the copper-brass gooseneck radiator in the accompanying photos. It's a dead-ringer for the original. You note that this radiator comes unpainted. Following manufacture (soldering) the radiator sees rapid surface rusting. It's not a big issue though;

Classic Industries' gooseneck repro comes unpainted. What you see is flash rust that occurs almost immediately following construction. When you receive it, the core should be masked off and the tanks media blasted. Then you can paint the entire works with quality radiator paint.

All stock Nova radiators have this mounting format (a pair of flanges on each side of the radiator). Some of the mounting hole locations on various stock radiators are different. Depending upon the radiator you select, the core support might have to be modified. It's not a big deal, however. In most cases, you just drill a couple of holes. Some examples might also need a weld nut added.

RADIATORS AND ELECTRIC FANS

It's a small thing, but some of Classic Industries' exact reproduction radiators even have the old GM "Harrison" stamped into the tanks.

Classic Industries simply recommends you glass bead the tanks and then paint the assembly with radiator paint.

The tanks and mounting brackets are exact copies of the original. This is a four-core HD radiator for a Camaro or Nova. In the photos, you can see the Harrison logo is accurately reproduced on the side tank. Another of the photos shows the gooseneck inlet at the top of the radiator (and yes, very late big-block Novas circa 1969 could in fact have a gooseneck radiator, just like a COPO Camaro).

Outlet Shapes and Sizes

Believe it or not, the shape and form of the radiator outlets might have a profound effect upon cooling. I don't have concrete proof of this, but I've witnessed one particular car (a high-horsepower 427 big-block) that went through multiple radiators in an effort to resolve a cooling issue. One was constructed by Ron Davis while others came from other manufacturers. The only (visible) external difference was the shape of the outlets. The Davis-built radiator had formed outlets with soft bends. The other had fabricated outlets with sharp bends (virtually a series of 45-degree joints). The car consistently boiled over with the sharp-bend-equipped radiator. With no other changes (aside from the radiator swap), the operating temperature was entirely satisfactory with the formed outlet radiator. The theory was that the sharp outlet corners restricted coolant flow.

A formed radiator hose (the type Chevrolet uses on its vehicles) usually delivers superior performance to one of the universal "fits-all" ribbed hoses available at the local discount auto parts stores. The belief is there is considerable laminar flow in the hose, and the ribs of the universal radiator hose disturb this flow. What is the solution? Simple. Watch out for cheap universal hoses, and be careful when selecting a radiator; smooth outlet bends are likely

Here's a good example of a lower radiator hose for a Nova. Several very good reproductions of factory formed hose are available today. Because of this, it makes no sense to use universal fit (ribbed) hose.

The same applies to upper radiator hoses. Classic Industries and others offer a wide choice of hose. Keep in mind that the layout of the radiator determines the radiator hose configuration. As an example, a gooseneck radiator mandates a different hose than a conventional neck radiator.

See the wire on the inside of the lower hose? The purpose is to keep the hose from collapsing. The wire support is found on most quality hoses.

much more efficient than sharp, angular turns.

Cooling Fans and Shrouds

In the hypothetical world, a fan wouldn't be required if a Nova was constantly driven at high speeds (definitely an enticing concept, but not exactly practical). Airflow from the vehicle's velocity would provide

CHAPTER 10

There are plenty of ways to cool a Nova, and of course a fan is mandatory. One outstanding option is this dual electric Spal fan setup from Ron Davis Racing Radiators. The fans are obviously set up in puller fashion. Note how the fans are tightly sealed to the radiator.

sufficient airflow over the radiator surface, with the result being proper cooling. After all, that's pretty much how World War II aircraft with liquid-cooled engines worked (good examples being the P51 Mustang, Spitfire, Warhawk, and so on). While this would be an ideal situation, it's seldom possible. Or realistic. Because of this, a fan of some sort becomes a necessary evil.

Given the fact that a fan is pretty much an essential commodity, it's probably a good idea to install one that works. The market offers several good-quality fans, ranging from OEM, factory-produced models to stainless-steel flex versions. Electric fans are common on late-model Chevys and are used with regularity on many modified Novas. The typical "standard" fan assembly is fixed. It rotates constantly with the water pump shaft. A thermostatic fan is just that: a fan that slows down when cooling requirements have diminished. This type of fan has seldom been used in North American passenger car applications of any sort (cost, size, and complexities being factors).

Flexible fans reduce their pitch as engine RPM increases (or, more correctly, as pulley speed increases). Fluid coupling fans (sometimes referred to as "viscous clutch fans") speed up or slow down, again, depending upon engine or pulley speed. Viscous, or "clutch," fans were regular fixtures on high-performance Chevys for years. But on factory big-block Novas, they weren't installed. Why not? There isn't sufficient room. All big-block Novas instead made use of fixed fans. Electric fans are simply remote units that depend upon the vehicle's electrical system for operation. Depending upon the application, electric fans can be manually switched or can operate via an integral thermostatic coupling. Of course, late-model cars all came factory-equipped with electric fans.

Certain types of fans require more horsepower for operation than others. Leading the pack in terms of least power absorption is the electric fan. They rely upon battery power to operate, but keep in mind that the battery will be drained when the unit is in operation. That means the charging system must keep up (basically, the engine must power the alternator demands instead of turning the fan, and it still must power the water pump

There's nothing wrong with a conventional fan, provided you include a tight-fitting shroud on the Nova. This is a reproduction fan for a 396 Nova.

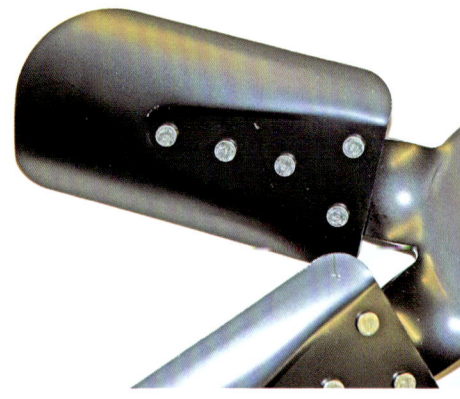

When looking at OEM-style fans, keep a close eye on the blades, and the rivets in particular. If a blade decides to depart, it can make a huge mess of your car.

138 CHEVY NOVA 1968–1974: HOW TO BUILD AND MODIFY

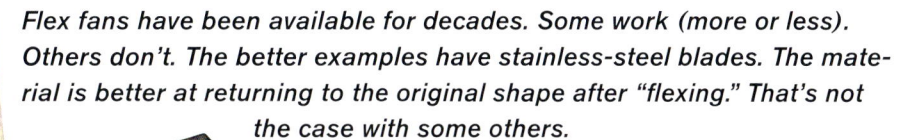

Flex fans have been available for decades. Some work (more or less). Others don't. The better examples have stainless-steel blades. The material is better at returning to the original shape after "flexing." That's not the case with some others.

and other accessories). In terms of conventional fans, both the flex fan and the "clutch fan" offer considerable advantages as far as horsepower losses are concerned. Obviously, a flex fan is far less complicated than its clutch fan stable mate, but it too has some drawbacks. Plenty of flex fan designs simply take a "set" at a given position following sustained use. The result, of course, is too little fan action and, ultimately, reduced cooling. Depending upon the Nova, one of the safest fan bets is the original equipment–style clutch or fluid coupling system. When the "clutch" mechanism is in competent operating condition, the fan works flawlessly, de-clutching as the engine speed or pulley speed increases. (Keep in mind that you don't have room for a clutch fan on a big-block Nova.) The outcome is more available horsepower when you need it.

When dealing with conventional fans, one area that you should think about is a phenomenon called "blade stall." In this condition, the fan attached to your Nova engine can in fact be turned too fast, like an aircraft propeller. A massive amount of turbulence is created, which effectively decreases airflow through the radiator. Obviously, overheating is the consequence, but fixing the problem might be more difficult. The only real solution is to reduce the speed of the fan, which can be handled easily with different-diameter pulleys.

When it comes to cooling you absolutely must figure out a way to bring the air to the cooler. The goal is to provide a constant supply of air through the radiator so that the coolant is reduced in temperature. Increasing airflow through the radiator improves cooling. A shroud that facilitates airflow is, therefore, almost mandatory on high-performance applications. Unfortunately, they are often missing on older Novas. Keep in mind, shrouds were often manufactured from plastic, so the condition typically degrades dramatically over the years. If you don't have a shroud or if it fits poorly, get the right one (that's a big hint if you end up sitting behind Old Faithful on a regular basis).

How does the shroud work? Basically, the shroud surrounds or partially surrounds the fan. It butts up tightly to the face of the radiator, effectively sealing the cavity. This isolates the pocket of air behind the radiator, allowing the fan to efficiently draw the required air through

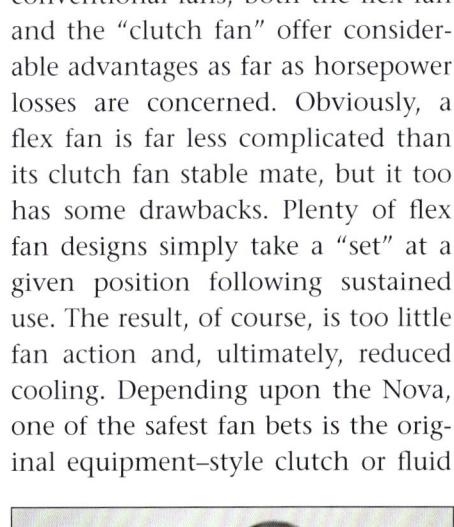

A factory fan spacer is pretty much mandatory on many Novas. It positions the fan as closely as possible to the radiator. That definitely helps with cooling.

A tight-fitting OEM-style shroud such as this is a big key to keeping your Nova cool. Typically, the fan blade tips are very close to the edge of the shroud. This directs all incoming air through the radiator. This example is from Classic Industries.

CHEVY NOVA 1968–1974: HOW TO BUILD AND MODIFY

Good reproduction fan shrouds have tabs molded in on each side. They are designed to accept a set of clips that affix the shroud to the radiator (just as Chevrolet did in the 1960s and 1970s).

Upstairs the shrouds typically mount to a bracket that is affixed to the radiator support. The top bracket keeps the shroud in place while the side tabs (with clips) keep the shroud tight against the radiator.

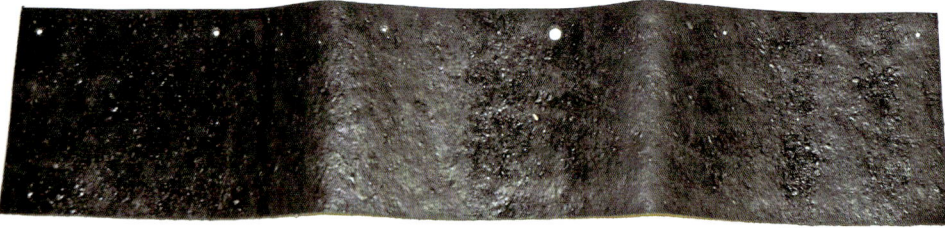

On factory big-block Novas, this rubber "flap" was fitted to the top of the radiator support. The idea here was to seal up the works so that air was forced through the radiator. If you have a big-block car and you're using a stock shroud, be sure to use this piece.

You can make use of an electric fan in any number of ways, such as using a single fan as a pusher, mounted in front of the radiator. This format works only if it's used in conjunction with a regular engine-driven fan.

Another option is to fit a pair of puller fans to the backside of the radiator. With this arrangement, be sure the plastic shroud fits tightly.

the radiator. If the shroud is not present, it creates a considerable amount of "dead" space behind the radiator that in turn destroys the effectiveness of the fan assembly. The bottom line is simple: If you don't run a proper shroud, you're asking for overheating grief. Classic Industries has a complete selection of quality reproduction shrouds for all Nova applications. They work.

You basically have two options in electric fans: a pusher fan or a puller fan. Chevrolet has used both configurations in modern passenger cars and light trucks, although puller fans are the most common. Sometimes electric fans are used in conjunction with an engine-driven clutch fan (typically, an electric pusher fan mounted ahead of the rad). This arrangement is particularly useful if heavy cooling tasks are mandated by the application (a good example is a pickup truck with a factory towing package). This might be a good choice for a Nova that's either blessed with a cooling challenge or sees double-duty as a weekend racer.

Companies such as Ron Davis Racing Products and DeWitts Radiators have spent considerable time researching cooling fans with these criteria. Davis offers a trio of fans: 12-, 14-, and 16-inch diameters.

All the above have a low-amp draw, but Davis points out that one of the other secrets to properly cooling a high-performance car is to effectively

Even though the fans overlap the sides of this radiator, the tight-fitting aluminum shroud directs all of the air through the radiator. As you can see, everything on the radiator backside is covered. This setup is from Ron Davis Racing Radiators. Not only is it good-looking, it flat works!

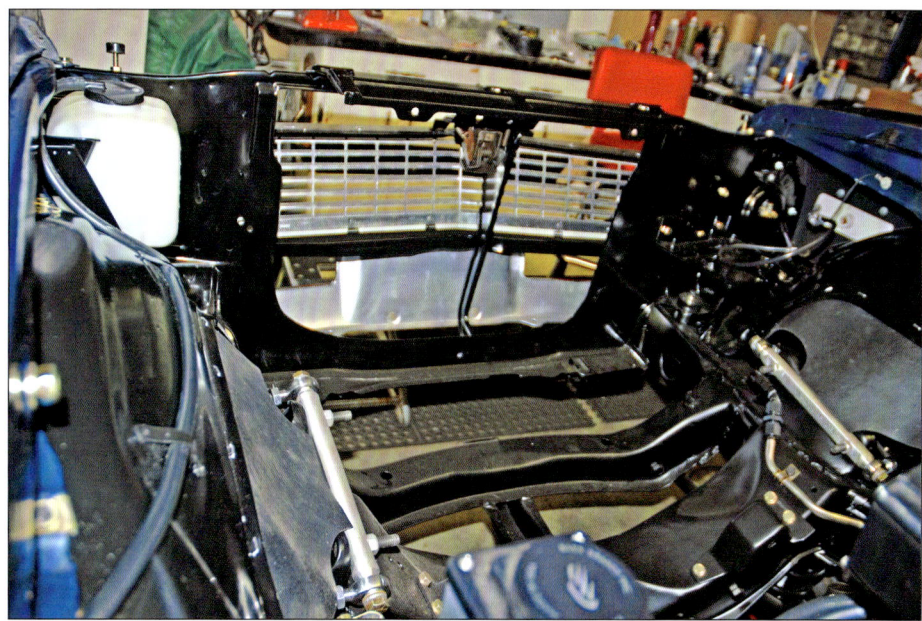

On this Nova, the radiator support was opened up to allow more air to flow through the radiator. Stock small-block Nova supports have an embossed outline of a big-block opening. You can simply trim it back to copy the opening for a big-block radiator.

Davis Fans			
Part Number	Diameter (inches)	RPM	CFM
EF 120	12	2,300	1,576
EF 140	14	2,400	1,828
EF 160	16	2,400	2,197

CHAPTER 10

seal the radiator to the fan. Typically, this is accomplished by way of an integral shroud surrounding the electric fan. The shroud simply allows the largest volume of air to be pulled through the radiator (usually in a pull through application). If you take the time to effective seal any gaps between the fan shroud and the radiator, cooling can improve. It's not that difficult to accomplish.

The best fan for your Nova depends upon the application and the space you have to work with. If you have the room, a Detroit-style engine-driven clutch fan with a full shroud is most certainly a good bet. Another really good arrangement is a dual electric puller system, complete with an integral shroud (as shown in the accompanying photos). The worst possible arrangement is an inexpensive discount store flex fan without a shroud, or a single pusher electric without a shroud (with these setups, you're asking for trouble). All other combinations fall somewhere in between.

When all is said and done, keep in mind one major point: There is virtually no way to "over cool" your Nova. And the more power your engine produces, the more cooling capacity you need.

It doesn't help you cool your Nova, but this new radiator drain petcock makes servicing the cooling system a bunch easier. This is a nice reproduction from Classic Industries.

Something else you shouldn't leave to chance is the water pump bypass hose. If you run a thermostat (and you should), don't leave the bypass hose off the water pump.

Remember those OEM radiator mounting points I examined at the beginning of the chapter? Here's the hardware used to mount the radiator. The pair of well nuts goes to one side and the pointed fender bolts are used on the other side. Again, reproductions such as these are readily available.

The most universal of thermostats is a 180-degree job. They work well on modified Novas because they keep the coolant in the radiator until 180 degrees. This allows time for the fans (and the radiator) to do their job, which is to reduce the coolant temperature before it goes into the engine.

These three radiator caps are all for a Nova. Each has a 15-pound rating. The one on the left is a reproduction, at top right is an original, and the one on the lower right is a replacement cap. For a modified Nova, the replacement RC26 on the lower right works perfectly.

CHEVY NOVA 1968–1974: HOW TO BUILD AND MODIFY

SOURCE GUIDE

Aeroquip Performance
Eaton Corporation
Hydraulics Group USA
14615 Lone Oak Rd.
Eden Prairie, MN 55344
952-937-9800
aeroquipperformance.com

ARP
1863 Eastman Ave.
Ventura, CA 93003
800-826-3045
arp-bolts.com

Aurora Bearing Company
901 Aucutt Rd.
Montgomery, IL 60538
630-859-2030
aurorabearing.com

Baer Brakes
2222 W. Peoria Ave.
Phoenix, AZ 85029
602-233-1411
baer.com

Belltech
300 W. Pontiac Way
Clovis, CA 93612
800-445-3767
belltech.com

Calvert Racing Suspensions
4530 Runway Dr.
Lancaster, CA 93536
661-728-9600
calvertracing.com

Chevrolet Performance
Parts available at your Chevrolet dealer
chevrolet.com/performance/overview.html

Classic Industries
18460 Gothard St.
Huntington Beach, CA 92647
800-854-1280
classicindustries.com

Competition Engineering
Moroso Performance Products
80 Carter Dr.
Guilford, CT 06437
203-453-6571
competitionengineering.com

Detroit Locker (Eaton)
Contact your Eaton Dealer

Detroit Speed
185 McKenzie Rd.
Mooresville, NC 28115
704-662-3272
detroitspeed.com

DeWitts
1275 Grand Oaks Dr.
Howell, MI 48843
517-548-0600
dewitts.com

Earl's Performance
1801 Russellville Rd.
P.O. Box 10360
Bowling Green, KY 42101
270-782-2900
holley.com

DTS Custom Service
4052 S. State Rd. (M-66)
Ionia, MI 48846
877-874-7327
dtscustom.com

Hollander
2955 Xenium Ln. N., Ste. 10
Plymouth, MN 55441
800-825-0644
hollandersolutions.com

Holley Performance Products
1801 Russellville Rd.
P.O. Box 10360
Bowling Green, KY 42101-7360
270-782-2900
holley.com

Hotchkis Sport Suspension
8633 Sorensen Ave.
Santa Fe Springs, CA 90670
877-466-7655
hotchkis.net

Hurst Performance
100 Stony Point Rd., Ste. 125
Santa Rosa, CA 95401
707-544-4761
hurst-shifters.com

Jerry Bickel Race Cars
141 Raceway Park Dr.
Moscow Mills, MO 63362
636-356-4727
jerrybickel.com

CHEVY NOVA 1968–1974: HOW TO BUILD AND MODIFY

SOURCE GUIDE

Lakewood
1801 Russellville Rd.
P.O. Box 10360
Bowling Green, KY 42101
270-782-2900
holley.com

Lamb Components
1259 W. 9th St.
Upland, CA 91786
909-985-1901
lambcomponents.com

Mark Williams Enterprises
765 S. Pierce Ave.
Louisville, CO 80027
866-508-6394
markwilliams.com

Mickey Thompson Tires
4600 Prosper Dr.
Stow, OH 44224
800-222-9092
mickeythompsontires.com

MandH Racemaster
800-299-8000
mhracemaster.com

MSD
1490 Henry Brennan Dr.
El Paso, TX 79936
915-857-5200
msdperformance.com

Nitto Tire U.S.A.
P.O. Box 6064
Cypress, CA 90630
nittotire.com

RobbMc Performance Products
1717 La Mirada St.
Carson City, NV 89703
775-885-7411
robbmcperformance.com

Ron Davis Racing Products
7334 N. 108th Ave.
Glendale, AZ 85307
800-842-5001
rondavisradiators.com

Russell Performance
2700 California St.
Torrance, CA 90503
800-416-8628
edelbrock.com

Spectra Premium
1421 Ampere
Boucherville, QC Canada J4B 5Z5
450-641-3090
spectrapremium.com

Strange Engineering
8300 N. Austin Ave.
Morton Grove, IL 60053
847-663-1701
strangeengineering.net

TRZ Motorsports
1651 Kelley Ave.
Kissimmee, FL 34744
407-933-7385
trzmotorsports.com

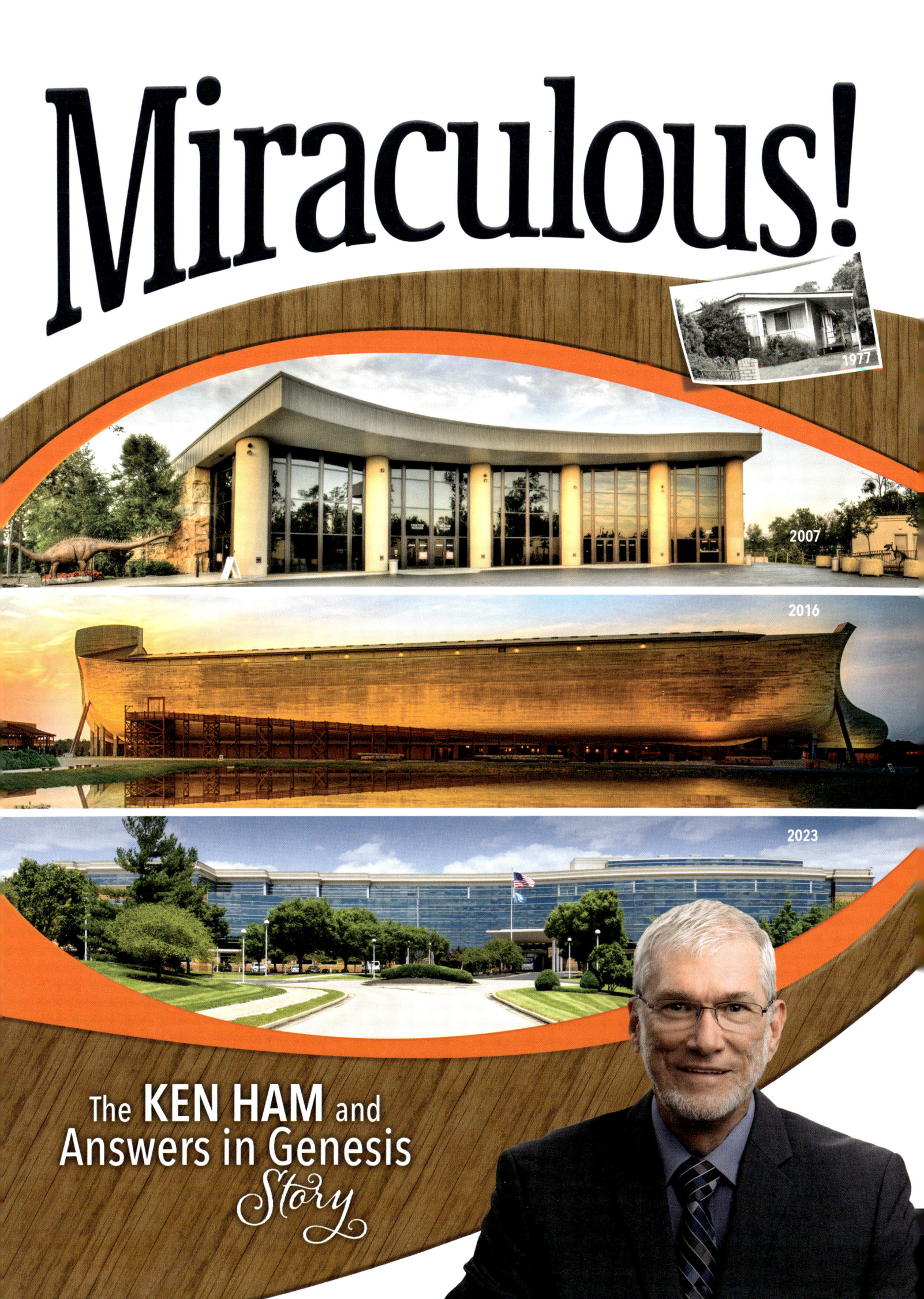

I would like to dedicate Miraculous *to five very special people.*

First, to my sweetheart Mally, without whom I could never have done what the Lord called me to do through Answers in Genesis, the Creation Museum, and Ark Encounter. Only God knows the sacrifice she has made over the years to enable this ministry to be where it is today. Her children and grandchildren comment on how selfless she is, and how she has such a generous and godly spirit. It would take a whole book (or many books) to write the account of what she has done over the years to support me in this ministry. As of the writing of this book, we are in our 53rd year of marriage and love each other more than ever. Her godly devotion to me and her family is evident to all. For her, it's always been God first, others second, and herself last.

Secondly, to two of the most outstanding, godly devoted men you could meet, Mark Looy and Mike Zovath, who God brought into this ministry to make up the three founders He anointed to build an organization dedicated to honoring God's Son and proclaiming the truth of God's Word and the gospel to the world. Since the founding of the ministry in December 1993, the three of us have stayed the course together as we have climbed mountain tops and descended into valleys in this journey of faith that God has used to impact millions.

Thirdly, to two very special people God brought into our lives: Don Landis, who became our founding chairman, and the late Dan Manthei, who became a founding board member. They deserve much honor for the dedication and sacrifice they have given to the ministry since its inception.

> being devoted to one another in brotherly love, giving preference to one another in honor. (Romans 12:10 LSB)

First printing: July 2025

Copyright © 2025 Ken Ham and Master Books®. All rights reserved. No part of this book may be reproduced, copied, broadcast, stored, or shared in any form whatsoever without written permission from the publisher, except in the case of brief quotations in articles and reviews. For information write:

Master Books, P.O. Box 726, Green Forest, AR 72638
Master Books® is a division of the New Leaf Publishing Group, LLC.

ISBN: 978-1-68344-381-0

ISBN: 978-1-61458-943-3 (digital)

Library of Congress Control Number: 2025940336

Scripture taken from the New King James Version®. Copyright © 1982 by Thomas Nelson. Used by permission. All rights reserved.

Scripture quotations taken from the (LSB®) Legacy Standard Bible®, Copyright © 2021 by The Lockman Foundation. Used by permission. All rights reserved. Managed in partnership with Three Sixteen Publishing Inc. LSBible.org and 316publishing.com.

Scripture marked KJV is taken from the King James version of the Holy Bible.

Scripture quotations are from the ESV® Bible (The Holy Bible, English Standard Version®), © 2001 by Crossway, a publishing ministry of Good News Publishers. ESV Text Edition: 2025. The ESV text may not be quoted in any publication made available to the public by a Creative Commons license. The ESV may not be translated in whole or in part into any other language. Used by permission. All rights reserved.

Scripture quotations taken from the Amplified® Bible (AMP), Copyright © 2015 by The Lockman Foundation. Used by permission. lockman.org

Printed in the United States of America

Visit our website for other great titles: www.masterbooks.com

For information regarding promotional opportunities, please contact the publicity department at pr@nlpg.com.

Introduction 6

1. Life Down Under 9
1951–1963

Ken Ham's parents and grandparents solidify his trust in the inerrant Word of God; he commits to trusting every part of God's Word.

2. Searching for Answers 25
1963–1971

Ken's family taught him and his siblings' discernment; the belief of evolution is at odds with the Bible; a book ignites answers.

3. Mally and Ministry 41
1971–1979

Ken and Mally meet and fall in love; teaching skeptical students; starting a ministry and making creation resources available.

4. Journey into Full Time Ministry 81
1979–1986

Wall to wall resources; driving throughout Australia to spread the truth; God clears obstacles, expands the ministry.

5. Coming to America 101
1986–1993

A difficult decision to stay or leave; the faithfulness of Mally; God begins to put in place people obedient to His call.

6. The Birth of AiG 123
1993–1995

Tale of two ministries; mailing mayhem ensues; Ken's face on envelopes; worldview castle diagrams; Kentucky and Answers in Genesis.

7. Building the Creation Museum 151
1995–2014

Led by a teacher, a history buff, and a retired lieutenant colonel; pushbacks, property, projects; courts, loans and debate.

8. The Ark Encounter 189
2004–2016

A bold vision; finding land; new battles; God comes through again; religious freedom; bond offering; funds in the nick of time.

9. Faithful God for 50 Years 235
2016–2025

Trusting God every step of the way; engaging a hostile culture; values, relevancy, diverse content streamed and shared worldwide; Answers Academy.

Introduction

Some might say that the Answers in Genesis ministry began fifty years ago with "fire in the bones" of an Aussie science teacher named Ken Ham who loved God's Word. And that would be true, but it's certainly not the whole story.

The whole story includes parents who taught their children to stand on God's Word, a wife who sacrificially loves Jesus, a myriad of men and women who were burdened to be part of proclaiming the message of biblical authority, and a faithful God who sovereignly orchestrated everything that made Answers in Genesis, the Creation Museum, and the Ark Encounter possible.

As you read the story of this unique ministry and watch it grow from humble roots in Australia to what it is today, there's a theme you'll see highlighted again and again: God's miraculous provision of resources and people at just the right moments. Even though there are certainly humans involved in the story—thousands of individual

humans in big and small ways—it's really the account of God's faithfulness. We could never have done this without His miraculous hand. And that's why I've always said AiG is not my ministry— it's God's ministry. He's the one who sovereignly built it, and He's the one who gets all the glory for what He's done through it.

It's a story about faith and the many lessons learned along the way in this exciting journey of mountains and valleys, encountering giants and Red Sea events, and much more in this ongoing spiritual war raging around us.

So, as you read, be encouraged that we have a God who isn't distant or deaf to our cries for help. Rather, we have a God who is actively and sovereignly working and who answers the prayers of His people at just the right time and in ways we never could have imagined. It's all truly miraculous.

To God be the glory!
Great things He has done!

Western Australia

1951 – 1963

AUSTRALIA IS NOT LIKE AMERICA

Embarrassingly, I found this out shortly after we arrived in America and I kindly offered to nurse someone's fussy baby. The awkward silence informed me I'd made a faux pas. Turns out, nurse means breastfeed a baby in America, not hold a baby like it does in Australia! I certainly never made that mistake again!

But it's not just the wildly varying weather, strange food (why do Americans have such an obsession with chicken?), and differing vocabulary (no one here says slacko, whinger, or bludger, all classic Aussie insults — oh that's another difference. We Aussies show affection by insulting each other!). The differences extend to our nation's histories. Australia was never a Christianized nation like America. We don't have the rich history of God's Word and Christian principles Down Under like in the U.S. While there are churches and Christians (and nativity scenes used to be displayed in shopping malls at Christmas), Christians have never had the influence they hold here. There is a need for missionaries to preach the gospel far and wide to reach those who've never heard the good news.

> "Probably only about 1% of 20 million people in Australia are truly born again." *Ken Ham Daily,* p. 280

MUM AND DAD ON A MISSION

My parents had a heart for the calling of these missionaries. When I was a child growing up in Queensland, a large state in northeastern Australia, Open Air Campaigners (a mission organization founded in Australia) would host evangelistic outreaches, to reach both churched and unchurched children. My mum and dad supported these missionaries financially and opened their home to host them so they could run programs in our local area.

My father, a primary (Americans would say elementary) public school principal, worked hard at his job, striving to please the Lord. His hard work meant he was promoted every three years, so we moved from place to place across Queensland. No matter where we moved, my parents would immediately try to find a church that preached God's Word faithfully and, if there was no Sunday school for the local kids, would get involved starting one.

A few years before she went home to be with the Lord, I interviewed my mother and asked her to give the details of a story she had told me as a young boy when visiting her parents in North Queensland. As a teenager, my mum was burdened for the lost and decided to start a Sunday school to reach the local kids. About 30 kids, from little ones right up to teenagers, showed up the first Sunday at the country hall a mile from her house. Mum wasn't expecting such a response, but several parents stepped up to teach the older ones and she taught the little ones from God's Word.

Norma Elizabet Ham
1928 — 2019

But there were two girls who lived two miles from the hall and were too little to come by themselves. My mother was so burdened for them to join she put a cushion on her bicycle handlebars, pedaled up to their house, put both little girls on her bike, and delivered them to Sunday school. Afterwards, she'd load them up again and cycle them back before going home herself — a five-mile round trip every week! Years later, in her 80's, she met those girls again, now as elderly women. One was still following the Lord because she had been so greatly impacted by those old Sunday school days. The other said she'd gotten away from the Lord but was coming back.

She impacted me (and all her children) in so many other ways too. I can still hear my mother's voice telling me, "God first, others next, yourself last," and "It's only what's done for Jesus that lasts." She not only drummed that into us, but both she and Dad lived by it. They never had much in the way of material goods, but they shared whatever they had. Sometimes when missionaries would stay with us, the missionaries wouldn't have enough money to travel to their next destination. My mother would go through her purse and my father's pockets, looking for what they could give them to help those missionaries continue impacting children in other places. They constantly sacrificed for the sake of the gospel.

It wasn't just money; they were generous with everything. If they replaced a piece of furniture and the old one still had use, they could never sell it. They would always find someone to bless with it (to this day my wife, Mally, and I can never bring ourselves to sell anything of ours — we always give it away, just like my parents).

> As a young child, when I first heard Mum tell me about this Sunday school she had started and her weekly trek with those two young girls, I remember thinking, "If my mother did that to reach people with the message of Jesus, what can I do to reach people?" It's something I've never forgotten. What an impact just that one action by my mother had on me and my life.

A PRINCIPLED MAN

My father was a serious man, firm in his convictions. Serving as the school principal meant he was always my principal, and he was well-known for his strictness. Never wanting to be accused of favoritism toward his own children, he was even stricter with us at school, disciplining us more than the other children. I would come home and complain to mum who would chide dad, but it didn't work. Next time I misbehaved, I'd again feel the sharp sting of a "wait-a-while" vine cane on my hand! (Yes, in those days the principal would hunt the tropical rainforest for the perfect cane for firmly, but kindly, administering discipline when needed.)

Dad was openly a Christian at work, holding his pupils to Christian standards of morality. Everyone knew his convictions and he took to heart — and quoted often — Colossians 3:23: "and whatsoever ye do, do it heartily, as to the Lord, and not unto men" (KJV). He had high academic standards for the children in his care and high personal standards because he knew whatever a Christian does should be done with excellence so as not to reproach the name of Christ.

He loved God's Word. I'll never forget the way his voice thundered as he quoted "thus saith the Lord," "have ye not read," or "it is written." He loved verses that emphasized the authority of God's Word.

Mervyn Ham, in front of his home at Kelceda St., Sunnybank Hills, Queensland.

One of my favorite photos is him sitting in his chair with his Bible open on his lap as he taught those who gathered at our home for a Bible study. Before my father passed away in 1995, my brother Robert asked why he loved God's Word so much. "My father died when I was 16 years old," he said. "I was without an earthly father, so I turned to the words of my heavenly Father." God's Word says it is strength to your bones, and he saturated himself in it and found God's strength.

And he didn't just love God's Word — he knew it and he loved to teach it. Another of my favorite pictures is him on vacation, sitting in a lawn chair outside our

Caravan camper, again with an open Bible in his lap. He was always reading and studying God's Word and knew it well. Romans 8:28 says, "and we know that for those who love God, all things work together for good" (LSB). It doesn't say all things are good — my grandfather dying when his son was just a teenager was not good. But God used that tragedy to drive my father to study and love God's Word and his love for Scripture impacted me (and my siblings) greatly.

Mervyn Ham camping near the Tweed River in New South Wales studying his Bible – one of my favorite photos of him.

As we moved around, Dad was always asked to serve as an elder or deacon once we were settled in the church. He and mum were always serving, starting Sunday schools, teaching Bible studies, my Mum cooking up a storm for a church event. Dad was also a lay preacher, often filling the pulpit when the pastor was away. He, like his father and grandfather, was a teacher and there was no better subject for him to teach on than God's Word (you can see where I get it from!). And he hated compromise; he would never knowingly compromise the Word of God. He loved God's Word too much.

I still smile when I remember that, whenever Dad preached in church, someone would inevitably come up afterward and ask if he could be the full-time Bible teacher. He was such a great communicator and had an ability to explain things so everyone could understand.

Mervyn doing some grilling for a group of Christian tourists.

Mervyn Ham conducting a Bible study at a home in Brisbane, Australia.

But his love for God's Word at one stage handed him the nickname "Merv the Stirrer" (his name was Mervyn). In my five decades of ministry, I've noticed when controversy arises, many people just want to smooth it over, not ruffle any feathers, and keep everyone happy. Not my father; he loved God's Word far too much to allow liberal theology to creep into the church.

I remember him leading my mum and all us children, Bible in hand, up to the front of the church after a sermon to challenge the pastor on a point of teaching that whiffed of liberalism. Whether it was evolution added to Genesis, a devotional the church distributed that taught a local flood, or naturalistic explanations for miracles — one pastor taught that the feeding of the five thousand happened because one little boy decided to share, which made everyone else open their lunches and share too — my father would open God's Word and stand up to false teaching.

He had what I call a "Nehemiah anger" about compromise on God's Word. In the Old Testament, the prophet Nehemiah grew righteously angry when he saw things that were very wrong, and he immediately set out to make them right. It's the kind of anger that says, "Why won't someone do something about this?" Dad would step up and do something — and that often got him into trouble, but he never minded. God's Word and its authority were more important.

I inherited that same "Nehemiah anger" from my father. As a science teacher touring children through secular museums, I would wonder, "Why must all museums teach evolution? Why won't someone build a creation museum?" I was righteously angry to see God's creation being used to promote naturalism (atheism) — and I did something about it! People sometimes get frustrated with me (as they did with my father) because I like to jump on problems straight away. But if I have the ability to fix something, why not do it straight away? I've always had that sense of urgency (like my father had) in dealing with issues.

SOME CHURCH HISTORY

In many parts of America, even small towns will have five or six church choices. In the rural towns I grew up in, there were often only one or two options, but my father would choose the church with the most faithful preaching, regardless of denomination. So, I was brought up Presbyterian-Methodist-Baptist-Brethren. I now see this as a gift from the Lord.

In Australia when I was growing up, denominational lines were not strong. With so few Christians and churches, denominations had to work together, or nothing got done. I found Aussie believers were much more accustomed to working with those of differing theological views.

Not so in America. In the U.S., you must be careful, as denominations are taken much more seriously. By growing up in a mix of denominations, God was preparing me for the unique, non-denominational work of running Answers in Genesis. Because I know how to "walk the denominational line" without getting into trouble, I've spoken at all sorts of American churches and been able to help the AiG ministry stay non-denominational. Knowing where to draw the lines between black-and-white "thus saith the Lord" and more gray denominational differences is hard, but my philosophy has always been, "Is this disagreement arising from differing interpretations of the text itself, or is it from bringing something from outside Scripture into your interpretation?" In other words, "Is it a biblical authority issue?" And that's how we draw the line; it always goes back to the authority of the Bible and God's Word vs. man's word! And if the disagreement starts with man's word, we'll stand on God's clear word.

Small seaside township of Sarina Beach on the Coral Sea, Queensland, Australia.

More Faithfulness

Queensland is a large state with miles of gorgeous sunny coastline, lush tropical forests, arid deserts, and acres of farmland, many growing that state's primary crop export: tall bushy sugar cane.

On one such farm, at the foot of the highest mountain in Queensland, Mt. Bartle Frere (a mountain I summited as a boy — the view from 5,285 feet is stunning), lived my mother's parents, in an old-fashioned farmhouse up on stilts. Nanna loved God and had a fervor for proclaiming His truth. During one holiday visit, we were visiting on the veranda when two Jehovah's Witnesses stopped by. They began sharing their message, but my 70-something-year-old Nanna pulled out her Bible and began preaching at them. They gave up on their message and started walking down the steps, but Nanna just went after them. I can still see her today, Bible in the air, preaching at them as they ran for their lives!

Mt. Bartle Frere

Grandad, David, Ken, Nanna, Norma, Robert, Rosemary, Beverley – taken at Mt. Bartle Frere, North Queensland.

When we were visiting my grandparents, my Nanna would often take my hand, squeeze it tight, and give me a big smile. When she let go, there would be some money in my hand. My grandparents never had much materially and lived very simply. Nanna didn't even own a washing machine — she cleaned clothes in a big copper drum filled with water that was heated with a fire underneath it, and she stirred the clothes with a large stick. But she loved giving us something so we could buy some lollies (candy) or put it toward something we wanted. I've never forgotten that generosity and love she showed, and to this day whenever we give our grandchildren something I feel my Nanna squeezing my hand with that special gift in it.

When Sunday came round, my Nanna and Grandfather would dress up for church in what they called their Sunday best. I remember asking my mother why we had to get dressed up for church. Her reply (which I'm sure she was taught by her mother) went something like, "If you went to visit the Queen of England you would put on your very best clothes. We are going to specially worship the King of kings, so we should not dress any less than we would for visiting the Queen."

My grandfather was a quieter, gentle man. He and Nanna were from Belfast, Northern Ireland. He had worked in the shipyards back when that city was known for its massive shipbuilding industry. It was there that the *Titanic* was built (but my grandfather never worked on that doomed ocean liner). They immigrated Down Under because of strife between Northern Ireland and Ireland at the time, eventually ending up on a sugarcane farm at the foot of Mt. Bartle Frere.

Grandfather played the fiddle and would play and sing Irish ditties to us Ham kids. I still remember one he taught me:

> That's as far as I want to go, oh as far as I want to go, I found a button in my stew and a pair of braces too. Said he, "oh won't you finish it?" I said "no, I don't want to find the braces, that's as far as I want to go."

Robert, Beverley, and cousin Jane

In his eighties, when he was losing his eyesight, I remember him telling me how much he was ready to go and be with the Lord. He had a faith in Christ that sustained him as his body failed and death drew near. That faith, of Nanna and Granddad, was passed on to my mother, who, together with Dad, passed it down to me, and it now lives in each of our five children who are passing it to their children who are now passing it on to their children! It's a legacy of faithfulness over six generations.

A Special Plan

During these holiday trips to the sugar cane farm, my Nanna would tell me, "God's got a special plan for you, Kenneth. You're going to be a preacher one day." She told me that so many times. As a young child, and later as a teenager, I was often very sick, dealing with serious health issues, and needed to be hospitalized more than once, beginning with an operation to remove my chronically re-infected tonsils and adenoids at a very young age.

When we lived in a very small isolated country town in the north, I once again needed a hospital, but the river had completely flooded the roads. During the rainy season in North Queensland I have experienced it raining an inch or two (25–50 millimeters) in just an hour. We experienced many floods, and I can remember my father driving a small car on flooded roads. But this one time the floods were so bad, my parents had to find someone with a rowboat who was willing to row me across a swollen river to get me to the hospital. After events like these, my mother would echo my Nanna, "God has something special for you, Kenneth. You're going to be a preacher someday."

Nanna

Oddly enough, this pronouncement kept happening. When I was about 12 years old, a family friend having tea with my mother shared, "You know, Norma, God's got a special plan for Ken. He's going to do something special one day." At the Presbyterian church we attended in Brisbane, I would be asked to read the Bible before the congregation sometimes and one specific lady would tell my parents, "Every time Kenneth gets up to read the Bible, God impresses on me that he's got something special for him." I heard this so many times from different people as I was growing up it almost seemed like God was telling me to get ready for something He had planned for my life.

During one of the children's outreach programs my parents helped organize in one of Australia's wettest towns, Innisfail, when I was about 10, I was burdened to commit myself to being a missionary for the Lord. The Open Air Campaigner missionary my parents had brought in to run a program in the church had a challenge for the children. He challenged us to ensure we committed our lives to the Lord and were willing to go wherever God wanted us to go and do whatever he wanted us to do. The missionary had a piece of paper with those words on it and asked those who made that commitment to sign that paper. I responded and said in my heart, "Lord, I am willing to go anywhere You want me to go and do whatever You want me to do." My sister Rosemary made the same commitment at the same time.

Little did I know, around the same age, a young girl called Mally (you'll meet her in the next chapter) likewise went forward at a Sunday school meeting saying, "Lord, you died on that cross for me. You did that for me, so I want to do whatever you want me to do and go wherever you want me to go." We both made the same commitment at about the same age! And God brought us together as His plan for the Answers in Genesis ministry. I've said it many times, and I'll say it again in this book, the ministry of Answers in Genesis, and the two attractions, the Creation Museum and the Ark Encounter, that impact millions of lives each year around the world, wouldn't be as they are if it wasn't for Mally being such a wonderful, godly, dedicated wife and mother. She has truly been one with me every step of the way — but I'm getting ahead of myself, more on that later.

Ken and Rosemary

Mervyn and Norma camping with four of the children: David, Beverley, Robert, and Rosemary.

There's no doubt various events in the 60's were pivotal to God preparing me for a ministry beyond what I could have ever imagined.

Yes, God was calling me to be a preacher — not a pastor like two of my younger brothers would eventually become, but a teacher of His truth in churches all around the world and a missionary halfway across the globe, in America.

God called me to this ministry, but ultimately it has nothing to do with me. God is the one who entrusted me with the ability to teach, opened doors of opportunity, and placed me in a family with a legacy of faithfulness that they passed on to me.

The story of Ken Ham and Answers in Genesis is really not the story of Ken Ham. It's the story of faithful parents and grandparents, a very special wife, and, above all, of a faithful God who took a boy from rural Queensland who loved His Word and used him to help pioneer the biblical creation message in Australia and, eventually, take it around the world. As I've always emphasized, this ministry is God's ministry, I'm simply a messenger.

Ken Ham at a beach in North Queensland.

Daily, as Christians, we are in an immense spiritual battle. We battle with the world and, sadly, we struggle with much of the Church too." *Ken Ham Daily*, p. 279

Beverley, Rosemary, Ken, and Robert taken at Mundoo, outside of Innisfail, North Queensland around 1961 – about the same time Ken committed to do what God wanted him to do and go wherever God wanted him to go.

Mervyn, Ken, Norma, Rosemary – 1955, taken at Mackay, North Queensland, while Dad was teaching at a school in a town called Sybil Creek

Ken's baby picture; he's probably around 9 months old.

Ken as a young boy.

Ken in school uniform for first year in High School 1965 Sarina, Queensland.

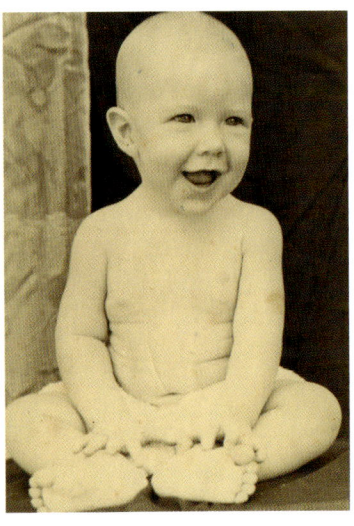

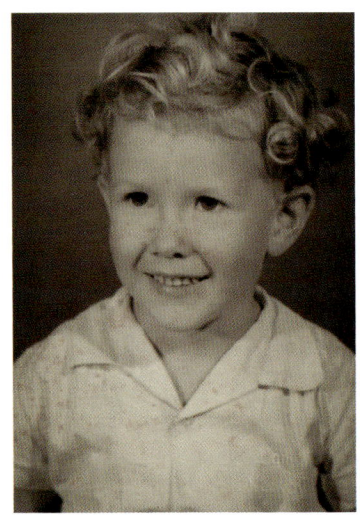

Born in Cairns, Australia October 20, 1951.

Mervyn and Norma Ham with their car and caravan they used to go camping. Taken in Carbethon St., Manly Brisbane where Dad's mother and sister lived.

Norma and Mervyn taken at Sunnybank Hills, Brisbane mid-1970's.

Robert, Ken and David taken in Sarina, Queensland around 1964.

Ken, Beverley, Robert, David, Rosemary – Siblings – taken in Sarina, Queensland.

There is a very small percentage of what we would call evangelical Christians in Australia. It is quite astonishing that my grandparents and parents were both outgoing born again, mission-minded Christians. I would call that Miraculous!

My Father's Bible

1963 – 1971

2 | SEARCHING for ANSWERS

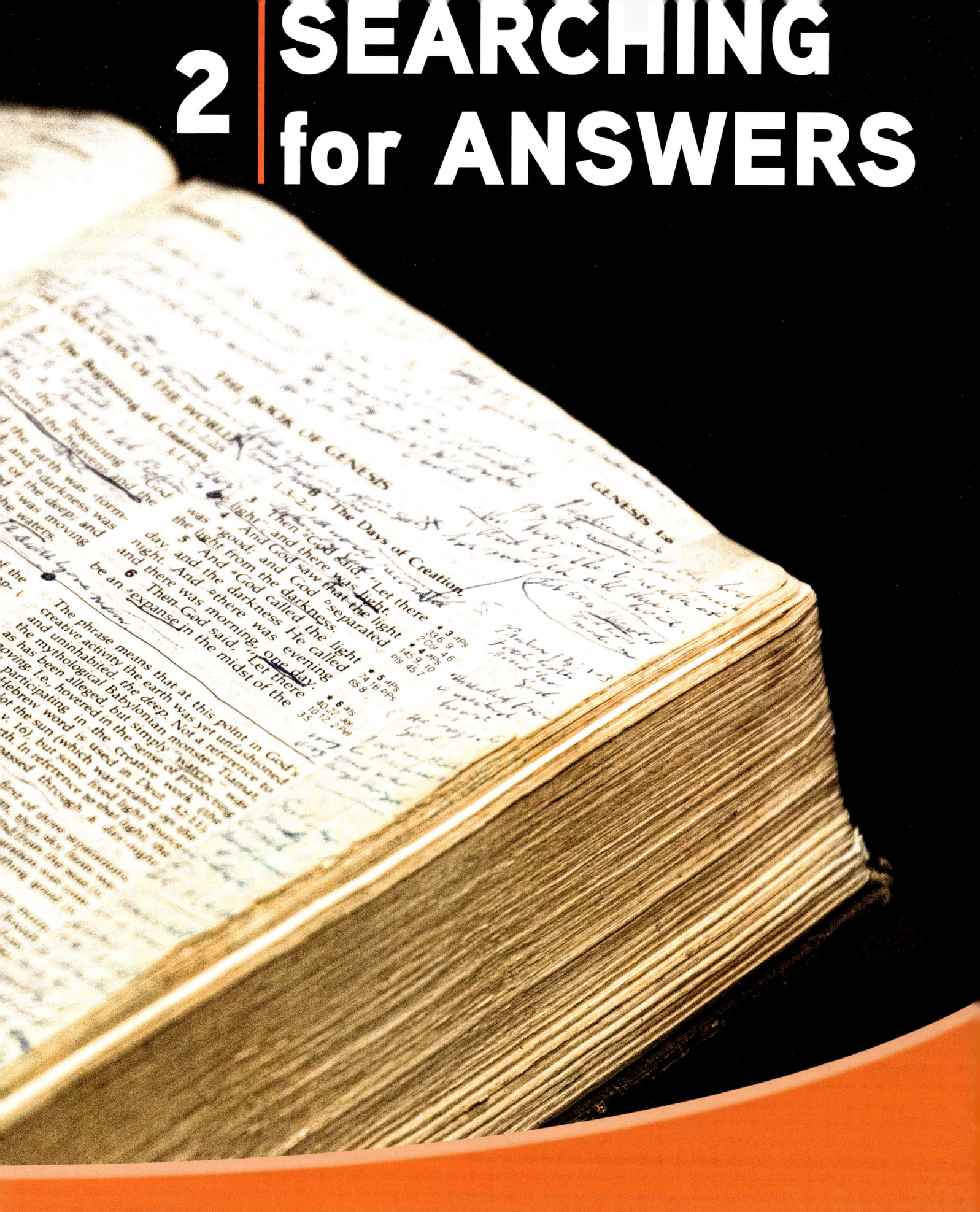

TRUE OR FALSE?

"It's all right, you can believe in evolution," the pastor preached. "God created, yes, He did, and the means He used was evolution. There's no conflict between science and faith. The Bible tells us God did it, science tells us how."

The first place you hear evolution taught as fact shouldn't be from a church pulpit. And yet, as a "going-on-13"-year-old boy, a sermon at a Presbyterian church in the quaint little coastal town of Sarina, was my first exposure to evolutionary ideas. And you can imagine how "Merv the Stirrer" reacted!

My father "hit the roof." Both he and my mother were so distressed, not because they knew all the scientific evidence against evolution (they didn't yet), but because they knew God's Word. That knowledge was enough to convince them that evolution was utterly false. We never returned to that church.

After the sermon — the last one we ever heard at that church — my father impressed on us kids that evolution undermines the authority of the Word of God. "As soon as you start saying one part of the Bible isn't true, that it's open to man's interpretation, then how can the rest be true?" Adding evolution to the Bible, he explained, is compromising God's Word, and we simply can't compromise God's Word. And, he went on, Genesis is the foundation for the rest of the Bible, and it's referred to as real history in other passages throughout Scripture. Yes, Dad knew the biblical arguments against evolution, but we didn't yet have answers for the so-called ape-men, dating methods, fossil layers, and so on.

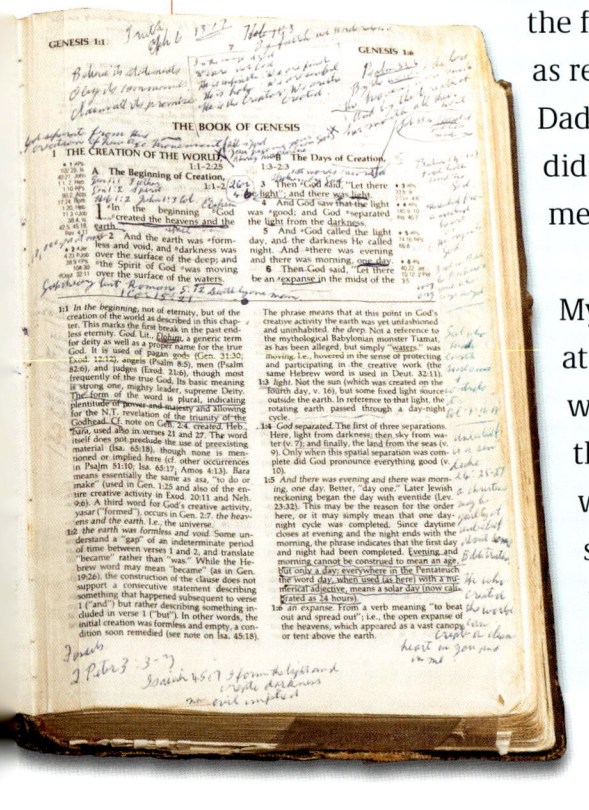

Dad's Bible and his written notes.

My parents also made sure we understood that we couldn't attend a church that compromised God's Word. That's why we never went back. All this had a great impact on me and the rest of our family. And here's something to ponder: when my mother was in her 80's, she told me she had met someone who remembers the time at that church when we left over the pastor teaching evolution — and it had a lasting positive impact on them!

Mum and Dad

Ken, Robert, David (baby), Beverley, Rosemary, Norma Ham, Mervyn Ham, Elsie Ham, (Mervyn Ham's Mother)

In the Creation Museum there is a display dedicated to my Mum and Dad.

MAKING A MONKEY OUT OF ME

Because of what happened at church, to make a humorous point about evolution, my parents decided to dress me for my school's costume party in brown overalls and an ape mask — yes, I went as an ape clutching a potted plant labeled "Our Family Tree." It was a spoof on evolution, and I remember other parents and teachers laughing. In those days, even people who weren't Christians mocked the notion that humans were related to the apes.

Dad wasn't above using humor to make a point.

The next year (1965) after the "evolution-from-the-pulpit" episode, I entered high school. The local high school had introduced new textbooks for science classes that emphasized evolutionary ideas, especially regarding human evolution and so-called ape-men.

My father warned me that, even though he didn't have all the answers from a scientific perspective, evolution wasn't true because it conflicted with God's Word — and we don't question God's Word! And we don't add to God's Word either — that makes man the authority and undermines the Scriptures.

Not a Science Textbook

Over the years I've had countless Christians tell me, "The Bible's not a science textbook." I always respond with, "I'm glad it's not!" When I entered high school, those new evolutionary textbooks taught human evolution as fact. Certain supposed ape-man specimens were trotted out as proof of our animal past and "vestigial" organs, like the supposedly useless appendix, poked at the idea of an all-wise Creator. After all, what kind of Creator leaves a body littered with useless parts?

At the time, I had no scientific answers for why humans didn't evolve from apelike creatures or why my appendix was actually evidence of God's wise plan for a beneficial bacterial hideout. But I knew the textbooks were wrong because they contradicted what I read in Genesis. My father was adamant that we take God's Word as written. He always said, "Just because you don't have an answer doesn't mean there isn't an answer — it just means we don't know it yet and we need to wait for the answers!"

His advice when an apparent contradiction between science and the Bible arose was this: carefully study the passage to make sure your interpretation isn't wrong. If you are sure you are reading the passage correctly, taking into account the grammatical-historical context and other relevant passages, then you don't question God's Word, you question man's word and wait for the answers.

And he was right. Looking back now, decades after high school, those examples the textbooks gave to "prove" evolution aren't really used anymore. Evolutionists have rejected a lot of those "proofs" and moved on to new so-called transitional forms and missing links. Take vestigial organs, for example. Once researchers bothered to look for a function for these supposedly "useless evolutionary leftovers," they found them! The most famous example, the appendix, is a home for beneficial bacteria. When a nasty bug or virus infects the digestive tract and wipes out the good bacteria, more of the good guys are waiting in the appendix to replace the ones that were lost. It's a great design in a fallen world.

It's a good reminder that man's word changes all the time. We're finite, fallible beings who don't know everything and we're constantly discovering new things and overturning previous wisdom. But God's Word never changes. That's why I say I'm glad the Bible isn't a science textbook like the ones we used in school — if it was, it would change every few years!

Over the years I've heard from many people that when the teaching of evolution came up at school or even in church or at a Christian college, they were counseled by their parents and Christian leaders to accept evolution as God's way of doing things. Many of these people have told me this ultimately caused them to question the trust they had in God's Word, and they walked away from the church. How I praise God for parents who understood how vital it is to stand boldly on the authority of God's Word and not compromise. And, yes, they were mocked for doing this. I recall many instances of people saying negative things against my parents because of their bold stand. But, wow, what an impact their commitment to God's Word had on me.

> "Just knowledge of facts will not save anyone. The power is not in any human reasoning but in God's Word and Christ's work." *Begin,* p. 231

NOTING THE NOTES

Something else my father taught me that I've never forgotten is this: whenever he used a study Bible, he would remind us that the text is inspired by God, but the notes are not. They're helpful, but ultimately, they're written by fallible people with feet of clay. We judge the notes based on the biblical text — not the other way around!

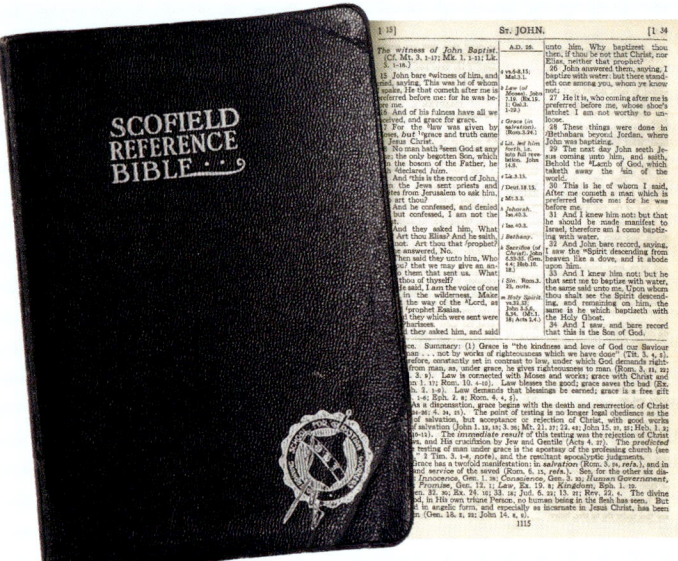

1917 Scofield Bible

For instance, the *Scofield Reference Bible* was a widely used study Bible. In his notes on Genesis 1:1 and 1:2, Scofield described the Gap Theory, arguing that there was a gap of millions of years between the events of Genesis 1:1 and 1:2 during which a "Luciferian flood" took place. This idea originally came from a young Presbyterian minister, Thomas Chalmers, as a way of fitting the long ages geologists were suggesting for the earth into Genesis. Scofield popularized it in his study Bible, arguing that the earth had been "made waste and empty by judgment" and that "the face of the earth bears everywhere the marks of such a catastrophe." Such an idea doesn't come from the text itself; it comes from adding man's ideas about the past into Scripture.

Dad taught us with examples like these that God's Word is the final authority — not man's opinions about what might have happened in the past.

During my high school years, I had biblical answers for why evolution and millions of years were incompatible with the Bible but no scientific answers. Those would come later. But even more important than those scientific answers was the rock-solid belief that my parents instilled in me that God is the final authority, that Genesis is foundational to the rest of the Bible so we cannot compromise God's Word with man's ideas or we lose our foundation, and that all of our Christian doctrine ultimately comes from Genesis.

Queensland University of Technology: City of Brisbane

FEEDING THE FIRE

In 1970 I left home for university, the Queensland Institute of Technology (later named the Queensland University of Technology) in sunny Brisbane, Australia, right on the South Pacific Ocean. Like my great-grandfather, grandfather, and father before me, I decided to become a teacher. (As an aside, our oldest daughter is now the founder and administrator of Answers in Genesis' Christian school, Answers Academy. You just can't take the educator out of the Hams!) Since I'd always loved science, I went for a bachelor's degree in applied science. And that's where I got hit with evolution yet again.

One professor explained that DNA, a complex information storage system with a language system, somehow came about by chance random processes. Such a claim didn't make sense to me, but I didn't have the information I have now to know how to question his evolutionary ideas.

My degree's emphasis was in environmental biology, which meant I was taught how man was using up earth's resources and destroying the climate. I was told the world was overpopulated and this would destroy mankind. And,

Al Gore at a TED Talk in 2006.

due to man's impact on the climate, many major cities in the world would be flooded — and there would be no more polar bears if we didn't make drastic changes. None of what I was taught back in the 70's about man destroying the earth has since happened. It reminds me of the more recent, but very similar, claims by Al Gore in *An Inconvenient Truth* — none of them have come true either! Remember that the next time you read a doomsday headline!

I was also taught about natural selection, adaptation, and speciation as part of the evolutionary process. I remember asking my professors why, if these evolutionary processes were actually occurring, all their examples were animals and plants that remained the same basic kind. I don't recall any of my professors being hostile because I questioned evolution. They knew I was a Christian and that didn't seem to bother them. Things were much different back then!

All through high school I'd been an outspoken critic of evolution, adamantly arguing with my friends that, from a biblical perspective, evolution is false. Now in Uni (Aussie slang for university) it was the same — I was so burdened that students were being taught evolution as fact. I can't explain why the creation/evolution issue gripped me from a young age. Over the years I've described it with this verse from Jeremiah:

> there is in my heart as it were a burning fire shut up in my bones, and I am weary with holding it in, and I cannot (Jeremiah 20:9 ESV).

It was like I had a "fire in my bones." I couldn't not speak about it to others. Those early days of learning evolution in high school were the beginning of the burden the Lord laid on me to be involved in this particular area, and throughout my time in Uni the fire blazed.

But still I had none of the scientific answers, I just lived with the conflict, knowing that none of it could be true if the Bible was true — and the Bible is true. Then Gordon Jones handed me a little booklet.

I was in my final year of university (1974), as I had now graduated with a science degree and had moved on to the University of Queensland for my education diploma. At that time, while in church one Sunday morning, the principal of a teacher's college, Gordon Jones, walked up to me after the service and said, "Hey, Ken, I've got this little booklet from England. I know you're interested in the creation/evolution topic, and I thought it might help you."

It was a small book (and is now part of the Ham Legacy exhibit at the Creation Museum), but it had answers. In a short summary, the booklet explained about fossils and the global flood, that Noah's flood was responsible for laying down the fossil record. It explained that the fossil record cannot be millions of years old, or it puts death before sin — that hit me like a ton of bricks. Of course you can't have death before sin!

As I've studied over the years, I've realized it's not just death before sin either. The fossil record is filled with evidence of diseases like cancer, abscesses, arthritis, and tumors. It's a record of death and disease. If that record is millions of years old, then God called all of that "very good" (Genesis 1:31) on the final day of creation. There are also fossil thorns that claimed to be millions of years old, but the Bible is definitive that thorns came after the curse (Genesis 3:18).

My Graduation picture from University in 1973.

You can't have millions of years of fossils before sin. Suddenly it made sense to me why we even have fossils — of course, the global flood of Noah's day would catastrophically form the bulk of those fossils.

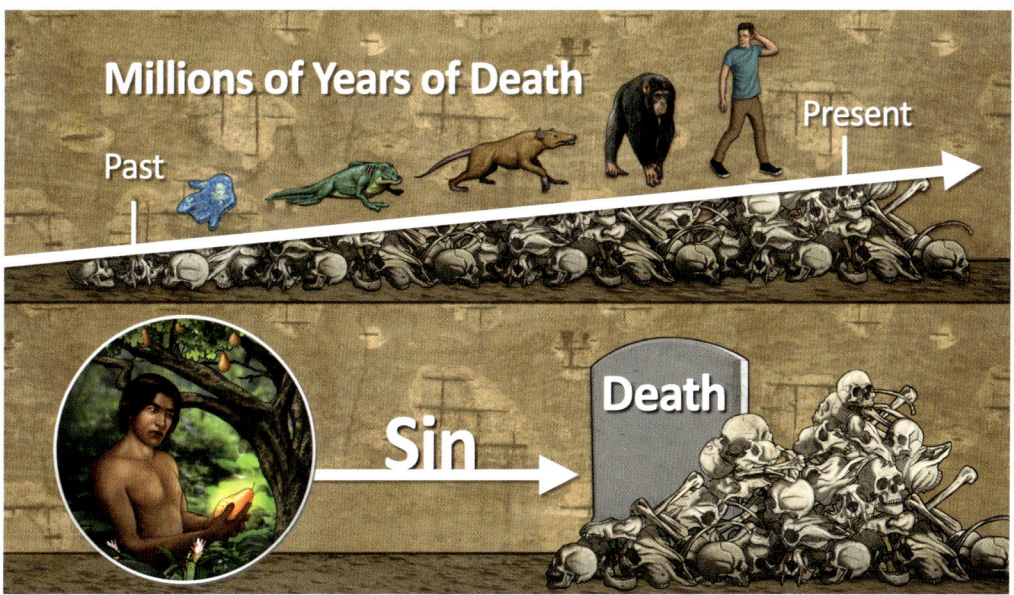

My father had always insisted the flood was a global event, even though he didn't understand the geological evidence to confirm it. He was adamant that the Bible taught that every high hill under the whole heaven was covered with water and that God promised, and said the rainbow after the flood would be a sign, that there would never again be another global flood. If the flood was just local, then God lied — there have been many local floods since Noah. As a child I remember him making points like this to church leadership who were distributing a devotional that taught Noah's flood was just a small, localized catastrophe (again, this is an attempt to fit millions of years into Genesis). As always, Dad approached it from a biblical authority perspective, but he'd never tied the flood in with the fossils. I was fascinated.

I finally had a few scientific answers, an explanation for the fossil record, and details about the assumptions being made when it came to the dating methods that supposedly give millions of years for earth's rocks. My journey of answers had begun.

A Book About the Flood

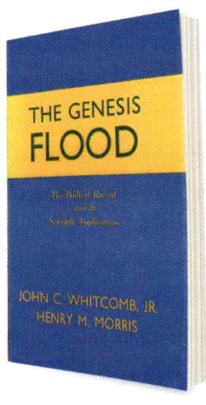

After I devoured the little booklet from England, Gordon told me, "There's a book produced in America, it's about the flood. You should try and get a copy of it. I've heard it's a really good book and really having an impact on people." The book he was referencing was *The Genesis Flood* by Dr. Henry Morris and Dr. John Whitcomb, the pioneering 1961 book that really sparked the modern-day creation movement. At the time, I didn't know what the book was called or who it was written by — I just knew there was a book on the Flood from America.

In downtown Brisbane, on an upper floor of an old-fashioned building, there was a Christian bookstore called The Gospel Book Depot. I decided to try to see if that small shop happened to have this resource I'd just learned about. I took the creaky old elevator up and went to the counter where a man came out to serve me. "Hi, someone told me there's a book about Noah's flood from America. I was wondering if you have it or if you've heard about it?" To my surprise he said, "I've got a copy of that book in the back." He disappeared and came back with *The Genesis Flood*. I bought it. And now I need to jump ahead from 1974 many years.

At one time in our ministry, we did an annual Australian tour with groups of Americans. During one such tour, we were in my college town of Brisbane, touring one of the animal parks where they did sheep shearing and had kangaroos, koalas, and other unique Aussie wildlife. Two ladies walked past, and one looked back, staring at me. After a moment, this elderly woman walked back to me. "I know who you are," she said. "You're Ken Ham. My late husband and I ran a Christian bookstore in Brisbane, The Gospel Book Depot."

"My husband," she shared, "had a real burden to have that book in our store. He couldn't explain it, he just knew he had to have a copy of that book available. It was for you — that's why God gave him that burden, He wanted you to get a copy of that book."

I thought, "Wow, you just never know what's going on behind the scenes." God is orchestrating things in ways we could never imagine, even down to giving a man a burden to order one specific book for his store, ensuring I heard about that book, and directing me to the right bookstore to obtain the book!

And this wasn't the only time God intervened in my life to get me on the path to where I am today. But before I get to that, let me say something important in relation to *The Genesis Flood* book. First of all, a caveat. I have met many people around the world who said *The Genesis Flood* saved them from the effects of the liberal college they were attending or helped them overcome the teaching of a compromising college professor. It's been said *The Genesis Flood* really started the modern creationist movement that has spread around the world and spawned many different creationist organizations.

The Genesis Flood and the important little booklet Gordon Jones gave me certainly helped me in giving additional biblical and scientific arguments confirming the global flood of Noah's day. But I do want to make it clear: it wasn't either of those books which directed me to believe in a global flood. It was the teaching of my father concerning the authority of God's Word and taking Genesis as it should be taken, as literal history, which gave me the foundation to believe in a global flood.

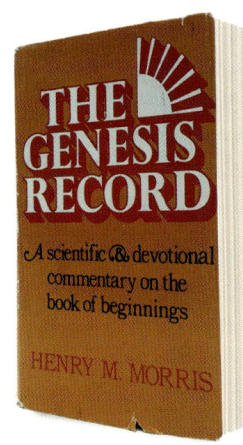

The "fire in my bones" to do something in regard to proclaiming the truth of God's Word beginning in Genesis was really the result of my parent's example of boldly and uncompromisingly standing on Scripture and their burden for the lost.

Now *The Genesis Flood* was certainly an important tool the Lord brought into my hands. That book introduced me to Dr. Morris and Dr. Whitcomb and also eventually led me to search out a copy of another of Dr. Morris' books, *The Genesis Record.* In a way, this second book had a greater influence on me than *The Genesis Flood* as it dealt with the same biblical authority issues concerning the relevance of Genesis that my father taught me.

Now back to the Lord's intervention in my life.

The Lord Directs My Steps

While I was in the early years of my science degree, I had a severe case of acne. And I don't just mean it was embarrassing or painful. It was so bad the bacteria entered my bloodstream, and I was hospitalized with sepsis. The doctors told my parents it was very serious. My mother told me later that she was so sure that God had a special plan for my life, to proclaim God's Word, that she believed I would recover — and I did. My mother was a prayer warrior. Although she trusted God to look after me, she also prayed day and night. I miss so much her telling me every time I called her over the years how she was praying for me and all her family members, even at night when she would wake up, she would pray fervently.

When I was able to leave the hospital, I headed back to where my parents were, far in the interior of Queensland's Outback in Mount Isa, a copper and zinc mining community (one of the world's largest mining complexes). For six months I worked in the warehouse for one of the mines doing jobs that were not too strenuous so I could regain my strength. I struggled with whether to go back to University and start my first year all over again to finish my degree, but I felt the Lord burdening me to do so. My father managed to get a transfer to Brisbane because of my health situation, so we all moved from the dusty desert interior to the sunshiny coast, and I started again on my degree.

I struggled with some of my classes due to the heavy evolutionary content. I was just so sick of hearing naturalistic processes of time and chance receiving the credit for God's incredible handiwork. It was so secular and atheistic, and I struggled to continue those courses, so I applied for a science job in a laboratory associated with the meat industry. I was interviewed and it came down to me and one other applicant — and that other person got the job. Looking back, if I'd gotten that job, I probably wouldn't be where I am today. God was in control directing my life!

God made sure I went back and finished my degree so I would become a teacher, and He made sure I didn't get what looked like a great job at the time. Looking back at my life, I almost feel like I had no choice in what I would do — God chose me for this ministry, and He made sure I did it! In our early years of marriage, I would tell my wife, Mally, "God's got something for me to do, I just don't know what it is yet. Maybe I'm supposed to go to Bible college or something, I don't know, but there's something I'm supposed to do!" God would later reveal what that something was, but I've always felt like God designed my life for me. And I believe that's true for all of us because God is sovereign over all our lives. And He was divinely guiding me down a path I never would've imagined.

Who was Noah? exhibit in the Ark Encounter.

At the Ark Encounter attraction, on the second deck of the life-size Noah's Ark, there is an exhibit entitled, "Who Was Noah?" This exhibit uses artistic license to suggest that maybe Noah was already a ship builder before God called him to build the ark. After all, when God called Noah to build the ark, nothing is recorded that suggests Noah didn't know how to do it. The exhibit goes on to teach that just as God prepared Noah for his future ministry in building the ark and being a preacher of righteousness, God prepares us through various circumstances for what He has called us to do.

Guests are then challenged concerning what God has called each of them to do. Looking back, I can see how God was preparing me and directing my paths for the enormous task He called me to do — even though at the time I did not know what this would all lead to.

Finding More Answers

After I devoured *The Genesis Flood,* I showed it to my father. He was thrilled to find the scientific answers he'd never had. I wondered if more such books existed and began searching, eventually discovering *Creation or Evolution?* a book by Professor Hannington Enoch, a zoology professor in India; *Chemical Evolution: An Examination of Current Ideas* by Professor S.E. Aw, a biochemist at the University of Singapore; and, eventually, *The Genesis Record*, another book by Dr. Morris. This last book took me even deeper into the theological relevance and foundational importance of Genesis, laying the groundwork for what would become my "relevance of Genesis talk," the backbone of the Answers in Genesis ministry, and the same basic talk I've been giving around the world for 50 years. It's also the basic message of my first book, *The Lie,* published in 1987 (updated and re-released in 2012 and then given a major update again in 2024).

> *I* had this fire in my bones for the truth of God's word and to get answers to combat the secular humanism that was starting to consume the culture. I randomly had a friend hand me a book that had answers and aligned with scripture. Then he told me about a book on the Flood out of America, he did not even know the name. I went to the Book Depot, and the owner felt the Lord leading him to stock such a book From America. One would have to say this is all *Miraculous!*

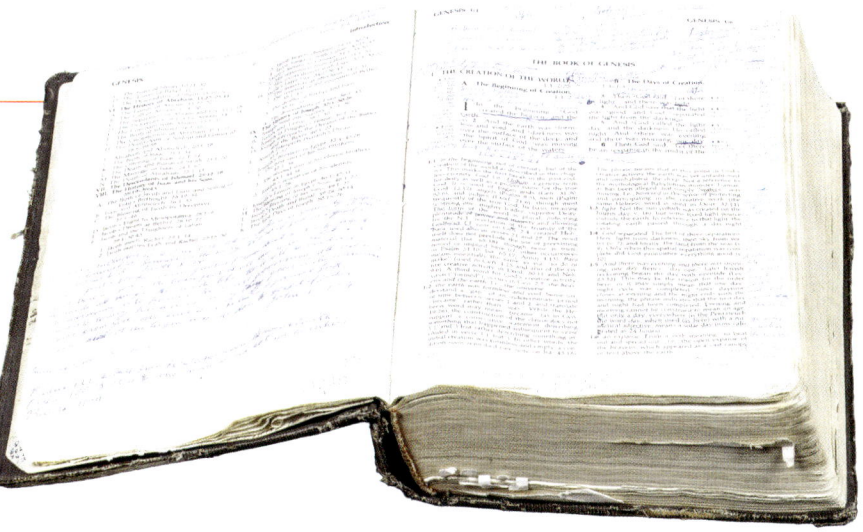

My father's Bible in the Legacy Exhibit on loan from my brother David.

> If I say, "I will not mention him,
> or speak any more in his name,"
> there is in my heart as it were a burning fire shut up in my bones,
> and I am weary with holding it in,
> and I cannot (Jeremiah 20:9 ESV).

"The family is actually the educational unit God uses to transfer a spiritual legacy to the next generation and to impact the world for the Lord Jesus Christ." *Ken Ham Daily*, p. 194

This was the start of my creation library in the 1970s. Today, AiG offers numerous resources to share the truth of God's Word with families and ministries around the world.

CENTRAL RAILWAY

This early photo of the Central Train Station in Brisbane is a reminder that trains in Australian cities have been an important part of public transport in people's daily lives. Trains played an important role in Ken and Mally's dating life.

1971 – 1979

3 | MALLY and MINISTRY

Mally at 6 months

Mally as a young child

Mally on the beach

"WOULD YOU LIKE ONE?"

After my family moved from Mount Isa to Brisbane, it was time to find a church home. My father picked Sunnybank Methodist Church, a small congregation in the Sunnybank suburb of Brisbane. That first Sunday morning as I walked up the steps, a shy young lady wearing a sash offered me a hymnal. This young lady was Miss Sunnybank Methodist — otherwise known as Mally — the winner of the local church pageant.

Everyone's heard the phrase "love at first sight," but I believe it really was for us. We both sensed something special when our eyes first met and, years later, Mally told me that she instantly thought, *"I really want to get to know him. I wonder what he's like."*

God brought us together for this ministry and we both just had an inner thought that something more than we could understand was about to happen. We had no idea of what God had planned.

Mally was well-known in the church for her selfless heart and love for the Lord. We weren't attending the church very long before my sister Rosemary and I were asked to serve as lay leaders in the church youth group. To my delight, Rosemary immediately nominated Mally (much to her shock and fear as she was very shy) to join us, she was immediately approved, and we began spending time together.

Myself, and Mally wearing the Sunnybank Pagent sash.

Mally with my Mum and Dad

Mally

WHAT'S IN A NAME?

Although everyone — myself included — calls my wife Mally, that's actually just a nickname, given to her by her mother when she was around 7 years old. Her real name is Marylyn, named after her mother, Mary. "Marilyn" was a popular name at the time, so she was named "Marylyn" with two y's instead of an "i" and a "y." "Marylyn" became "Mally" when she started attending school. Other children called their mothers "Mum" and Mally copied them, switching from "Mummy" to "Mum." So, her mother responded with, "If you're going to shorten my name to Mum, I'm going to shorten yours to Mally" — and it stuck! Most of our friends and acquaintances are shocked when they hear her real name is Marylyn as they've never heard her called that by anyone. The only person who really continued using Marylyn was her father (who was very formal in his approach) who didn't like calling her Mally.

While most people know me as Ken, you'll always hear Mally refer to me as Kenny. My mother, sisters, and brothers called me Kenny, my father sometimes called me Kenneth (my actual name), and everyone else called me Ken. When we came to America, as people heard Mally calling me Kenny, others started calling me that too. So now my close friends sometimes call me Kenny, but most people know me as Ken.

A RELATIONSHIP TAKES OFF

"In those early youth groups days, I began to think Kenny was flirting with me. We attended a barbecue together, Kenny driving his father's car and us girls in the back, and he began addressing me like he was a pilot, 'And we've reached cruising altitude at 20,000 feet. I'm your pilot, Captain Kenneth Ham, and, Ms. Stewardess, what's your name?' Later, I heard him play piano for the first time. He was really good and had a silly way of playing that made me laugh. Between his jokes and piano skills — he had my full attention." —*Mally*

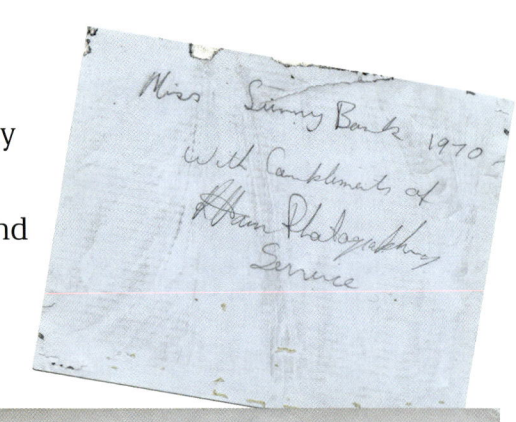

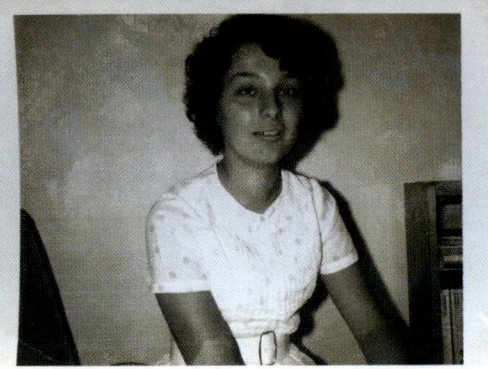

During our first youth leaders meeting, on a rainy day when my hair was as curly as anything, Kenny pulled out his Polaroid camera and took this snap. I was so shy and wondered why he was taking my photo — then he wrote on the back — Miss Sunnybank with compliments of Ham Photography Service — and gave it to me. I kept it all these years.

Early each morning I took the train into town to attend my classes at the university. Suddenly Mally decided she was really dedicated to her job at ANZ Bank, just over the river in South Brisbane, and needed to get there early via the early morning train — the same one I would catch. Bright and early that morning she hopped on the train and two stops later, I climbed in with my sister, Rosemary, who needed to go to town that day too. We saw Mally, chatted for a bit and got off. A few days later I met her again on the train, we chatted for the 30-minute commute and planned to ride the train together the next morning. But in the days before cell phones, how was I to know which train car she'd be in? She told me when the train came to my stop, she'd hold open the door and I'd know what car to jump into. There were no electric trains with automatic opening doors in those days.

Each morning, the train would pull into the station where I was waiting, and I would see a door open, and there she was! We'd chat on the train ride, and when we arrived at the train station at South Brisbane where we both got off, we'd walk together to the bank where Mally worked. I would then go over the bridge to walk to the university. Eventually we'd sit at the park next door and keep talking. I'd stay until the last possible second and then rush off, running all the way to the university to avoid being late.

Our romance was slowly blossoming on these train rides, even though we'd never even been on a proper date. And apparently it was obvious to the other daily commuters that we were falling for each other. One morning the early train broke down and everyone from that train had to ride a later train, packing every car with people standing in the aisles. Mally had a seat, but the train was filled with double the normal occupants and there were no other seats and hardly any room to move. Determined to make sure I could still find her; she climbed over and around the seats and pushed through the crowds of people to open the door as they came into the station. I saw her and hopped in. We noticed the crowds parted for us to go back to Mally's seat together, and someone had stood up to make sure there were two seats for us. Then everyone clapped as we sat down. Apparently, our daily visits hadn't gone unnoticed!

One of Ken and Mally's favorite train rides to Kuranda from Cairns in North Queensland

After spending time together leading the youth group and riding the train each morning, we finally went out on a real date, a double date to a drive-in movie. Actually, my sister Rosemary dared me to take her out! Now here I am wanting to impress this young lady by taking her to a movie — that's what you did in those days. I can't remember what the movie was, but at a drive-in theater, you park and then unhook the speaker from a post and clip it on the window of your car. At the end of the movie, I was so nervous, I put the car in gear (yes, we had manual cars in those days — no automatic transmissions for most vehicles), took off, and there was a loud bang. I had pulled the speaker out of the post. So, I backed up, placed the speaker back on the post and left! I'm sure many others had a similar experience at such drive-in theaters ... right?

Drive-in Theater

Mally and I also started a singing group, Faith Proclaimers (I'm sure you've heard of us — not!), that performed at various churches around Brisbane and country areas. Mally was an alto, her sister sang soprano, and my younger sisters and some other friends also joined. I played piano for the group and even composed a few songs for us to perform (I do still have an old cassette audio tape of our group). It was a joy getting to do various ministries alongside this sweet, shy young lady. And, yes, she was really shy. The first time I introduced Mally to my mother, she said to me later, "Does she talk?" My godly mother loved Mally and looked on her like another daughter. They had a wonderful relationship.

Faith Proclaimers, Mally, 2nd from left

This is the car Ken was driving when he proposed.

Visiting the marina where Ken proposed.

Manly Boat Marina at Brisbane, Queensland, Australia

WANT TO GET SEVEN ICE CREAMS?

On October 22, 1971, about ten months after we met, Mally and I drove to "the Manly mud flats," a giant expanse of mud when the tide is out, but a beautiful blue marina when the tide is in, to enjoy the sunset shining on the water (the tide was in!). While parked in front of the ocean, I asked Mally, "How about we get together and then we can get seven ice creams someday instead of just two?"

Now that proposal might leave you scratching your head a bit — it's not exactly a normal "Will you marry me?"! But Mally knew exactly what I meant. You see, when my mother was pregnant with my youngest brother (who is nearly 20 years younger than me), she told us kids the news by saying, "You know how, when we go to the ice cream shop, we ask for seven ice creams? Well, now we have to ask for eight!"

Strangely enough, we started out needing to ask for two ice creams and made it all the way to seven, just as I'd asked her all those years ago. The Lord gave us five beautiful children.

At that time, Mally's father was not a believer, and he didn't think anyone, let alone "a religious nut," was good enough for his darling daughter. Out of respect for him, we kept our engagement unofficial until he finally relented in March of 1972 and gave us his blessing. Then I bought her a ring. I was a student and didn't have much money so it was a tiny diamond — tiny! But she loved it. And much later in life, we bought a new ring with a bigger diamond (not too big), but she made sure this tiny diamond was part of the setting.

Then on December 30, 1972, on a sweltering Aussie summer day, we were married in a church with no air-conditioning. A marriage made in heaven? Definitely! God brought us together for a ministry that we had no thought of at that stage. It was what I call an "arranged marriage." God arranged it. It was as if He said, "You two are getting married and there's no option." That's the sovereignty bit! The human perspective is that we believed we were made for each other.

Before we were married, I would often tell Mally that I believe God has something special in store for me, but I didn't know what it was. I kept thinking about what my Nanna would say to me, that God was calling me to be a preacher. And, as I've stated, others through my younger years told me that God had something special in store for me. But what would it be? We had no clue.

Our wedding day!

MALLY'S TESTIMONY

While neither of my parents were Christians when I was a child, Mum packed us all off to Sunday school every Sunday morning at Sunnybank Methodist Church. One Easter morning, when I was around 11 years old, a guest speaker brought in a flannelgraph and shared the account of Christ's death and resurrection with the Sunday school class. When I realized what Christ did for me, I made a promise, "If you did that for me, I will go anywhere and do anything for you." The speaker asked any of us children who had prayed to come forward. I was incredibly shy and was very scared to go up, but I told the Lord if one other person went up, I'd go too — I just couldn't do it by myself. Well, the Lord must have wanted me to go forward because the whole class got up and went!

> "Faith is an indispensable element of the Christian life, important in all aspects of our belief and hope." *Divine Dilemma*, p. 108

Around the time when Kenny and I started dating, the Lord saved my mother at Sunnybank Methodist Church under the teaching of Pastor Rod Lippiatt. He was a great Bible teacher, and I am so thankful he led my mother to commit her life to Christ.

Years later, when Kenny and I moved to America, my dad was very unhappy about it. He'd already had a sister-in-law move across the world and he hated to lose me too, especially for Christian ministry. He said it was history repeating itself for a family member to move from Australia. But Kenny brought us back to Australia every year to see our families and, when

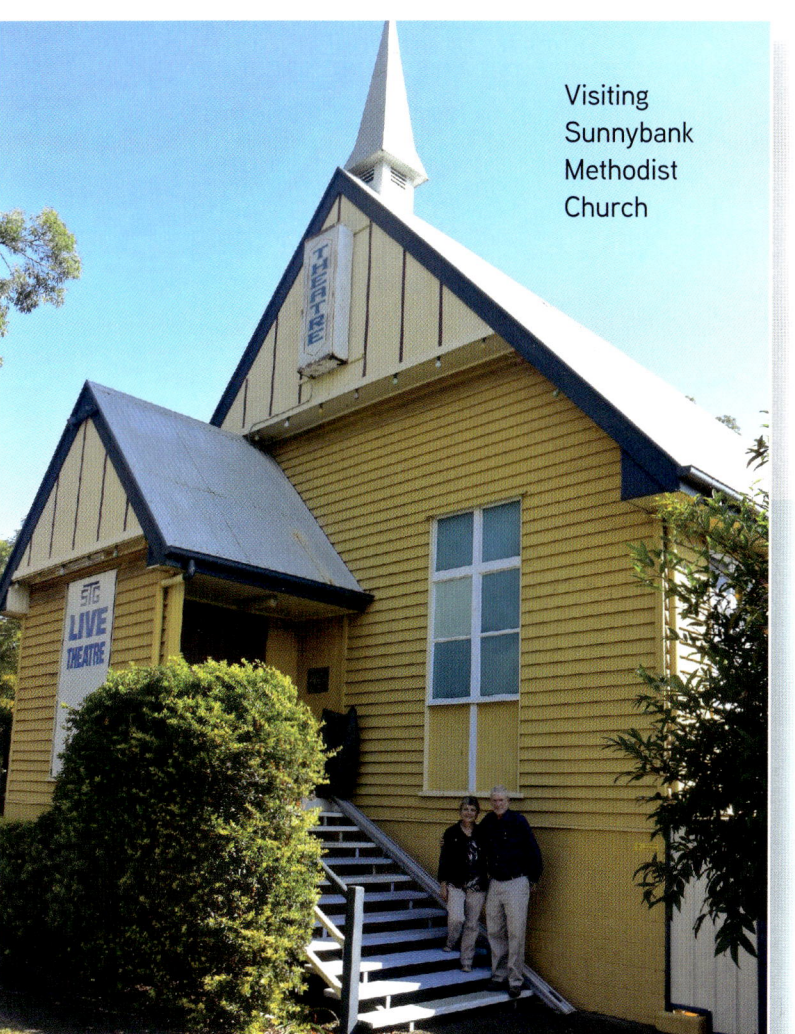

Visiting Sunnybank Methodist Church

Mally's Mum and Dad

Mally and Mum

Mally's Dad

Mum and Mally

Mally with her 3 siblings, Christine, Robert, Michelle, and her Mum and Dad.

Dad saw the way Kenny treated me by looking after me (I would say he looked after me like "gold dust," which means treating me as very precious), and ensuring I would come back to visit with family, it really meant a lot to him. My father wanted someone perfect for his daughter. It meant so much to me when one day Dad told Kenny he had totally accepted him and loved the way he looked after me. Knowing my father, it was something very, very special that he said that. Both my parents made the trek to America several times over the years. During one visit, we took Dad to Calvary Baptist Church in Covington, KY with us and, at the end of the service, after a powerful message from Pastor Charles Wagner that ended with a challenge to respond to the gospel and a prayer an unbeliever could pray to receive the free gift of salvation, Dad turned to me and said, "I prayed that prayer." … We praised the Lord for His kindness in saving my dad that day.

My father was not one to talk about spiritual matters — he was a very private man and kept everything "close to the vest," as we say in Australia — so this was a big deal, a miracle really.

—Mally Ham

THE DALBY YEARS

Ken and Mally standing in front of the Caravan that was parked beside Ken's parents' house.

As I was still a student with various education costs to pay for (even though I had a teaching scholarship), money was tight and, to save on rent, we moved into my parents' Caravan next to their driveway.

Mally continued working at the bank and I kept up with my studies and, eventually, we saved enough for a proper apartment. In 1973 I graduated with my science degree, and in 1974 I finished my diploma in education; I was ready for my first teaching appointment.

That appointment came in 1975 to the small town of Dalby, three hours west of Brisbane. Surrounded by various grain crops such as wheat and barley, cotton farms, and pastures, it's part of the Darling Downs area of Queensland. It is such a beautiful area, and we loved it.

We immediately found a church — Dalby Baptist Church. That welcoming community embraced us, and one special couple, Buster Jiggens (he passed away in 2024) and his wife Marian (she passed away in 2025) and their children really took us in as their own family. Some of our best, lifelong friends, including the pastor and his wife, were made during our time at that church. We thought we'd stay in Dalby for a very long time. Whenever we visit Australia, we always take a day to visit with our special

friends in Dalby. We meet for lunch and catch up on all the news. Our group has slowly decreased over the years as God has taken various people home to be with Him. But it's great to see the younger generations embracing us as friends. Yes, Dalby will always have a special place in our hearts.

I began teaching science at the local high school and immediately offered to lead the school's Christian group that met once a week during lunch. Some of my students saw my name listed as the leader for this group, so, assuming I must be a Christian, at the first science class I began to teach, challenged me. One of them said "Sir, we saw you're a Christian — how can you be a Christian when we know the Bible isn't true?" I asked why they thought the Bible wasn't true and they replied, "Well, because of what our textbooks teach us about evolution."

Another student piped up, "Noah couldn't get all those animals on the ark!"

"Well, how big was the ark?" I replied.
"I don't know."
"How many animals did he need?"
"I don't know."

These students "knew" the Bible couldn't be trusted but didn't really know what the Bible said or what answers were available for their objections. The "fire in my bones" intensified by degrees and I began developing tools to give these students answers and teach them how to think. I already had the books I'd found the year before, but I began to search for other books that dealt with the creation/evolution issue.

Ken standing in front of Dalby High School.

I would teach what was in their textbooks, including evolution, but I would show the difference between the observational evidence (e.g. fossils) and the interpretation of that evidence, showing them both the evolutionary and biblical creation interpretation. While I didn't use these words at the time, I was showing them the difference between observational and historical science.

Ken at Dalby High School

Observational science is directly testable, observable, and repeatable. It's this kind of science that builds technology and makes medical innovations — and, by and large, creationists and evolutionists agree on this kind of science.

Historical science is very different. This kind of science deals with the past by interpreting the observational evidence in the present. But because we weren't there, and we can't repeat the past, historical science is not directly testable, observable, or repeatable. So, the lens through which you view the evidence (creation or evolution; a young earth or millions of years) determines your interpretation. In a different way to how I do that today, I was teaching them all about the limitations of science in regard to origins. I also showed them how science confirmed the interpretation of the evidence based on a biblical worldview. The message, and the wording, has matured over the years but I was teaching these students how to think by drawing a comparison between fact and interpretation. These students would then go to their other classes and some of them would challenge the teachers who taught millions of years, asking how they knew these long ages were accurate. Those teachers would then come and get upset with me! But I wanted these young people to understand that no one was there in the supposed distant past, so it's an interpretation, not an observation. I still teach kids this today when I encourage them to ask, "Were you there?" when confronted with millions of years or evolution. No! None of us were there but we know the God who was there, and He has given us His Word with the perfect eyewitness account of history.

During one class I told the students about the Tower of Babel, that all humans trace their ancestry back to Noah, then back to Adam, so there's only one race, the human race. After class, three young ladies from the Aboriginal community began asking questions about Babel and the biblical truth that there's only one race. My teaching had struck a chord because the Aboriginals had suffered from others racist ideas.

All the evidence a scientist has exists only in the present.

In Charles Darwin's book *The Descent of Man*, published 12 years after *Origin of Species*, he wrote that the dark-skinned Australian Aboriginals were closer to our ape-like ancestors than lighter-skinned Europeans and were really "missing links" in our evolutionary family tree. Scientists were even commissioned to send people to Australia, to hunt Aboriginals, skin them like animals, boil their skulls, and ship the specimens back to museums. This legacy of racism had impacted these young ladies, and they were so hungry for the biblical truth of their ancestry from Adam, through Noah, and the event at Babel that created the different people groups as the human race was separated by language and, later, geography as they dispersed, eventually making it all the way Down Under. It meant so much to them to know all humans were really one family and all related to each other. I was gaining a reputation for being the "creation teacher."

The fire I felt just kept burning hotter. Not all the teachers appreciated this though! What I did wouldn't be tolerated today, but we had much more freedom back then.

> "I speak on the necessity of a Genesis that is understood in the way it was intended to be, as historical narrative teaching literal history." *Six Days*, p. 27

A "Romans 8:28" Event

I was collecting creation books ("every book under the sun" as Mally puts it) to equip myself with answers to the questions my students were bringing forward. And God gave me the opportunity to study these books in a rather unique "Romans 8:28 all-things-work-together-for-good" way. In those early teaching years, I owned a small motorcycle (a trail bike). Riding with a friend one day, I slowed down to take a corner, skidded in the gravel, and my bike toppled, twisting and snapping both bones in my left leg. We were out in the country, and the people who owned the nearest farm (Bev and Esther Skerman and family) actually attended our church and they became lifelong friends too. They brought their Ute (like a pick-up truck) and took me to the hospital.

Those were different days. The local GP came to the hospital, and I remember him standing at the end of my bed and lining my leg up so the nurse could start putting the plaster of paris around my entire leg. I just hoped my leg was on straight!

> And we know that for those who love God all things work together for good, for those who are called according to his purpose. (Romans 8:28 ESV).

My first teaching appointment at Dalby High School – I broke my leg in a motorcycle accident – I am here pictured with all the teachers at the school for that year.

At the time we had what was called a "panel van," which was a car with a front seat and the rest was open. We had a company fit out the back to have a bed and allow us to put up a tent we could back up to. This was so we could go camping.

Well, now we had a problem. Mally didn't have a license to drive. She had never driven a car. I had tried to teach her, but it didn't go well. She said I didn't have any patience and certainly not the patience of Job, she claimed. Well, the Lord solved that problem! My broken leg meant now someone else had to teach her to drive so she could get her license.

First, we found Mally was too short to see over the hood in the panel van we had. So, we had to trade that in and buy a smaller car. It was made by Holden and called a Torana. And it had a "stick shift" (manual transmission). Our dear friend Buster volunteered to teach her to drive. And he did! She obtained her license in this country town, which meant she had to show she could drive around the block and stop at a stop sign.

As I was laid up with a broken leg, I was able to read and study my creation books more deeply to make sure I had answers for the students. So, God used this event to help me get educated on the creation/evolution issue as I needed to be.

At this stage, Mally thought I had gone crazy over the creation/evolution issue. She saw a change come over me and she didn't understand it at that time. She now says with a laugh, "I thought you were bonkers." She remembers one time driving me from Dalby to Brisbane, stopping in the town of Toowoomba at a bookshop where I asked her to buy me "a creation book." She said she had no idea what she was doing and went in and bought a book that looked like it had something to do with creation.

She said she first began to notice a big change in me in 1974 with that first little book (we call it the "yellow book") that I was given that detailed how there can't be death before sin. She noticed that for me, after reading that book, it was like a light bulb going off and suddenly I began to see things in a way I hadn't understood before. Mally did a commercial course at high school, which meant typing, shorthand, and bookkeeping. She left high school at grade ten to work in the bank and eventually became a teller. She said she didn't understand science and so didn't understand all the issues as I talked with her. But she certainly understood the biblical issue of no death until after sin.

Mally watched me become increasingly consumed by this issue and realized it was becoming a real passion.

God was preparing me for a new chapter in our lives. Our Dalby church had a "youth exchange" program where young people from country churches would go into the city and lead a service, and young people from that city church would come to the country and lead a service. I was asked by the pastor to lead the youth exchange in 1975. This involved me having to give the sermon. Because of the fire in my bones the Lord was intensifying, and the fact that many people in the church had students at the school being taught evolution, you can guess what I decided to speak on.

Of course I picked my favorite topic: creation and evolution, toppling the "icons of evolution" like the horse evolution sequence, so-called missing links, and ape-men. So, it was in our little Baptist church in Dalby in 1975 that I gave my first-ever creation talk before heading for Brisbane with the youth to give it again at a city church. People told me how fascinated they were with my sermon; I received enthusiastic responses.

> Because of the fire in my bones the Lord was intensifying, and the fact that many people in the church had students at the school being taught evolution, you can guess what I decided to speak on.

As I gave the same sermon in Brisbane at Petrie Terrace Baptist Church, I couldn't help but notice one man who sat, listening intently, with a huge smile on his face. After the service he shook my hand and exclaimed that he loved my talk, not only because of the scientific evidence I presented, but because of my emphasis on biblical authority. Steve Gustafson (an attorney) made a huge impression on me, greatly encouraging me after this talk. Several years later, in 1977, he would help us draw up the legal papers for our creation ministry, and would become one of its main board members. Isn't it amazing how God providentially ordains us to meet those He wants to use for His service?

After this first talk of mine, I was invited to speak at several other Brisbane churches, and I would always hear the same comments afterward, "We've never heard any of this before!" Some believers even told me, "I thought I had to believe evolution — I didn't know I could believe Genesis!" I was so burdened with a "Nehemiah anger": why isn't someone doing something about this lack of knowledge?

Steve Gustafson

Ken teaching

During this time, I would take my students on field trips to natural history museums. They were always filled with evolutionary content, taking God's incredible creation and using it to indoctrinate students against the truth of God's Word. Just as a point of interest, one of the places I would take students on excursions was called the Beerwah Reptile Park. It was just a small park. The man that ran it was the father of Steve Irwin, who became famous and known as "the Crocodile Hunter" with a popular TV program. That small park turned into the Australia Zoo, located in Beerwah, Queensland (north of the city of Brisbane).

As I visited museums and saw all the evolutionary signs, the "Nehemiah anger" welled within me and I wondered why we couldn't have a museum like this that taught creation, giving glory to God, instead of evolution. My burden for a creation museum actually began in 1975–76 but God wouldn't grant my desire until 2007 and on an entirely different continent — but I'm getting ahead of myself. We had a much smaller move before God directed us to uproot completely and move across the world! But all along the way God was using people and circumstances to fuel a fire in my bones that has never been quenched.

Before I close the Dalby chapter of our lives, I want to point out that God used those humble beginnings, teaching in a country school, not only to increase the "fire in my bones," but to bring some of my students to Himself. Over the decades, I've met at least three of my former students, all of whom became Christians later in life and pointed back to those days in my science classroom and the answers they were given. Wow, praise the Lord!

Well, we had intended to stay in Dalby a long time, but one Sunday morning Mally and I were sitting in the car outside the church waiting for the doors to be open. Those that know me won't be surprised to learn we were early — I always try to be early for any

> "It has been a subtle switch of religions in the school systems, secular media, and secular museums — from a Christian worldview to a secular humanistic religion."
> *Gospel Reset,* p. 121

engagement, as my father was like that. The joke at our ministry is that I get to the airport three days ahead of my flight! There are times when Mally and I are sitting in church and she says to me, "I'm glad we got here early or we wouldn't have a seat," as we look at the empty auditorium. Anyhow, as we were sitting in the car, we looked at each other and said, "We aren't meant to stay here anymore." I can't explain it, but it happened. Somehow, at the same time, we both had the same burden — we are meant to move somewhere else. That thought was very emotional for us as we had made such wonderful friends — some of the best friends ever in our whole lives. We didn't want to move away from them. But we knew we had to be obedient to how God was directing us regardless of our own personal desires. As my mother taught me, "Always put God first, others second, yourself last."

Ken and his Dad at Kelceda St., Sunnybank Hills — Ken had just started the creation ministry.

The Lord laid it on our hearts that we needed to go back to Brisbane, so I asked for and was granted a transfer to a school in the city, and we prepared to leave our dear friends for life back on the coast in the big city.

One of the last books I signed to my Mum before her passing.

Our first home in Brisbane.

A Ministry Is Born in Brisbane

Two weeks before our moving date, our first son, Nathan, was born (1976). Mally cared for him while family and friends helped us pack everything and move to Brisbane. We moved in with my parents until we could find a house — they had a room under the house that gave us some independence. Our Brisbane home, just down the street from my parents, was a small three-bedroom ranch home with a tiny kitchen. It was quite small, and we were aghast when we found out it would cost $19,000 — and we had to borrow most of that from the bank. It had a very small patio out front — little did I know that this patio would eventually become important, and, in a way, the birthplace of Answers in Genesis.

In Brisbane I taught science at three different high schools, teaching the required evolutionary content in the textbooks but, as before, teaching the students how to think, the problems with evolution, and the biblical creation interpretation of the evidence. I first taught at Brisbane's prestigious Brisbane State High School. I asked for a transfer after the first year to a school in the suburbs, Acacia Ridge State High School, where kids from our church attended.

Now at this time, I was even more passionate to teach my students the truth about creation and the problems with evolution. The teacher in charge of all the science teachers, called the "Subject Master," heard that I was questioning evolution and teaching creation (though I still taught the kids what was in their textbooks so they would pass their exams) and became very upset. He asked the school inspectors to have me transferred to another school. Even in the 1970s I was facing discrimination for what I believed and for simply encouraging students to think critically about what they were learning. I found the students loved the way I taught and loved to hear about creation and the problems with evolution.

However, regardless of how good you are as a teacher, or how positively the students respond to a teacher, when the authorities didn't like the worldview I was teaching, they wanted me out of there. So, I received a transfer to another high school, Salisbury State High School. Coincidentally, the principal of this high school was a well-known Christian. So, I'm sure that had something to do with why they sent me there!

While in Dalby, a missionary with a ministry called Scripture Union that sent workers to speak in schools, learned of my passion concerning the creation/evolution issue. She then told me about a high school teacher at Brisbane Boys Grammar School who had a similar passion. His name was John Mackay, so I attempted to contact him.

At some stage we made contact and agreed to get together.

John had a degree in geology whereas my degree is in biology. So together we launched the first-ever Australian creation apologetics conference at a church in Brisbane in 1977. I can't remember all the details, but I think 100–200 attended. At that time, we focused mainly on science, giving believers answers regarding the age of the earth, fossils, and the flood, although I also taught a section on the issue of no death before sin. This will begin to explain why in most of my presentations I make sure I have a section dealing with no death, disease, or thorns before sin.

Now I always say that if I heard myself giving those first talks now, I'd never hire me to work at Answers in Genesis! But it was a start and God would, over time, mature the message into what it is today. It was a pioneering ministry in Australia for the creation apologetics message.

John Mackay

I brought the creation library I'd built in Dalby with me, displaying the few books I had such as *The Genesis Record, Bone of Contention,* and *The Genesis Flood* on a table in the back. Conference attendees flipped through the books, "How can we get these books? We need these books!" people would say. But I only had one copy of each, and they were rather hard to come by. And, again, that "Nehemiah anger" flared up, "Why isn't somebody doing something about this need?" True to my nature, and that of my father before me, I decided I better do something about it, since no one else was!

I talked with Mally about starting a bookstore to make these books, and others we could find, easily available. She didn't blink an eye. To her, if that's what God was calling me to do, she would totally support it. She didn't know what would happen when boxes of books from overseas eventually piled up in our living room, bringing cockroaches into the house! (It's just as well we didn't know all that.)

I knew a Presbyterian minister (Guido Ketnis) who had a Christian bookstore in his house, and I said to Mally, "If he can do that, why can't we?" Yes, God uses all sorts of circumstances in our lives to direct us.

I had also heard about Evangelistic Literature Enterprise (ELE), an organization that was located in Geebung, Brisbane, which imported a variety of Christian books to Australia from America. I made an appointment with them, explained that I wanted to be able to place creation materials in the hands of Christians, and they agreed to help us start this bookstore and import books into Australia. Sid Hunter (who is with the Lord now) was the leader of his organization, and he said he would help us in any way he could. He was so gracious and generous with his time and information. It's almost like God told him to do whatever he could do for us. God had all the right people in place.

Creation Science Supplies (CSS) was started as a partnership between me and John Mackay in 1977. I contacted Steve Gustafson (the attorney I met at the church in Brisbane in 1975), and he did all the legal work for us for free. Later

The early beginnings of a catalog.

Steve changed the organization from a partnership to a non-profit called Creation Science Foundation. And, of course, he became the first board member, other than John and myself.

The bookstore was called Creation Science Supplies, but we called our teaching ministry Creation Science Educational Media Services. A mouthful to say! But we were novices! I've learned a lot about branding and marketing over the years and cringe at things we did in those early days. But at the same time, God used all this to teach us and prepare us for the future. In essence, the embryonic beginning of the Answers in Genesis ministry began as a book ministry to get literature into people's hands and an associated teaching ministry.

Ever since those very early days, I have had a passion for resources, and Answers in Genesis has always had an emphasis on producing and distributing creation apologetics and biblical worldview resources for families and churches. I had to wait years for answers, and I didn't want others to have to wait. Many other believers were hungry for resources that

> "I pray you will be equipped to train up a generation that will stand on God's Word with boldness and will not be intimidated by the secularist giants that come against them." *Will They Stand?*, p. 15

> "My people are destroyed for lack of knowledge" (Hosea 4:6).

simply weren't available to them, and seeing that lit a fire in me to ensure everyone had access to answers. I've often tied that passion to this verse, "My people are destroyed for lack of knowledge" (Hosea 4:6). The fire in my bones continued to grow.

Now we had a problem. We needed a little bookstore to store the books ELE was importing for us, so we stepped out in faith, obtained a construction loan, and my brother-in-law, Paul Whincop (who is a builder), filled in our little patio, turning it into a room we could sell books out of. The existence of our little bookstore began to spread by word of mouth in churches. Also, John and I were asked to give talks in churches, Bible studies, and Sunday schools, so people began to find out about these now available books.

God blessed Creation Science Supplies, and the small number of books we had begun to sell. People were so excited to have answers. I remember many people being amazed at the answers that were now available in these books, and they wanted to help us in any way they could. God was preparing people for the time He would burden them to support us financially to be full time in the ministry — which happened in October 1979.

No Isn't an Option

Many of the resources we were seeking to offer through CSS were published by the same group: Master Books out of San Diego, California. ELE couldn't get those books for us, as Master Books had an exclusive arrangement with one specific Aussie company, S. John Bacon. But S. John Bacon only had a handful of copies of each book we needed — that wasn't going to work! Harold Slusher, an American physicist from the Institute for Creation Research (ICR), was coming to speak in three of our larger cities, Sydney, Melbourne, and Adelaide, and we needed to have resources available to sell after his talks. Again, I contacted Master Books and again I was turned away due to their exclusive contract with S. John Bacon. "It's hopeless," I thought, "I won't be able to get these books since S. John Bacon doesn't have them!" I pleaded with the Lord to enable us to get these books as ICR, founded by *The Genesis Flood* co-author Dr. Henry Morris, was known as the leading creationist organization in the world.

Well as I always say, responsibility and sovereignty always go hand-in-hand.

I wasn't ready to give up (I don't take no for an answer — there's always a solution). I had a copy of a publication called *Creation Research Quarterly*, a scholarly journal produced by young earth creation scientists in America. The journal listed many of these scientists, none of whom I knew. But I went to the post office and began sending large numbers of telegrams (yes, telegrams — this was long before email!) overseas to each and every scientist listed in that journal, begging them to please contact Master Books for us and ask them to sell us these much-needed books.

Not long after my bulk telegrams, George Hillstead, the then manager of Master Books, called me, "Mr. Ham, I am getting phone calls from all these people who received telegrams from you. What is going on?" I said, "We need your books! The agency you work with has no real inventory of creation materials, there's a speaker from ICR coming over to deliver some lectures, and we need resources!"

Years later I found out that I'd caused quite the commotion at the publisher — one of Master Books shareholders and board members Dan Manthei, heard about my telegrams and told George, "Oh for goodness' sake, George, let the kids get the books." If you knew Dan, that's how he would speak.

Dan, also a board member at ICR, would eventually become one of Answers in Genesis' founding board members and a dear personal friend until his passing in 2023. I was privileged to be asked to speak at his funeral. We miss him and the wisdom he brought to our ministry so much.

Well, George agreed to give us one order. I considered how many books were likely to sell during the tour, which titles people would most need or want, and I added up our order: $20,000 U.S. dollars. Now the exchange rate in those days was in Australia's favor, and what we found was the exchange gave us enough money to cover the freight cost. This meant we only (ONLY!!!) needed $20,000. That's a lot of money today — but that was an enormous amount of money for a schoolteacher in 1978. Where was that going to come from? Mally and I only had two hundred dollars in the bank and that was needed for daily living expenses. But this is where divine sovereignty and human responsibility come together.

Looking back, I can hardly believe we did it, but we stepped out in faith, and after prayer, placed an order for $20,000 worth of books. We really didn't know where the money would come from. We began calling and writing

> "It only takes one generation to lose a culture. The change in the culture is devastating and catastrophic from a Christian perspective."
> *Divided Nation,* p. 9

letters to friends and family, sharing the vision for these books, and asking for donations or loans. And people generously gave donations or interest free loans. No one even drew up paperwork, they simply trusted that we would repay the loans. And after the last donation had come in, and the bill was nearly due, we counted it all up: we had $17,000. It was an incredible miracle, but it was $3,000 shy of what we needed.

We prayed and pleaded with the Lord to somehow provide us with the rest of the money. I'm sure George Hillstead (who later became a close friend) would have been horrified to know we placed such an order with no money to pay for it! I just didn't tell him that piece of information. In fact, I look back and think, "What on earth made me order $20,000 worth of books with no money?!" Well, it had to be the gift of faith the Lord gives, and He empowered me to do it even though my human self would not normally do such a thing.

Mally and I sat out in front of the house, discussing the shortfall and praying for God to meet the need. It was the first of many what I now call "Red Sea moments" in the history of this ministry. You'll see many of them throughout this book. When the Israelites reached the Red Sea, they had the Egyptian army behind them and the expanse of the sea before them — they couldn't go back, and they couldn't go forward. There was only one answer: God must act on their behalf (and He did — by miraculously dividing the Red Sea so the Israelites passed through on dry land and then drowning the enemy army). Throughout my five decades in ministry, we've faced many such moments and each time they seem to get bigger. This was the first. And God delivered us.

As we sat praying about that $3,000 a car pulled up and a man we had met at a local church I spoke at got out of his car and walked up to us, saying, "My wife and I really want to help you guys get this ministry to Australia going and get these books into the country. It's just so important, so here's a check for your ministry." The check was for exactly $3,000. We were overjoyed that God had His hand in this situation and was blessing our step of faith. To this day I can still see that car pulling up and that man walking up to hand us the check.

> "God's Word is attacked in so many ways, and our kids need to be trained to stand firm on God's Word." *Divided Nation,* p. 125

But now we had another problem: we had the books, bought and paid for. But how would we drive them from Brisbane nearly 10 hours to the first of Dr. Slusher's lectures in the city of Sydney in New South Wales, then another 7 hours down to Melbourne in Victoria, then 8 more hours over to Adelaide in South Australia, and then 21 hours back home? I was discussing this need with someone at church when another man walked up, "Hey, Ken, I've got a truck you can borrow."

> **Red Sea Moment**
>
> "My wife and I really want to help you guys get this ministry to Australia going and get these books into the country. It's just so important, so here's a check for your ministry." The check was for exactly $3,000.

So, we loaded that truck to the brim with boxes of books and followed Dr. Slusher on his speaking route, selling resources at every church. By the time we left Adelaide for the long trek home, the truck was empty. We'd sold everything!

When I reached home, I called George at Master Books with the news, "We've sold it all!" He was in shock. Master Books then decided to break with the exclusive agency of S. John Bacon to give us the freedom to import as many books as we needed. We had paid Master Books using the money given and loaned to us, and now were able to use money from the book sales to pay back the loans from family and friends and use profit from the sales to order our next lot of books. After all the enthusiasm for resources I'd seen, I knew we needed to always have books available after a talk. After all, most people might remember a small percentage of what a speaker says; they need literature and resources to take home with them to ensure they can root what they've learned deep in their heart and share it with others.

Nathan was three and Renee was just a few months old.

Another Step of Faith

As the 1970s were drawing to a close, I was invited by more and more churches to present on creation apologetics. I would wrap up teaching at the high school Friday afternoon. Mally, my accountant and order-fulfiller, would have the books packed for me. I'd drive overnight to Sydney or even Melbourne, give talks on Saturday and Sunday morning, then drive home, ready to teach again Monday morning.

Looking back, I don't know how we did it — and with two young kids at the time (two more came after this and then God gave us our American daughter in 1988). But Mally never complained; she never has through all these years of ministry. She has always supported me 100% and done everything she can to ensure people hear the message and obtain resources. I've always said this ministry wouldn't be what it is today if it wasn't for Mally and her many (many!) sacrifices behind-the-scenes. Years after these events, she shared with me her own insecurities she had at the time but hid from me so I wouldn't be distracted from the ministry God called us to.

Creation Science Supplies, and my speaking schedule, was becoming all-consuming. Our bookstore soon outgrew the little patio room, overflowing into the living room, the bedroom, the kitchen — everywhere was filled with books. And all those boxes of books attracted more than just Christians hungry for answers, they brought in cockroaches. Mally wasn't thrilled about that (to put it mildly) but, again, she never complained. I don't know how she did it, allowing the house to become laden with boxes of books in almost every room.

A very early book table in Australia.

CSS wasn't just selling books at speaking events; we were shipping them across Australia as people had heard they could buy books from us.

The very first order we ever sent out warranted a phone call from the recipient when it reached its destination. She called me to inform us that, "I got the books, but you should know, just for the future, that the books arrived outside the package that you mailed them out in." Apparently when I filled the package with books, I didn't do it correctly and during shipping it burst open, all the books came out, and the post office had to tie them together. I realized I needed to talk to experts to learn how to ship books. And there is quite a science to it all.

With all of the traveling, speaking, and the growing number of book sales, we were faced with another step of faith: I couldn't continue teaching Monday–Friday and speaking every weekend. It was simply too much for our family. It was either one or the other. But the fire was burning in my bones — I couldn't not speak on this issue.

We knew that I needed to resign from teaching and go into full-time ministry if we really wanted to do this. It was a huge decision. We wrote letters to family and friends, asking, "If we enter full-time creation ministry, will you support us financially?" Many responded with, "Yes!" But, of course, there were no guarantees anyone would follow through and we had no idea to what extent they would support us. And, keep in mind, donations to churches and non-profits in Australia, have never been tax deductible. So, there was no tax deduction incentive like there is in America. People gave generously and sacrificially without a tax deduction. We prayed and went back and forth, back and forth, "Do we go from a job with a guaranteed salary to, well, having no idea what will happen?"

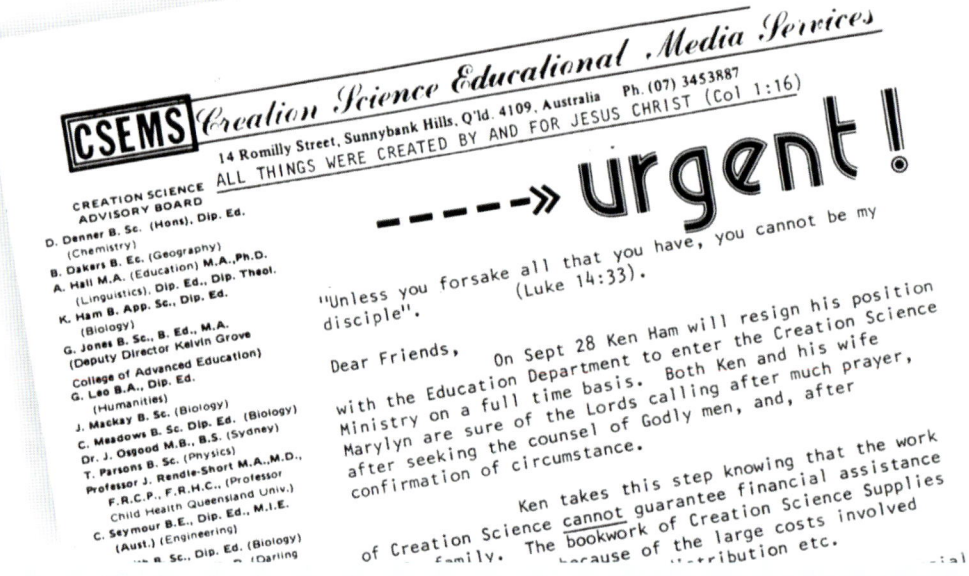

In April of 1979, Mally and I, and our family, along with John and Anne Mackay and their family, attended the Easter Convention at Kingswood, a convention center in the town of Warwick. We'd been asked to give some talks on creation and Genesis, so we took boxes of books with us to sell. Another speaker at the convention was Harry Mitten from New Tribes Mission (now called Ethnos360). During his talk, he suddenly stopped, looked at me and John and said, "You know the Lord is calling one of you to go full-time into this creation ministry. So, when are you going to obey the Lord and do this?"

I was shocked and this really burdened me. Mally and I talked about it all the way home. Later we realized it was all part of God guiding and directing us; part of His providential ways of steering us in the right direction.

Eventually, in October 1979, we decided to take the step of faith. I resigned from my position as a high school science teacher and prepared to enter full-time creation ministry.

Now that sounds simple, right? But there's a complex story behind all this, a story that reminds me that life is not always that simple, and with our own human struggles, and trusting God's sovereignty, it's not always a direct easy path. And sometimes I believe (and have experienced) God allowing obstacles in our way as a test of our faith.

As we were agonizing over whether I should resign from a secure job with steady income, we kept talking to each other and praying and seeking an answer from the Lord. In a way, I could say that we were 98% sure when we told the Lord we were willing for me to resign and go full-time. Yes, we were willing to do this, but there was that niggling 2% that we hadn't, in all honesty, committed to.

At this time, we decided to make the two-and-a-half-hour trip to Dalby to visit our friends. While we were traveling, Mally was reading Matthew chapter 6 out loud for both of us.

And then she came to these verses:

"Therefore I tell you, do not be anxious about your life, what you will eat or what you will drink, nor about your body, what you will put on. Is not life more than food, and the body more than clothing? Look at the birds of the air: they neither sow nor reap nor gather into barns, and yet your heavenly Father feeds them. Are you not of more value than they? And which of you by being anxious can add a single hour to his span of life? And why are you anxious about clothing? Consider the lilies of the field, how they grow: they neither toil nor spin, yet I tell you, even Solomon in all his glory was not arrayed like one of these. But if God so clothes the grass of the field, which today is alive and tomorrow is thrown into the oven, will he not much more clothe you, O you of little faith? Therefore do not be anxious, saying, 'What shall we eat?' or 'What shall we drink?' or 'What shall we wear?' For the Gentiles seek after all these things, and your heavenly Father knows that you need them all. But seek first the kingdom of God and his righteousness, and all these things will be added to you" (Matthew 6:25–33).

Red Sea Moment

Right then we knew God was speaking to us. We prayed and for the first time said, "Lord, we really mean it, one hundred percent, we are willing to do this." It was like a big load being lifted off our shoulders. We made the decision.

It was October, the middle of a teaching term. The school year was divided into four terms in those days. I went to the principal and said I wanted to resign, explaining why. He understood but said it wouldn't be fair to the students as they wouldn't have a teacher, and he didn't know how one could be found. I asked him to at least think about it and call the education department to see if there was a possibility of a replacement. They called him back and said they had just received a request from a science teacher to transfer to Salisbury State High School. The principal told me to go ahead and submit my resignation. I did and started putting things in place. I sent letters to various family and friends, telling them what we were doing and asking if they would help us financially. My parents said they would help us, others said they would do what they could.

Now not long after all this happened, the principal contacted me, "That teacher withdrew his request to take your place. Could you reverse your decision to resign?"

Mally and I were somewhat distraught over all this. Together, we went over all the steps we had gone through and the commitment we made to the Lord. We had seen the provision of that teacher as the Lord saying "yes" to my resignation. We both agreed that if the Lord had led us so clearly, it wouldn't be right for me to now reverse direction. We both believed it might be a test from the Lord to see if we were following Him and really ready to walk this path of faith. So, we decided to continue our plan to leave teaching, praying that God would provide a teacher for those students. And you know what? It wasn't long after that we heard from the principal that another teacher had applied to teach my former class and would be there for the students.

When I resigned, my retirement (superannuation) payout was about $3,000. With that, Mally and I purchased a plain paper copier, an electric typewriter, and other equipment. We needed this equipment to set up the ministry.

And people began to send us money, a little here and a little there. Some people gave us clothing. One family owned a fruit and vegetable shop. They started leaving a big box of fruit and vegetables on our front steps every week. They did this for a very long time. The Lord was providing for our needs, and that's all God promises to do: to provide our needs.

Mally (like myself) has never been interested in money or material things. To us it's all about putting God first in everything.

You see, as you read this very involved story, it's really a love story. It's a story about two people who love God with all their hearts, who love God's Word, who have a love for people to hear God's Word and the saving gospel, who love each other deeply, and who love to do all they can to help raise up younger generations who will stand boldly for the Lord.

My Faithful Helpmate

Although few people meet Mally at the Creation Museum or Ark Encounter, or during the meet-and-greets after I speak, this ministry is as much the fruit of her sacrifice and dedication as it is mine.

I've seen many men's ministries over the years be destroyed because the wife was not supportive and willing to make (sometimes very great) sacrifices. Mally certainly had plenty of reason to complain, but she never has. This ministry would not be here if it was not for her sacrifice and support — sacrifices most people will never know that she made.

She once told me that she was like Ruth, the young Moabite widow who made this promise to her beloved mother-in-law, "For where you go I will go, and where you lodge I will lodge. Your people shall be my people, and your God my God" (Ruth 1:16 ESV). And she has been like Ruth, totally supportive of the ministry, wanting to do what is right before the Lord. (And that's another part of the story I will tell later concerning the topic of Ruth. That verse had great bearing on our decision to leave family and friends and move to a totally different country.)

Not only has she sacrificed and supported me, but she also counsels me. She's the one who sometimes has to tell me, "No, Kenny, you can't do that. I feel the Lord would have us do this." Mally offers such wise counsel in both my life and in the lives of our grown children (and now grandchildren!).

Mally also never gets flustered (or at least never shows it). I'll never forget one time, when our kids were little, Renee, our eldest daughter, dropped a brick on our eldest child, Nathan's, thumb and squashed it. To me it looked just like a mashed piece of flesh with blood everywhere. I was freaking out, but Mally just calmly

began to clean it up, not flustered at all. Whenever I am stressed or freaking out over something happening in our lives or in the ministry, she lets me "go on" for a bit and then she calmly "walks me off the ledge." She has been more of a blessing to not only myself and our children and grandchildren, but to this ministry more than most will ever know. But God knows.

When I think of Mally I am reminded of this verse,

> "Her children rise up and call her blessed; her husband also, and he praises her" (Proverbs 31:28).

Had a chance encounter with a young shy lady at church. Then riding the train together for many months to school and work. Standing with me for over 30 years at Answers in Genesis. Now 50+ years of marriage made in heaven, I would call that Miraculous!

HAM BIRTHS!

Mally and I have unique stories about the birth of each of our kids. Some of these are quite humorous to look back on, but they weren't at the time. Here is Mally's take on things.

Nathan —born November 10, 1976, 8 lb 14 oz

Our eldest child was my longest labor, seven hours, and a forceps delivery because his head got stuck. After this rather forceful delivery, he had a great big hematoma on his head (a mass of clotted blood due to the blood vessels bursting from the trauma of the pressure on his head). It looked like a great big lump. Kenny reckons little Nathan had two heads—it looked that bad—but I just saw a little baby.

So what if he had a lump on the side of his head, I thought he was the most adorable thing ever. Because his eyes were swollen, when Kenny's youngest brother, Stephen (just a little child at the time) saw him, he asked, "Mum, is he Japanese?" (Actually, my great grandfather was Chinese, from Canton in China).

Renee —born February 22, 1978, 8 lb 2 oz

About 15 months after Nathan's birth, our daughter Renee was born. Kenny's uncle was in town and I was a week past my due date. Uncle Charlie teased me, "well, you better hurry up and have this baby!" That night I woke up around 4:00 am with really strong labor pains. I told Kenny, "something's going on!" We really didn't know what to do as childbirth books inform you the contractions will be erratic at first and then calm down. We were waiting for them to calm down, but it never happened; they just got closer and closer and stronger and stronger.

Well, then 15-month-old Nathan wakes up, and he's running around, crying and screaming in the lounge (living) room, I'm in labor and can't get off the couch. Kenny called for an ambulance, which took ages to arrive. Kenny and his mum kept popping outside to look for it when suddenly I realized the baby's head is being born. I yelled and Kenny came running (if he hadn't been fast enough, I would've had to deliver her myself—she wasn't waiting!). So Kenny delivered Renee. He had no idea what to do with that tiny baby but he'd seen doctors on movies hold a baby up and spank its bottom, so he did that! And she cried—so that worked.

It was now five in the morning (yes, this labor was only 45 minutes total!), and Kenny's mum recollected that one of her neighbors was a midwife. She came and delivered the placenta, asking if we had any shoelaces we could tie off the cord with. In my head I knew where they were, but it didn't connect with my mouth. I just couldn't seem to tell her where some were, so they used Kenny's old laces right out of his shoes! I thought, "oh my goodness, that is not exactly sterile." But it all worked out and the ambulance finally arrived and took us to the hospital where a doctor asked Kenny, "well, is baby a boy or a girl?" Kenny answered, "I don't know! I didn't check!" But I knew it was a girl; our first daughter.

Danielle — born September 14, 1982, 8 lb 1.5 oz

Our third child, our daughter Danielle, is four and a half years younger than Renee. My water broke early in the morning and Kenny immediately called for an ambulance and pleaded with them to come immediately. They whisked me off to the hospital. I got all settled in but I still wasn't in labor, nothing had started yet beyond my water breaking. But I warned the doctor that I'd had Renee in just 45 minutes.

We waited, the doctor waited, and nothing happened. Just as the doctor was leaving, I started having some back pain. Ten minutes later I was in full labor. The doctor had just arrived at his office, was informed I was in active labor, so he turned right around and came straight back. As he walked in the door Danielle arrived, barely giving him time to catch her. She too took only 45 minutes to be born. I started to realize I had this propensity to give birth very quickly. The doctor used the term "precipitous labor."

Jeremy — born September 29, 1984, 7 lb 11 oz

Almost exactly two years later our fourth child and second son, Jeremy, arrived. This time we scheduled an induction for September 30 to ensure I'd be at the hospital for this delivery. Well the day before my induction date was our niece's first birthday so I made some food and went to the party. Then I went grocery shopping, did the laundry, and cleaned the house in preparation for having a baby the next day.

At 8:30 that night I told Kenny I had a twinge in my back—not a labor pain or anything, just a twinge. He went "bonkers" on me, calling the doctor asking what to do, "she's got a twinge!," then calling the ambulance and telling them they didn't arrive in time for Renee so please hurry. I just wondered what was wrong with him—he was going crazy!

The ambulance arrived within a few minutes and Kenny was going on about how last time we didn't make it, please get a move on it, get us to the hospital ASAP. And I wasn't even in labor!

Suddenly I had my first labor pain, and we began timing them. But we only got to the third contraction—and it didn't stop! The only way to stop the pain was to push so I did. We had passed through the city and were going up a hill on the other side when the driver realized I was having the baby, pulled over under a tree, told Kenny to come and help, and opened the ambulance doors. And Jeremy was suddenly born. We could see the city lights below us, it was very pretty! So Jeremy was born underneath a Port Jackson fig tree with a lovely view of the city of Brisbane. Whenever we visit Brisbane, we stop at "Jeremy's tree." From the first labor pain, Jeremy took only 11 minutes! That was scary.

Fig Tree in Brisbane City Australia where Jeremy was born.

Kristel — born February 25, 1988, 8 lb 11 oz

On January 22, 1987 we moved from Australia to San Diego, California for Kenny to work with the Institute for Creation Research. A year later I was due with our fifth child. Kenny's parents were visiting and, of course, Kenny was traveling all over the place speaking and hosting conferences. One weekend, he was in Chicago speaking and his mum was staying with me. I was absolutely paranoid that the baby would come that weekend and only his mum would be there to help me—all I could remember was how both she and Kenny had panicked big time when I had Renee on the couch.

I thought, "Oh my goodness, my last baby arrived in just 11 minutes, I'm in a foreign country, and Kenny's parents are in town! Lord, please give me a sign for when I should leave for the hospital." That day we were supposed to go shopping at a local mall, but I felt strongly that I should go see my doctor, a Christian who was on the board at ICR. I took that as the Lord's direction and went. My doctor said I was ready to pop and sent me straight to the hospital, joining me after his office hours and starting an induction at 5:00. I remember him sitting in a rocking chair, calmly reading the newspaper after starting the induction. Well, the peace didn't last long! At 5:38 our California Girl, Kristel, was born. We called her Kristel Ruth—the name Ruth has special meaning as you will discover later in our story.

Kristel, Mally and Ken

1979 – 1986

4 | JOURNEY INTO FULL TIME MINISTRY

ORDAINED AND SET APART

We had stepped out in faith and gone full-time into ministry, commissioned by the laying on of hands during a special service at our Brisbane church home, Sunnybank Baptist Church. Gifts from friends and family, along with book sales at my speaking events, were paying our basic living expenses. But the ministry had needs — expensive needs, including the purchase of a new (to us), larger vehicle for ferrying myself and the books around Australia.

We had already taken out a loan to put an extension on the back of the house. That enabled us to get the books (and the cockroaches!) out of Mally's living room and kitchen. But even that extension wasn't enough — the books were spilling back out into the house again. The Lord provided a building we leased not far from our house and, taking yet another step of faith, we moved into this warehouse. Around that time, we discovered we weren't really allowed by the city by-laws to sell books out of a residential home (whoops!). But, thankfully, no one complained about all the people stopping by to pick up books, another evidence of the Lord blessing and protecting our fledgling ministry. Yep, we were novices at starting an organization!

The first expansion of the ministry in our house in Australia as we had an extension at the back of the house and moved out of the small front patio we had filled in.

In those days, I would have long socks and shorts — normal for office and even for speaking.

In 1977 when we first started the ministry officially, my brother-in-law Paul filled in the small patio on the front porch of our home in Sunnybank Hills Brisbane. We soon outgrew that and the next year we obtained an additional loan to build a large extension on the back to house the ministry.

But now the ministry had a warehouse, and we had that expensive problem of the need for a larger vehicle that could bring enough books for speaking events at multiple churches in little country towns sprinkled between Sydney, Melbourne, Adelaide, and even Perth (46 hours, or 2,600 miles, away on the other side of the continent!).

A nearby used car lot had the perfect vehicle for us: a diesel minibus called the Toyota Coaster. We could take out the seats and pack the back with boxes of books. The sale price? $13,000 — a fortune to us. The ministry certainly did not have the money to afford it. But we really needed it. So, we prayed.

The vehicle the Lord miraculously provided by the businessman who called us after we were praying for a vehicle. We modified the back of this Toyota Coaster to carry books and equipment. I travelled thousands of miles all over Australia in this vehicle as I spoke at churches and conferences.

A mechanical ribbon typewriter I used to type letters and make stencils for our duplicators (mimeograph machines) which would duplicate our newsletters, etc.

One evening we met with our board, attorney Steve Gustafson, John Thallon, an accountant, and Professor John Rendle-Short (affectionately known to all of us as "Prof"), at the time professor of child health at Queensland University, to discuss the ministry and pray for this need. While we were meeting the phone rang and I grabbed it. A businessman, Greg Peacock, who had heard me speak at his church was on the line, "Hey, Ken, you spoke at my church' and it really impacted me. I have a little extra money from my business right now. Do you have any specific need at the moment?"

The Toyota that Greg Peacock bought.

Red Sea Moment

"Yes, we have," I replied. "We are just gathered together praying for a larger vehicle so I can take more books to churches and conferences."
"How much is the vehicle?" he asked, "I've got around $13,000."
It was the exact cost of the Toyota Coaster.

He wrote us a check and the minibus was ours. The Lord had provided exactly what we needed, exactly when we needed it.

This is the second vehicle we bought to travel around Australia to churches and conferences. It was a Toyota Coaster and we took out many of the seats and set it up with shelves to carry books and equipment. This is the vehicle we bought when business man Greg Peacock called to us if we had any needs as he had $13,000 to give and that was the price of the vehicle.

Down the road, Greg would eventually become a board member, taking over as chairman when Prof John Rendle-Short due to age, could no longer be as involved. And I put many miles on that Toyota Coaster until one day, on a tour with Dr. Gary Parker, we blew up the engine!

Greg Peacock

One Talk Changed Everything

The ministry was growing quickly. I was being invited to speak in churches across the nation, and in each church, I would highlight why evolution was not true, from both the Bible and science, and why we could trust what the Bible said about creation. I usually shared about dating methods, fossils and the flood, ape-men, or other icons of evolution. But in 1979 I was invited to a church about an hour away on the Gold Coast, a trendy beach area loved by tourists from around the world.

At that church I decided to do something a little different (looking back it was the Lord who burdened me to give this new talk). I noticed that after my presentations people were excited and interested but I was often asked, "Why does this matter? Why is Genesis such a big issue?" Dr. Henry Morris's *The Genesis Record,* a commentary-style book on those early chapters of Genesis, highlighted why Genesis matters, powerfully showing that Genesis 1–11 is the foundation for the rest of the Bible, for all our doctrine, and for the gospel. If you reject Genesis as literal history, you destroy the foundation of our Christian faith.

I sat down at the typewriter and developed a message I called "The Relevance of Genesis," using quotes from Dr. Morris along with other books I had and incorporating the basic principles my father had taught me. At that church on the Gold Coast, I basically read my message in a dynamic teaching style — and the response was incredible. Person after person came up to me afterward sharing some version of, "I never realized how important Genesis is! Wow, I really do need to believe in a literal Genesis." I knew I had hit on something that opened people's eyes to the need for answers. After that "relevance talk," they hungrily snapped up more books than I had ever seen and attended all my other talks to get the scientific answers.

That was a lightning bolt moment — I needed to give a relevance talk first (with a few scientific answers sprinkled throughout) and, when people realize that creation/evolution isn't just some academic debate or side issue, they're hungrier than ever for answers. And they can find those answers in the books, giving them something to take home and read and re-read to ensure they remember all the answers.

From then on, I continued to develop my "Relevance of Genesis" talk, giving it at every church where I spoke. I would share why we need to believe in a literal first Adam because he's tied to the literal last Adam, that marriage, the sanctity of life, and the truth of one race are all founded in Genesis, that evolution and millions of years puts death and disease before sin, undermining the gospel, and, of course, that the real issue is biblical authority: will we start with God's Word and allow Him to be the authority or will we undermine God's clear Word by starting with man's ideas and reinterpreting the text to fit with man's ideas?

To help communicate these truths, I used an overhead projector. I had used a projector during my teaching career and recognized it was a great communication tool. I developed a lot of transparencies (in black and white to start with) with all my points listed on them. As our ministry grew, an artist, Steve Cardno, came on board, and developed illustrations for me, including the first "castle diagram" to explain the real nature of the origins battle. That castle diagram has become iconic for the Answers in Genesis ministry, and I still use an updated version of it today.

Eventually I was traveling with boxes of overhead transparencies and became an expert at using a stack nine inches or so high, knowing how to skip and rearrange transparencies while I was talking. That takes a lot of practice. I no longer need a nine-inch stack of transparencies — I use a computer with hundreds of Keynote slides instead!

Speaking in the early days (late 70's) using an overhead projector.

Red Sea Moment

That relevance message is still the basic message I give now, decades later (and it's the message we train every AiG speaker to give). It's the message that built this ministry. Really, it changed everything.

And the response was overwhelming — exponentially beyond what I had been hearing before. I remember one person described it as "a conversion experience all over again." Nearly 50 years later, I still hear comments like that. It really is a "light bulb" moment for so many people and, really, this message the Lord gave me was sort of a prophetic moment in my life and a huge turning point in our ministry.

Several years later I would transcribe that talk via a Dictaphone into my first book, *The Lie,* originally published by Master Books in 1987 in preparation for my ministry in the United States. In those days there was no voice to text on a computer (and I personally didn't have a computer anyway). To transcribe my talk, I recorded the audio with the Dictaphone and then one of our staff members, Carol VanLuyn, later listened through headphones and typed it all out on an early computer. Then I went back through it and enhanced the manuscript so it would work as a book. That book is really the core message of the ministry: why does Genesis matter? It was also the talk that would later be filmed in America and shown in hundreds of churches as The Genesis Solution. The relevance message would eventually be portrayed as a major exhibit at the Creation Museum in northern Kentucky. I can't count the number of times I've now given that talk or a version of it, but it must be thousands and thousands of times. Even though I've modified it over the years, and I have many different versions of a relevance of Genesis talk, the same basics are always there. And in those early days it took off like wildfire, resources started selling like crazy, and that caught the attention of my contact at Master Books: George Hillstead.

My first book, *The Lie.*

Carol VanLuyn possibly typing *The Lie* on an early computer, back in the late 1980s.

An Aussie in America

We were ordering large quantities of books from America, so many that we were selling more books Down Under than Master Books was selling across America!

Ken holding up an early edition of *Dinosaurs Those Terrible Lizards*.

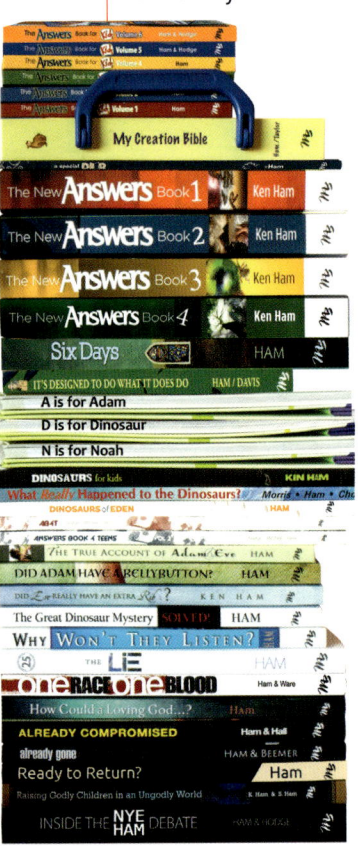

Here are a few of the many books written by Ken.

I've always had an emphasis on resources, even in those early days. It's so vital that we get materials into people's hands so they can remember what they are learning. People will remember some of what you tell them, but not everything (even Mally, who's heard me talk thousands of times, says she learns something new every time she hears me!). After I finished speaking, when I would watch mums and dads flock to the book tables, I would get excited. Those parents were getting equipped, and they'd pass those answers onto their children.

Jumping ahead a bit, I know I'm now getting old because it seems every day someone who looks middle-aged will tell me that they grew up on AiG's dinosaur books, curricula, or other resources and now they're using those same books, and our newer resources, with their children. These resources have a generational impact.

Even the Apostle Paul, when writing to the young pastor Timothy, asked him to bring his cloak and "above all, the parchments" (2 Timothy 4:13 ESV). The printed word matters and becomes an invaluable resource for looking things up again, refreshing yourself, or passing answers along to your children.

Resources have always been a major focus for me, and my new "relevance talk" was selling an exceptional number of books, arresting the attention of Master Books. In response, George invited me, and fellow board member Professor Rendle-Short, to come to America to meet with him. We braved the 16-hour flight and indescribably disorienting jetlag to go halfway around the world to sunny California.

We met with Master Books over my first ever American meal in El Cajon, California, a Grand Slam at Denny's®: pancakes, eggs, bacon, and maple syrup (I think such a meal cost $1.99 in those days!). I'd never had pancakes for breakfast before. Over the stacks of fluffy flapjacks, George expressed interest in an American tour where I would visit churches giving my relevance talk and offering resources. He wanted to see Master Books resources flying off the tables there like they were in Australia — people needed these answers, but they also needed someone to tell them why they needed these answers. And that's exactly what my relevance talk did.

After meeting with George, I had the opportunity to meet a man whose writings had impacted me more profoundly than anyone else's, other than my father: Dr. Henry Morris. He kindly took us out for dinner at a local Mexican restaurant. I'd never had Mexican food in my life. It was so foreign to me that when the server brought out a bowl of red stuff and chips, I had to ask what it was for! Dr. Morris, a very quiet man, dipped a chip in the salsa and popped it in his mouth, "That's what you do with it."

Dr. Henry Morris

"Okay," I thought, "Got it." I copied him and was nearly thrown to the floor from the spice — I'd never had anything hot like that before! Since I had no idea what anything on the menu was, Dr. Morris ordered for us and, well, I thought it was the most revolting food I'd ever eaten in my life. I have since "acquired a taste" for Mexican food and have even learned some Spanish like tortilla, taco, and enchilada. Mexican food is now one of my favorites!

> "The gospel message hasn't changed, but the way in which it needs to be presented in a secularized culture does need to change." *Gospel Reset*, p. 10

Over dinner we slowly got to know each other a bit as I shared what we were doing in Australia. I found Dr. Morris a very humble man. He was fascinated with the enormous sales of his books in Australia. I think he was amazed that a science teacher from Australia was selling his books all across the continent. Never did I think at that stage I would one day work for him for seven years in America. By the end of that first trip to America, I had agreed to come back and do a speaking tour for Master Books.

Traveling, Speaking, and "Chance" Meetings

My first short speaking tour was in 1981. During that tour I was interviewed on a live Christian radio program, KECR, out of a dingy, dirty part of El Cajon, by a man named Mark Looy. In those days, radio stations used reel-to-reel tapes, and watching Mark interview me, while spinning those tapes, pressing buttons, moving things around, and doing who knows what else, was like watching the Wizard of Oz at work! Mark would interview me again several times and, just to once again show how God works, several years later Mark would become one of the three founders of the Answers in Genesis ministry (the third being Mike Zovath), moving with me to Kentucky in 1994. God planned all along to bring us together for a special calling that we did not know at the time.

In 1984 I arrived back in America for another speaking tour with John Mackay, including a stop at a church in St. Louis, Missouri. In the 1970s–90s there were many small, local creation groups across the nation and these groups would often host events and bring bigger speakers in to present. One such group was the Missouri Association for Creation (MAC) who invited me to St. Louis to give my relevance talk. Afterward I met two men who were very active in MAC: Dr. David Menton and Walt Stumper. They loved the relevance message and were eager to introduce themselves. We all hit it off. Now, if you've followed our ministry over the years, at least one of those names probably sounds familiar: Dr. David Menton.

Dr. Menton had a PhD in biology from Brown University and was an award-winning anatomy professor

Mark Looy

Walt Stumper and Dr. David Menton a few years after I met them.

at Washington University School of Medicine at St. Louis for 34 years. He was also a consulting editor in histology (the anatomical study of microscopic structures) for *Stedman's Medical Dictionary*, a standard medical reference work. And he was a staunch creationist — a fact that was known throughout the university at the time — and very active in his local creation ministry since the mid-70s, giving entertaining and informative presentations on science and the truth of God's Word. He had an outstanding gift of communication.

A name that might not sound familiar to those outside the ministry is the other man I met that day, Walt Stumper, at the time an academic librarian, a great friend of Dr. Menton's, and an active member of that same creation ministry. He became involved when, at a church banquet on his one-year wedding anniversary, his pastor told him, "Everyone needs to be involved in ministry, and I have a job for you." Walt's ministry position was to help MAC by bringing books to meetings and events and selling them. At the time, Walt hadn't read any of the books and was basically a theistic evolutionist who hadn't really thought about the issue. But he began reading the materials, was convinced of the young earth creation position, and pretty soon Walt had a library of materials in his home and knew of just about every book available covering issues of Genesis and creation/evolution.

> **Red Sea Moment**
>
> Over the years I've been asked how we find the talented people who work for the AiG ministry. Well, the truth is, it's like how the animals got to Noah's ark — God brought them! Mark Looy, David Menton and Walt Stumper.

A "chance" interview introduced me to Mark Looy and another "chance" meeting after one U.S. speaking event introduced me to Dr. Menton and Walt. Years later, Dr. Menton would travel with me, speaking, and eventually after he retired Associate Professor Emeritus, he would come and work for AiG for 20 years until his second retirement and then passing in 2021. Walt would likewise join the AiG family, first working in our outreach department, then transitioning to become our full-time librarian. He built up a wonderful research library, with a variety of valuable collections, and also assisted AiG's Christian school, Answers Academy, in starting their school library before his retirement in August 2024 after 24 years serving with us. The legacy of both these men lives on at Answers in Genesis.

Phoenix Festival, May of 1986; people perusing the product tables.

Filming at the Phoenix Festival that eventually became *The Genesis Solution*.

I left St. Louis and spoke at various other churches across the country, dipping my toes, so to speak, in the American waters. During that visit, George even took John and I on our first ever visit to Disneyland. I never thought I would actually visit that theme park. Today I don't encourage people to visit such woke places — people need to come visit the Ark Encounter and Creation Museum instead! But the speaking events were going better than I ever expected. We were receiving an amazing response, so Master Books invited me, along with John Mackay, back for more American tours.

During that time, I was connected with a ministry called Films for Christ, a group founded by Stan and Marion Taylor, producing very unique 16mm films such as *The World that Perished, Footprints in Stone, The Great Dinosaur Mystery Solved,* and, eventually, a very impactful series on origins featured the late Dr. A.E. Wildersmith. Stan had a burden to make films dealing with the origins issue. The only other films I can think of at the time that dealt with science were produced by the Moody Institute of Science. These Moody Science Classics films, created and hosted by Dr. Irwin A. Moon, were extremely popular in churches, but no one was making films dealing with Genesis and the creation/evolution issue. All of Films for Christ's videos complimented the books we were selling and the ministry we were doing in Australia. We were able to gain rights to distribute those films Down Under and began showing them across the nation. That meant I had to take a 16mm movie projector along with my overhead projector as I traveled. Eventually we transitioned to selling VHS tapes and then DVDs. And now DVDs are on the way out and people stream videos. Technology sure has changed.

Well, in 1986, Films for Christ wanted me to do a U.S. speaking tour on their behalf — this time lasting six months! Mally and our children came with me to

The church where we filmed *The Genesis Solution.*

the Phoenix, Arizona, area. We lived with Paul and Star Taylor (Paul was the creative genius behind many of the films Films for Christ produced) and their family, enrolling our children at a local Christian school in Tempe. We bought a vehicle and Mally learned to drive in America. I'm glad she learned to drive in Australia in 1975, even though I had to suffer that broken leg for that to happen! She was stressed as she was driving (to her) on the wrong side of the road. But she was willing to do it! And I made sure the car had an automatic transmission to make it easier for her. Mally never complained, even though she was living in a foreign country, and I was away a lot of the time. She saw it as her ministry to support me in any way she could.

For six intense months I traveled across the U.S. in a van with a trailer loaded with books, alongside Dale Mason, who worked at Films for Christ and had married Stan and Marion's daughter, Karen. Dale, many years later, would become a VP at Answers in Genesis until his retirement in 2024. He was also the founding publisher of our award-winning *Answers* magazine.

During this tour, Films for Christ asked if they could film my relevance talk for another documentary they were producing. At Grace Community Church in Tempe, Arizona, I was filmed for the first time on 16mm film, a popular and economical way of filming back in the 1980s. A year later they nixed the idea of a documentary and decided to release my relevance message in full, accompanied by (at the time) cutting-edge animations. *The Genesis Solution* (which included an animated introduction with cartoon versions of me and a kangaroo!) was shown all across the U.S. and around the world, impacting hundreds of thousands, maybe even millions, of people and really helping launch our future Back to Genesis conferences.

Meanwhile … Back in Australia

In between these American tours I was still traveling around Australia speaking and hosting conferences. The ministry had grown so much we now rented both sides of the warehouse, doubling our space. We purchased a larger truck to fill with books to bring to conferences. And that larger, very high-backed truck was the cause of quite the commotion one day.

The first building on Bradman Street, Acacia Ridge (the section on the right with the garage door) the ministry moved into after moving from our house in Brisbane. We then expanded to the left side with the second garage door.

This was the first vehicle we obtained to carry books and travel to churches and conferences around Australia. Because of the high back it was a little unstable when it was fully loaded. It's also the vehicle that caused me to rip the roller door out of the building because the door was partly down and I didn't see it and the truck had such a high back.

I had backed it down the steep hill into the warehouse and filled it with books. I then had to rev up the four cylinder engine and push the gas pedal to the floor to give the truck enough "go" to get me back up that hill. Well, I forgot how tall the truck was — and that I had only pulled the roller door up about halfway! I shot out of the door and crash; it sounded like an explosion as the truck ripped through the door. All the neighbors heard it too, running down the street to see what had happened. I was so embarrassed but, looking back, it was rather funny. I drove that truck many miles all around Australia. As I went to church after church, I would carry heavy boxes of books into the church, set up, and then pack up what was left over at the end. I believe all that lugging around of books is how I did my back in. To this day I have chronic back problems and pain that I've had for over 40 years.

One of the most popular series of books we sell now is called the *New Answers Books.* In four volumes (and an unofficial fifth volume) we answer the most-asked questions people have about science, the Bible, creation/evolution, and more. It's really our classic apologetics series and has sold over 800,000 in the series. The origin of this series began in those early days in Australia.

As I traveled from church to church, I found people would ask the same basic questions over and over again: Where did Cain get his wife? How do you explain the dinosaurs? Were the days of creation ordinary days? What's wrong with believing in evolution and millions of years as a Christian? I came up with the idea of producing a magazine-style publication with answers to these most-asked questions. This then grew into a book that we kept adding to, eventually producing multiple volumes. We still have a copy of the first Answers publication in our library.

Published in 1990

Ken with Dr. Gary & Mary Parker

After returning to Australia in mid-1986, we then hosted a series of conferences across Australia, inviting top American creation speakers such as geologist Dr. John Morris, biochemist Dr. Duane Gish, and biologist Dr. Gary Parker to travel with me. During one tour with Dr. Parker (he was at ICR at the time and would join AiG during our early years), a Christian group wanted to record the five or six core talks both he and I were giving. Those talks were filmed at a Bible college in Katoomba, outside Sydney, and turned into the VHS series, *Understanding Genesis,* which were then sold all across Australia and America.

Esther and John Thallon

Prof. Rendle-Short and wife

And I had not forgotten my burden to build a creation museum. During these Australia years (I believe the particular event was sometime in 1980–81), board member John Thallon (another life-long friend, along with his wife, Esther), who knew of my desire for a God-honoring museum, suggested we find a property and pray that the Lord would let us build such a facility. We found a property between Brisbane and the Gold Coast, not far from a petrol (gas) station that was built to look like a spaceship (oldies from that area in Australia would recognize where that would have been). We stood on the property and prayed that God would let us build a creation museum. Well, God answered that prayer in 2007 in Kentucky when the Creation Museum was opened. It's a reminder that God's ways are not our ways.

During this time, I was also doing speaking tours in England. Prof. Rendle-Short (who was awarded the Order of Australia by Queen Elizabeth for his pioneering work on autism) grew up in England, having graduated from Oxford University. Prof was so burdened by the compromise with evolution by many of the church leaders and pastors in England that he pleaded with me to go there and give my relevance message. We did a number of tours, resulting in a Creation Science Foundation ministry being set up in England with a dedicated servant of the Lord, Graham Scott (who is now with the Lord), serving full time in that country. Before Prof, at age 90, went to his heavenly home in 2010, he pleaded with me to always keep a light shining for the creation apologetics ministry in England. I have done my best to fulfill the promise I made to him. Today our UK ministry, currently headed up by Simon Turpin, still proclaims the relevance message across England, the UK, and Europe.

A Life-Changing Invitation

Back to our six-month tour of America in 1986. George Hillstead shared with Dr. Henry Morris the incredible numbers of books we were selling. Dr. Morris couldn't believe the numbers and George kept insisting it was because of the relevance talk — it fired people up and they excitedly swarmed the book tables. Dr. Morris decided to attend my talk at Scott Memorial Baptist Church in El Cajon, California, to see what all the fuss was about. "I just can't understand how you're selling so many books! I need to come and hear what you do," he told me.

He came and heard my relevance talk, observing how, after I finished, the book tables were swamped. He was perplexed, meeting with me afterward, "I just don't understand. I give the same message you do" — remember my relevance talk was partly based on his work from *The Genesis Record* — "but I never sell books like that. I talk to people about the presuppositional importance of Genesis and having the right paradigm to be able to understand evidence. I don't understand how you sell so many books!" I had to smile to myself, "Yes, Dr. Morris gives the same information, but it's not given the same way. He's a scientist and doesn't have the same layman communication style I have, even though he is a great communicator!" Over the years I've noticed that many scientists have amazing information (though often rather technical), but it's not their gifting to bring it down to a level that the average person can understand and be motivated by. People just don't "get it" the same way sometimes, even if the same basic information is taught. The Lord has gifted those men and women differently — and we need both!

Well, Dr. Morris recognized that the scientists at ICR just weren't getting the same response, but people really needed these resources. He was one of the founders of Master Books and recognized the importance of getting printed material into people's hands. So, he asked if we would be willing to leave Australia and come to America for a few years to work at ICR, speaking in churches, and really helping get the message out there.

It was yet another huge decision and we would agonize over it for months: would we leave our homeland, our family, and our friends, for America?

> *When God gave me the relevance message many years ago it changed everything. It brought the importance of this foundational message of Genesis to the laypeople of the church. It made them hungry for more information which brought them to the book table. The book table helped finance the ministries in Australia and the early days of Answers in Genesis. This truly was the hand of God, this was Miraculous!*

The Answer Book Timeline

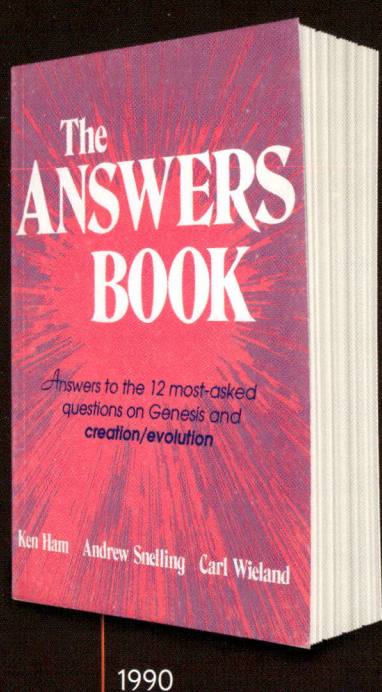
1990

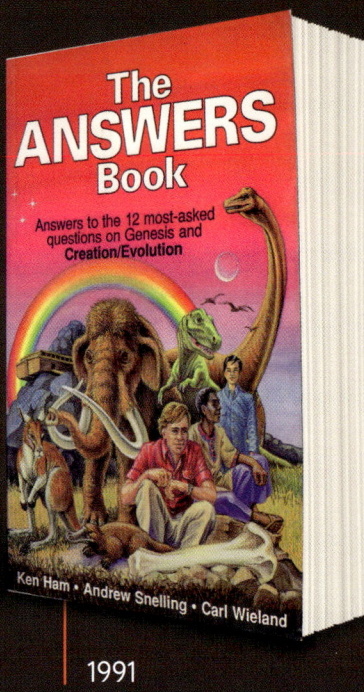
1991

1999

2000

Evolution … intelligent design…creation…or a little of all three? What do you really believe – and why does it matter to your life, your family, and your faith today?

Christians live in a culture with more questions than ever – questions that affect one's acceptance of the Bible as authoritative and trustworthy. Now, discover easy-to-understand answers that reach core truths of the Christian faith and apply the biblical worldview to these subjects:

- Genesis
- UFOs
- The Days of Creation
- Death & suffering
- Millions of years ago
- Noah's Ark & Flood
- Evolution
- Fossils
- Dinosaurs
- Starlight and time
- Carbon dating
- …and much more.

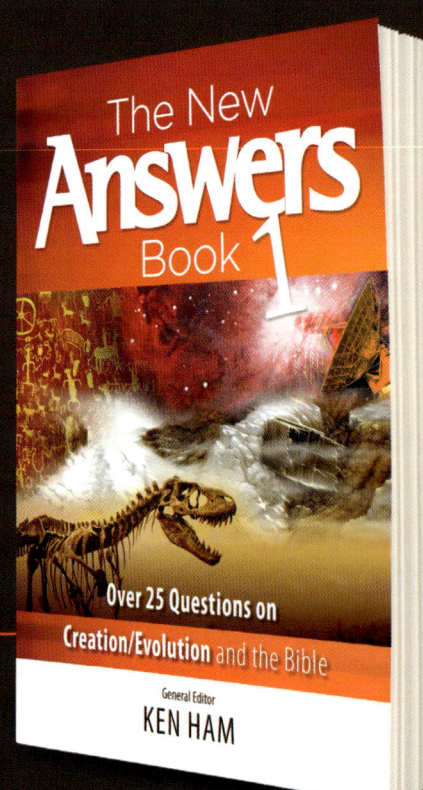
2006

"When I first began speaking across Australia in the late 70's and 80's, and also in the USA during the early 80's, I found people would ask me questions about Genesis, creation, evolution and associated topics. Now I began to find that people tended to ask the same basic questions wherever I went, over and over again. This inspired me to produce a magazine-type booklet with written answers to a number of these questions like, What happened to the dinosaurs?, Where did Cain get his wife?, How could Noah fit all the land animals on the Ark?, Why can't Christians believe in millions of years? And many more.

Over time, this booklet was expanded to become a paper book, and as time went on turned into five substantial books called the Answers Books Series. These became the best-selling apologetics books ever!"

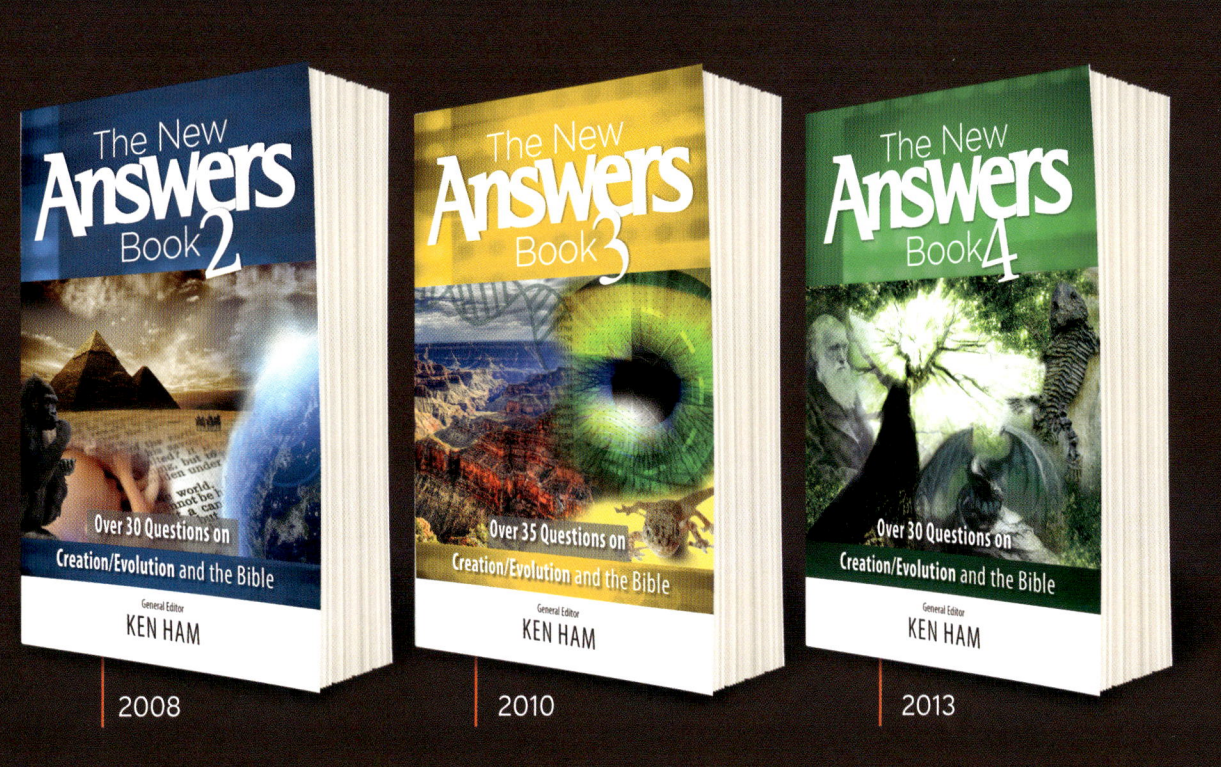

2008   2010   2013

5 | COMING to AMERICA

Florence, Kentucky

WHERE YOU GO, I GO

"Do you take this woman, to have and to hold, in sickness and in health, for richer or poorer, for better or for worse, till death do you part?" Mally and I were at a wedding where a pastor friend of ours was officiating his son's wedding. But our thoughts were distracted as we agonized over the decision of moving to America. It was a massive decision to leave everything we knew — our family, our friends, our church, and the Australian ministry we'd built with our own blood, sweat, and tears (and prayers — lots of prayers!). How could we tell our parents we were taking their grandchildren halfway around the world? How could we leave all our brothers and sisters and their children? And what about all our wonderful friends — how could we leave them? We simply couldn't decide what to do. We needed the Lord's clear direction.

> "A major reason for so many of the problems in Christian families today is that fathers have not taken their God-commanded responsibility of being priests in their household." *The Lie,* p. 143

As pastors are apt to do, Pastor Grieger turned the marriage ceremony into a mini-sermon, addressing his new daughter-in-law, "I want to talk to you about Ruth, from the Bible. Ruth said to her mother-in-law, Naomi, 'For where you go I will go, and where you lodge I will lodge. Your people shall be my people, and your God my God.' Be like Ruth with your husband—his God is your God—you both serve the same Lord—and where he goes, you go, you support what the Lord has called him to."

I don't know if the starry-eyed newlyweds heard any of his wisdom, but Mally did. She turned to me, saying, "Kenny, that's me— I'm like Ruth. Where you go, I go, what you do, I do. I support one hundred percent what you are doing and what God has called you to do. I'm part of this too."

A SIGN FROM THE LORD

At this same time the church we were members of relocated farther out of the city, so we, along with several other couples from our previous church, joined another church nearby, Salisbury Baptist. The pastor, Norm Weston, had the habit of welcoming people into membership by asking each person to share a brief testimony about themselves before the congregation.

Now Mally, as shy as she is, was certainly not looking forward to having to say anything. Over the years I've coaxed her to say a few things publicly, and she's agreed to a handful of interviews, but she likes to be behind-the-scenes, far away from the spotlight. She's always said she just wants to be a wife, a mother, and a grandmother.

> But Ruth said, "Do not urge me to leave you or to return from following you. For where you go I will go, and where you lodge I will lodge. Your people shall be my people, and your God my God (Ruth 1:16 ESV).

She was actually quite terrified about saying anything in front of the church, but that's what Pastor Norm would always do when welcoming people into membership — ask them to give a brief testimony.

She was stressing out about this, as she didn't know what to say. But after she heard Pastor Grieger talk about Ruth, she exclaimed, "Kenny, since I'm like Ruth, what if I shared that for my testimony? I could just say a little bit about Ruth." I thought it was a great idea.

Now keep in mind we were seeking the Lord constantly, agonizing over what we should do about the ministry opportunity in America. I think one of us even said something like, "I wish God would just send us a letter to tell us what to do."

Sunday morning, we showed up for church with our short testimonies ready. No one had seen them yet; we'd only shared them with each other. But we didn't need them. The pastor decided to do something totally different that morning. Because so many new people were being welcomed into membership on the same day because of that church relocation, instead of having us share, he stood before each newcomer and shared something about each of them with the congregation. When he arrived at Mally he looked at her and said, "Mally, I've been watching you with your children and with Ken. I know a lot about you as I've known Ken's parents for many years. I know you have a huge decision to make about whether or not to move to America. Now from all I've seen from you, you know who you remind me of? You remind me of Ruth. Ruth said

Ken and Mally

to Naomi, 'Where you go, I will go, and where you lodge I will lodge. Your people shall be my people, and your God my God.'"

We were stunned; no one but the two of us knew about our post-wedding conversation or that Mally had planned to share that exact thought at that service. No one knew — but God. He knew. And we immediately recognized it as a sign from Him; we were to go. Peace settled in our hearts; God was calling us to America.

Throughout our lives, so many events like this have occurred as God has showed us the direction we should go. Events like this made us realize more and more that God had His hand on us, and on this ministry, He called us to. He was directing us in ways we never dreamed.

A Tale of Two Anniversaries

We broke the news to our families and our Australian ministry team. Our ministry board agreed to loan me to the Institute for Creation Research for seven years — a long time, but not forever. Our church held a special service, commissioning us as overseas missionaries. We sold our house, gave away many of our belongings, and made tearful farewells to our family. "Don't worry," we said. "It's only for a few years. We'll be back soon!" (That shows how little we knew of what the Lord's plans for us were!) We stowed our luggage and settled into our plane seats, knowing we'd need to keep four young children happy on planes for the next 18 hours as we flew across the world, stopping, as flights from Australia usually did during that time, in either New Zealand or Hawaii to refuel.

On January 22, 1987, we arrived in Los Angeles, California, tired, overwhelmed, and very happy to be out of the airplane. I've always found it interesting that we started our life in America on that particular day — the anniversary of the deadly U.S. Supreme Court decision that legalized abortion across the nation. Praise the Lord that horrendous ruling, which cost 66 million unborn babies their lives, was overturned in 2022 after 49 years).

Little did I know that many years later, we would build a Creation Museum, and in 2020 that museum would open a stunning exhibit, Fearfully and Wonderfully Made, the world's most powerful and unique pro-life exhibit. This exhibit, featuring a series of phenomenally detailed baby models at various stages of development, an accompanying developmental timeline, biblical and scientific teaching, and touching personal stories, is overturning the bloody legacy of Roe v. Wade by showing thousands of guests each day that every life has value, life begins at fertilization, and abortion is taking the life of a human being made in the image of God (it's murder).

So the anniversary of a barbaric ruling that refused to recognize the right to life that every person made in God's image deserves, is also the anniversary of a family obediently following the Lord to a new country and God blessing that obedience, resulting, by His grace, in a ministry that is ardently pro-life and is reaching millions of people each year with the message that every life — from the moment of fertilization — is made in God's image and is fully human and therefore deserving of life.

In Roe v. Wade, 7 of the justices voted in the majority. Justice White, a Catholic, and Justice Rehnquist, a Lutheran, dissented. January 1987.

Fearfully and Wonderfully Made expanded exhibit in the Creation Museum, October 2022.

We were now in America. We began our new lives in a rented home and eventually obtained a loan to purchase a home. That was not as easy as it sounds. When you arrive in America with no social security number, no American credit cards (at that time our credit cards only worked in Australia), and no U.S. bank account, every little thing you try to do is extremely difficult, complicated, and stressful. It seemed like we were fighting in an awful battle, but eventually we were able to get through it all.

••

Next up: settling our eldest two children into school. We found a Christian school for them. Despite the added cost of private Christian education, we were committed to having our children enrolled in a Christian school. Several years earlier, in 1982, when it was time for 5-year-old Nathan to first go to school, both Mally and I had a real burden not to send him to the public school system. Back in those days, there was no such thing as homeschooling and, in Australia, really no Christian schools either. But we'd heard of a school a pastor was starting in his Brisbane church, so Nathan attended there until we moved stateside. None of our five children ever went to the secular education system; they have all either been to Christian school or homeschooled. This heart for Christian education comes, again, from the burden I saw in my parents: a burden to raise up generations who trust in Christ and know His Word. That's why they ran so many evangelistic programs. We wanted the same thing for our children and were dedicated to training them up for the Lord as God directs us in His Word. We both felt this was best done by partnering with a like-minded Christian school. Not all schools are like-minded — we struggled to find such a school, and once we even pulled our kids after only six weeks! Mally and I are both so thrilled that our children have this same burden for their children and that it led our daughter Renee in 2017 to found a biblical worldview Christian school for Answers in Genesis in Northern Kentucky called Answers Academy. But that's another story of faith and miraculous provision from the Lord.

ICR FACULTY PROFILE

NAME: Kenneth A. Ham
DEGREE/SCHOOL: B.App.Sc., Queensland Institute of Technology, Australia; Diploma of Education (science teaching); University of Queensland, 1975
ICR TITLE: Director of Seminars and Conferences;
FAMILY: Wife, Mally; five children
BORN: October 20, 1951, Cairns, Queensland, Australia
BIOGRAPHY: Ken Ham, one of the featured speakers at ICR's popular "Back to Genesis" seminars, has been at the forefront of the modern creationist revival in both the United States and Australia. A dynamic communicator with a good sense of humor (along with a charming Australian accent), he has the unique ability to make the creation/evolution conflict relevant to the life of the average Christian, as it speaks to the important issues of today.

This message is conveyed very forcefully in Ken's acclaimed film, *The Genesis Solution*, produced by Films for Christ, which was nominated, in 1988, as best Christian film documentary. It also is the theme of many of his popular books, including *The Lie: Evolution* and *The Decay of the Nations*. His most recent book, *D is for Dinosaur* was written—with his wife, Mally—not only for his five children, but as a teaching tool for other parents and teachers.

Ken holds to a very firm conviction that "the Scriptures are authoritative in all areas, and that the book of Genesis, in particular, is foundational to Christian faith and practice. By going back to Genesis, we can do much to overturn the evolutionary philosophy which so dominates our society."

ICR headquarters in Santee, California (ICR eventually moved to Texas).

Back to Genesis Begins

I began working with Dr. Henry Morris and Dr. Duane Gish at the Institute for Creation Research, speaking at churches across the nation. Unlike the "old days" of Aussie speaking, I could fly instead of drive to many of these events. Mally and the kids liked this as it meant I wasn't gone for weeks at a time as was the case when I spoke in Australia. Even though I was speaking more than ever, we actually saw more of each other, thanks to America's hub of airports, larger population, and churches in closer proximity to each other.

The ministry in Australia had given me a lot of experience at organizing meetings. For instance, before each event I would organize the book order and get it ready to be shipped out, then I would head for the airport or drive to the church by myself. I would set up the book tables, train volunteers to sell the resources after the event, then head into the sanctuary to organize my transparencies, overhead projector, and the screen (and troubleshoot any of the myriad problems that

can arise with technology, such as too much light from windows washing out the screen). After the event was over, I'd repack up whatever was left, fold up and put away tables, and load up the truck. I remember a few churches where the pastor would say, "Well, just lock up when you leave," and leave me to the tear down. It certainly wasn't glamorous work being a one-man operation out in the field those first few years, but this equipped me to be ready for the next stage of the ministry in the USA. It didn't take long for those in authority at ICR to realize they needed to get me some help, as the church ministry was growing considerably.

Not long after we arrived in the USA, our ministry in Australia suffered a leadership crisis and the staff begged me to please come back and take over. They were worried the ministry would shut down. Mally and I were disheartened — we'd just arrived in America and were excited for what God would have us do here, but we also loved our Aussie ministry. We prayed and felt strongly we were where the Lord would have us be; we reminded ourselves of all the ways the Lord had clearly directed us, and we were convinced that the devil didn't want us to be in America. So, as hard as it was, we made the decision not to return to Australia at that time to rescue the ministry. We would have to trust it to Him.

And He was faithful. Geologist Dr. Andrew Snelling (who would later join AiG in America until his retirement and return to Australia in 2024) took over temporarily and Dr. Carl Wieland, the founder of the precursor to *Creation* magazine, stepped in after a few months to lead the organization on a permanent basis, though I would remain a director until 2004.

Henry Morris and John Whitcomb

Ken and Dr. Gish just a year before Dr. Gish's passing.

Ministry in America was producing fruit, speaking engagements were increasing, and I had a vision for Back to Genesis conferences, mega-events I couldn't pull off on my own. I had been interviewed several times now by Mark Looy in the dingy little Christian radio studio he worked at, including a 1987 interview shortly after I began at ICR. After the interview, I told Mark that I was speaking soon at a local church in Santee. He showed up and brought his wife, Renee, along. At that time, Mark was also on contract at ICR to write their Scripture, Science, and Salvation radio program. Clearly, he cared about creation apologetics and the relevance of Genesis. Indeed, he did — a Dr. Duane Gish presentation on scientific evidence for creation, given to just a handful of students in Mark's Christian high school years had changed his worldview 180 degrees, giving him a confidence he'd never before had in God's Word.

> "…it was vital that the pastors defend the Book of Genesis to the students. After all, if the first book in the Bible can't be trusted in their eyes, why should any other?" *Why Won't They Listen,* p. 18

I approached ICR about hiring him to help organize these Back to Genesis events and eventually he was pulled in part-time, very quickly becoming full-time. It was time for our first test for my Back to Genesis vision.

John Morris and Ken

Ken Ham, Don Rohrer, Tim Rizor, Rick Homesley, Steve Austin, and John Morris at a Back to Genesis Conference in Virginia.

Here's how such a program went: we would invite pastors from across a particular area to a breakfast and show them *The Genesis Solution* movie (my relevance talk in cutting edge — at the time — form), helping them understand why this issue mattered and why their congregations needed answers. Many of these pastors would then agree to show that movie in their churches on a Sunday morning or during a special evening service and promote our Back to Genesis conference coming to the area. A few weeks later we would come back to the area and host the conference — and hopefully hundreds of people would attend. And they did!

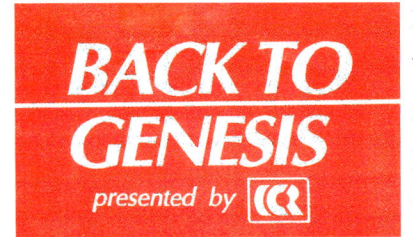

Our first pastors' breakfast was in Connecticut and drew 200 pastors. The subsequent conference in a local high school auditorium saw 2000 people show up — the idea had worked! Showing The Genesis Solution had whetted the appetites of pastors and their congregations and they were eager to learn more. Our Back to Genesis events quickly grew, becoming the largest conferences ICR had ever done, easily filling 1000–2500 seats. We would even host special school assemblies on Monday morning — kids in the morning, teens in the afternoon — for hundreds of Christian schools and homeschool students. Our largest event was in 1993 in Newark, Delaware, where over 6000 children and teens attended our morning and afternoon programs. People were amazed that I could keep kindergarten through fifth grade students' attention for an hour and a half, and middle and high school students likewise for an hour and a half of teaching at their level — and they all have fun! God gave me a gift of communication which enables me to speak to different age levels in ways they will enjoy and understand.

What also surprises many people (this was true back in the 1990s and is still true today) is that the more liberal areas of the U.S., such as Washington, Oregon, and California, usually saw the biggest crowds — and sold the most resources as they basically swept them off the tables! People living in spiritually dark areas are hungry for answers and encouragement from God's Word.

Strangely enough, these events were helped on by the release of a 1986 action-comedy film, Crocodile Dundee, featuring Paul Hogan as a bushman from Australia's vast Outback. By the time we arrived in America in 1987 this movie was popular, introducing Americans to some Aussie culture and, of course, the amazing Aussie accent. At the time, my hair was fairly dark, and with my beard and strong accent, well, as a few pastors put it in their introductions of me to their congregations, I was the man who "looked like Abraham Lincoln and talked like Crocodile Dundee." People loved the accent! I've had people in America tell me, "It doesn't matter what you say, we just love to hear you saying it." Actually, that gives me open doors to say many things they need to hear.

Because I was from Australia, when Crocodile Dundee made Australia popular, I would sometimes dress up with Aussie clothes for a talk I did on creation with Australian animals and fossils, etc. The hat has corks which in certain western areas are used to keep the flies off your face.

Mark was handling the organization of these events, but I needed help on the road. In 1993, Don Rohrer, ICR's business manager, told me about a longtime friend of his, a U.S. Army infantry Lieutenant Colonel named Mike Zovath. Mike was retiring and wanted to be involved in Christian ministry. Apparently, he hadn't thought much about joining ICR in particular, but he couldn't get rid of this little thought that he ought to send his resume to Don. Well, when he did, Don thought he'd be great for helping me out on the road, as Mike had worked in plans and operations for the last few years of his military service. I met him and he was soon hired to travel with me and be part of what we were doing.

The Lord was blessing the seminars tremendously — tens of thousands were being impacted, the relevance of Genesis message was spreading through churches and families, and we were praising the Lord.

Mike Zovath

MINISTRY MOMENT

I had known ICR's Don Rohrer since second grade. In 1992, when I was retiring from the army, my family and I stayed at his house in San Diego for a week before heading to South Carolina for my retirement. During that time, I met this Ken Ham I'd heard about, and Don handed me two cassette tapes of Ken's messages to listen to on the long drive. We listened and were blown away. Despite attending church all our adult lives, five years of Bible college, and being on ICR's mailing list for years, we'd never heard anything like this.

While driving through Arizona "the light came on" as Ken talked about no death before sin. I'd never heard this before, and both my wife Susan and I were hanging on every word. After just those two cassette tapes, I was all in. I'd never thought of working at ICR before, but three weeks later I was working with Ken. Those days of long hours, hard work, and constant travel were some of the happiest days in my adult life so far. I loved it.

To me, Ken's message that I heard over and over again as we traveled was the most important message anybody had ever preached. Not just because of the creation/evolution issue, but because it was about biblical authority. His stand on creation was just a consequence of his stand on biblical authority and that was the message people needed to hear!

—Mike Zovath

A New Chapter Begins

Toward the end of our seven-year commitment, Mally and I began to feel that our time at ICR might be coming to an end. For quite some time, we prayed about it, seeking the Lord's direction, "Should we stay with ICR? Should we go back to Australia? What should we do?" I knew Dr. Morris' heart was that ICR would be a scientific research institution with a graduate program. But our laymen's ministry, and the Back to Genesis events, were quickly becoming what ICR was known for and the largest part of the ministry. I saw this as a positive thing — we could fund their research with the revenue from Back to Genesis events. But Dr. Morris was concerned it was overshadowing research and would keep them from being known primarily as a research institution. We had two very different ideas for the future. Now that's not to be taken as a negative; God gave two people different burdens.

"Do you think I should leave ICR and follow the burden God has given me for the direction of apologetics ministry?" I asked Dr. Morris. He agreed that might be best, so a few days later I slipped my resignation under his door before heading out for another speaking event, with no idea of what would happen, if anyone involved with Back to Genesis would come with me, or exactly what Mally and I would do. However, we did have the blessing of the Australian ministry to stay in the U.S. where we were seeing so much fruit, if we believed the Lord was clearly leading us to do so.

And still my vision for the creation museum Aussie board member John Thallon and I had prayed and asked God for stayed with me, intensifying during my time with ICR. I had come to realize that Australia was not the place for such a museum; America, the home to millions of Christians, was the place to build it. Here we would have more visitors to make such a place viable and find it much easier to raise the necessary funding as America had a large Christian philanthropic base. America was really the center of both the business and Christian world. Mally and I began to realize we wouldn't be going back to Australia.

I pitched my idea to Mark Looy and Mike Zovath, "What if I stay here in America," I said, "and we start a creation ministry, dedicated to reaching laymen with the message of biblical authority and the truth of God's Word? And what if we build a creation museum here in America as a major part of that ministry?"

They loved the idea. With Back to Genesis ending at ICR, there was really no place for them in that ministry so, with no hard feelings on anyone's side, Mike, Mark, and I parted ways with ICR to establish our own creation ministry: Creation Science Ministries (the temporary name we gave to the ministry until it was changed to Answers in Genesis in late 1994). But where would we locate this fledgling ministry and build our museum? I was thinking somewhere in the middle of the country, maybe St. Louis or Kansas City.

For my last weeks with ICR, Mark booked a few speaking events, stringing them together for maximum efficiency in my travels. Mike and I were to hit Akron, Ohio, before continuing on to Massachusetts, then New York, and then home to California for Thanksgiving. Mike's wife had grown up in Columbus, Ohio (about two hours southwest of Akron) and Mike had been stationed for many years at Fort Knox, south of Louisville, Kentucky. He'd driven from Columbus to Fort Knox and back many times, and knew the Florence area of northern Kentucky well, including the close proximity of the Cincinnati airport hub. He kept suggesting that area for the new ministry we were founding, so between speaking in Akron and heading for Massachusetts, we swung by Florence, Kentucky, a city right on I-75, one of the busiest north-south interstates in the U.S. The first place we visited was the spot everyone scopes out when they're considering a move — the airport, of course!

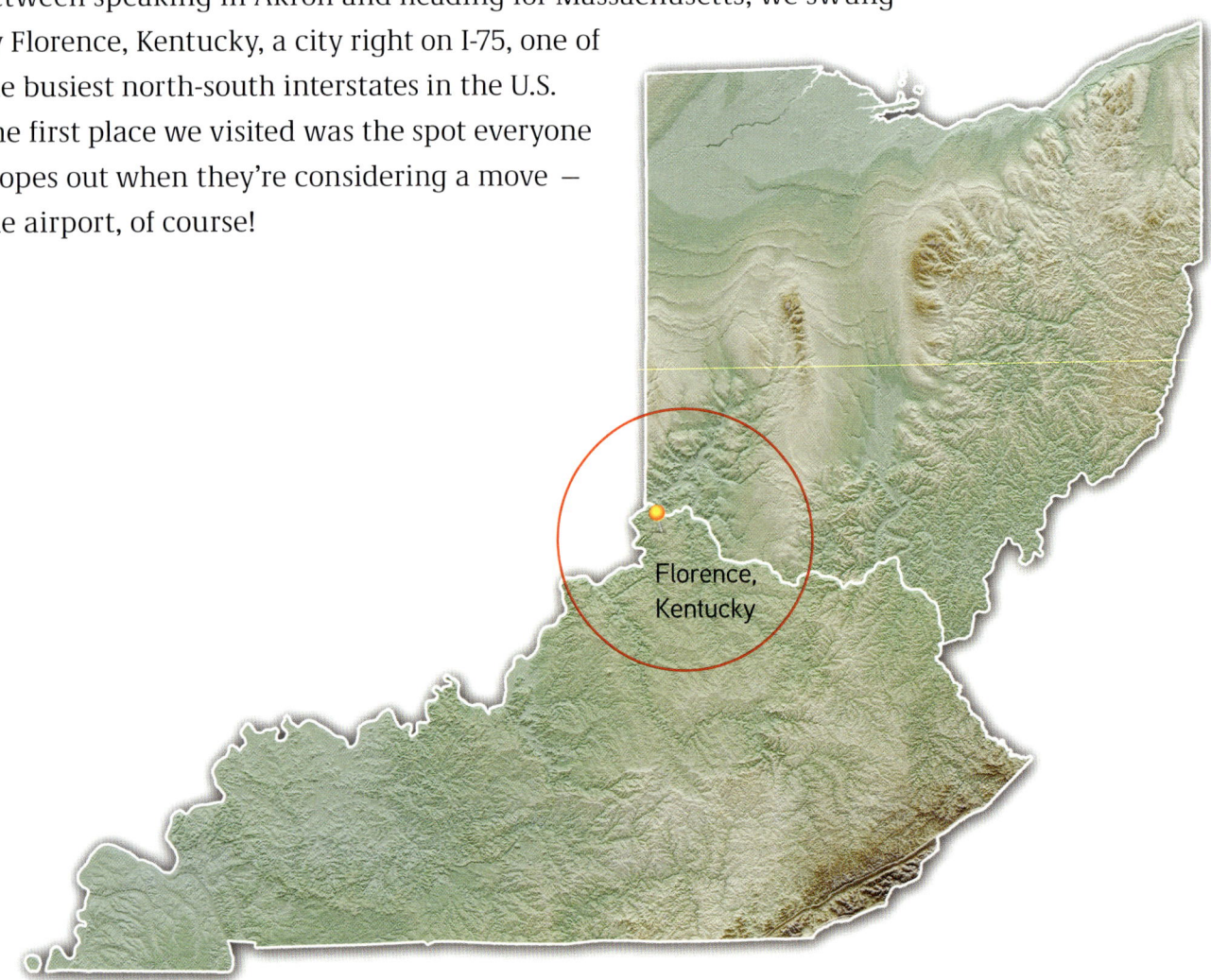

Since airports were my second home, I cared what the airport was like! San Diego airport was a zoo, always stressful and congested. Cincinnati's airport was a central hub with flights all across the country and yet it was calm, with plenty of parking. The area was within a day's drive of two-thirds of the U.S. population. And, driving down Florence's "main drag," Mall Road, home of the iconic red-and-white-striped "Florence Y'all" water tower, I noticed lots of shopping — Mally would be happy!

During that first visit, northern Kentucky was hit with a massive snow storm that shut I-75 down for two days — we were stuck. It was my first time driving in snow and Mike says I tested the anti-lock braking system on the rental car at every stop sign as we looked around the area. But, despite the cold, I liked the area, and Mike was happy it was somewhere close to his wife's family.

Reading a USA Today paper Mike noticed that Cincinnati was voted the number one "livable" city in the U.S. Mark then called, "Hey, did you see that Cincinnati, Ohio, is the number one city to live in? You need to check it out." He'd purchased a big thick book that emphasized all the positives of Cincinnati and why it received the rating it did. (I don't think Cincinnati has ever been rated that highly since!)

That did it — all three of us were in agreement: Florence, Kentucky, would be the new home of Creation Science Ministries and future home of a creation museum.

Please Tell Me How

I've often been asked by people who are just in awe of what the ministry of AiG has developed into, with two world-class attractions, "How could all this happen?" To me the answer is so complicated I can only explain some of it. You see, all along the way, God was building a complex web of people and events, like bringing Mike Zovath and Mark Looy to ICR so the three of us could become the founders of the Answers in Genesis ministry. This web is so complex, only God could explain it. As Mike has said many times, *"It's a God thing."* There's no other explanation. Some people He brought for a short time, others to stay longer, some for all their lives, but God was doing something miraculous as this ministry was constructed in ways we did not envisage, and we still stand amazed as to how it all happened.

Life for Mally & Children

Those early months of moving to the U.S. were very hard — it was a very different culture — but the Lord was kind. The house we purchased was next door to a woman who attended a Salvation Army church. She quickly became "Grandma Jo," sort of an adopted grandmother for our kids. I think the Lord placed her next to us because He knew I needed it!

Years ago, when Kenny first began speaking, he left me Easter weekend to go with John Mackay to speak in Sydney, ten hours down the coast. I had a 6-week-old baby and a 17-month-old toddler. I had never been alone before and really didn't know what I was going to do. Well, John's wife, Anne, decided to bring her two little kids over and have a girls' weekend. We had a blast, but I realized that this weekend was just the first of many and I couldn't be babysat every time Kenny went away. "Lord," I prayed, "I claim Psalm 4:8, 'In peace I will both lie down and sleep; for you alone, O Lord, make me dwell in safety.' If you want me to do this, Lord, I need you to look after me."

I prayed that prayer nearly 50 years ago and the Lord has been looking after me — I know that without a doubt. I have never been afraid while Kenny is gone, and the Lord has always cared for me.

Over the years I've been asked how our marriage survived Kenny's intense traveling schedule and the overwhelming demands of ministry. We've been married over 50 years and we both just adore each other — to me, he's my darling Kenny and I would do absolutely anything for him and he for me.

So how did our marriage survive? Well, I knew, without a doubt, the Lord had called us — not just Kenny, but both of us — to this ministry. My job was to look after the home front and, right from the beginning, the Lord laid it on my heart that I was to do everything I could for Kenny so the Lord could use him in a mighty way. It's one of the reasons I know He brought us together!

Any time things were hard, and I would question what we were doing, the Lord would remind me of the promise I made to Him as a child, to go anywhere and do anything for Him. Sometimes I chaffed at that — I was only a child when I made that promise, what did I know — but He would remind me anyway, and by His grace I've kept that promise and He has blessed our sacrifice.

Over the years, we've experienced so many ministry trials and battles, including friends turning their backs on us. When people hurt Kenny or me, and I want to become bitter or unforgiving, I just keep reminding myself that God is in control. He holds all things together and none of us would be here except that He is still on the throne. And He will be with us no matter what.

During these difficult ministry times, I remind Kenny that we're all broken and, though I don't understand why the Lord uses any of us when we are so sinful and so full of pride, He graciously does, and we just have to cling to Him because we can't do anything without Him. I always point my Kenny darling to the Lord, reminding him that we're going to get through this with the Lord's help.

And by His grace we have for over 50 years!

—Mally

Forms, Exams, and Permanent Residents

To come from Australia to work in America for ICR I, of course, needed a work visa. We procured it before coming and upon arrival we all applied for green cards. In 1988 we planned a trip home to visit our families, fulfilling a promise I made to Mally's parents that I would bring the family back to spend time with them, and fulfill some speaking engagements the Australian ministry had for me. We had our tickets in hand and were to fly out in a few days when our attorney informed us, we could not leave the country without jeopardizing our green cards and risking not being allowed back into the U.S.! What would we do? I had speaking engagements all lined up, people counting on me in Australia, and I had made that promise to Mally's parents.

I had recently been on a tour of the Grand Canyon with ICR and had met a man on the trip who I remembered worked for the immigration and naturalization service in El Cajon, where we lived. I called him up, "We have a problem. Are you able to help? We have three days before our flights leave."

He paused, "Let me investigate." The next day he called me back, "Ken, can you all come down to the Immigration and Naturalization Service office tomorrow?" He gave me a time and a name to ask for. The next day we headed to the office, standing in a long line waiting to ask to see the specific person he'd told us about. At this stage in immigration, we'd filled out all of our forms, done our medical exam, and completed the biometrics capture of our fingerprints and photos. When it was our turn, we were taken downstairs where files were stacked to the ceiling. The man we'd been told to ask for had our files. He flipped through them, "So you want your green cards, hmm? Okay," stamp, stamp, stamp, "put your hand on your heart and say after me, 'I promise to obey the laws of the land'...okay, hand me your passports,"

> We can't see things from an eternal perspective. Only God can. Only God can foresee all the events and orchestrate plans beyond our comprehension. He is God! We need to ponder that every day!
> *Divine Dilemma*, p. 147

stamp, stamp, "okay, here are your temporary green cards. Your permanent cards will arrive in the mail." And just like that, we were permanent residents. It was a miracle. The Lord sent the right person at just the right time to help us out of a difficult situation. We flew out for Australia the next day.

You know, sometimes I think we live complicated lives, so often it seems we live "on the edge." Certainly, our lives are never dull! It's like we are constantly in a war — oh, we are, a spiritual battle God has called us to be soldiers in. And what a continuous battle it had been — but there was much more to come.

> *My 7 years at ICR taught me so much about business, events, and the American audience. I learned a lot from Duane Gish, John and Henry Morris about Scripture and how it confirms the creation account in Genesis. One would have to say my time at ICR was Miraculous!*

MINISTRY MOMENT

I was privileged to work side-by-side with Ken at ICR. It was there that I first saw his genius and visionary ideas. Not all geniuses are visionaries, but Ken was blessed to be both. The Back to Genesis seminars Ken and I organized for seven years were tremendously popular, often attracting thousands of young people and adults. As a result, the ICR ministry exploded in growth from 1987–1993. Ken and I also helped launch a daily radio feature, Back to Genesis, during our ICR tenure, which was to air on more than 1,000 radio stations.

As Ken and his Australian ministry were about to end the loan to ICR and see Ken return to Australia, the board down under asked Ken to remain in America where he was seeing so much fruit and start a sister organization of the Australian ministry. Ken informed me of these discussions, and asked if I would join him in this venture, especially to organize region-wide seminars and start a new media ministry. I agreed, though I realized that with three young children (one still in diapers) this would not be an easy undertaking as we packed up and moved 2,000 miles, leaving several family members back in California.

Yes, it was an emotional time to leave so much behind, but I never doubted for a second that God had blessed Ken with vision and remarkable teaching ability, so it was easy in that sense for we knew that God was behind this venture. Now, my wife Renee was a trooper. She never hesitated because we knew God had blessed Ken with a message that was relevant to the country, and we saw peoples' lives being impacted nationwide. That was in 1993, and we've never looked back.

—Mark Looy

Since its first release in 1987 *The Lie* has gone through several updates and revisions.

The covers have been redesigned as well.

1987

1994

2012

2024

1993 – 1995

6 | THE BIRTH of AiG

THE BIRTH OF AIG

It was one of the most embarrassing moments of my life. In December of 1993 we officially incorporated Creation Science Ministries, named after the ministry, founded in Australia, and prepared to move from sunny California to Kentucky, home of bluegrass, rolling hills, and horses (and snow—so much snow! I think we got more snow that first winter than I've seen in the 30+ years since!). But first we had to let people know about this new ministry so they could support it, and we could schedule conferences.

Master Books had a large mailing list of people who had purchased books from them in the past. Since they mostly published creation science materials, their mailing list seemed like a good place for our fledging ministry to begin getting the word out. Master Books agreed to let us send our first mailing out to their list of 130,000 households.

Dan Manthei, one of the founding members of Master Books and a board member at ICR, was thrilled with what we were doing and his family foundation generously agreed to fund our first mailing, a huge blessing.

"We need to put your photograph on the front of the envelope," Mark Looy advised as we discussed the design of this mailing.

> "...historical science (the beliefs about the past) is fallible; it is God's Word that is infallible."
> *The Lie,* p. 94

I protested, "No, I do not want my face on all the envelopes!"

"People don't know what Creation Science Ministries is yet. But anyone who has heard you speak will be much more likely to open the envelope if they see your face."

So, over my continued objections, our first mailing went out, each envelope emblazoned with a black-and-white photo of me. Mark also advised we set up a PO box to receive any undeliverable mail ensuring we began with a clean, up-to-date mailing list.

A few weeks later, Mally and I packed up all our worldly goods into a trailer, buckled five kids into the van, and drove across the country, arriving in Northern Kentucky on March 4, 1994. The very next day I stopped by the post office to check the PO box, just in case there was anything there. Inside were a couple of items, including a card from the post office telling me to come inside for my returned envelopes. We had rented a large PO box. "Why on earth do they need me to come inside?" I wondered as I opened the door and headed for the counter.

The staff behind the counter immediately froze and silently stared at me until someone exclaimed,

> "Oh, there he is! This is him," Then everyone started laughing. I was more confused than ever by the sudden fanfare.
> "We have some return mail for you," a clerk offered helpfully.
> "Oh, thanks. Where do I get it?"
> "What are you driving?"
> "Uh oh. What kind of a question is that?"
> I was bewildered, "I have a van."
> "Well, that'll help. Just drive around the side."

At the side door I was shown enormous piles of returned envelopes. No wonder they knew who I was — they'd seen my face staring at them from the front of 18,000 returned envelopes! And the return mail kept pouring in for quite some time after that! It took days for our kids to open each envelope, remove the reusable envelope from inside, and set them aside for future use.

Turns out Master Books hadn't kept their mailing list up to date and many people on the list had either moved addresses or moved to their heavenly home. That was so embarrassing for me at the time, but it's a good joke 30 years later.

Despite all the returned mail, many people sent in checks to support the new ministry and now we had our own mailing list (which we've scrupulously kept up to date!) to continue growing our support base. And grow it did! Amazingly, many of the families who received that first mailing still support the ministry today.

Settling In

After the debacle at the post office, it was time to find a house. We'd sold our home in California, but housing prices at that time weren't what they are now. Our home in Santee wasn't worth very much and most of the sale price went to the bank. We drove away with around $3000 towards our new home in Kentucky. That certainly wasn't enough for a down payment!

When Mike and I had first scoped out Florence, Kentucky, we'd seen an area with a bunch of houses under construction, so we started our search with these houses. We could get one, but only if someone would agree to guarantee the loan. I didn't know what to do but I called my Uncle Charles Harwood (my mother's younger brother). He was a warrior for the Lord, very outgoing in his faith and supportive of what we were doing (he's with the Lord now). "Uncle Charles, will you help us get this ministry off the ground in Kentucky by enabling us get a home by co-signing a loan for us?" He graciously agreed and soon we had a home in the Bluegrass State to settle into.

Next up, we needed an office. Mike and Mark, still in California, were working out of their homes, moving into Phil and Mary Chivers' San Diego house (that couple was helping with the distribution of Creation magazine) when their homes sold. The offices had taken over the Chivers entire lives with magazine distribution in the garage and Mark's office set up in their old Care Bears themed nursery. We were all looking forward to a northern Kentucky office space!

Our search for a rental turned up two possibilities: available for purchase, the old Boone County Jail House, a large building with small rooms, small windows, and very thick walls due to it having served as, well, a jailhouse! Available for rent was a large empty building with plum-colored carpeting in a little strip mall that housed a pharmacy and a few other shops. Schwartz Drug Plaza was owned by the pharmacist, and he rented out the other units. We inquired about the open unit — he charged $6 a square foot — but we were upfront that we were a brand-new Christian ministry, and we didn't have the money yet, but we would as the ministry grew.

First house in Kentucky.

First office in Florence, Kentucky.

This elderly pharmacist, who was rather crusty and negative toward Christianity, looked at us and said, "You're trusting in your God, then I'm sure your God will supply it for you," and gave us the lease. And he was right — God supplied what we needed.

Eventually, the media heard about us and wanted to know why we were in Kentucky and what we planned to do. I agreed to an interview, sharing about what we believed and about our conferences, then announcing that we were going to build a creation museum in Kentucky someday.

"Where are your offices?" they asked. "Over there," I waved in the direction of our leased unit, "right by the porn shop."

Wait — what? They looked shocked. I was trying to say, "pawn shop," as that was the store next to our unit, but with my Aussie accent I, to this day, cannot say "pawn." It comes out every time sounding like, well, a very different word!

Creation Science Ministries Becomes AiG

That December of 1994 we met for our first face-to-face board meeting in Jackson Hole, Wyoming, at Rocky Mountain Lodge. It was beautiful; the snow-capped Tetons in the background were a majestic sight. Gathered were the three founders — myself, Mark, and Mike — and our four other board members, Dan Manthei, Don Landis, Carl Kerby, and Peter Strong. Dan, I knew from my days at ICR, Don was a pastor in Wyoming whose church I had spoken at (he's now the president of Jackson Hole Bible College, a wonderful one-year biblical worldview creation college). Carl was an air traffic controller who I met at an event in the Salt Lake City area (today he runs his own ministry, Reasons for Hope), and Peter was a businessman from Seattle who came highly recommended from a friend of Mark's as an asset to the board.

We met to celebrate what the Lord had done in our first year of ministry and how He'd been faithful to financially support our endeavors. Even though the Australian ministry had agreed to serve as a sort of "safety net" in case we needed financial assistance in the early days, we never needed to ask for financial help, and we praised the Lord for that. But another reason we'd gathered together was to discuss a new name for the ministry.

Creation Science Ministries was only a temporary moniker. We wanted something that emphasized that we weren't just a creation/evolution ministry — that was simply a consequence of our belief in the authority of Scripture. We were first and foremost a biblical authority ministry and we wanted that reflected in the name. Besides, "creation science" was too close to "Christian science," the name of an unbiblical cult.

Our very first board meeting in Jackson Hole, Wyoming. Peter Strong, Dan Manthei, Mike Zovath, Carl Kerby, Ken, Mark Looy, and Don Landis

During my Australia ministry days, we'd put together a magazine-style publication called *Answers,* which answered the most common questions I heard on the road. That publication grew into a book (and today is five books). So, we'd already been using the term "answers," a reference to 1 Peter 3:15 which commands us to always be ready with an answer for the hope we have.

In 1986 we'd produced a video series titled *Understanding Genesis* and our ICR conferences were called *Back to Genesis.* When we left ICR we changed the name of our events, pulling from our *Answers* publication and *Understanding Genesis* to become Answers in Genesis events. One of our seminars was filmed in Akron, Ohio, in 1993 and sold as a VHS series called *Answers in Genesis.*

As the board discussed a new name for the ministry "Answers in Genesis" was suggested — and it stuck. It got away from the word "science," which implied technical and only scientific issues, and emphasized that Genesis is where the answers to the questions of our day come from. Yes, Genesis 1–11 is the foundation for all doctrine, for the rest of the Bible, and, in fact, for everything. The answers will always be in Genesis!

> But sanctify the Lord God in your hearts: and be ready always to give an answer to every man that asketh you a reason of the hope that is in you with meekness and fear: (1 Peter 3:15 KJV)

In early 1995 we introduced Answers in Genesis for the first time as the name for the ministry.

Early Ministry Endeavors

That first year of ministry was a full and blessed one. One early staff member described it as "jumping aboard a freight train, with the staff holding on by the fingernails!" Throughout the course of 1994 we hosted over 100 events and reached over 86,000 people across the nation. Our first major conference was held in March 1994 (yes, the same month we moved to KY!) in Denver, Colorado, where 2,200 adults and over 4,000 students attended. There were so many people at that event, 60–70 kids sat at my feet on the stage because there was nowhere else to put them!

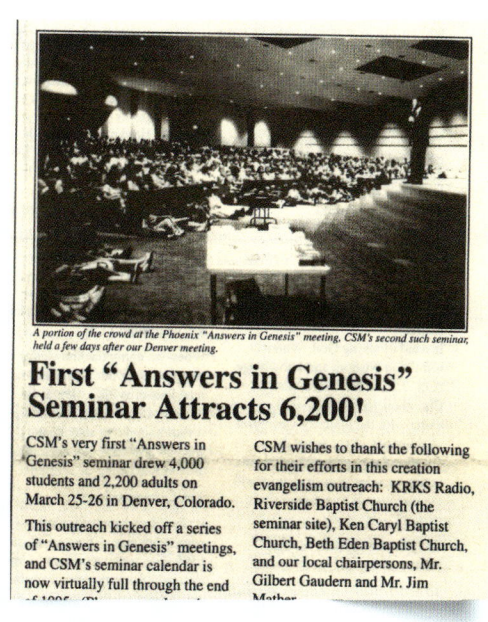

A portion of the crowd at the Phoenix "Answers in Genesis" meeting, CSM's second such seminar, held a few days after our Denver meeting.

First "Answers in Genesis" Seminar Attracts 6,200!

CSM's very first "Answers in Genesis" seminar drew 4,000 students and 2,200 adults on March 25-26 in Denver, Colorado. This outreach kicked off a series of "Answers in Genesis" meetings, and CSM's seminar calendar is now virtually full through the end CSM wishes to thank the following for their efforts in this creation evangelism outreach: KRKS Radio, Riverside Baptist Church (the seminar site), Ken Caryl Baptist Church, Beth Eden Baptist Church, and our local chairpersons, Mr. Gilbert Gaudern and Mr. Jim Mather.

Ken is very accomplished at playing the piano.

Including their time at ICR, Ken and Mark have probably recorded about 10,000 radio programs together.

Halfway through my talk, my projector "clunked," and half the screen disappeared. Then it "clunked" again... and the other half of the screen disappeared! Mike had to run and find a new projector, wade through all the kids, and set it up, but despite the lack of seating and technical difficulties, we received a tremendous response.

At another early event, Mike and I took two brand-new, still in the box, overhead projectors with us. Mike set up one projector and then left it to go and chat with some of the event organizers only to hear me say, "I don't think this thing is supposed to be smoking this much!" Smoke was pouring out of the machine. The lens was off by about a quarter of an inch and was melting the plastic, filling the air with smelly smoke. That was quite the way to start a major seminar!

That April we hired our first employee: Kathy Ellis, a connection through a friend who knew someone who went to her church. Her husband, Wilbert, took Mark out for pizza and kept embarrassing his wife by insisting Mark needed to hire her as his secretary. Well, the pizza bribery worked, and Kathy was hired to work in our office — an office with only one phone line (in those days phones had cords!) stretched from our "computer room," across a hallway, and down into Mark's office. Kathy turned out to be a great hire. She remained with the ministry for 30 years, eventually serving as VP of our administrative team, until her retirement in 2024. Well, mostly retirement! We did get her to come back at times to "download" her 30 years of knowledge to others.

In October we launched a daily radio program, Answers...with Ken Ham,

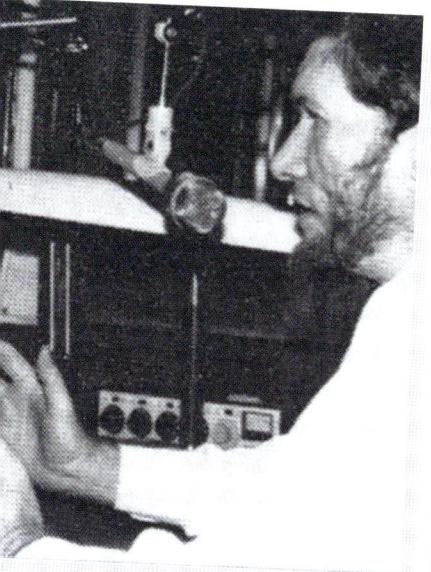

Vicki Eggert, Kathy Ellis, and Mary Chivers. Kathy was our very first employee.

Ken and the overhead projector days.

60-second short. A prominent advertising agency, Ambassador, had worked with us during the Back to Genesis radio program we'd done with ICR (we did around 2,000 episodes of that program), and agreed to help us launch a new series. We viewed Christian radio as strategic; not only were we getting answers out by the radio waves, but if a radio station was already carrying our program, they were usually happy to advertise a seminar coming to their local area.

When we arrived in Kentucky, we reached out to Calvary Baptist Church in nearby Covington as they had a recording studio in their building. I'd done a seminar at the pastor's Bible college but that was about all they knew about us, and yet Pastor Charles Wagner graciously agreed to let us use their studio free of charge. In August we sent out 900 CDs featuring the very first episodes of Answers...with Ken Ham, 45 episodes in all. CDs, rather than the more conventional press tapes, were a more expensive method but we wanted to show radio stations we were serious. Forty-five stations immediately picked up the program and by the end of the year that number had risen by nearly 100. Each month our ministry received over 1,400 calls just from radio listeners.

I'm still doing that program today, over 8,000 episodes later — though these days it's sent out digitally. CDs are yet another thing of the past! It's now carried on nearly 1,000 stations and now there's even a Spanish version, *Respuestas Hoy,* heard across the US and Latin America. Every time I do a meet and greet, I meet people whose first exposure to the AiG message and ministry was those 60-second spots — some people have even come to faith in Christ from hearing those programs and then going to our website to learn more.

We were also distributing Creation magazine, produced by the Australian ministry, advertising subscriptions first during ICR events and now during our Answers in Genesis seminars. After we arrived from Australia, Mally and I had distributed the magazine from our house with our kids and some friends stuffing and labeling the envelopes for mailing. When that got to be too much, Mary Chivers, originally from Master Books, took over from her home in San Diego. It was clear very quickly that being headquartered in Kentucky and distributing the magazine from a garage in California was not going to work. We needed Mary to come with us, but, understandably, she didn't want to move so far away.

One day, before the move to Kentucky, we got our new CSM logo and all three of us were so excited about it. As Mary listened to us chat enthusiastically about the logo and the impending move, the Lord pricked her heart to come with us. Her husband agreed to the move, and we were able to continue distributing Creation across the U.S., not only getting answers out there but providing some much-needed revenue for the ministry. Phil and Mary remained involved with the ministry until Phil's passing and Mary, now Mary Carmack, and her husband Steve worked in the ministry for some time and are still supporters to this day.

By 2006 we noticed that magazine subscription numbers weren't what they once were with over 50% of subscribers declining to renew after their first year. We surveyed our subscribers and discovered they still wanted a magazine, just something with a different emphasis. We decided to launch our own magazine, focused on culturally relevant biblical worldview teaching and practical apologetics application, with biblical and scientific teaching on origins and biblical authority. It would also include a children's section. We'd call it *Answers*.

Answers was a hit. Today, while most print magazines are dying out, *Answers* is going strong with a small, but very dedicated and talented, team producing each quarterly issue. *Answers* also comes as a digital version and now includes a separate 32-page kids' magazine, *Kids Answers* (which is also available as a separate subscription), and it has won dozens of awards. The Lord has truly blessed that publication. As technology continues to change, who knows what modifications will be made in the future.

First *Answers* Magazine

A Fight for the Ministry

Despite the blessings and exciting growth, that first year was not without its battles. When we arrived in Kentucky, we set the ministry up as a non-profit and began receiving tax-deductible donations. That September we received a disturbing letter from the IRS that said something to the effect of, "We don't believe Creation Science Ministries meets the new rules for non-profits. It seems you are merely promoting your own materials to make money under the guise of a non-profit organization."

The IRS had implemented rules to exclude frauds and hucksters from starting "non-profits" to sell their own materials and make huge amounts of money. Since a large part of our ministry was selling materials, including my books such as *The Lie,* the IRS was suspicious of us, and we had to fight to keep our non-profit status. Without that status we couldn't send donation receipts out at end-of-year. It was critical that we keep our non-profit status. But things got dicey when an IRS representative from Washington, D.C., said he was going to recommend denying our application, but we could always file an appeal. We did not want to fight an appeals battle. We were sweating bullets — how could we convince the IRS we weren't a bunch of charlatans; we were just trying to start a ministry?

I called up Don Rohrer at ICR for advice and he recommended a lawyer in San Diego who was very brash, rather cocky, and very confident he could help us — if I would agree to one thing: giving all the royalties for my past and future books to the ministry. This lawyer said the core issue was the IRS didn't want the directors of the ministry making money off of book sales (even though authors typically do receive royalties from published works). Master Books was struggling financially and wasn't paying royalties at that time but carte blanche giving them up — including for any future books — was a big financial consideration. But Mally and I didn't hesitate. If the ministry needed us to, as Mike put it, "sign over our kids' college fund to the ministry," we'd do it. The lawyer drew up the proposal, the IRS was placated, and there was great rejoicing in October when the approval notice officially arrived. The ministry would continue, and we praised the Lord. Years later, we found out such a rule does not apply to non-profits like they insisted — but such were the battles we've faced over the years.

Over the years I've been accused by various atheists and secular groups of being a charlatan, only in it for the money. One time, I received a letter chastening me for my supposed net worth of over $54 million! Well, that was news to me! We dug around and, sure enough, there's a website listing my net worth at $54 million. It seems they assumed I own the Creation Museum (it is owned by the non-profit Answers in Genesis), and they determined what they believed my net worth is off of that. Because of that one silly article, we've had a number of people ask why my net worth is so big. We did have one of our attorneys try to get this false information removed but, for many reasons, that turned out to be nigh on impossible. So, we've just had to live with that false information out there, and trust most people know you can't believe everything you read on the internet!

When it comes to finances, I stand before the Lord with a clear conscience — I certainly haven't made millions of dollars. From the beginning, finances have been a step of faith for me and Mally, but God has always been faithful to meet our needs, and we've followed my parent's example of being generous with what God has given us. Our treasure is in heaven because, as my mum always said, "It's only what's done for Jesus that lasts."

He Makes Dreams Out of Nothing

It was still 1994 and we were in Mt. Vernon, Ohio, for a conference. I'd heard about Buddy Davis over the years because we'd had a few articles back in the 80's in *Creation* magazine featuring this guy from America who sculpted dinosaurs and believed what the Bible taught about history. Buddy and his wife, Kay, had brought his dinosaurs to the conference and displayed them on the stage. After I spoke, this kindly, humble man came up to me, introducing himself as the guy who sculpted dinosaurs and inviting all of us back to his rural log cabin. Buddy and Kay had a business renting Buddy's stunning dinosaurs to shopping malls or for other special events. But when I shared with Buddy that we had a burden for building a creation museum but couldn't figure out how to start it, his eyes lit up. He said he and Kay had talked about how they'd love to see his dinosaurs displayed in a museum that honored God. I immediately saw his dinosaurs as the key to making the long dreamed of museum a reality.

That meeting at Buddy's log cabin was really a turning point in regard to the building of what is now the Creation Museum. You see, dinosaurs have always fascinated people, especially children, but they are almost always used as a teaching tool for evolution and millions of years. Meeting Buddy and seeing his world-class dinosaur sculptures really opened our eyes and got us excited about what we could do at the Creation Museum.

While at his cabin, I saw Buddy had a guitar hanging on the wall and asked him to play. He shook his head; he'd sort of given up music after pursuing a career in country music and not "making it." I finally convinced him that night to play, and he sang his original song, "He Makes Dreams Out of Nothing."

> He makes dreams out of nothing,
> And he makes the dreams come true.
> He has given you a vision,
> You must hold on to the view.
> If you but ask you shall receive,
> But in your heart, you must believe.
> He has a victory for you,
> And he'll make sure your dreams come true.

I was so moved as Buddy played, I just blurted out without really thinking, "Buddy, when we open the creation museum, I want you to sing that song." At this point we had no plan, no land, no money — just a dream of a museum that would point families to their Creator. Thirteen years later, Buddy sang that very song during the grand opening of the Creation Museum.

After that first meeting, Buddy and Kay were quickly involved with the ministry, eventually traveling with me. Buddy would display his dinosaurs (and we'd dream of the day when we could display them in our museum), he'd give concerts, and together we'd teach families and children.

Over the years, Buddy composed many songs based on my talks, including one on godly men (inspired by my family and parenting talk), one on six days based on my "relevance of Genesis" talk, one on the truth of only one race pulling from my "One Race, One Blood" presentation, a song about the 7 C's of History drawn from our museum exhibits, and even a funny song about cats (after I spoke about how much I dislike cats!). But his signature song — kids just love this song — is "Billions of

Dead Things," a song about the fossils that were laid down during Noah's Flood based on my saying, "If there really was a worldwide flood, what would you expect to find? Billions of dead things, buried in rock layers, laid down by water, all over the 'earth.' And that's exactly what we see!"

One time Buddy sang his "Billions of Dead Things" song at a church concert when I wasn't there. Afterwards, a man came up to him and said, "Did you know there's this Australian guy who stole the words of your song and uses them in his talk?" Buddy loved to make the audience laugh by telling that story when we were on stage together.

Yes, the Lord granted Buddy his dream of writing and producing music. Families and kids have always loved both his songs and Buddy himself — he was so "homely" (the Aussie way of saying comfortable or "down-to-earth"), kind, and friendly.

Buddy's dinosaurs became a major exhibit in the Creation Museum called "Buddy's Dino Den." People of all ages love Buddy's dinosaurs and all the teaching that goes with them to explain these creatures using a truly biblical worldview. The largest dinosaur he sculptured was T-rex. It is so large we had to bring it into the museum while the building was in the early stages of construction.

One reason Buddy was so good at sculpting was because he was also a taxidermist. This skill gave him a knowledge of animal anatomy. Buddy was also an avid hunter. He loved to hunt deer and other animals for food and to mount their heads. Once he took me squirrel

hunting — he loved squirrel stew — telling me to be very quiet and just stand still until we saw squirrels. He had the gun. We were out in the woods, and I was trying to be very quiet. I thought I would just lean up against a nearby tree...and suddenly the whole tree came crashing down making an enormous noise. Buddy looked at me in disgust and said, "That was a dead tree, you don't lean on a dead tree. Let's go home, you frightened all the squirrels away."

Buddy was such an avid hunter, I would tease him, "What are you going to do in heaven where there will be no death and so you can't hunt animals and eat them?" His reply, "Well I believe in heaven I will go hunting and shoot the animal and then it will get back up and wave at me!"

Buddy was more than "just" a major inspiration for the Creation Museum with his dinosaurs, a talented singer-songwriter, or a ministry partner — Buddy became one of the closest friends I've ever had. He and I were like brothers. I'm not as close to most people as I was to Buddy. In 2024, after three years of dealing with serious health issues, Buddy went to be with the Lord. It is really sad to see him leave this earth, but he's left an incredible legacy, and it will go on and on. Buddy was one of a kind!

Over the years, Buddy and I traveled the world giving our Dinosaurs, Genesis, and the Gospel program (later renamed Dinosaurs and More) to children and families. During this one-and-a-half-hour program, I would do biblical worldview and creation teaching and Buddy would sing songs, perform a few illusions, and we'd banter back and forth, joke around, and poke fun at each other. Kids loved it.

Buddy, Mike and Ken, 1997

Well, the last time we gave that program was in the Answers Center at the Ark Encounter just a few weeks before the stroke that began his health issues. After

Buddy making a very large T-Rex.

we finished the program, and he was preparing to leave, Buddy turned to me and said something like,

"Ken, I just want to tell you, I can't say enough, how much being part of this ministry has meant to me. I can't explain enough how much this ministry has done for me. It's been so phenomenal for me to be involved with it. It's been my life. I just can't thank you enough for what this has meant to me."

As he said that, I had this sinking feeling that it almost sounded like a good-bye. I just wonder if the Lord prompted him to say that, because not long after that he had a stroke and could no longer speak or communicate. It was as if the Lord had said, "Your time of active ministry has ended but it will continue on through Answers in Genesis and the legacy you've left."

Yes, there comes a time when we finish this work on earth and God calls each of us home. This doesn't make sense from an earthly perspective — I just think of how much more ministry Buddy and I could have done together — but God is in control and Buddy had fulfilled the mission God called him to. And now he is totally healed and worshiping the Lord in his heavenly home.

Red Sea Moment

Meeting Buddy Davis in Ohio after a conference was the hand of God. Then he invites us to his cabin afterwards and we have the time to go, it was odd to say the least. Then him playing the song "He Makes Dreams out of Nothing" was truly a Red Sea Moment!

> To really understand Buddy's heart, here's a transcription of the prayer he prayed at the end of that last program he and I did together.

This is my favorite part of the program, where I get to give this message. Wow, what an honor I have. Don't we have an awesome God?

Are you saved? Are ya? Have you asked Jesus to be your Lord and Savior? If you have not, you need to do it. It will be the most important thing you ever do in your life. Know where you're going to go to when you leave this planet, you better — and you can! You can live eternally in heaven where it's better, the Bible says it's better than anything we can imagine and, let me warn you, hell is worse than anything you can imagine. There's no gray area; you're going to be one of two places. And you better make sure you're going to be in heaven, and you can take care of that right now!

But it's gotta be the real deal, you've gotta mean it. Don't mean you're going to be perfect, none of us are, but you gotta be sincere. And if you've never prayed this prayer, now's the time to do it. And it's not the words we say, it's the Holy Spirit's going to touch your heart, and I really pray he's touching your heart big time right now, because I want you to be in heaven. It's going to be awesome. You be there — make sure you're going to be there!

Just say these words right here, "Lord God, I know that I have sinned against you. I have not obeyed you perfectly and I repent of that — that just means turn from my sin — I love you and trust you with all my heart. I believe that your Son Jesus died on the Cross for my sin and rose from the grave. I trust in Jesus alone for salvation" — guys, there's no other name but Jesus — "thank you for forgiving my sin, saving me, and make me part of your family. In Jesus' name, amen."

AnswersinGenesis.org Launches

"Ken, we need a website." "A website? What's that?" I thought, "That's fine, Carl, that's your little thing, you go and do it."

Believe it or not, in 1995 the internet was not yet "a thing" — Google wouldn't even officially begin until 1998! I had no idea what the internet and websites were, but Carl was excited and really felt we needed a website and email (I didn't know what that was either). I thought perhaps it would someday help us reach more people, so Carl Kerby began working on ChristianAnswers.net, a seven-ministry mega site featuring answers to core questions from various ministries. Naturally, we took the creation/evolution questions.

Turns out, the internet was rather a big deal! On May 16, 1997, we purchased the domain AnswersinGenesis.org and Carl began plunking out HTML in-between shifts as an air traffic controller. That's right, our website wasn't started by a computer guy — it was started by someone who really didn't know much about computers! But today that website is one of the most accessed Christian websites in the world, reaching tens of millions of people every year.

Since the early days of our website, we've focused on producing fresh new content every day. Mark Looy got that strategy from a broadcasters' convention in Washington, D.C., where Mark Cuban — before he was famous — gave a workshop to about 20 people on the internet's potential. He said a website should focus on staying fresh so people would keep coming back to see what was new. It was good advice, and we still follow that same strategy today.

Even if we didn't know it then, that website was a major key to the success of the ministry, keeping us at the cutting-edge of technology. Our AiG website has had hundreds of millions of visitors from 220 different countries, with hundreds of thousands of views of just our gospel page alone. Oh, and three of the first employees we hired to help with the website — Frost Smith, Linda Saur, and my son, Jeremy — are still with the ministry working on the website as of the writing of this book.

AIG website then and now.

God Calls My Dad and Robert Home

Dad's voice sounded tired as he said, "Kenneth, I won't be here when you come home. It's better for you to give your talk at the conference — I'd rather you be giving the message God's called you to give and be talking about God's Word. That's the most important thing. That's what we trained our children to do."

• •

It was June of 1995, and I'd just learned my dad's heart was not doing well, he was in the hospital, and it looked bad. His heart had often troubled him, forcing an early retirement at 55 after a major heart attack and multiple bypass surgeries. If I wanted to see him before he died, I needed to hop on a plane now. But I was scheduled to speak at a big homeschool conference in Indianapolis, Indiana. I called home to find out what Dad would want me to do. He wanted me to stay and give my talk. It was more important to him that people heard God's Word, so I headed for Indianapolis as planned.

I was in my hotel room June 9th, 1995 the evening the conference began. The phone rang; the call was from Australia. My brother called to tell me the news that Dad was now with the Lord. With a heavy heart I hung up and immediately answered another call, this time a radio station calling to interview me. I completed the interview, left the hotel, walked across the parking lot to the convention center, mounted the stage, and gave my keynote address, including dealing with the death and suffering issue starting with Genesis.

Seated in the large audience was a firetruck manufacturer named Joe Boone, along with his pregnant wife and young child. They had never heard a talk like that before. Years later Joe would tell me my address turned them around as a family and they basically committed their lives to the Lord that night and began homeschooling their children. Over the years, I've actually had others tell me something very similar about that particular talk at that conference. Perhaps there was a special anointing on me that night surrounding the death of my father. Whatever the reason, the Lord mightily used that evening to impact many people.

Ken and Joe Boone

Shortly after that talk, and the birth of their second child, Joe and his wife found out that she had a brain tumor. It would take her life nine years later. Joe says that talk I did on death and suffering really helped his family during that horrible time. Years later, Joe would sell his business of making equipment to rescue

people from fires here on earth and join a different kind of firefighting operation — one to save people from eternal fire! Joe now serves as the president of AiG.

People ask me how I could hold it together and speak after my father had just passed away. Well, at times I'm the type of person who can "pigeonhole" something. I just put it up there in the "too hard" basket and I'll deal with it later. I think that's how it worked that night. I was honoring my father's wishes; this is what he wanted me to do, and I knew that he was in heaven with the Lord.

I've had to do a lot of pigeonholing over 50 years of ministry. As you can imagine I've had to go down through many valleys and then up to the mountaintops and then down into the valleys again. It's only my trust in God and the never-ending support and counsel of my wonderful godly wife Mally that I've been able to get through those valleys. Mally's depth of spiritual understanding continues to amaze me day by day.

In God's gracious timing, we had an Australian tour booked in just a couple of weeks so we were able to leave a week earlier and go home for the memorial service. At the service all six of us Ham kids got up and shared a testimony about Dad. Although we all said very different things, we all really said the same thing: how much Dad encouraged us to stand on the authority of the word of God.

At the end of the service a friend said, "I'm going to go home and ask my kids 'What are you going to say about me when I'm dead?' Because what your kids said about your dad is what I want them to say about me. I want to impact them spiritually."

My dear younger brother, Robert, who passed away seven years to the day after my father, told me about a conversation he had with Dad while he was dying in the hospital. He asked Dad, "Why did you love God's Word so much?" Dad answered "My father died when I was only 16. Because I didn't have an earthly father then, I turned to the words of my heavenly Father and read them over and over again." Yes, Dad saturated himself in the Word of God.

When the group of Americans joined me a week later for their Australian tour, I brought them to my parents' house, as planned, for a meal and special Aussie desserts (people loved meeting real Aussies and having these kinds of authentic, homey experiences). Before he'd passed away, my father had built a little wooden Noah's ark to float in the swimming pool. It was painted black to seal it on the outside. He put weights in the bottom, and he was going to have it floating in the swimming pool with the American flag on one side and the Australian flag on the other side for the American group. My mother gave me that ark and today it's displayed in a little glass case in our Legacy Lobby at the Creation Museum as part of the Ham Family Legacy exhibit. It's featured alongside my father's Bible, open to Genesis.

That Bible had been given to my brother, David. He went "off the rails" and away from the Lord, but the Lord brought him back to himself and now he's a Christian on fire for the Lord. As he was greatly impacted by Answers in Genesis, I asked David if he would consider loaning that Bible to our creation museum someday as part of an exhibit highlighting the legacy of our parents. It was a very emotional request for David, that Bible meant an awful lot to him. But he decided that would be a great way to honor our parents and allow the world to see our father's Bible. Over the years, I've seen many people standing in front of that sobering exhibit, some with tears running down their cheeks. I've asked some of them, "What does this legacy exhibit mean to you?" As one couple answered, "it really challenges us as to what legacy we are leaving in our children and in this world."

My father knew of the vision we had for building a creation museum, but he never saw any of the plans or the construction of it. Nor did he ever hear us talk about building a life-size Noah's ark. But he knew how important it was to believe God's Word and I'm thrilled his legacy lives on in our attractions.

The ark made by my dad.

Heartbreak and Hope

My brother Robert preached a message a couple of years before his major health issue began called "The Experience Trap." In this message he dealt directly with the very issue he was being confronted with himself. It was like he was giving the sermon to himself.

Audio tapes of a sermon Robert preached called, "The Experience Trap."

Robert and Ken

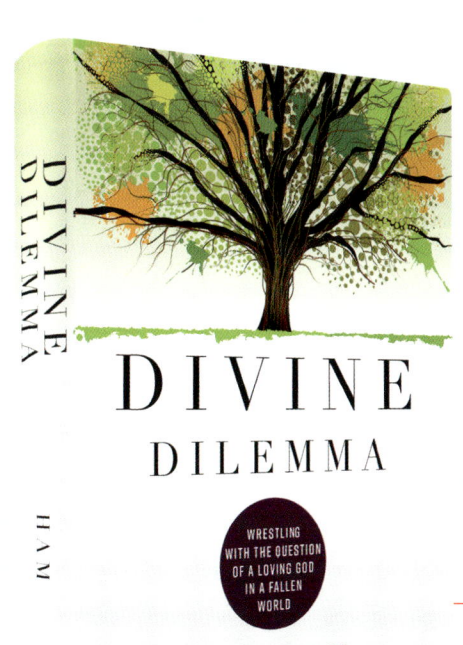

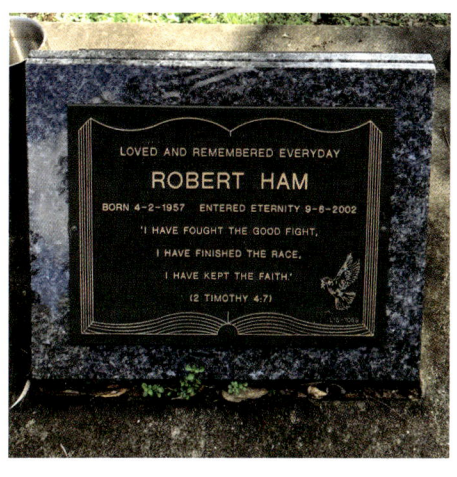

Robert's gravestone

A book Ken wrote chronicling how his godly mother dealt with the death of her husband and son.

Another Crisis

In 1996, the ministry hit another crisis: Master Books was in trouble, heading for bankruptcy. They were really the only young earth creation publisher in the country, and we needed them to stay in business so we could continue to have resources to sell. They decided to sell the company but who would buy a struggling publishing house, featuring mostly technical, scientific works? I knew for them to succeed they needed to put an emphasis on more laymen's materials and less technical works. If they did that, I knew we could sell them because, well, all the laymen's works were flying off the tables at our events!

Tim Dudley, the president of New Leaf Press, was interested in the purchase. The deal was nearly finished when…it fell through. We were crushed. George Hillstead from Master Books called, "Ken, you've got to call Tim and try and change his mind." I picked up the phone to call Tim. I vividly remember standing in my bedroom in our Kentucky home, staring out the window at the bleak winter scene, praying while the phone rang that Tim would say yes. He picked up.

"Tim," I pleaded, "I promise you, if you buy Master Books and publish our books, we can sell a lot of books. You just need a different philosophy from the current strategy. Together we can have a huge impact on this culture and the Kingdom." I did my best to help him catch the vision for what we were trying to do for the Lord and then we waited.

> On February 1, 1996, to our massive relief, Tim purchased Master Books. You'll notice they're the publisher of this book, nearly 30 years later. Yes, they're still the largest publisher of young earth creation materials and all of my books over the years have been published through them.

Tim Dudley and Ken standing by massive timber while the Ark is being built.

Controversy, Fruit Flies, and God's Blessing

The ministry continued to grow. That year, 1995, we first announced in a newsletter to our supporters that we were going to build a creation museum. (We still didn't know how or where the money would come from!) We began searching for land but, in the meantime, moved the rapidly growing ministry from the strip mall to an office building and a warehouse on Industrial Road. It gave us some much-needed space, and, for the first time, we had a real warehouse! Master Books didn't need to drop ship resources to our events for us anymore; we could now pack and ship our own orders.

But that building didn't come without its challenges, namely fruit flies. Yes, fruit flies! Our rented office building was connected to a large warehouse where a company was recycling used plastic soda bottles. And you know what that means? Lots of sugar residue in millions of bottles. And what did that do? Attract millions, maybe billions, (it seemed like trillions!) of fruit flies that infiltrated our office building and tortured all of us working there.

Today we have a beautiful office building with a wonderful working environment for our office staff. I sometimes think about the staff who come today, wanting to work in such a nice place, but to get where we are, there was quite a long journey. And like the Israelites we have battles to fight and lots of things to learn as He leads us little by little to do bigger and bigger things. And the fruit fly battles were just one little part of this journey. And it certainly makes us appreciate so much more what God has provided for us today.

| Industrial Road Office

In the fruit fly-infested section of the warehouse we rented, we also stored some of Buddy's dinosaurs. Opposition from atheists to the museum plans kept us constantly in the local news and, as the controversy grew, we made national and then international headlines. When media arrived to interview us about our plans for a creation museum, I would take them into the warehouse and show them Buddy's dinosaurs, saying, "We're going to use these to teach families about the truth of God's Word."

Atheists hated that we were going to use dinosaurs — which they sort of view as "theirs" — to teach children about the Bible. The opposition grew so fierce that a local, who didn't know us well, was so concerned about the way we were being attacked that his family gave $1 million towards the project! What a blessing.

By 2006, our radio program was being heard on over 800 U.S. stations and hundreds more overseas, our website had taken off and had even won the "Best Ministry Website" award from the National Religious Broadcasters, and our staff had reached 100 people scattered between four offices. That year we did over 300 events, sometimes speaking before six different audiences during a trip to one city.

Mexico Mega Conference with 6,000 in attendance just North of Mexico City in 2019.

Living in Babylon Conference, Australia 2024.

In early 2007, we launched Answers Worldwide, expanding our international outreach with overseas speaking tours, apologetics training for international Christian leaders, and translated materials in over 70 languages. Today we're continuing to grow our international footprint with offices in the UK, Canada, Australia, and Latin America. And we're harnessing the power of AI to speed up the translation process and create videos that feature our speakers who are suddenly able to speak any language in the world! It's amazing how technology is allowing us to reach the nations for the Lord.

Yes, the Lord was growing the ministry, and it was time for our dream to come true. The Lord answered the prayer John Thallon and I had prayed on a little piece of land near Brisbane in the 1980s. He gave us our creation museum.

> *When New Leaf Press bought Master Books that was a huge deal. New Leaf Press was an established Christian publisher and knew how to produce books. They were also willing to publish any and all books ICR or AIG wanted published. That was beyond Miraculous!*

1995 – 2014

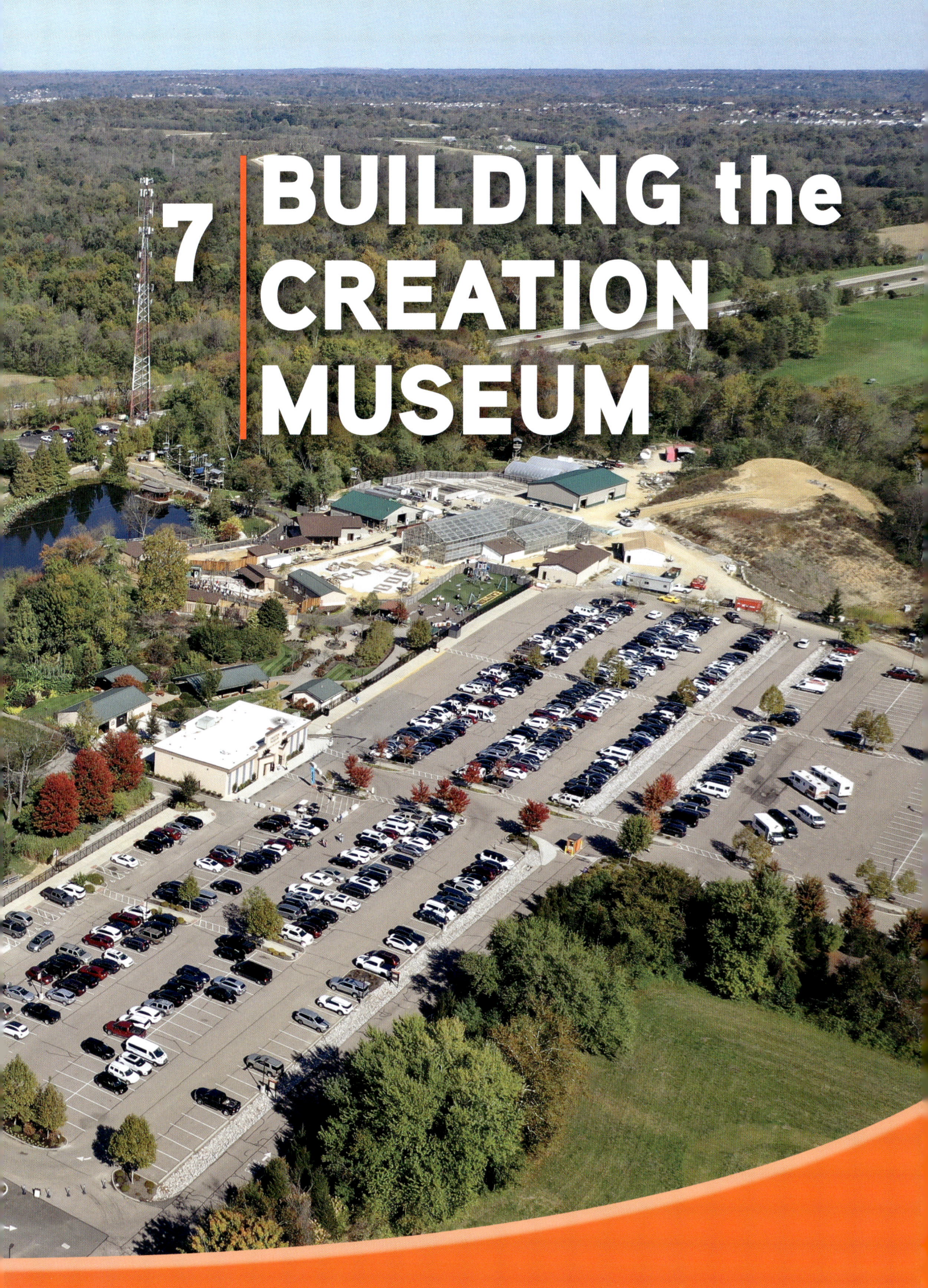

7 | BUILDING the CREATION MUSEUM

The Three God Chose

Imagine you've been asked to assemble a team to build a large Christian ministry from the ground up, including a world-class Creation Museum and the world's largest free-standing timber frame structure, a life-size Noah's Ark. Well, you would definitely want:

- A science teacher with an entrepreneurial spirit brought up in a Christian home in Australia
- A history buff who loved participating in quiz shows, has lots of random, general knowledge, and is great at PR
- A retired lieutenant colonel from the U.S. Army who knows how to plan battles

...right?

Actually, you would probably think that's a ridiculous selection of men, but those are the three men God chose to found Answers in Genesis and build the Creation Museum and, eventually, the Ark Encounter.

One time I was speaking in Michigan, and a professor who attended my talk, and lectured at a university on business start-ups, shared this with me: "When I think about the three of you starting this ministry, you actually have the three different types of people it takes for a successful start-up: a visionary, a marketer, and the doer." God brought three unlikely men together. One is an entrepreneurial visionary and marketer (me), one is great at PR and marketing (Mark), and one knows how to get things done (Mike). Apparently, those are the classic characteristics needed to accomplish something like this, and God, in His wisdom, brought us all together.

Ken, Mark, and Mike around 1995.

The Battle Begins

To build our Creation Museum we first needed land to put it on. A small, rural plot of land came up for sale in our area and looked like the perfect spot for a museum, only 10 minutes off the interstate and large enough for a 30,000-square-foot building (an arbitrary number we chose). We signed a contract, contingent on our attempt to get it rezoned. (We didn't tell anyone we didn't have any money yet. We knew the Lord had called us to this, and He would provide.) Zoning didn't seem like it would be much of an issue. We only needed the zoning commission and then the Fiscal Court to approve our request.

The zoning commission unanimously approved it, assuring us that the Fiscal Court rarely stopped projects that the commission approved. It seemed like the land would be ours, and we were already dreaming up fundraising ideas.

Then a local group of atheists heard about it. They immediately opposed our purchase, turning our desire for a museum that honored God into a political issue. Their vocal opposition soon made the papers, and it seemed we were headline news day after day as the battle wore on. Because of all the opposition, a zoning meeting was called, in which one lady accused us of being a cult. "He's Jim Jones," she cautioned the court, pointing her finger at me. "He's coming to get our kids!"

Gathered with the atheists and other secularists was a liberal pastor, adorned with a large wooden cross around his neck (presumably to make it obvious to the court and the papers that not all professing "Christians" were on our side). The late Pastor Charles Wagner, whose church we attended, approached this pastor afterward with, "You should be ashamed of yourself. Take that cross off."

To this day it greatly saddens me how much opposition we've received from people who claim to be fellow Christians and yet they compromise God's Word and fight to keep us from being able to equip Christians with answers and share the gospel with a lost world.

In other meetings, we were accused of violating the so-called separation of church and state by trying to build a private museum on private property funded by private donations! So ridiculous.

Another person blasted us as trying to undermine the museum at nearby Big Bone Lick State Historic Site, the birthplace of American vertebrate paleontology. At the salt lick at Big Bone, mammoth, mastodon, and other megafauna fossils had been uncovered in the days of Thomas Jefferson, giving the area the name "Big Bone." This state park was reasonably close to our desired property, but we'd never heard of it. After being accused of trying to undermine this state-run evolutionary "museum" we went and checked it out.

It wasn't really a museum; it was a park visitor's center that featured a gift shop and a few bones, artifacts, and signage in glass cases in the basement. Atheists still claim we tried to undermine Big Bone Lick and the evolutionary teaching in the visitor's center.

The fight dragged on with meeting after meeting, each one highlighted by the media who, I'm sure, were enjoying all the drama. At the final meeting the Fiscal Court members (three of whom were liberal-leaning) voted down our zoning request, a rare happening as the zoning commission had unanimously voted yes. We had lost our property. Though somewhat discouraged, that wasn't going to stop us.

A reporter asked me afterward, "So, Mr. Ham, does this mean the end of the Creation Museum?"

"Absolutely not," I confidently replied, "God's called us to do this so we're going to find a better piece of property."

What You Meant for Evil

One of our employees was tasked with the challenge of finding another piece of property for the Creation Museum. He found a beautiful 50-acre farm, right by an I-275 exit. (I-275 is the loop that goes around Cincinnati, with the bottom part of the loop going through Northern Kentucky and then a bit of Indiana.) The farm was close to the Cincinnati Airport and featured a beautiful lake. We found out later that when I-275 was under construction, the contractors parked their big construction vehicles on the property and raised the dam to make the lake as a "thank you" to the property owner.

There was plenty of space for our museum with room to grow. The asking price was $500,000 which was more than we had since, well, we really didn't have *any* money to put toward land.

The 50-acre farm close to the Cincinnati Airport which featured a beautiful lake.

"We'll give you $500,000 but could we pay it off at $100,000 a year for five years, interest free?" we asked the property owner. I don't know why we even thought to ask for such a preposterous deal. He certainly could have found someone who could pay the full price right away. Shockingly, he agreed. I have no explanation for why he agreed other than the Lord must have put it in his heart to accept our crazy offer. It was part of us stepping out in faith, but, as I always say, we have to step out responsibly but in faith, nonetheless. However, we knew we had another zoning battle ahead of us.

In preparation for the sale, the farmer had the property rezoned industrial. We needed it zoned for a public facility. Such a zoning would be better for the local area than a large, smelly factory or warehouse bringing in trucks and industrial waste. But would the fiscal court agree?

The Lord was already working on our behalf. Because of the debacle on the Fiscal Court over our first piece of property, two locals ran for Fiscal Court election solely on the platform of the injustice we had suffered. And, despite one of the two being completely unknown as a public figure, they both won! That was another God thing. There is no other way to explain it. Since one original court member already supported us, we now had a majority. This time our zoning request was approved. Not long after, both of those new Fiscal Court members moved out of the area. God had them there for this time to be in the right place to ensure the Creation Museum project would go ahead.

After that, some of the same people who'd opposed us the first time—three women in particular—sued us. Because the county had approved our zoning, the county attorney now had to defend us in the lawsuit. During one of the depositions, one of the women suing us was asked why she was so against us building a Creation Museum.

"I have three reasons," she said. Now you might not believe me when I give her reasons, but they are on record, and I was there and heard this for myself. These were her actual reasons for opposing the rezoning of this farmland from industrial to public use:

1. When it burns down (not "if" but "when"), it'll send all these ashes into the air, and all the houses in the area will burn down.

2. All of the dust the visitors will kick up will cause viruses to spread and make people sick.

3. The dinosaur roars will keep us all awake at night. (At this one the county attorney nearly fell of his chair.)

Those were her reasons for so staunchly opposing us. The depositions were sent to the judge, and we all arrived to plead our case. The judge called us, the plaintiffs, and all the attorneys into his chambers ahead of hearing the case. He looked at the plaintiffs and said, "All I can tell you is you need to have better reasons than what I've seen in all this documentation, or I am going to rule against you."

In the courtroom, the plaintiffs took the witness stand and repeated their interesting reasons for opposing us. I was put on the witness stand and questioned, and our attorney questioned them, and finally it was time for the judge to make his decision.

He addressed the plaintiffs, "I told you in my chambers if you didn't have anything better, I'd be ruling against you." And he did. The property was rezoned. After many months of battles, we could build our museum.

It was a long battle, but we prevailed.

We closed on the museum property on May 4, 2000.

The whole situation still reminds me of Genesis 50:20.

> As for you, you meant evil against me, but God meant it for good (Genesis 50:20 ESV).

Satan intended to stop the Creation Museum from being built, but God used that opposition to give us an even better piece of property in a far better location with visibility from the interstate where thousands of vehicles drive by each day.

Instead of the 30,000-square-foot museum we had planned on building, we decided to build a much bigger building totaling 75,000 square feet for the museum with another 30,000 square feet for offices. And we had room for growth, as over the years we have developed our stunning botanical gardens, a zoo, three parking lots, a beautiful four-greenhouse conservatory, zip lines, and more to come! And it was all a miracle from the Lord. The museum welcomes so many visitors today that our offices moved to a new location in March 2025, and those additional 30,000 square feet will be turned into more museum space!

Now for the Next Step

Now came the question of exactly how we were going to build this thing. We didn't know the first thing about building a museum nor did we have any money to build it. But that "fire in my bones" was burning intensely. God was calling us to do this, so we knew He would direct us on the right path.

We figured the best place to start was with a building. A friend of the ministry offered to use his architectural skills to design the building for us. He eventually moved our project over to a mechanical engineer at a major architectural firm who asked his higher-ups if they would do the architectural work for free. They agreed! It was another miracle.

We continued to spread the word that this museum was really happening, sending out mailings to our supporters and hosting banquets across the country, asking believers to join with us financially in this exciting project. They responded enthusiastically, and we saw God provide both miraculously and through the generosity of His people over and over again. The museum would cost $27 million (we didn't know that at this stage) and, while we did receive several six-figure gifts, 75% of the funds came from supporters who gave an average of $130. Yes, God was faithful to use many thousands of people to provide for our needs.

When people asked us what we would put inside the museum, we showed them photos of Buddy Davis' dinosaur models. Buddy had sent many of his dinosaurs to our warehouse so when the media visited, we were sure to show off these dinosaurs. We had no idea how we would display them or how we would incorporate biblical teaching; we just knew somehow this would happen.

I sometimes wonder what would have happened if we told people we had no idea how we were going to do this, and no idea what would happen inside the museum. In one sense we were amateurs, but we all knew God had called us to accomplish this, and we had to trust Him.

We decided to host our first event on our new property: a small prayer meeting to thank the Lord for His kindness and ask for His continued blessing. At this point we hadn't done anything to the property. It was just a field with tall grass and the remains of some decaying cow patties from the previous occupants. As we were praying, a police car pulled into the field. "A neighbor called and reported an unlawful meeting," the sheriff deputy informed us. "I didn't know we needed a permit to host a prayer meeting on our property," I protested. "I'm all for you guys. I'm supportive of what you're doing," he replied, "but I have to come out here and give you a warning because there was a complaint. Just make sure next time you get a permit." From then on, we made sure to get a permit before hosting any events or prayer meetings on our land. That same neighbor has tried a number of things over the years to harass us, including turning up at zoning meetings to object.

Prayer Rally, November 20, 1998

Groundbreaking
March 16, 2001

Groundbreaking

When we had raised enough money to begin construction, we held a groundbreaking ceremony on March 17, 2001—and we had a permit! It was a freezing cold day but around a thousand of our supporters turned out anyway. We brought in a trailer with one of Buddy's dinosaurs on it. Buddy sang, I spoke, and we all prayed. Then all of the board members picked up gold-painted shovels and rammed them into what felt like permafrost. It was a huge moment—decades in the making and a gracious gift from God.

We didn't have all the money needed for the entire project, but we had enough to start and believed God would provide as we continued to fundraise and share what we were doing. This was the first large Creation Museum in the world, so people were excited to get behind the project. However, it took a lot of hard work, traveling across the country to conduct various fundraising events.

Then came the day the first fire hydrant was installed. That was what Mike calls "a significant emotional event" because it meant this was real. It was the first immovable structure on the property, and Mike turned to me, "Ken, look at this—

On a cold March day, Buddy sang at the groundbreaking.

we're really going to build this thing!" It meant so much to us, we took a picture of the both of us standing beside the fire hydrant! Now that sounds funny looking back on it, but after all we had been through, this really was an incredible event for us. I'm sure none of our staff today would want to get a photo taken with a fire hydrant, but this was part of our history, part of our pioneering days, and a symbol of how God was making this happen.

Foundation work began and after what felt like millions of years (foundation and preparation work always takes forever!), another "significant emotional event" took place as the steel for the lower level was raised into place. The museum was taking shape!

As the construction continued, our offices attached to the back were finished so we could move our 100 staff members from four different office buildings (including the fruit fly-infested one) on to one location in September 2004. Who would have thought a major stepping stone would be to have offices without fruit flies!

Mike will say that I drove our construction manager, Kevin Marksberry (who still serves with AiG at the writing of this book), crazy during this time as I kept bringing supporters and friends of the ministry in to tour the museum as it took shape. Apparently, this wasn't the best for OSHA workplace safety rules (we all wore hard hats!), but I was trying to help us raise enough money to keep building our museum!

First fire hydrant on site, August 2002.

MIKE ZOVATH

Ken will tell you that the construction of the museum building—the planning, the permits, working with the architects and contractors—was all on me. He says he could never have done it, so the Lord raised me up for that task. I tell everybody that the three of us founders drew straws to see who would have to do the museum. I got the short straw. I had never been involved in such a large construction project, and I kept wondering, "What am I doing?"

But in reality, I got the best job in the ministry from the time we started until now. The joy of coming up with ideas and having a team of creative, talented people coming up with even more ideas has just been phenomenal.

—Mike Zovath

God Provides Again

The building was quickly taking shape, but what about exhibits? Whenever anyone asked about our plans, as I stated earlier, we showed them Buddy's world-class dinosaur models and they were enamored. I can't stress enough how pivotal those dinosaurs were to the success of the ministry. We didn't know what we were doing. We just thought we would build a building and then figure out what to put inside eventually, but those dinosaurs made it look like we knew what we were doing! God really used them in a special way to bring about the museum. God had brought Buddy into our lives at the right time and had prepared Buddy and his wife Kay for this ministry.

And that's when God, in His sovereignty, brought along Patrick Marsh. It was 2001 and Patrick was in Japan, working as the senior designer for an amusement park. A family member saw an article about our Creation Museum and sent him the newspaper clipping. As a Christian and a creationist working in a secular field, he was intrigued, emailing us his résumé and the offer to be of service to us in designing our museum.

As we looked at his qualifications, our eyes almost popped out of our heads: He had worked for Universal Studios™ on their *Jaws*™ and *King Kong* attractions, had coordinated a team of 50 designers for the 1984 Olympic Games in Los Angeles, and had helped design the unveiling of the refurbished Statue of Liberty in New York Harbor in 1986. To say he was qualified was an understatement. We couldn't believe God had dropped someone of his caliber into our laps.

"We need to pray about this," Mike said. Two seconds later we emailed Patrick back. He responded, letting us know he would be flying in from Japan to Indiana in about a week or two and, if we were interested, he'd stop by and check out what we were doing. We replied that we would love to talk to him when he got here. Right after Mike sent that email, Patrick's computer crashed. He never received our response. He was a mere three hours from us in Kentucky, thought we weren't interested, and headed back overseas two weeks later.

When he arrived back in Japan, Mike's email finally dropped into Patrick's inbox. This time he called us, and we set up a time for him to meet with us. Mike will tell you it was "love at first sight." He was exactly what we needed. Patrick had a heart for the ministry, the skills, the vision, and the experience to fill our building with world-class exhibits.

But we had unknowingly committed "an unpardonable sin," as far as Patrick was concerned. "You don't build a building and design a museum to go in it," he cried when he saw our completed blueprints. "You design the exhibits and then build the building to fit what you want to do with the exhibits." Oops!

Patrick and Mike reviewing plans

Years later, as we were designing the life-size Ark project, I said to Patrick: "Remember when you said you don't design a building and then fit the exhibits inside, but you design the exhibits and then design the building for those? Well, do you realize God was preparing you to design exhibits in an already designed structure because God has already given us the dimensions of the Ark in the Bible?" Patrick just smiled.

On his own dime Patrick took our museum blueprints and headed for a craft supplies store. Two days later he left a white model and a note on Mike's desk before heading back to Japan. It was a model of our museum, with the interior laid out with a gently sloping ramp that allowed us to utilize the space two or three times. It was an ingenious idea and, for the first time, we had a 3D model of our museum and the beginnings of a plan

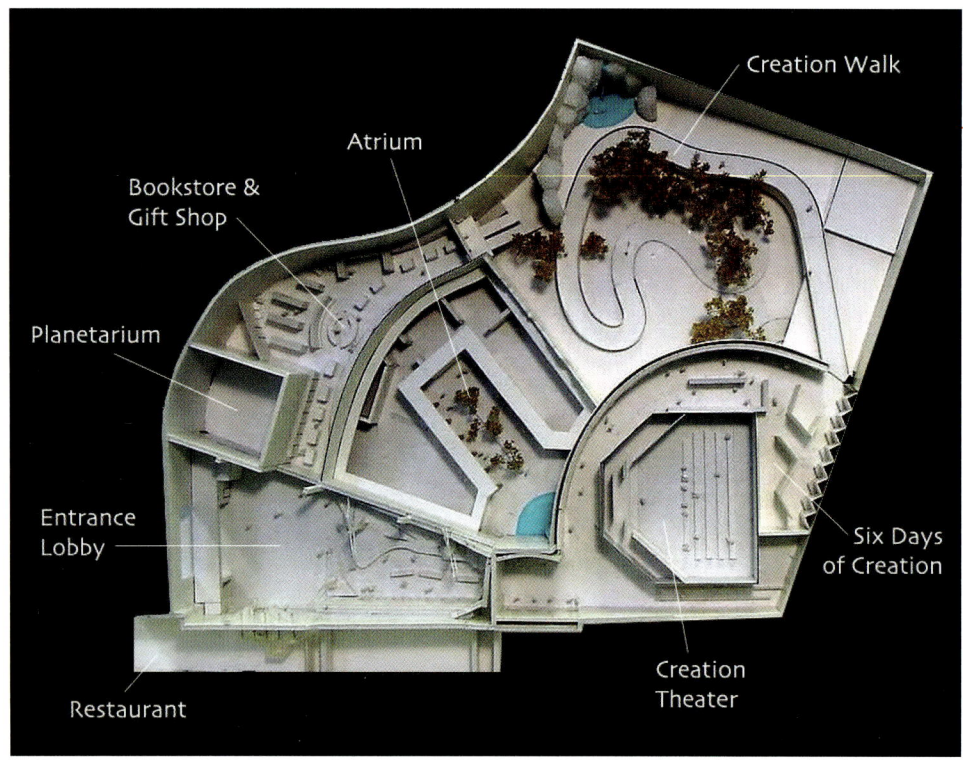

Patrick's beautiful model that he made for Mike.

for the exhibits. When his plane landed Patrick had an email in his inbox: *"You're hired. When can you come?"*

Patrick was truly a miracle. He went home to be with the Lord after a brief illness in 2021. I miss him as a friend and ministry partner, and the phenomenal design team he built up misses his friendship, guidance, and wisdom terribly, but his legacy lives on through the attractions he brought to life. What a gift from the Lord!

I've often wondered what would have happened if Patrick had not come into the picture. From my fallible human perspective, I realize the Creation Museum would not be anything like it is today. From the perspective of God's sovereignty, God had planned to bring Patrick along at the right time, preparing him to do something special for the Kingdom. Patrick and his wife were once Buddhists, and they were married in a Buddhist ceremony! But God grabbed hold of them and opened their hearts to the truth. When Patrick talked with us, he said he wanted so much to use his talents for the Lord and do something significant for the Christian faith. He basically pleaded with us to let him come and design the exhibits. We told him we couldn't pay what the secular theme parks pay, but he said he wasn't interested in money. It was more important for him to use the talents God had given him and all the experience he had to help proclaim the truth of God's Word.

Patrick Marsh
(1944–2021)

Patrick and Ken during the days of construction of the Creation Museum.

The Exhibits Take Shape

"What's your budget for exhibits?" Patrick asked us once he was back in Kentucky. We didn't really have one, but we thought we could do everything for about $4 million. We already had Buddy's dinosaurs and some cool exhibits we'd purchased at an auction in Baltimore from an aquarium that had closed. He loved Buddy's dinosaurs but informed us our aquarium exhibits were junk and useless. Ugh! *"I'm glad Patrick is making the decisions about exhibits now and not us,"* I thought.

"I can do something that will be Disney® -level, but it's going to cost $14 million." *Gulp.* That meant we needed to raise $10 million more, and it would delay our opening by a few years. But it would make our museum world-class. We went to our board, they approved the new budget (I praise the Lord for this group of godly men who were willing to step out in faith with us), and we got to work fundraising. Our advertising agency, JDA (now called Prolific) headed up by Brad Benbow, had a brilliant idea: sell lifetime memberships to help raise money. Our donors were excited for the opportunity, and that really helped finance the exhibits.

Meanwhile, Patrick got to work designing the museum exhibits. He asked what my overall message for the museum was to be. I had a burden for two things: I wanted a linear view of history so guests could understand the chronology and big picture of history, and I wanted to give our guests the right foundation to be able to interpret the world correctly. Dr. Gary Parker and his wife, Mary, had written a book called *Dry Bones and Other Fossils* that featured four C's: Creation, Corruption, Catastrophe, and Christ. In other words, it covered major events of history and ended with the gospel.

It was the chronological approach I'd always had a burden for and it gave the right foundation for understanding the gospel. *"Well, seven is God's perfect number,"* I thought, so I expanded

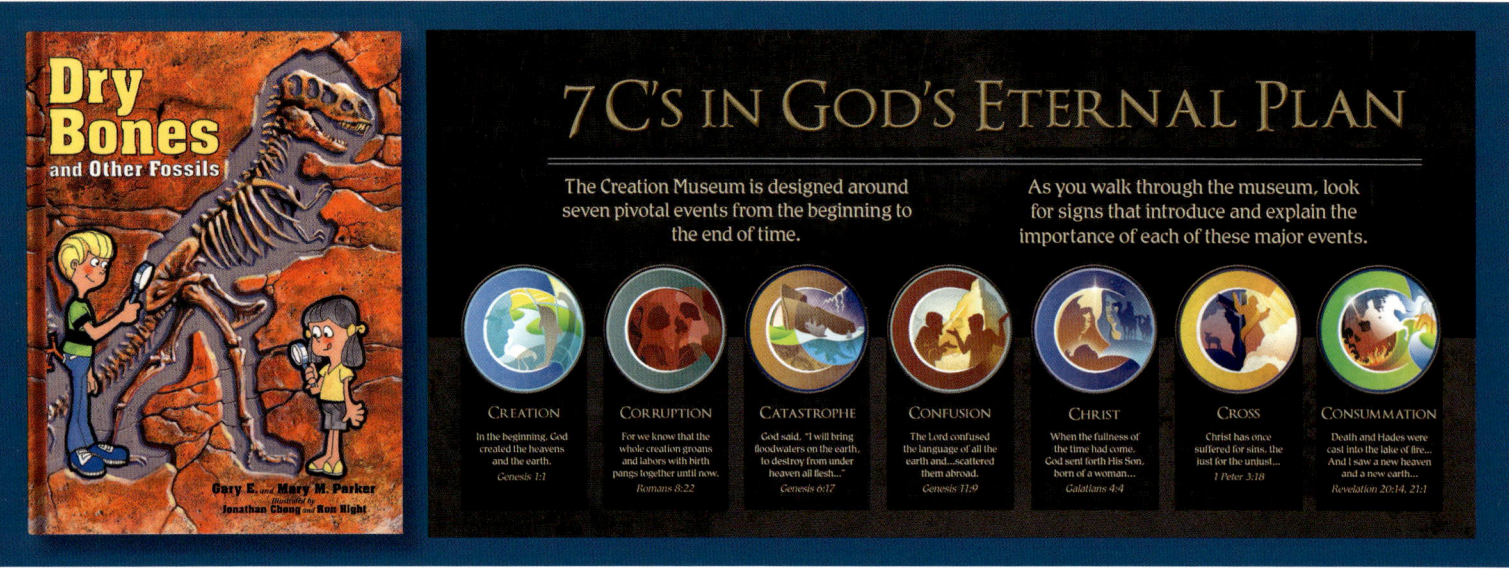

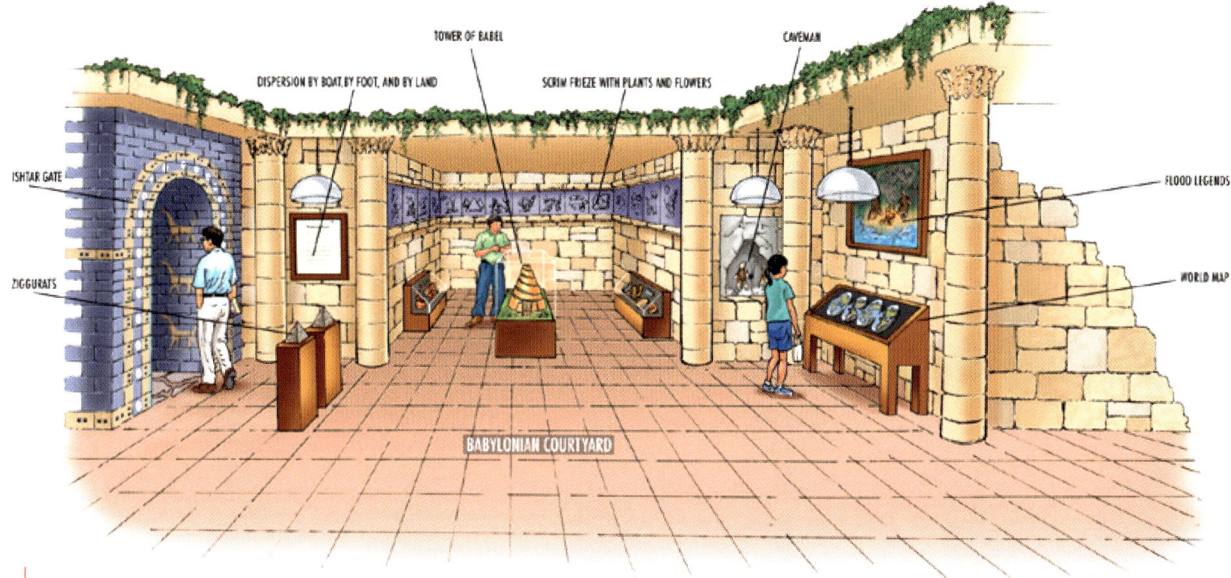

Early rendering of a proposed exhibit associated with the 4th C, Confusion, in the 7 C's walkthrough.

Dr. Parker's 4 C's into the 7 C's of History: Creation, Corruption, Catastrophe, Confusion, Christ, Cross, and Consummation. It was really a summary of Genesis to Revelation. I wrote a script based on this idea and gave it to Patrick. He then took it and brought it to life with a 7 C's walkthrough which began with a "starting points" room to emphasize there are two starting points for interpreting the evidence and building your worldview: man's word or God's Word.

The 7 C's walkthrough became the heart and centerpiece of the museum, and it will always remain so. It's such a powerful way of summarizing biblical history and giving guests the right worldview.

In order to fulfill his vision, Patrick needed talented designers and wasn't sure he would be able to find them in the Cincinnati area as there's no connection here to any major theme parks. Mike told him, "Well, God dropped you in our laps. Don't worry, He'll provide others." And He did. Patrick was blown away by the level of talent God kept bringing us.

Patrick possessed such world-class skills that he attracted a team of incredibly talented artists, fabricators, sculptors, carpenters, script writers, and welders. Usually, it's only places like Disney® or Universal Studios™ that attract that kind of talent! And because we had our own team, we could produce exhibits at a fraction of the cost. Nearly every original exhibit in the museum was produced in a little design studio in what is now Legacy Hall at the Creation Museum. (In those days it was our warehouse.)

Early concept of the walking through the 7 C's of History.

Those early days were the beginning of our incredibly talented design team that still exists today and continues to design and build world-class exhibits at both attractions. At the time we had no idea how extraordinary God's plan was. Because of this team, not only could we build the Ark and fill it with stunning exhibits, but we could continue to upgrade our exhibits and build new ones such as our *Fearfully and Wonderfully Made* pro-life exhibit or the world's most accurate scale model of first century Jerusalem. We didn't know all this was to come, but God did, and He prepared the team for it. I just stand in awe of what God has done.

Have you noticed God's sovereignty and provision is a theme through all of AiG's history? God had been and still is doing things at different times, burdening different people, and directing circumstances in an incredible complex web of details to bring about the building of the Creation Museum and then the Ark Encounter. As Mike has said so many times, "It's a God thing." Yes, it is. There is no other explanation.

> When the Ark was opened, a CNN reporter asked me, "How did you find all the talent to do all this?" An answer popped into my head: "Well, just as God brought the animals to Noah, so He has brought all these people to us." Yes, it's a God thing.

Designing such phenomenal exhibits slowed the museum construction down, pushing our opening date several years into the future. Some secular media attacked us on that point, claiming we were failing because we didn't open when we had planned. (We had no idea what we were doing. That original date was really just a guess.) But I'm pleased it was later than we planned. The museum was levels beyond anything we expected when we first dreamed of it, and that was only possible because of Patrick and the team he assembled. God's plan was so much better than ours. It's a reminder that His ways are not our ways, and His thoughts are way above our thoughts. Yes, Isaiah 55:8–9 often comes to mind when I think of what God has done over the years.

The talented design team that built the Fearfully and Wonderfully Made exhibit.

| A concept drawing comes to life.

> For my thoughts are not your thoughts, neither are your ways my ways, declares the LORD. For as the heavens are higher than the earth, so are my ways higher than your ways and my thoughts than your thoughts (Isaiah 55:8–9 ESV).

As construction steamed ahead, we realized the museum was not going to be large enough. We had planned for about 100,000 guests a year. A study by researcher Britt Beemer (who is now with the Lord) of America's Research Group said we should expect 400,000 guests in our first year. We pivoted, enclosing the outside portico to increase our space, and enlarging the restaurant.

Growing the Grounds

As the construction and exhibit design took shape, Tim Schmitt and his small team, under Patrick's direction, were preparing the grounds. When Tim would design a garden or landscape for a client, he would ask for their personal preferences on color, texture, size, and seasonal interest. But this was different—he was designing for guests from across the country and even around the world. "When the guests arrive," Patrick directed, "we want them to feel comfortable, to feel a sense of peace as they walk around." (That's called "decompression" in the attractions world.)

The beautiful landscapes and plants enjoyed by families at the museum grounds.

Tim divided the garden into various sections: a rainforest, a butterfly garden, a woodland, and so on. But before a landscape looks good, it looks awful. At one point, Tim was tearing up the ground to put in waterfalls and we were a bit dubious. Mike said it looked like something from his army days when they would dig trenches as a defense against tanks. "Have you ever built a waterfall this big?" I asked Tim. "No," he admitted, "but it's the same concept as a little one, just bigger." Patrick could see the vision, but Mike was still unconvinced. It really did look like Tim was just destroying the property. But we left him to his work.

After the initial site development, which also included a zoo or petting zoo area, Tim began selecting trees, shrubs, and ornamentals to fill everything out. He wanted to use plants people were not used to seeing every day to grab their attention, showcase some of God's unique creation, and direct glory to God's amazing design. Unlike the artists working inside, Tim's designs would take decades to complete because plants don't grow up overnight. When the rainforest garden went in, he enthusiastically told us that someday we wouldn't even be able to see the museum through this garden. It would be so lush and tall. The little sticks of plants he had put down were so small that this idea seemed rather far-fetched, but he was right! At opening, the ground was maybe 10% covered with plants, but today we have an incredibly lush garden that envelops guests as they wander down the trails, enjoying the waterfalls, bridges, and peaceful sights, sounds, and smells.

One of my favorite things to do is take off my AiG name tag and walk through the gardens, listening to what guests say. Repeatedly, I hear them exclaim, "Wow, this is so beautiful. Can you imagine God creating this plant? He's so creative." All the glory goes to God, and I wouldn't have it any other way.

Remembering Sheila Selby

Sheila Selby was an avid gardener who absolutely loved the Creation Museum. Before her passing in 2010, she had visited from Pennsylvania for several weeks each year to help with landscape design and development, personally planting thousands of plants. She even donated the funds for our beautiful koi garden as well as a much-needed skid steer and utility vehicle—both of which the ministry still uses as of the writing of this book. Sheila and Tim Schmitt used to talk about someday growing our own flowers in a greenhouse. When she passed away, she left funds for us to construct two of those greenhouses. We now have twelve greenhouses, named Sheila 1–12.

These greenhouses grow the 60,000 annuals and tropicals we seasonally plant throughout the grounds, allowing us to propagate and quickly grow new plants, and we even have one heated and cooled geothermally that grows massive amounts of greens for our zoo animals year-round.

Yet Another Crisis

Opening day was set: Memorial Day, **May 28, 2007.** Designers were feverishly working to finish up the last of the exhibits, but there was another problem. We had a lot of expenses, particularly payroll for all the staff working tirelessly to finish everything. Cash was really tight as in, well, we had none. We estimated it would take $3 million to finish up the last exhibits, bring in inventory for the bookstore and gift shop, purchase food and supplies for the restaurant, and hire staff for opening day. But where would we get $3 million?

We asked the bank for a loan. They turned us down. We tried another bank and another and another. No one would touch us. They had no idea what a "Creation Museum" was, so how could they loan money for it? Discouraged, we called a board meeting to pray and brainstorm what on earth we were going to do.

Unbeknownst to us, a staff member knew someone on the board of a small, local bank called Heritage Bank. While our board and we founders were meeting and praying, he called the board chairman, who was a Christian (as were all their board members), and asked if he would meet with us. That president who "just happened" to have been on the original zoning commission that approved our zoning application, knew all about us.

"But what about all the red tape?" I asked apprehensively. "It can take weeks for this sort of thing to be finalized." He agreed they would cut the red tape and get it for us straight away. His board likewise approved our request, they rushed it through, and right when we needed it, we had our $3 million. That board chairman,

> ### Red Sea Moment
> "What do you need?" he asked as he looked around the almost-finished Creation Museum.
> "We need $3 million to open," I answered.
> "Well, I'll have to ask the board, but I think we can loan you the money."

Arnold Caddel, who was also the founder of the bank, is now with the Lord. But God had him and the other board members at the right place, at the right time, to enable the Creation Museum to become a reality. Yet again, we were on the edge of the Red Sea with the Egyptians closing in and if God didn't show up, we would be stuck.

Over the years I've noticed that these Red Sea moments get bigger and bigger. It started out with that $3,000 check, which felt absolutely enormous at the time. But God promises if you are faithful in little, He can trust you with much (Luke 16:10). We have stepped out in faith over and over through the years, and each time it felt enormous, but then the next time was a bigger step and then a bigger step, and no matter how big the step, God has always been faithful. But remember, we step out in faith responsibly but trust God's sovereignty. Responsibility and sovereignty go hand-in-hand.

Red Sea moments are incredible—when you are on the other side of them! In the moment, it's stressful and scary and, well, exhausting! Over my fifty plus years of ministry it seems like we have climbed so many mountains and gone into so many valleys. And then climbed more mountains and walked through more valleys. And the mountains get higher, and the valleys get lower—and sometimes I just pray, "Lord, can't we just stay on the mountain for a little while?"

It's like the Israelites crossing the Jordan River. Then they had to fight Jericho. And then battle the town of Ai. And then go into the land and fight more peoples, including giants. Fighting is wearying, and I'm ready to have some peace in the land for a little while! But we keep doing battle, trusting God for the strength to continue what He's called us to do because He is worthy of our devotion, sacrifice, and trust through it all. And that fire in my bones just doesn't quit!

At Long Last the Dream Comes True

May 28, 2007 dawned bright and hot. Our designers, who had been working non-stop for weeks, were slapping the last of the paint on the walls. Our dedicated staff had been working nights, even sleeping in the exhibits so they could get back to work bright and early the next morning. Everyone was exhausted and beyond excited that opening day had finally arrived.

We opened our now iconic dinosaur gates, and the cars began to flood in. Over four thousand people showed up. Thanks to Mark Looy's coordination, a massive media presence (secular and Christian) turned up to cover the opening. Cameras and reporters were everywhere, guests were lined up, and staff buzzed about in anticipation of our first visitors flooding the building. The excitement was palpable.

Then the protesters showed up. The same troublemaking group of atheists who had fought so hard to keep us from obtaining any land on which to build were granted permission from the neighbor (the same one who called the police on our prayer meeting years before) to set up a protest. They had a tent and a rock band and homemade signs emblazoned with insults and epithets like "Dumbing down children is child abuse," "You evolved (but not enough)," "Receive now the curse of Ham across the street," "Ham's hellish heliocentric heresy," "God protect me from your followers" and "Religion is the root cause of all terrorism." They even rented a light aircraft which buzzed back and forth over the museum dragging a banner which read, "DEFCON SAYS THOU SHALT NOT LIE."

Ironically most of our guests thought *we* had rented the plane to troll the atheist group. No one realized it was all their doing. Eventually someone with connections at the airport reported the plane, which was in violation of FAA regulations because of how close the airport is to us, and the plane had to leave. At one point the protesters wandered onto the property, and we offered them some ice cream as the day was very hot. We later crossed the street to offer some water bottles. We wanted to make sure we were obeying Proverbs 25:21–22:

> If your enemy is hungry, give him bread to eat, and if he is thirsty, give him water to drink, for you will heap burning coals on his head, and the Lord will reward you (Proverbs 25:21–22 ESV).

Mark and I were busy with media interviews that day as reporter after reporter, some friendly, some not, plied us with questions. (Between the private ribbon cutting ceremony on May 26 and opening day, over 100 credential media showed up.) I remember a CNN reporter cynically asking me, "Okay, what are you really trying to do here? What's your real motivation?"

"To stand on the authority of God's Word, proclaim the gospel message, and see people saved and won to the Lord Jesus Christ," I promptly replied.

"So, you admit it then!" he cried triumphantly.

"Admit what?"

"You admit you're deliberately trying to get people converted to Christianity!"

"Absolutely! That's what it's all about."

He looked rather stunned, "Well, that's refreshing." Apparently, he interviewed people all the time who are fighting for the family or against abortion and when he asks them for their real motivation they'll say "traditional family values" or some such thing. "Why don't they just come out and say they're on about the Bible or about Christianity as you did?" he exclaimed.

Over the years I've found it really lowers the guard of the secular media when we're upfront with them about why we're doing what we're doing. Of course, we're on about the Bible and we want to see people saved! We're not hiding it. I think many people in the secular media see Christians as sneaky, trying to underhandedly slip their Christian beliefs in. No, we boldly proclaim the Christian message from the rooftops. And that's how we should be.

Another reporter, this time at the opening of the Ark Encounter, in an attempt to get a soundbite for a splashy headline, opened the interview with, "Are Muslims going to hell?" That's not the question I was anticipating! I responded with, "Well, anyone who doesn't trust the Lord is going to hell whether they're Baptist, Presbyterian, Lutheran, Catholic, Mennonite, Muslim, Methodist, Hindu, Sikh, Orthodox Jew, or any other denomination or religious group. If a person has not repented of sin and received the free gift of salvation offered through the Lord Jesus Christ, they will be separated from God for eternity in a place the Bible calls hell. What about you? Where do you stand?" Yes, I believe Christians should be bold and unashamed about what they believe!

Another reporter, a man in a wheelchair with characteristics of someone with cerebral palsy, also visited on opening day, asking all kinds of questions. Later, when his mocking report came out, we found out he was an atheist and did not have cerebral palsy or need a wheelchair. He faked the whole thing just to see how we would react!

But despite the sixty or so protesters and some not-so-friendly media, it was an amazing day. Our supporters were so excited to be there. Guests were lined up out the front and wrapped around the side of the building and, it being a hot day, I felt bad, thinking they must be miserable standing and waiting in all that heat. I walked up and down the line, greeting them and asking how they were. No one minded the wait or the heat at all. They were just thrilled to have a Creation Museum to visit. It was an incredibly special day.

May 28, 2007: Ken, Mark, Patrick, Mike and Don Landis (Chairman of the Board)

It was a goosebumps day when the Creation Museum opened in 2007. Ken's dream had come true. It was thrilling for me not only because I moved to Northern Kentucky to help Ken create the museum, but because I helped raise the funds for the $30 million high-tech museum and got several dozen media outlets to visit on opening week, including CNN and other national TV networks. What a privilege to be part of what the Lord did!

—*Mark Looy*

We had this huge throng of people that came for opening day, and I was so glad. I wrote my speech weeks ahead of time just to make sure that it wasn't jammed up right at the end, and I'm glad I did. It was such an emotional time. Buddy sang his song "He Makes Dreams Out of Nothing" just as Ken had requested him to do the day they met. We knew it was coming, but when he sang that song, it was emotional, and I was tired from all the work and the years of planning. Well, this tough old lieutenant colonel shed a tear or two.

—*Mike Zovath*

Mike speaking at the Grand Opening.

Mark, Ken, and Jason Lisle taking questions from media.

"Teddy Bear Ken"

Two days before our official opening, we had a private ribbon-cutting ceremony with our board, our families, some supporters, and a few media outlets. That was also a special and emotional day as we cut the ribbon and Buddy, at long last, played his guitar and sang "He Makes Dreams Out of Nothing" in front of the completed museum.

Now, as I've shared, I'm not generally a very emotional person, but my wife will tell you that underneath what I show the public there's a "soft teddy bear" (and she's right). I don't show it often, but when you open the world's first major Creation Museum and think back to the vision that began during your teaching days, prayers over a piece of property in Australia in the 1980s, the seemingly insurmountable battles fought to open the museum, and all those supporters cheering in excitement, well, you can't help but get choked up. And I did. (We all did!)

I especially choked up when I gave my speech and turned to thank Mally for standing by me through everything, never complaining of the time and energy I had devoted to this, and encouraging me when the media smeared me and said nasty things, like I was Hitler reincarnated and other nonsense. (That seems to be a mantra they still use today with people they don't agree with.) I would have loved for my parents to be there, but my father was already with the Lord. My mother had visited America and seen it under construction, but her health was such that she could not attend the opening. The emotions of the moment almost got to me, but I gathered myself together and finished my address.

Mally being honored.

Ken speaking about a dream come true.

Buddy singing "He Makes Dreams Out of Nothing."

Those emotions still get to me today when I go to the Creation Museum and the Ark Encounter even though I'm at one or the other (or both) almost every day. When I drive in and I see the museum or the life-size Ark, the beautiful grounds, and all the families learning about God's Word and the gospel, I can't help but think, "Wow, God actually let us do this amazing thing!" A God thing!

I often meet people — and when I say often, I really do mean often — who ask, "How could all this happen?" They point out that everything is the quality of Disney® or better. It's mind-blowing to them how this could ever come to be. It's so complex to try and explain all the Red Sea moments where God moved on our behalf, all the times we boldly

> "Christians must be prepared to make an intelligent defense of the gospel by arming themselves with knowledge and an understanding of the forms unbelief takes in these days." *The Lie,* p. 136

stepped out in faith, and all the battles God fought for us. I often liken it to a spider web. If you look closely at a web, it's complex with threads going all over the place and yet there's a beautiful pattern to it. Answers in Genesis, the Creation Museum, and the Ark Encounter are like a spider web because there are all these different threads of people God brought along, circumstances encountered, battles fought, and things we had to do, but it all comes together in a miraculous way like a beautiful pattern.

Shocking Research Makes Waves

The museum was a huge hit with 3,000-4,000 visitors coming each Saturday throughout the summer months. By November we had already welcomed our 250,000th visitor, nearly seven months ahead of projections. By our one-year anniversary—celebrated with a fireworks display—we had crossed the 400,000 threshold Britt Beemer's research had told us to expect. By the following anniversary, over 700,000 people had visited, and we hit the one million mark a month before our third anniversary.

As people and media visited the Creation Museum, one of the comments we heard over and over was, "The quality of the building and exhibits way exceeded our expectations!" Some of them told me that Christians are usually associated with "cheesy" quality, and they didn't expect Disney® quality at a Christian attraction. But because God brought Patrick along, the quality *was* Disney® and Universal Studios™ quality. In fact, in many ways, I think it exceeds their quality.

When the Ark Encounter opened, I gave a CBS reporter a tour. He stopped between the second and third decks and said, "You said this place was the quality of Hollywood." I affirmed that, yes, I had said that. He replied, "This is not the quality of Hollywood; it's way above Hollywood. For a start, the wood is real."

> "...most Christians today are intimidated by the world because they do not know how to answer questions challenging their faith and the truth of God's Word in today's increasingly secularized culture." *The Lie*, p. 138

Many have told us that the quality of the Creation Museum (and now at the Ark Encounter too) has helped set a standard for Christian facilities, challenging Christians to do all they can to be as good, if not better, than the world in the quality of their work. And it should be. After all, we are proclaiming the most important message in the universe.

But other things were also happening in the early days of the Creation Museum. Christian researcher George Barna released the statistic that two-thirds of young people were leaving the church by the time they reach college age, with very few returning. From my years of experience on the road, talking with pastors, church leaders, and young people themselves, I had an inkling why this was happening. But we wanted research to back it up. We turned to Britt Beemer and America's Research Group for answers.

Their research team crafted a detailed survey and interviewed 1000 young people who had grown up in the church but had left to find out why. We published the results in 2009 in my co-authored book *Already Gone*. Other than *The Lie*, I believe that book has had the greatest impact on the Church regarding our ministry. I can't tell you how many pastors have told me they read that book and were convicted to introduce apologetics and biblical worldview teaching into their churches.

One of the most shocking results of the research was finding that children who went to Sunday school tended to be worse off spiritually than those who never attended Sunday school. This confirmed the concerns I had always had about most Sunday school material. It tends to be shallow, with moral truths drawn from a collection of "Bible stories." Few curricula teach apologetics, equip children and young people to defend the Christian faith, or answer the skeptical questions of the age. And now we had the research to back up my concerns. Someone needed to do something about it!

So, we did. *Already Gone* was a turning point in our ministry in so many ways, especially regarding curricula and other resource development. We put together a team to write and produce a unique Sunday school curriculum that emphasized apologetics, biblical authority, doctrine, and worldview and is laid out chronologically just like we have in the Creation Museum with the 7 C's.

That curriculum has now been used in thousands of churches, and I've heard from countless pastors who say it's revolutionizing their congregations. Praise God!

Craig Baker (AiG board member) Ken, and Tim Dudley in the Master Books warehouse.

Ham vs. Nye

"I asked Bill Nye, 'the Science Guy,' if he'd be willing to debate you, and he said yes. Would you be prepared to debate him?"

The interview with the Associated Press reporter had been pretty standard and had gone smoothly so far when suddenly he threw out the offer of a debate with the well-known science personality, ardent evolutionist, and secular humanist (he is really an atheist), Bill Nye. I've never seen myself as a debater and was very much put on the spot, but a glance at Mark Looy, sitting quietly in the corner, confirmed what I already thought—I had to say yes. I voiced my willingness to "get into the ring" with Nye, thinking nothing would probably come of it. Boy, was I wrong!

A few weeks later we were in contact with Bill's agent to organize a formal debate to be held at the Creation Museum on February 4, 2014. It was a stressful event to plan and with everything that went on behind-the-scenes (conditions became very complicated) we weren't sure it was going to happen, but we finally had a set-in-stone contract and made the announcement. Tickets to the event sold out in minutes. Atheists were up in arms, furious that Bill would give us that kind of publicity. Christians were excited and began planning watch parties. Media clamored all over us for details, with over 70 representatives from secular and Christian media securing a press pass for the event.

Our AV team worked tirelessly to ensure the event could be successfully livestreamed to the world (and that there was a backup plan in case the original plan failed—and then a backup for the backup!). The night of the event, Kentucky saw a massive

snowstorm. We were worried Bill wouldn't be able to make it, but a driver picked him up and brought him safely to the museum.

We estimate a minimum of seven million people tuned in live and now it's been viewed over 25 million times. We can't know exact numbers because we heard of hundreds of churches, universities, Christian schools, homeschools, and even a number of public schools gathering to watch together, but there were millions of views while it was live. Facebook reported that the debate was the #1 trending topic on their platform for hours before it began and likewise for half of Twitter's (now X) trending topics. It was the talk of the nation, even internationally!

It was a huge responsibility and weight for me, knowing millions were watching me answer the question, "Is creation a viable model of origins in today's modern scientific era?" Hundreds of people contacted me beforehand, urging me to include this or that point in my presentation. I certainly didn't have time to include them all (nor did I want to—some were … interesting), but I met with our researchers, and we brainstormed what we thought were the key points, including the difference between observational and historical science, highlighting creationists who are successful and brilliant scientists, and, of course, preaching the gospel message. I didn't want to just throw a bunch of evidence for creation at Bill and the millions watching. I wanted them to see that the issue wasn't the evidence at all; it's about the interpretation of the evidence based on your starting point of man's word vs. God's Word.

The most iconic moment of the evening occurred at the end of the debate when Bill was asked, "How did the atoms that created the Big Bang get there?" and then "How did consciousness come from matter?" His answer to both: "That's a great mystery!" My response was instantaneous because, unlike secularists who have no real answers for questions like those, Christians can confidently say, "There is a book …" that gives us the answers.

After the debate, I asked Bill Nye if we could be friends and stay in contact even though we disagreed on the origins issue. Sadly, he said no (though I would meet him again two years later when we opened the Ark Encounter—more on that in the next chapter). Many people, though, continue to pray for Bill Nye's salvation. Personally, I believe Bill knows the truth but like the rich young ruler in the Bible, he is not prepared to give up his atheistic, evolutionary beliefs as he would lose fame and friends. Yes, continue to pray for him as long as the Lord grants him life and breath.

I truly believe the debate was a historic moment in Christendom, and the ripples are still being felt. I'm not exaggerating when I say I hear weekly from people who tell me they watched the debate when

> "Most church-going adults cannot adequately defend the basics of their Christian faith or basic doctrines, let alone defend the faith against the skeptical questions of this scientific age."
> *Already Gone,* p. 48

they were kids, that they saw it in college, or that they just watched it recently and that it had a huge impact on them. I've even had many people testify (including those who said they used to be ardent atheists) that the Lord used that debate to bring them to Christ. The number of people who were introduced to our ministry and the Creation Museum for the first time rose exponentially. It took our ministry to levels we never imagined and very quickly—at just the right time. I believe God specially orchestrated that event so millions would hear the gospel and a defense of the Christian faith but also to introduce millions of new people to our ministry.

I certainly would never have thought of that idea on my own or even have wanted to do it. God put it all together and forced me to do it, and the results were spectacular and pivotal in the success of our next God-given dream—building a life-size Noah's Ark.

> *Some* 30 years ago I prayed with John Thallon that the Lord would allow us to build a Creation Museum some day. Well that day finally came and the timing of the Lord is perfect. *Miraculous!*

Evolution of Our Logo

2004 – 2016
Ribbon cutting, July 5th, 2016

8 | THE ARK ENCOUNTER

WHY BUILD AN ARK?

"When you guys get this done, you need to build an ark!"

At the Creation Museum as guests walk through history, they leave the fallen world of "Corruption" into the next C of history, "Catastrophe," and a reconstruction of 1% of Noah's ark. Before the museum opened, as I brought guests through that particular point of the walkthrough, someone would always exclaim that our next project needed to be a life-size Noah's ark.

• •

Ever the visionaries, we had already discussed the idea with Patrick who was enthusiastic about it—but we needed to build the museum first. Mike warned me to stop telling people we wanted to build the ark, or they would get excited about that and donate to that project instead of the museum.

Like my intense desire for a Creation Museum, the thought of an ark goes back to my Australian ministry days. One of the most common questions we received was, "How could Noah fit the animals on the ark?" This question came from two misunderstandings: 1) the size of the ark and 2) the biblical teaching about kinds.

Because of the silly "bathtub arks," as I call them (you know, the ones that have giraffe necks sticking out the chimney!), that people grow up seeing on children's nursery walls, in children's Bibles, and in Sunday school decorations, they think the ark was small and crowded with modern animals. They don't realize the ark was huge and Noah only needed two of every kind of land animal (seven pairs of some), not two of every species. That means Noah needed less than 7,000 animals. (When we did open the Ark Encounter, atheists protested outside the grounds, and one of their mocking signs was a picture of a bathtub ark!)

> "I am the door. If anyone enters by me, he will be saved and will go in and out and find pasture" (John 10:9 ESV).

• •

I also realized the Flood account was integral to the creation/evolution and biblical authority discussion because the Flood would have laid down the rock layers and fossils—the very things evolutionists interpret as evidence of millions of years of slow processes and evolutionary change. The ark, with its one door of salvation from God's judgment on sin, is also a powerful picture of the gospel and the one Door we must go through to be saved.

Of course, in those early days I never dreamed of building an ark, but we wondered if someday we could build an office and warehouse that somehow could be used to show people how big the ark was. In the meantime, helium balloons spread out to show the length, width, and height of the massive ship during our family camps sufficed. But with the experience of building the Creation Museum, we realized maybe we could do more than just the 1% shown in the museum. Maybe we could do 100%.

May of 2005 the Leadership Team and AIG board listed building an Ark as strategy #1.

Our Next Priority: Noah's Ark

In 2004—three years before the museum welcomed its first official visitor—we briefed our board on our ambitious idea for the future, and in 2005 we voted to make it our next priority as part of our strategic plan. In 2007, after the successful opening of the Creation Museum, our design team began plans for a life-size Noah's ark themed attraction. While design work took shape, we searched for land. Originally, we had planned to build it on our museum property, but research from America's Research Group threw cold water on that idea: Over a million people a year would come if we built it. We needed much more land.

This new property needed to be within easy driving distance of the museum. We could go north to Ohio, west to Indiana, or further south into Kentucky. One Indiana county tried to court us—they wanted the tourism dollars such a project was sure to bring—but Kentucky offered an attractive tourism tax incentive, tipping the scales in their favor. Then our real estate agent called us out to a beautiful 800-acre property in Williamstown, KY right off of I-75. It was perfect. And it had only two owners—a developer and a corporation—both of whom could be quiet about our purchase. After all the drama surrounding the Creation Museum's attempt to acquire land, we wanted to keep this purchase out of the public eye until we had the land secure and could make the big announcement to our supporters that we were building Noah's ark. (We knew that local atheists, who follow everything we do, would oppose this project. I think we give this tiny group of God-haters purpose and meaning for their existence. Our ministry is a way for them to show their utter intolerance of anything Christian.)

This 800-acre property was in Grant County (a different county than the

Overhead shot of the 800 acres purchased to build the Ark.

Creation Museum) and, while obtaining the property was not without some drama, the local county worked with us to ensure the property could be developed into a themed attraction. After all, it would be a phenomenal economic boom for the county. Within a few short months, that 800-acre property was ours, and we praised the Lord.

On December 1, 2010, we announced to the public that we were building a full-size reconstruction of Noah's ark to open in the summer of 2016. The entire attraction was to be called Ark Encounter, so-named as guests would have an encounter with Noah's ark, an encounter with God's Word, and (for non-Christians we pray) an encounter with Jesus Christ.

The media was abuzz once more with outlets from around the world carrying the story (and sometimes badly mangling it, leading to a rumor that persists to this day that state tax dollars were used

to build the Ark. They weren't. But more on that soon). Other outlets wrung their hands, insisting the money should be spent on the poor. (We've heard that many times over the years.) This accusation is so hypocritical. For example, none of these same outlets criticize Hollywood for spending hundreds of millions of dollars making a movie instead of feeding the poor. It reflects the anti-Christian sentiment of the media, the intolerance of anything Christian, and the discrimination leveled against us because of our biblical message. But we responded to the controversy as best we could and then ignored it, getting to work at what God had called us to do.

The Answers in Genesis board praying on the site where the Ark was to be built.

God Provides Again

No one had ever attempted a project like this. How would we even begin? Where would we find someone with the skills and the desire for such a niche project? You can't just go to any architectural firm and assume they know how to design Noah's ark! We needed a life-size—that meant 510 feet long, 85 feet wide, 51 feet high—Noah's ark, designed as a wooden ship but built as a building according to modern building codes. That meant ADA compliant, HVAC, elevators, restrooms, exit stairs, and more. And, while we couldn't get gopher wood (no one knows exactly what it is!), we did want the structure to be made of wood.

Again, the Lord went before us and sovereignly brought about the right people. A friend of the ministry had worked on a few projects with an architect named LeRoy Troyer. LeRoy had designed a 51,000-square-foot, three-story timber frame farmer's market near Elkhart, Indiana, and skilled Amish workmen had constructed it. Soon we were standing with LeRoy in that farmer's market, looking at a timber frame building nearly the height and width of the biblical ark. "Wow!" we thought. "We can really do this!" For the first time the idea of building a life-size wooden ark felt real.

Visiting the Farmer's Market building the Amish built in Northern Indiana

Inside beams of the Farmer's Market were very impressive in size and scale.

LeRoy had gathered some Amish craftsmen together to hear our vision. I pulled out my overhead projector and shared the purpose of this project; It wasn't just to build an architectural marvel (though it would be that); we wanted it to be evangelistic, filled with biblical teaching and apologetics, as a testimony to the world that God's Word is true. When I finished, one of the Amish men stood up, exclaiming, "I believe God has been preparing us our whole lives for this project." They were all in.

After several planning meetings, LeRoy took Mike into his office, pulling a wrinkled set of blueprints from a cabinet. It was rough architectural plans for Noah's ark, designed by LeRoy at Notre Dame's architectural school in the 1960s, when LeRoy was in his twenties. Mike was in shock. God had directed us, not only to someone who had the skills for a complicated architectural design and connections with the Amish craftsmen we needed to build it, but who had always wanted to build a Noah's ark. God was giving him the opportunity of a lifetime to bring his dream to life fifty years later. Wow, God is amazing! Yet again, he had dropped the right people into our laps.

Soon after the Ark opened, LeRoy told me it was the highlight of his life. "I believe this is what the Lord raised me up for. This is what He trained me to do. This is my life's work and now I feel my life's work is complete." In 2018, just two years after the Ark's opening, LeRoy (aged 81) went home to be with the Lord after a brief battle with leukemia.

| LeRoy being presented with the Ark print.

Before he passed away, several members of the Ark's design team took a beautiful print of the Ark, signed by the whole Ark team, and presented it to him, telling him, when he gets to heaven, "Say hi to Noah and tell him you built one too." He passed away a week later. Yes, God had provided LeRoy at just the time we needed him, and his architectural legacy points thousands of guests each day towards God's Word and the gospel.

> **Red Sea Moment**
> Once again I stand in awe of how God had been preparing people for tasks in this ministry that, at the time, none of us were even aware of. God sent us LeRoy Troyer.

And the Battles Begin

"Taxes" probably don't sound very exciting, but we were about to enter another major battle. We had selected Kentucky as the future home of the Ark Encounter in part because of a tourism tax incentive offered to anyone who would build a tourist facility, providing the state's research showed a certain percentage of people from other states would visit. In other words, build an attraction, people visit, and the attraction receives a rebate on sales tax generated within the facility up to 25% of the project cost over 10 years.

I'll repeat that just to make sure you understand, as misinformation and lies about this program persist to this day. No one's income taxes are used for this incentive, and none of the incentive is paid to build the tourist facility. Basically, the program goes like this (and it's a brilliant strategy to bring tourism dollars to the state): If you build a tourist attraction to bring economic benefit to the state, then if approved after a detailed appraisal by experts selected by the state to confirm it will benefit the state, then the state will pay a certain percentage of the capital costs back to the organization from sales taxes generated within the facility. In other words, the tourist facility has to generate the funds for the incentive through sales tax paid within the facility only. Because of all the dollars then coming into the state through sales tax (and, of course, the taxes on hotel rooms people stay in, restaurants guests eat at, gas stations they fuel up at, and so on), there is a massive net gain economically for the state. Since 92% of those who visit the Ark (and the Creation Museum) come from outside the state, our attractions, as of the writing of this book, have generated billions in economic benefit for the state of Kentucky.

Back to our tourism incentive battle. The then Kentucky governor, Steve Beshear, was originally enthusiastic about our Ark project. He even appeared alongside us when we announced it and shared that the

> "Though it is often difficult to see the good while the bad events are happening, it doesn't take too much imagination to see the potential for good in all that happens, particularly when we look not just at the outward circumstances, but when we focus on how God uses the outward struggles to conform us to Christ on the inside." *Divine Dilemma,* p. 152

state tourism cabinet had approved our tourism incentive, easily fulfilling the requirements, and only needing confirmation of its economic benefit by an independent consultation for final approval (which was confirmed). We applied for the incentive, easily fulfilled all the requirements, and were approved.

Then the secularists showed up. These atheists were already furious about the success of the Creation Museum and certainly didn't want to see the Ark built and the Christian message boldly proclaimed. So, they began a misinformation and intimidation campaign. Even though we corrected them *ad nauseum* they screamed from the rooftops that taxpayer dollars were going toward building a Christian attraction. Even many in the media picked up this blatantly false story. By twisting the tax incentive from "a rebate on sales tax generated within the attraction after the Ark opens" into "tax money to build the Ark" they created an angry frenzy within their own groups and the media. And then they began to pressure the governor and other state officials, intimidating them with false claims that the Ark Encounter somehow didn't qualify for a facially neutral incentive because we were Christians, hiring Christians, and teaching Christian things!

On December 10, 2014, the state, under Governor Beshear, reversed course, halting our final approval on the grounds that we must not discriminate in our hiring (i.e., we couldn't have a statement of faith that applicants had to sign) and we couldn't preach the gospel at our attraction.

In a letter from the state Tourism, Arts and Heritage Cabinet, we were told, in regard to a job posting on the Answers in Genesis website for a CAD Technician designing exhibits in the Ark Encounter: Based on the job posting outlined above, the Commonwealth doesn't believe that Ark Encounter, LLC will be complying with state and Federal law in its hiring practices. Therefore, we are not prepared to move forward with consideration of the application for final approval without the assurance of Ark Encounter, LLC that it will not discriminate in any way on the basis of religion in hiring for the project and will revise its postings accordingly.

The specific items they objected to were listed in their letter: one of the goals of employees will be 'edifying believers and evangelizing the lost'. As part of the application process, applicants are required to provide, in addition to traditional employment information, the following:

1. Salvation testimony
2. Creation belief statement
3. Confirmation of applicant's agreement with the AIG Statement of Faith, which states that it is imperative that all persons employed must abide by and agree to an itemized list of fundamental Christian beliefs, including a statement on marriage and sexuality.

So, the Kentucky state government was discriminating against us because, as a Christian organization, we required employees to be Christians and adhere to our mission and Statement of Faith.

Speaker of the United States House of Representatives Mike Johnson

We contacted a religious freedom group and an attorney who specialized in constitutional law, Mike Johnson (yes, that Mike Johnson, future Speaker of the House), agreed to represent us in a lawsuit against the state that was clearly violating our First Amendment rights. On February 5, 2015, we launched a legal battle, fighting for religious freedom—including the right for Christian organizations to stay Christian by hiring only Christians. It was clear viewpoint discrimination by Kentucky state officials.

In July we presented our oral arguments before the judge. And on January 25, 2016 the federal court handed down its ruling: We had won! The court found evidence of clear religious discrimination, stating "that the Commonwealth's exclusion of AiG from participating in the program for the reasons stated – i.e., on the basis of AiG's religious beliefs, purpose, mission, message, or conduct, is a violation of AiG's rights under the First Amendment to the federal Constitution." The court also upheld, on the basis of Title VII of the 1964 Civil Rights Act, our right to religious preferences in hiring as a Christian ministry. On April 25 the state's tourism board voted unanimously to approve us for the rebate.

It was a major battle and a huge victory, setting a precedent in federal court that Christian ministries cannot be excluded from facially neutral programs because of their Christian beliefs, and they cannot be forced to hire non-Christians. Praise the Lord for a fair ruling! (By the way, I'm sure the atheists who tried to stop our getting this incentive because we're a Christian group hiring Christians wouldn't hire a Bible-believing Christian like me to be part of their atheist group!)

But the misinformation continued. To this day (2025) we still hear and see in print the claim that taxpayer dollars funded the building of the Ark Encounter. But that's utter nonsense. Not one dollar from

> **Red Sea Moment**
>
> We won! The court found evidence of clear religious discrimination... on the basis of AiG's religious beliefs... a violation of AiG's rights under the First Amendment.

the state went toward building the Ark. Rather, we received a rebate on sales tax we generated within the attraction only after we opened. And keep in mind we had to have the funds to build the facility and open it before we could start generating the money for the rebate that is paid over 10 years. But it's not shocking that atheists will lie and slander to try and get their way. After all, they don't have the authoritative Word of God as their standard.

Another laughable bit of misinformation that was (and sometimes still is) repeated by atheists was "no one would visit the Ark" and we'd be shutting the doors within a few years. Atheists would show up when the Ark was closed and take pictures of a vast, empty parking lot, then post those photos on their blogs to try to show how the Ark was failing. Others gleefully planned what they would do with our empty building, throwing out ideas like a casino. But, of course, they were wrong.

Attendance projections were met, and we soon surpassed expectations at both the Ark and the Creation Museum (attendance at the museum doubled). Hundreds of millions of dollars have been added to the state through full hotels (many new hotels have been built to house Ark guests), restaurants, gas stations, and more. It has certainly been a boon for the state even though (as of the writing of this book) we are rarely, if ever, mentioned by the state when they promote Kentucky as a tourist destination.

But taxes weren't the only battle we faced.

The Egyptians Were Closing In

It would take about $120 million to build the Ark, a truly staggering number. Unlike the museum, we couldn't build it slowly as the money came in. We needed to build it all at once, so we needed about $100 million to even get started. We came up with a fundraising plan - $38 million in donations and lifetime boarding passes (like we'd done for the Creation Museum) and a $62 million bond offering.

These are some whiteboard notes from an AiG board meeting trying to figure out how we were going to fund this project.

Donations began pouring in. People were excited about the idea of a life-size Ark and, having seen the quality of the Creation Museum, they knew we would do it well. By the end of our first fundraising year (2011), we had raised over $5 million – only $33 million more to go from donations and passes! As I shared, when you remove the few large donations we received, the average donation to the Creation Museum was $130. And it was similar for the Ark—$230. Thousands and thousands of families gave, and together we were slowly able to raise the $38 million we needed in donations and lifetime passes.

The remainder needed to come from the $62 million bond offering. Interested supporters could purchase bonds and would receive interest from us, paid out over a number of years. Rather than a donation, it was an investment on their part. Many of our supporters were excited about the idea, and commitments for the bond offering began coming in until we had much more than we needed.

But then, once again, the atheists attacked, with one leading atheist even pretending to be interested in the bond offering so he could get all of the relevant documents. I once had someone tell me, "When you stand on the devil's toes, he reacts. You guys must be kicking him in the shins!" Yes, Satan was doing everything he could to stop our work. These atheists attacked the bonds, trying to get the government to shut us down by demanding we be investigated and falsely claiming the city of Williamstown was somehow on the hook for the bond payments if our project failed. (We saw a letter of complaint by an atheist group sent to the government.) In response, the government sent two representatives to investigate us. They even falsely accused us when they arrived, but we had done nothing illegal. Of course, that didn't matter to our opponents. The atheists smeared us any way they could and a young journalist writing for the prestigious Bloomberg News wrote three patently false articles maligning us. Because of certain rules regarding the bond offering, we couldn't respond publicly. We could only sit helplessly by as brokers refused to work with us, stopping clients who had agreed to purchase bonds from fulfilling their purchase.

As the lies spread, a deadline loomed. We had only one week—a mere seven days—to get to $45 million minimum. If we didn't

NEW ISSUE
BOOK-ENTRY ONLY

*In the opinion of Bond Counsel, interest on the Series 2013 Bonds (as hereinafter defined) is **not** excludable from gross income for federal income tax purposes. Interest on the Series 2013 Bonds is exempt from Kentucky income tax, and the Series 2013 Bonds are exempt from ad valorem taxation by the Commonwealth of Kentucky and any of its political subdivisions. See "TAX MATTERS" and APPENDIX C hereto.*

NOT RATED

CITY OF WILLIAMSTOWN, KENTUCKY
$62,000,000
Taxable Industrial Building Revenue Bonds, Series 2013
(Crosswater Canyon, Inc. Project)

Dated: Date of Initial Issuance

Due: As shown on inside preliminary pages

The City of Williamstown, Kentucky (the "Issuer") is issuing its Taxable Industrial Building Revenue Bonds, Series 2013 (Crosswater Canyon, Inc. Project) (the "Series 2013 Bonds"). The Series 2013 Bonds are being issued pursuant to §§ 103.200 to 103.285 of the Kentucky Revised Statutes, as amended (the "Act") and a Trust Indenture dated as of December 1, 2013 (the "Indenture") between the Issuer and U.S. Bank National Association, as trustee (the "Trustee"), to provide funds which will be loaned to Crosswater Canyon, Inc., a Kentucky nonprofit corporation ("Crosswater Canyon") and Ark Encounter, LLC, a Missouri limited liability company ("Ark Encounter, LLC" and together with Crosswater Canyon, the "Borrower") for the purposes of: (i) financing a portion of the costs of constructing, installing and equipping the initial phase of a biblically-themed educational and entertainment complex to include a replica of the Ark of Noah and related facilities (the "Project"), as more particularly described herein; (ii) capitalizing a portion of the interest due on the Series 2013 Bonds and including April 1, 2016; (iii) funding an initial deposit to a debt service reserve fund with respect to the Series 2013 Bonds, all as more fully d reach that number by February 25, 2014, we would have to refund all of the bonds, and the Ark project was either dead or significantly delayed. But we were now $13 million short because of the impact of that shockingly false Bloomberg article. How could we raise $13 million with brokers having reversed course and lies flying around? It was the biggest Red Sea moment we had ever experienced.

I addressed our staff, all of whom were earnestly praying, "If God's in this—and I believe He is—then somehow He is going to make this happen. Our duty is to do everything we can in the natural (responsibility) and leave the supernatural (sovereignty) up to God."

Taking their human responsibility seriously, and trusting God's sovereignty, our advancement team and I worked tirelessly contacting supporters who had expressed interest or had purchased bonds, letting them know the situation. And our supporters stepped up, purchasing extra bonds, including one foundation that invested an additional $4 million (the maximum they could legally do) to get the total down to a single digit: $9 million. I called one foundation that had expressed interest in supporting our ministry. They said, "Do all you can to raise funds and, when you're convinced you can't do any more, call us with where things are at."

The deadline of Tuesday at 5:00 p.m. loomed before us. We found some more supporters who brought the number down to $7 million.

Red Sea Moment

Then I called that foundation back, and they said they would fund the final $7 million. Whew! A miracle. But that wasn't the end of the problem.

A model was built of the overall area of the Ark project. We could start to show donors and create awareness of the project.

Monday morning dawned and we had enough pledges to fulfill the $13 million, but it all needed to be in the bank by 5:00 p.m. the next day. With countless people praying, the Lord cleared the obstacles and by 4:34, the bond trustee called to inform us every dollar was locked into the account. The email Joe Boone, our now president but head of our advancement team at the time, sent out to several of us when the news came, will tell you how we all felt: "It's been a harrowing day of ups and downs, but with only minutes to spare before it had to be re-done, everything came through. They almost put the defibrillator on me a couple times. But … PRAISE JESUS – IT'S ON!!!!!!!!!!!!!!!!!!"

It was truly miraculous. A big Red Sea event! And I mean that. Without God's intervention it never would have happened. It was yet another "God thing." The Lord had thwarted the plans of the enemy, and construction could begin. It was a tense week, the worst Red Sea moment of them all, but on the other side, when the Egyptians closing in had been swept away, there was so much rejoicing among our staff and supporters. To God be the glory!

The atheists had mocked our bond offering—and continued to after it was done—saying it would never work, we would go bankrupt, no one would ever get a return on their investment. But they don't know the power of our God. The Ark wasn't merely a human endeavor. God was going before us. And not only did we pay off all the bonds, we did it early!

The leadership and board members had a 'pound the peg' event to celebrate construction beginning on May 7, 2014. Ken, John Whitcomb, Mike and Mark are in the front row.

The columns that the Ark would sit on dwarf Ken and Mally.

God Is Our Rock

As we've worked on these projects, there have been many times we've just had to smile at God. Once I was talking to the construction workers who were putting in the concrete piers for the Ark to sit on. To install them, they had to drill down to the bedrock. I realized the whole Ark is sitting on the rock. The Bible teaches God is our Rock, and I thought, "You know, there's some interesting symbolism here—a sermon really: Our reminder to the world of the truth of God's Word is sitting on both the rock and the Rock. We too need to stand on the Rock, Jesus Christ, and the rock of His perfect Word."

> The LORD is my rock, my fortress, and the One who rescues me; My God, my rock and strength in whom I trust and take refuge; My shield, and the horn of my salvation, my high tower—my stronghold (Psalm 18:2 AMP).

It took many months of planning to come up with the completed blueprints to build the Ark.

LeRoy Troyer and Ken standing on a viewing platform for the general public to view the Ark.

CONSTRUCTION BEGINS

As I told Patrick, we had the dimensions and basic shape of our next project handed to us by God in His Word so there would be no planning the building around the exhibits. He would have to do it backwards again, but this time he had experience! And, together with the architects, he came up with another ingenious design.

The Bible mentions three decks, so we would have three decks of exhibits with long, sloping ramps between floors allowing guests to move easily up and down between the decks, while also providing stunning views by looking up or down in certain places to catch the scale of the structure even from inside. Along the decks would be bays, and each bay would house an exhibit (or part of an exhibit). At the end of decks 2 and 3 would be a theater. A long ramp, snaking back and forth, would bring guests into the Ark from underneath, and dim lighting, storm and animal noises, and tightly packed cages would immediately immerse guests in the experience.

Deck 2 would highlight life inside the ark with a workshop, blacksmith shop, library, and more, along with more animal cages filled with life-like sculpted animals, a cutaway of a miniature ark, teaching on biblical kinds, a special spooky kids walkthrough, and the dramatic door exhibit of the one door into the ark.

The third deck would walk guests through what the living quarters on the ark might have been like and then introduce them to Flood geology, the post-Flood ice age, and other more science-focused topics. The theater on the third deck would present the gospel message through the story of a young reporter coming to visit the Ark.

Patrick Marsh with Orie and Ernest Lehman (brothers) who oversaw the Amish and Mennonite team that did all the timber framing on the Ark.

That was the plan. And in May 2014 we officially broke ground on our 800-acre property just off I-75, exit 154, in Kentucky. Massive earthmovers cleared half a million cubic yards of dirt for the Ark site and another million cubic yards for the sprawling 4000-car parking lot. Then contractors dug 20–25 feet down to the bedrock to ground the concrete piers that the Ark would sit on.

After that, the massive amount of timber began to arrive, brought in on 1,300 tractor trailers. In June the first of the "bents" (large wooden "u"-shaped beams) was installed, starting in the middle and working out toward the bow and stern. The timbers, milled in Colorado, had only an eighth of an inch tolerance to fit into big metal brackets produced in Pennsylvania—and not one of them was out of tolerance.

The timber work was done by talented teams of about 90 Amish and Mennonite craftsmen from a variety of states. Some of these men arrived on a Monday, worked through Thursday, then went home for the weekend. Others rented homes in the area and brought their families with them. Two men, Ori and Ernest Lehman, headed up the construction. Back home they drove horse and buggies but on the construction site they used computers and cell phones. They became life-long friends. (In fact, we have many friends and supporters from the Amish and Mennonite communities.) Nine months later, the timber frame structure was finished, an astonishing 3+ million board feet of timber all in place.

There were hundreds of people involved in this project, which is a reminder that Noah could have hired, and likely did hire, other people to help him. Not everyone who worked on the project were Christians, nor did they really understand what we were doing. They were just there to work a job and collect their paycheck. But, just as the Lord brought believers to work for us, so He brought those talented, unbelieving contractors. And many of them were curious about why we were building an ark. As they worked side-by-side with Christians and heard the message of God's Word and the gospel, we heard of people who were saved. Yes, even during the construction phases God saw fit to save lost people! The spiritual impact had already begun.

> "For various reasons, many creation scientists believe there may actually be only 1,000, or even less, land-dwelling, air-breathing kinds. So, there would have been plenty of room on the Ark." *Creation to Babel,* p. 82

Workers lining up the massive Engelmann Spruce posts.

MINISTRY MOMENT

Our plan was to start installing bents in the middle and working our way out in both directions, so that way we could block off the middle and get tradespeople in to start interior work right away, rather than having to wait for the whole structure to be built. It was a great idea except it meant we never got rid of plumbers, electricians, drywallers, floor installers—they were there in each other's way the whole time. And they were in the way of our design teams as we tried to install the exhibits! We were building them off site and installing them as construction progressed because we had a very tight timeline, opening July 7, 2016.

We sort of shot ourselves in the foot with the day we picked. We just had no idea how complicated it was going to be because we assumed we would have the bays to ourselves to get out exhibits installed. But that was not to be! I remember our teams trying to install an exhibit only to be shooed away by contractors putting down more bamboo flooring. In a perfect world we would have built the Ark, invited all the trades in to do their jobs, and then came in afterward to install exhibits. But that was not reality! The good news is, in spite of the challenges, it all got done in the end and by God's grace we opened on time with help from the government and city officials. We received temporary occupancy to allow people inside the Ark just hours before the opening ceremony. Now that was stress!

Mike Zovath

This picture shows the initial construction as well as the outline of what would be the rest of the Ark when completed. The piers that it would sit on were 12½ feet tall, and there were 102 such piers from the bow to the stern of the Ark when construction was completed.

"As we study through the first 11 chapters of Genesis, we learn that the first verse in Genesis is **foundational** to the first chapter, and the first chapter is **foundational** to the first eleven chapters, and the first eleven chapters are **foundational** to the rest of Genesis, and Genesis is **foundational** to the rest of the Bible. Indeed, Genesis 1–11 is **foundational** to all Christian doctrine and to the Christian worldview." *Creation to Babel,* p. 10

These logs are Engelmann Spruce that were harvested out of a forest in Utah. They were responsibly harvested because they were already dead trees that were just taken out of the forest before they rotted.

Laying out and assembling the bents for the Ark.

Ken Ham, LeRoy Troyer, and Mike Zovath watch as the first bent is successfully lifted into place.

On June 15, 2015 the first bent was lifted into place.

The first two bents took two weeks to assemble and lift into place. The Amish and Mennonite team were eventually able to do two in a week's time.

The Ark construction with eight bents fully in place.

The Ark is built 100% out of wood except for the steel plates that you can see in this picture where the beams connect. For wind loads and other codes we were required to have these plates added as part of the overall construction of the Ark.

The utilities, heating and cooling, restrooms, elevators and electrical grid are all in these towers. The towers also help with wind load on the Ark.

The Answers in Genesis board and leadership visiting the construction site of the Ark.

Several very large cranes were on site for many months to lift the bents into place. These Engelmann Spruce logs were 50 inches in diameter and 48 feet long.

Ken and Mally with a few of their grandchildren.

> But who is able to build him a house, since heaven, even highest heaven, cannot contain him? Who am I to build a house for him, except as a place to make offerings before him (2 Chronicles 2:6 ESV)?

The stern starting to take shape.

Initial concepts for the Ark Encounter.

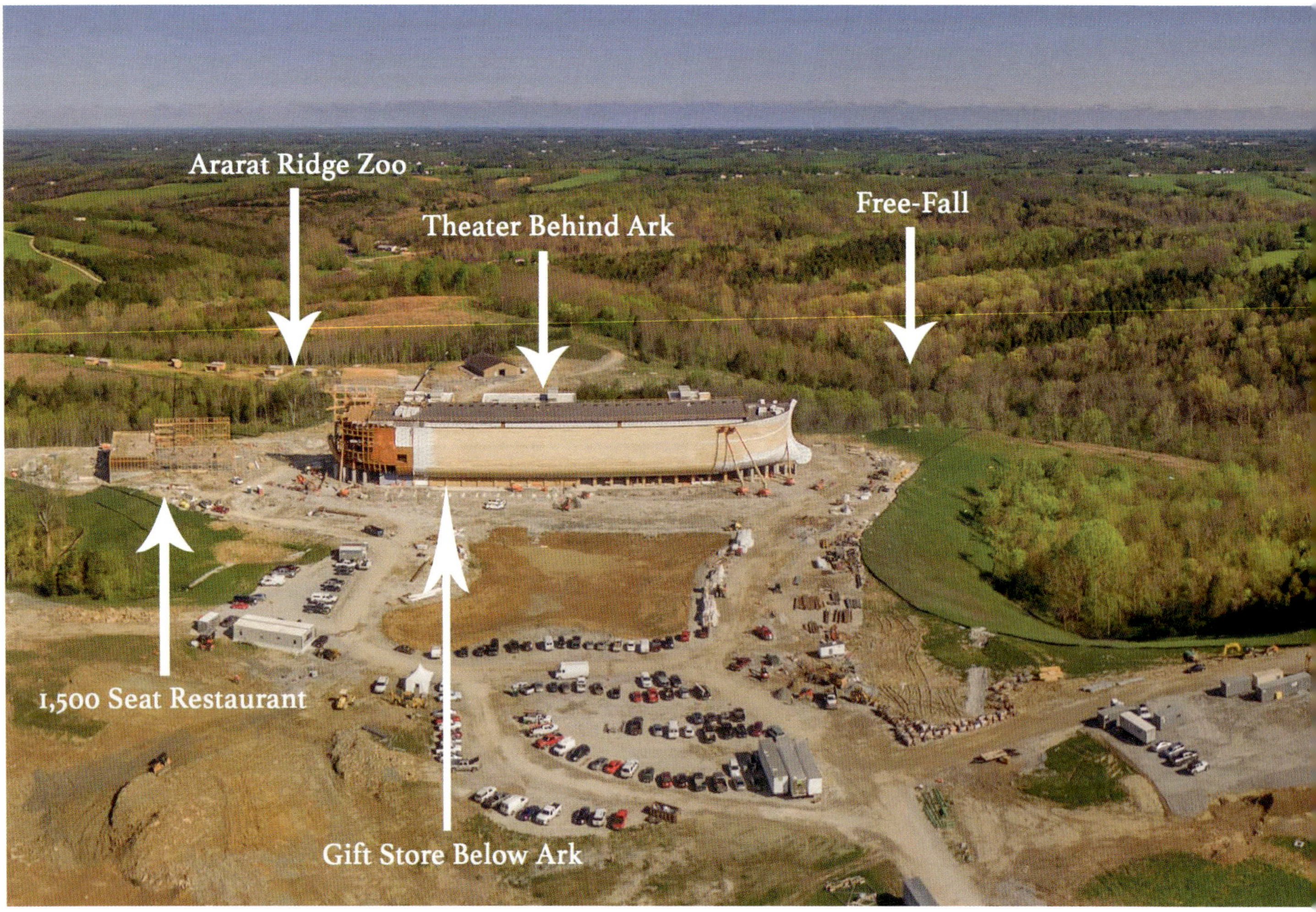

Ararat Ridge Zoo

Theater Behind Ark

Free-Fall

1,500 Seat Restaurant

Gift Store Below Ark

Ken with Dr. John Whitcomb, one of Ken's heroes, announcing the opening day of the Ark Encounter.

The opening date was 7-7-2016. Genesis 7:7 says, "And Noah and his sons and his wife and his sons' wives with him went into the ark to escape the waters of the flood."

Allen Greene developed this plan view of the space to show where props will be placed.

This elevation drawing provides a sneak peek into what the finished exhibit might look like from the guest's perspective.

Although some exhibits, such as the blacksmith area on Deck Two, do not have much teaching content, it still required the attractions design team to research the feasibility of a forge on a wooden vessel to create a realistic scene.

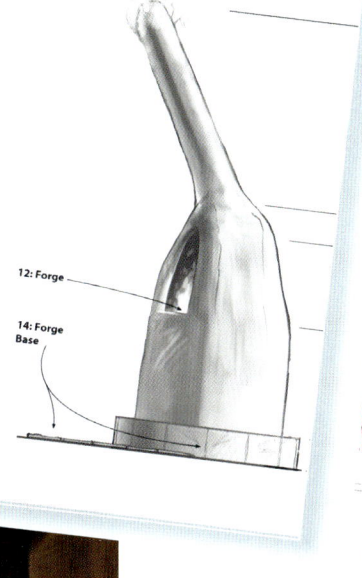

These sketches of the forge helped the technical designers and fabricators craft the physical prop.

This sketch calls attention to 70 props, signs, and design elements that needed to be created for the exhibit.

The colored drawing shows what the exhibit would look like when it is completed.

Bringing Noah's World to Life

While half a million cubic feet of dirt was being moved in Williamstown, it was full speed ahead on exhibit design at our design studios. Our research from America's Research Group, and my personal experience, had given us a good idea what questions people would want answered, queries like, "How could Noah fit the animals on the ark?" "How many animals did he need?" and "How could he feed and care for them?"

Patrick met with the exhibit designers and project coordinators to determine how to best answer these questions and more, while also immersing people into life on the Ark. They would teach through signage, prop-filled displays, dioramas, and videos. The team brainstormed, deciding which exhibit would use which combination of mediums.

And over time the original design was refined. For example, on deck 3, in what is now the Can We Trust the Bible? exhibit, two theaters were originally planned with back-to-back showings. The idea was guests would watch the first show, move into the second theater for part 2, and the first theater would fill with the next wave of guests. We soon realized that this would create a bottleneck at the end of the experience, and many guests would skip it, so we shifted to open theaters on decks 2 and 3 and a stunning comic-book style exhibit at the bow end that draws guests in with a story and teaches basic Bible apologetics and the gospel.

The exhibits that fill over 100 exhibit bays are simply stunning. The exhibit artists wanted the Ark to be more than just an impressive structure. They wanted it to be an immersive experience that brings the Bible to life, adding "flesh and blood" so to speak, to Noah and his family. What might it have been like to spend over a year on an ark surrounded by two of every kind of land-dwelling, air-breathing animal?

Minute details of everyday life—like feeding the animals, cooking food in a kitchen, growing lettuces with light from above, and relaxing after a day's hard work—are shown in vivid and intricate detail. Gifted artisans created handwoven blankets and tapestries, carvings, hanging planters, and handcrafted furniture, all based on research from the ancient world and imagination of what it might have been like on that epic voyage. I believe the attention to detail not only humanizes the biblical characters but revolutionizes people's view of the past. They weren't dumb brutes but people just like us who created beautiful things, had culture, and had interests and hobbies.

And then there's the animals. Dozens of sculpted animals (two of each, seven pairs of some) fill wooden cages and ceramic pots throughout the first two decks. Some are more familiar, like representatives of the giraffe, deer, or rhino kinds. Others are unfamiliar, such as *Simosuchus, Pakicetus*, and *Cotylorhynchus*. The

animals, familiar or not, are based off fossils buried during the time of the Flood. For example, our giraffes look like giraffes but with shorter necks and stocky bodies. Noah didn't take two *Giraffa camelopardalis* (and the nine subspecies that exist today) on the Ark. He took two representatives of the giraffe kind. After the Flood, they spread out and adapted to different environments, giving us the iconic safari giant and the shy forest-dwelling okapi. To depict the ark giraffe kind as accurately as possible our artists sculpted it based on fossils of the now extinct *Shansitherium*.

The animals were sculpted over many painstaking hours, first from a digital 3D model then either a modified taxidermy form or in pieces from a block of foam sculpted by a CNC machine and assembled by the artists. Over many weeks the artists added fur, scales, hairs, eyes, claws, skin, and other features, turning a piece of foam into a creature that looks like it might just blink and move to the other side of its cage! For some of these creatures, each hair had to be placed one by one by hand. It was an almost overwhelming amount of work, but the results take guests' breath away.

> "Our children are caught in this ever-changing climate of cultural opinion....God's Word is attacked in so many ways, and our kids need to be trained to stand firm on God's Word."
> *Divided Nation*, p. 125

People have often asked why we didn't use taxidermized animals. Well, they are today's species, but we needed representatives of the land-dwelling, air-breathing kinds on the ark. Today's species have developed from those kinds that were on the ark. To help people understand this important concept of "kinds," and to be as biblically accurate as possible, our designers had to develop unique kinds of sculpted animals for the Ark exhibits.

Those exhibits then needed to be installed. The deadline to open the Ark was so tight exhibit artists would sleep in various places throughout the Ark, catching a few winks before grabbing coffee and getting back to work. On the night before the ribbon cutting, two days before we opened to the public, artists worked into the wee hours of the morning, installing signs and finishing last-minute touches. As artists one-by-one drifted home to catch a couple hours of sleep, a massive mess was left behind. It certainly didn't look like we would be ready for opening the next day! But our amazing housekeeping team came through and somehow cleaned everything up before guests arrived.

Workers feverishly working to install exhibits in the Ark as the opening date approached.

MINISTRY MOMENT

"Where are the lights?"

As the content manager for the attractions, I have written and supervised the creation of hundreds of signs, including a sign for "the door" exhibit on deck 2. Our design team wasn't initially planning to have a sign at the door, but Ken had other plans.

After church one Sunday, Ken handed a note to one of our project designers, Jon Taylor. Ken had written a draft for the sign himself. We ran it through the approval process, and the printed sign soon arrived at the Ark. Knowing Ken wanted it up as soon as possible, I convinced a couple of our graphic designers to help me install it immediately. When we entered the Ark, we found out that Ken was about to lead the first tour up the brand new Ark ramp and bring them through the door on live video.

We rushed to finish the installation before Ken's group arrived, pulling it off with eight minutes to spare. Before Ken opened the door, I whispered to one the graphic designers, "As soon as Ken sees the sign, he's going to ask, 'When are we going to get lights on that thing?'" Sure enough, the first thing Ken said to me when his livestream was finished was, "When are we going to get lights on that thing?" It now has lights!

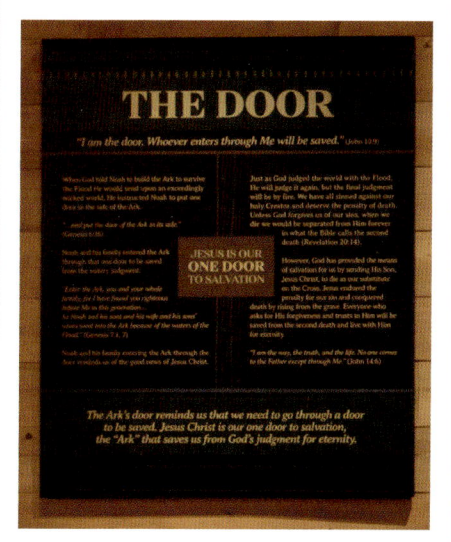

• • • • • • • • • • • • *Tim Chaffey*

"ON THE COUNT OF 3...2...1!"

On July 5, 2016, we hosted a special ribbon-cutting ceremony before a crowd of 7,000 supporters whose generosity had made this massive undertaking possible, along with 150 different media and a few dignitaries. The board members and Dr. John Whitcomb (co-author of *The Genesis Flood*) laid twelve stones as a symbol of what we were doing at the Ark. After the Israelites crossed the Jordan River, they set up twelve stones of memorial as a sign to future generations of what the Lord had done. And that's what we were doing—reminding future generations of God's just judgment on sin and His mercy in offering us an Ark of salvation, the one Door, the Lord Jesus Christ.

The day was a festive one, less emotional than the museum opening had been. We had activities going on throughout the property, and it was a joy to watch guests enter the full-size Ark for the first time. Everyone was blown away. We had to serve box lunches that day because we hadn't yet received occupancy for the restaurant. (We were praying hard about that one. It arrived the next day, right before our grand opening to the public.)

Word quickly spread and by September we had already welcomed over 325,000 guests—the number the state of Kentucky thought we would reach by our first anniversary if the attraction had creationist content. Motor coach bookings were flooding in for the next spring and fall, and guests were coming in waves, 6,000 at a time on weekends. (Our record as of the writing of this book is now almost 11,000 on one day!) Our numbers have continued to climb, with over a million visiting each year, and we receive rave reviews.

Ken gathering his thoughts before he is to speak to a crowd of 7,000. Pondering all the work, legal battles, fund raising it took to get this moment. The many years of planning but the day is here. Praise the Lord.

••••• Post-visit surveys indicate that over 60% of guests feel their visit "extremely" or "very much" strengthened and better equipped them to defend their Christian faith. And these same surveys indicate 6.3% of guests make a decision to follow Christ after visiting. That's 63,000 souls per million guests (and that number might be low as we hear testimonies of people who became Christians months after their visit, long after they had filled in a survey). All we can say is praise the Lord. It is His work, and we are so grateful to play a small part in His eternal plan of redemption.

Lieutenant Governor Jenean Hampton standing next to Ken

Ken addressing the large crowd of supporters and media at ribbon-cutting.

Over 100 national and local media came by to the ribbon-cutting event.

The three founders and others, holding the ribbon during the ceremony.

MINISTRY MOMENT

Are We on the Moon?

When I see pictures of the ribbon cutting, I cringe a little because it looks like the Ark landed on the moon! There's rock everywhere, no vegetation—not even grass. We had hydroseeded around the lake so we would have at least a little green, but it rained for two straight weeks before we opened, and there was nothing we could do to make it more hospitable for our guests. You would never know it now though. The grounds are beautiful and, as they mature, they will only become more so.

It was a scramble to be ready for opening day, but we did it! We knew it would take 2–3 more years to get the Ark to where we wanted it, but on that day, we could take a deep breath and celebrate what the Lord had done. When I visit the Ark, I still tear up and get goosebumps. It's an impressive structure, and to think I had a little part in it is mind-blowing. What a blessing to be part of such a God thing!

Mike Zovath

There's More to Come

I still stand in awe of what the Lord has done. I never would have imagined as a public school teacher in Australia that someday I would be standing before a life-size Noah's ark that a ministry I co-founded had built. It's tremendous and a true gift from God. He brought it about, and as we continue to faithfully serve Him, He will continue to use and grow this ministry into the future.

> "What do these stones mean to you?" Then you shall answer them … And these stones shall be for a memorial to the children of Israel forever. Then Joshua set up twelve stones in the midst of the Jordan, in the place where the feet of the priests who bore the ark of the covenant stood; and they are there to this day (Joshua 4: 4–7, 9 ESV).

The Second Debate

The day after the Ark opened to the public, July 8, 2016, Bill Nye once again visited us, this time to take me up on my public offer to give him a guided tour through all three decks. He agreed on the condition that he could be accompanied by his video crew who were working on a documentary. We knew we wouldn't be favorably portrayed but agreed under our own condition—our video crew could also be there.

The day of the tour, a massive storm moved into the area. It poured rain, thunder boomed, and lightning struck nearby. To break the ice, I asked Bill if he liked our special effects. Before a large crowd of onlookers, and surrounded by boom mics and cameras, I guided Bill through the Ark, starting on deck 3. (He insisted on going through the Ark backwards, from the top down, starting with the science exhibits.) For over two hours we "sparred" back and forth, with Bill confidently stating things like it's "not crazy" to believe "we're descendants of Martians," that evolutionarily we're related to bananas, that when you're dead, "you're done," and that right and wrong is "based on what I think as a member of the human tribe." Over and over, I challenged Bill on his beliefs and, once again, shared the gospel with him. At the end, I asked if I could pray for him and he said he couldn't stop me, so I prayed.

We then released the "second debate" in full on our YouTube channel. It's received millions of views, and those two debate videos are still our most watched videos. They've had a tremendous impact.

The beautiful rainbow garden in full bloom at the Ark.

MINISTRY MOMENT

Our first horticulture task for the Ark construction was clearing 80 acres of trees—three guys with three chainsaws over three months clearing 80 acres of trees and brush for the Ark, the grounds, the zoo, and the parking lot. We then began some minor excavations for the grounds and the zoo, expanding our team to include site development as we worked in sunshine, rain, and snow to construct the beginnings of the Ararat Ridge Zoo, behind the Ark, in time for opening.

I then created a diagram of the grounds featuring bubbles, representing where I was planting flowers, shrubs, and trees. There weren't really any measurements; I just spray painted the ground to get a visual of what it would all look like, imagining how much shade and what kind of aesthetic these little trees would produce in 30 years. One challenge in landscape design at the Ark is everything looks dwarfed by the sheer size of the structure. But in 20–30 years our little trees will be gorgeous, big shade trees, and guests will stroll through an alleyway to Ararat Ridge Zoo. But that all takes time. You can't speed up the growth of trees.

At a worldwide attraction like the Ark, the grounds are vital. It's the first thing you see when you arrive, and it must inform the guest, "This is world-class." I'm thankful Ken and Patrick have always seen the grounds as vital to the success of the attractions.

Tim Schmitt

To build this Ark so many things had to happen and the only thing one can say is it was the hand of God. First, the leadership and board to even consider such a huge project was incredible. Then you had to have someone to build it, LeRoy Troyer and the Amish and Mennonite men that made it happen. Then once again you had to have someone like Patrick to cast the overall vision for the exhibts. One would have to call this *Miraculous!*

AiG staff through the years.

The beginning of this ministry started off very small. It was we three founders and Kathy Ellis day one.

But over the years we grew gradually as the Lord blessed us.

I can't begin to tell you all the amazing people that the Lord has brought to us.

You can see we had steady growth in the 90's and early 2000's.

When the Creation Museum opened, we grew fast and added a lot of staff.

Since the opening of the Ark Encounter, we have not been able to get everyone together as we now have over 1000 full- and part-time people.

1995

1998

2001

2003

To God be the glory.

2009

2016

2016 – 2025

9 FAITHFUL GOD for 50 years

BEYOND FIFTY YEARS

As I write this book, it's exactly 50 years since that first talk at Dalby Baptist Church in Australia. Fifty years sounds like a long time. When you say it as "half a century," it sounds unbelievably long. And yet it's been half a century since the "fire in my bones" produced my first-ever creation apologetics presentation. And what a fifty years it has been!

When the Ark Encounter opened in 2016 our ministry made headlines around the world. We were thrust into the spotlight in ways even the publicity of the Creation Museum hadn't done. The ministry grew by leaps and bounds as new staff joined us, new departments were started, and other visionaries throughout the ministry brought forward ideas and projects. It's been exciting, and it thrills me to think of where this ministry will go in the future.

The future can also be a bit scary. After all, many Christian ministries started out the same way we have—with a commitment to the truth of God's Word and a desire to proclaim the gospel. But, over time, the wrong people infiltrated those ministries, the mission became cloudy and began to drift, and many a ministry has died, a shell of what it is was, or still continues today having no impact for God's Word or the gospel. Consider, for example, that most of today's Ivy League schools—Harvard, Princeton, Yale, and the like—were founded as Christian schools. You would never guess that today!

I take the risk of mission drift very seriously and, as a ministry, we have done everything we can from a human responsibility perspective to protect the ministry. (For example, having a robust and highly detailed statement of faith all employees must sign each year and having an editorial review board that checks content for accuracy and mission focus.) Then, after doing what we can, we trust the ministry to God's sovereignty and look for the right people to put into leadership positions to move this ministry into the future.

But really, it all comes down to people! I've seen those who started strong on God's Word grow tired of the battle and wane in their vigilance to keep a strong stand. Other organizations get complacent as they become successful and have financial stability. Some succumb to peer pressure and allow staff in who may be weak in their stand on God's Word and so on. There are so many pitfalls. So regardless of all the safeguards someone puts in place, it really does come down to people.

• •

MINISTRY MOMENT

Three Founders, Still Together

Mark, Ken, and I have been together going on 32 years. I just can't believe it has been that long. We get asked, from time to time, "How have you stayed together all these years? It's very unusual!" Well, in my mind, the three of us were not competing against each other.

Neither Mark nor I could preach, talk, and teach the way Ken does. Mark is so smooth with the public relations stuff, and he's got a memory like a steel trap. He can remember somebody's name, what they were doing, and who their kids were from a quick meeting at an event 20 years ago. You can't even try to compete with that so there's no "ego conflicts" between what Ken and Mark do. And I can't do any of that stuff, but what I can do is push stuff through and spin plates. Ken doesn't want to do that—and he's too busy anyway. And Mark doesn't want to do it because he's got other administrative things to take care of. So, I've been "getting stuff done" since the "old days" when I would go to our seminars and set things up for Ken. And I could never please him, I would think I had it perfect, and he would want the projector moved 6 inches. I just kind of gave up, got as close as I could, and waited to see what he wanted to change.

Over the years we've all had a lane, and we've stayed in our lane almost the whole time. It also helps that all three of us have a good sense of humor and we can poke fun at each other a bit. (When things got tense, Mark would come up with some pretty funny one-liners.) But, as I've said before, I have the best job of the three of us. God has given us incredibly top-notch teams

who love what they do, and it's a joy working with them at the design studios. It's been the ride of a lifetime, and I couldn't ask for a better life. It's been so much fun, and it's a blessing and a joy seeing people respond to the message that's portrayed in the Creation Museum and the Ark. I pray that the Lord looks on my life with favor as I have tried to please Him. I know there are many people that have worked tirelessly with us who will hear, "Well done, my good and faithful servant."

Mike Zovath

The Impact Grows

The previous chapter ended in 2016—nearly a decade from the present. But much has happened at the attractions and the ministry in that decade. When we built the Creation Museum, we planned for our warehouse space to be at the museum. Well, the ministry grew to a size where that simply wasn't enough space, and we moved it off site. (Our warehouse staff—with help from robotic chucks—now ship tons of materials each year.) That freed up a significant amount of space. I had always wanted a way of giving our presentations to Creation Museum guests, and

Expanding warehouse space and downstairs at the Answers Center.

the deserted warehouse was the perfect opportunity. We turned it into an auditorium (the very auditorium my debate with Bill Nye took place in). It was phenomenally successful and another opportunity to impact guests. Over the years, we outgrew even that space, and the technology and overall look were aged so, in 2022, we completely renovated Legacy Hall with state-of-the-art lighting and acoustic treatments, an LED wall, and a reorientation of the stage and chairs to increase capacity.

Warehouse turned auditorium

Once the Ark Encounter opened, we had a burden to build an auditorium at the Ark. Originally, we planned for a smaller auditorium behind the Ark, but we quickly realized we needed something much more substantial: a 2,500-seat auditorium and a full lower level with a science lab, a kitchen, and space for breakout sessions, special dinners, and smaller events. Such a facility could become a conference center, not only for our ministry but also for other ministries.

We shared our burden with several different foundations who, catching the vision, gave several large gifts, enabling us to build our Answers Center. It opened in 2019 and has been one of the greatest ministry assets we've ever had. That building has hosted sold-out women's and men's conferences, pastors' conferences, our Spanish-language (Dia Latino) and Deaf outreaches, homeschool experiences, the world's largest Christian music festival (40 Days of Christian Music), Broadway-quality live stage productions, and more. And, as we predicted, many other Christian ministries, large and small, have hosted their events in the Answers Center. It's had a tremendous impact.

Classrooms downstairs at the Answers Center.

Defending Christian Love

Over the years I've often thought of Genesis 50:20, "As for you, you meant evil against me, but God meant it for good." Yes, God often works by taking what Satan means for evil and using it for good. I've seen that over and over throughout the years, including at the University of Central Oklahoma (UCO).

In 2018 I was invited by a Christian group to speak for them on the UCO campus in their Constitution Hall on "Genesis and the State of the Culture." They had trouble getting the school to even agree to having a "controversial" speaker like me come, but eventually the school granted permission, and I signed the contract, adding the date—March 5—to my speaking calendar.

Now before I share what happened, consider that, since 2014, this school has hosted an annual drag show called "Glamazon," featuring men dressed as provocatively clad caricatures of women. The school also hosts an annual "Safe Sex Carnival" and "Sexy Haunted House" event that involves lewd activities and encourages licentiousness. They claim to be "committed to an inclusive educational [environment]" that fosters the "free exchange of ideas." Now, with all that information in mind, you can probably guess where this story is heading.

Yes, the LGBTQ group, headed by an activist professor, put pressure on the school to rescind my invitation. They

caved, cancelling the contract because of my supposed "hate speech." That "hate speech," I would later find out, was the biblical teaching that marriage is between a man and a woman.

Well, word soon got out to the media and residents of Oklahoma—none too pleased with how their tax-payer funded college was trampling on the First Amendment rights of students—reached out to certain politicians, and pressure was put on the college, this time to invite me back. It blew up so much the college president personally called me, reinstating the invitation but now as a public presentation at the university. What was supposed to be a small private talk to a group of Christian students became a packed-out public talk with Christians and non-Christians from the university, media, and the local community attending (and people watched online). I was also allowed to bring one of our scientists, Dr. Georgia Purdom, along with me to give a scientific presentation. We reached so many more people because of the controversy caused by the LGBTQ group.

And that group was front and center when I gave my talk. Knowing they'd be there—and would be hostile, accusing me of hate speech—I gave a talk that was basically an overview of what Christians believe and why. I highlighted the 7 C's of History, the foundational history that gives us our worldview, showing that, because I believe the Bible, I have a different foundation from those who do not believe the Bible. For example, I handled marriage by showing that because I believe God created us male and female, and created marriage from the beginning as recorded in Genesis, He gets to define marriage. Those who don't start with God's Word will have a different worldview, and we will never agree on the worldview level until we can agree on the foundational level. "Having a different worldview doesn't mean I hate anyone," I shared, "it just means we have different starting points." I covered other topics like abortion and racism in a similar way. Actually, when I spoke against racism, sharing that we're all one family, I received resounding applause. And because I was giving an overview of what Christians believe and why, I also clearly presented the gospel message.

At the end of the presentation, I had non-Christian professors tell me they appreciated the way I presented what I believed because it took the emotionalism out of the argument.

I emphasize even more in all my talks that as Christians our worldview is founded in Scripture and if someone else doesn't have the same foundation, they're not going to have the same worldview.

Dr. Purdom and Ken taking questions at the university.

Before we spoke, we invited people to write down any questions they had and hand them in as Dr. Purdom and I would be doing a Q&A afterward. One of the questions I received was from a member of the LGBTQ group who asked:

"I sought the Lord and churches for why I feel attracted to the same sex. I found the church nor churches' traditional view on [LGBTQ] fit my experience of hearing the Lord speak directly to me. Science, not the church, gave me peace. How can you say my experience of still being a child of God isn't valid?"

Here's how I responded: "Well, if the God of the Bible is the same God that spoke to you then His written Word is not going to be contrary to what His spoken Word would be. So therefore, you and I must have a very different view of Genesis because what you're saying He spoke to you and said is different to what I believe Genesis is saying. Until we sort that out, we're never going to sort out our conflict at the worldview level. Now that doesn't mean we hate each other or anything like that, because as Christians we're commanded to love people. But you and I obviously have a different view of Genesis, so we need to sit down and talk about why that is. I'm certainly willing to do that with you." That person never came up to talk afterwords but she (the LGBTQ group at the presentation were all females)—and everyone else in the audience and online—heard that defense of a biblical ethic and how God's spoken Word will never contradict His written Word.

2020 (Enough Said, Right?)

We entered a valley of despair, where we wondered what God was doing, in March 2020. (I'm sure many of you readers can relate!) And, yes, God used that COVID year for good. Right as our busy season was beginning, like the rest of the world, we were suddenly shut down, first for "fourteen days to slow the spread" and then it dragged on indefinitely, totaling three months.

I wanted to continue ensuring we were communicating with our supporters during lockdown while everyone was stuck at home, so I asked Maria, one of our talented graphic designers who is also a talented photographer, to begin recording all sorts of behind-the-scenes videos while the Ark and Creation Museum were closed to the public. We filmed dozens of such videos, and our supporters loved them. The teaching and fun educational content meant so much to them during that hard time. And that led us to finally take a step we had thought about for a long time: creating a streaming platform.

As threats of "de-platforming" by secular companies grew, we wanted to ensure our content was protected for the future. DVDs were on their way out so that wasn't a viable option; we needed a streaming platform. In a matter of weeks (the Lord was so gracious to enable it), we launched Answers.tv, an affordable subscription-based streaming platform for all of our AiG videos. So even through the terrible problems everyone experienced through 2020, God was working for good. That streaming platform has over seven thousand videos as of the writing of this book, with more programs added each week.

| COVID, sitting six feet apart.

I'm often asked how we survived financially after being shut down for three months. It was a struggle. It broke my heart that we had to temporarily lay off 80% of our staff, but without the revenue from the attractions, especially after coming out of the slow winter months, we simply could not afford to pay salaries. The whole situation had a tremendous impact emotionally on all our staff. Thankfully, with all of the stimulus checks and other programs, most of our staff actually received more money during those months then they would have while on salary. The Lord provided for the ministry and our laid off employees. And many of them came back as soon as we could hire them again.

But God also provided through our donors who gave generously. Before the shutdowns, a foundation had given us a large grant toward one of the projects at the Creation Museum. We asked if they would be willing to redesignate those funds to enable us to survive through the shutdown and they agreed—and then later replaced those funds so the project could also continue. What a blessing!

Just a few of the many programs available on Answers.tv.

> I am the door. If anyone enters by me, he will be saved and will go in and out and find pasture (John 10:9 ESV).

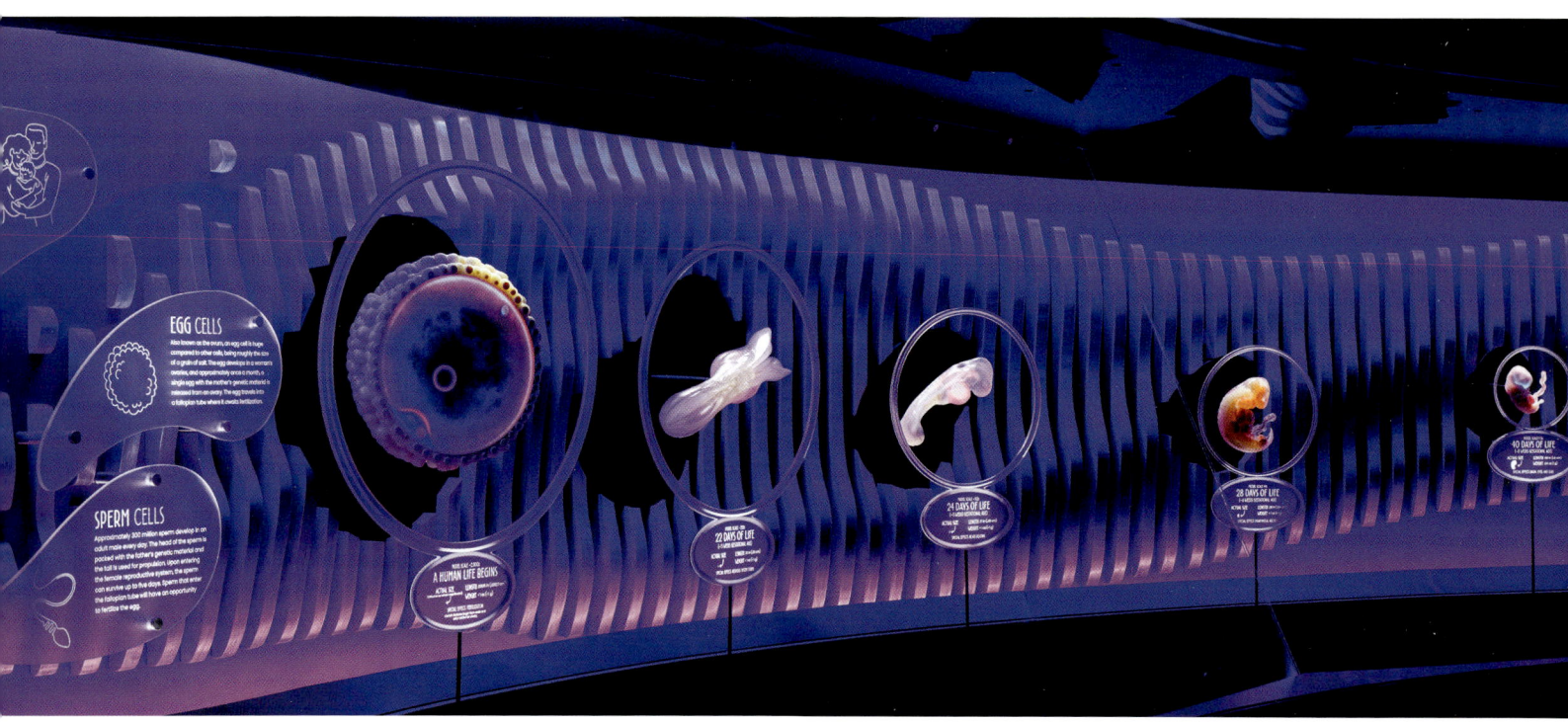

Saving Little Lives

Since the opening of the Creation Museum and Ark Encounter we've made countless enhancements and upgrades to the exhibits, including redesigning the first one-third of the museum walk-through to accommodate the increase in guests once the Ark opened. But one of the most stunning new exhibits we've added has to be our Fearfully and Wonderfully Made pro-life exhibit at the museum.

The year 2020 was an election year and abortion was a huge talking point in the media (consider that *Roe v. Wade* would be overturned in 2022). We've always been a pro-life ministry, passionate about the sanctity of human life and unafraid to call abortion what it is: the murder of a child. But we didn't have an exhibit at the museum dealing with this vital issue. So in 2019 we started talking about such an exhibit and decided we wanted it open before the 2020 election. That took some creativity on the part of our designers!

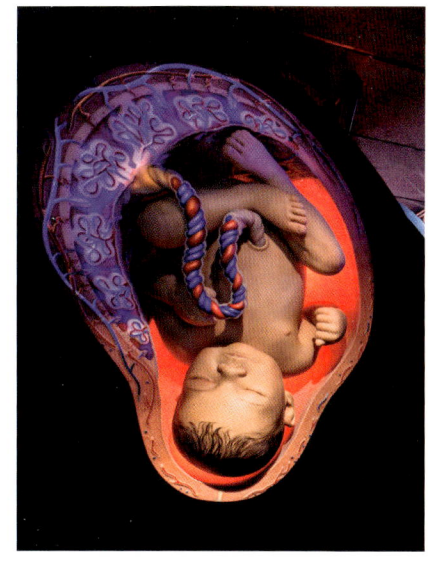

They first crafted a temporary exhibit, set up in Legacy Lobby at the museum while they continued working behind the scenes on a permanent exhibit and began the necessary renovations to our Palm Plaza area where Fearfully and Wonderfully Made would live (and, eventually, Borderland: Israel at the Time of Jesus, too). The permanent exhibit opened in October 2022.

It is stunning. The baby models, showing the various levels of development as an unborn child grows in his or her mother's womb, are beautiful and hyper-realistic, highlighting God's incredible design and the wonder of life. Biblical and scientific teaching clearly portray the truth: life begins at the moment of fertilization and every human life is made in God's image and has inestimable value.

Everyone Wants to See the Ark

Bill Nye

Tim Tebow

Barry "Butch" Wilmore, who spent 9 months on the International Space Station.

Over the years, we've had many famous visitors tour our attractions from atheists such as Bill Nye, Christopher Hitchens, and Bill Maher (he snuck into the Creation Museum offices back in 2007—we've since learned the importance of a good security team, and our Department of Public Safety is truly second to none) to athletes such as football quarterbacks Tim Tebow and Ben Roethlisberger, musicians such as Ozzy Osbourne and Nicole Scherzinger, astronauts Barry "Butch" Wilmore and Charlie Duke (who walked on the moon), politicians such as now Secretary of Defense Pete Hegseth, former presidential candidate and acclaimed neurosurgeon Ben Carson, Senator Rand Paul of Kentucky, Speaker of the House Mike Johnson, former representative of Congress and presidential candidate Michele Bachmann, and other well-known personalities including best-selling *Left Behind* author Tim LaHaye, Demi-Leigh Nel-Peters who was Miss Universe 2017, and even a Nigerian king!

One exceptional visitor toured before the Ark Encounter opened to the public: former U.S. president, Jimmy Carter (he passed away in 2025). He was a friend of our architect, LeRoy Troyer, through their mutual involvement with an organization called Habitat for Humanity. President Carter loved working with wood, so LeRoy invited him to tour the Ark and marvel at all the incredible woodwork involved with the structure. He and his wife visited and agreed to an interview with some media. I had to smile when the reporter asked President Carter—who we knew

Astronaut Charlie Duke third from the right.

Steven Curtis Chapman, and former Kentucky Governor Matt Bevin

Mike Johnson, Speaker of the House

to be a theistic evolutionist who did not believe in a literal Genesis—what he thought about the message we were putting in the Ark. He immediately responded by telling the reporter he believed in evolution.

After the tour, we all went to Cracker Barrel for lunch and chatted. I didn't bring up the topic of evolution or anything like that. We just talked to him about his life and, of course, he talked to us about how wonderful the timber frame Ark structure was. So, he loved the timber framing; he just didn't love the message that we would be putting in the Ark.

Ken with Jimmy Carter

A Big Step Forward

I remember the day we moved into the Creation Museum offices. We were so thrilled to be in one place (and away from the fruit flies!). The offices seemed huge, more than enough space for our staff of about 100. Well, we've now outgrown that space and, as I write this, we are splitting at the seams, but the Lord has provided wonderfully for that need.

For years, as I've driven the I-275 loop around Cincinnati, I've seen this beautiful large building Cincinnati Bell built and then Toyota bought and expanded into their national headquarters. As I would drive past that particular building, I was burdened, "Lord, why can't Christian organizations like us have a building like that for our offices?" I even mentioned that thought to a board member one time as we drove past, "I'd love to see AiG have a building like that someday. We could do so much with it!"

Our new offices that we moved into spring of 2025.

Fast forward a few years and Answers in Genesis had a growth problem—a good problem to have but a problem nonetheless. Answers Academy, our Christian worldview K-12 school, started by my eldest daughter Renee, had opened in 2017 and had rapidly outgrown the church facility they rented. They desperately needed a home of their own but there was nothing suitable available.

Our AiG offices were bursting (as were the offices at the Ark), with staff rotating work from home some days so desks could be shared between staff members. The Creation Museum needed a new and bigger restaurant, and we wanted to design some exhibits especially to impact children. We discussed, and even received approval, to build a large building in the front parking lot of the museum. Maybe we could move our staff over there and convert the offices into a children's space and larger dining venue. Well, that would cost many millions of dollars and take years to fundraise. We were stuck.

Then one day I noticed that the Toyota building was up for lease. Toyota had moved their headquarters to Texas, and a Fortune 500 company wanted the building. But then came the pandemic, and that changed everything. With staff working from home, suddenly office space wasn't nearly as desirable and the company that wanted the building pulled out. Now, in 2023, 200,000 square feet of office space was up for lease. But, of course, there was no way we could get such a building, so I put the thought out of my mind.

Soon after, we met with our marketing agency, JDA, to create a strategic plan for the future of Answers Academy. This plan included not just physical growth in the number of students, but we also want to have an online aspect to impact homeschoolers and other schools. (Very few Christian schools teach biblical worldview. We want to change that, and Answers Academy can be the "model school" to do so.) Brad Benbow, the head of JDA, suggested a commercial real estate agent who could help us. I couldn't get that Toyota building out of my head, so I mentioned it to him, just in case.

The real estate agent checked it out. "It's the only suitable building in the area" was the conclusion of his research. "Maybe they'd be willing to sell it." We all went to check it out and while we walked through, Mike Zovath and I realized at the same time that we needed to reevaluate everything. This building could be the answer to our prayers, not only for the school but also for our offices.

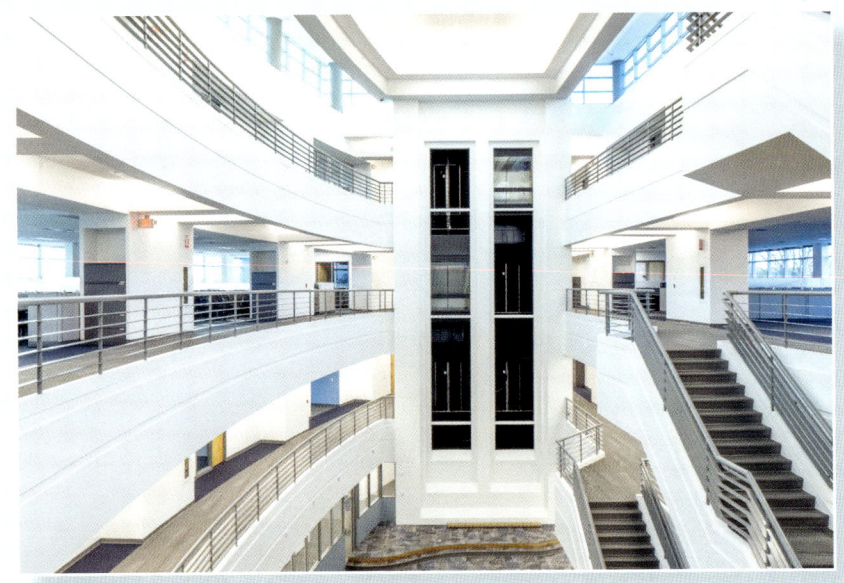

One-third of the building could become an entirely separate building and house the school, allowing it to quadruple in size. Eventually the grounds could house athletic fields, a gym, and even a preschool building. The other two-thirds would fit our offices, a much-needed studio for social media filming, and so much more. Because the pandemic had lowered the value of commercial real estate, the building would cost a fraction of what it would cost to build new and it wouldn't take years of fundraising, getting permits, designing, and building. Through a series of miracles, the owners agreed to sell the building, we secured funding, and the building was ours.

Since then, the Academy side has been fully and beautifully renovated, and the school has moved in and quickly grown. The offices were also renovated, and our staff started moving in department by

> Now to him who is able to do far more abundantly than all that we ask or think, according to the power at work within us, to him be glory in the church and in Christ Jesus throughout all generations, forever and ever. Amen (Ephesians 3:20–21 ESV).

department beginning in March 2025. We've broken ground on a new restaurant at the Creation Museum and have a vision to turn the Museum office space into a children's museum. The move also allowed us to demolish one of our downstairs classrooms to make space for a new identity exhibit on the biblical truth of male and female. Someday, Lord willing, maybe we can use the permission we obtained to build a building in the front parking lot to expand the museum. Who knows what the Lord will do in the future?

I find it fascinating that for years I was burdened for that one specific office building, out of the hundreds in our area. It's almost as if the Lord was letting me know that there was something special about that building. Then, when I least expected it, this building became a part of the Answers in Genesis ministry, giving us a tremendous facility for our international headquarters. God truly gave us "more abundantly than all that we ask or think" (Ephesians 3:20). Praise the Lord for "nothing will be impossible with God" (Luke 1:37).

> "... an atheist said to me, 'I don't care if they find a big boat on Mt. Ararat and drag it down the main street, I will not believe in Noah's Ark.' This reminds me of the scoffers in 2 Peter 3 who 'willingly reject' (or deliberately disbelieve) creation and the Flood." *Ken Ham Daily*, pp. 58-59

For nothing will be impossible with God (Luke 1:37 ESV).

Tearful Goodbyes

In November 2019, Mally and I were in Australia as my mother passed from her nursing home into her eternal heavenly home. As I reflected on her passing, I was reminded of a video I had recorded with her a few years earlier, where I asked about her life so I could pass those stories on to our kids and grandkids. In response to a question about death she answered that she was ready to go. "Well, you don't die," she explained. "You know, you just go through the valley of the shadow of death. You just walk through the shadow—you don't go into it—you walk through the shadow, and you go to be with the Lord. Have you thought about that?" Even as she approached the shadow of death herself, she couldn't help teaching me from God's Word!

My mum lived to be almost 92 and she would tell people, "I had 90 good years." She didn't care for the last two years in a nursing home, but her health was such that it was necessary. And she "redeemed the time" by sharing Christ with the other residents and the staff any opportunity she had. But she was ready to go home and be with the Savior she loved so much. One time, when she was in her 80s, living in a unit in a retirement village, my sisters, who checked on her every day, couldn't get in contact with her. My sister, extremely worried, rushed over to find mum collapsed on the floor. She had fallen in the night but hadn't

pressed the emergency button on the device around her neck. "Why didn't you call for help, mum?" my sister asked, to which my mother replied calmly, "Well, I thought this was the time Jesus was coming to get me, and I didn't want to stop it." And when I visited, she often wasn't even wearing the emergency button, but she would smile and say, "Oh, I know where it is if anything happens." I just shook my head. Yes, she was ready to go home and be with Jesus. What a testimony to the peace that comes from knowing the One who has conquered death, emptying it of its sting.

Buddy Davis

Patrick Marsh

Dr. David Menton

My parents aren't the only ones we've lost over the years. Many of our dear friends in Australia, and here in America, along with other close family members, have now gone to be with the Lord. Through the decades, the Lord has brought thousands of people to Answers in Genesis as full-time, part-time, or seasonal staff members. Each has had a huge impact, some even serving right up until the Lord called them home. I hate to single anyone out (that's the hardest part of writing a book like this—space just doesn't permit the mentioning of everyone the Lord has used in big and little ways throughout the decades), but I do want to mention a few saints in particular who have now gone home with Jesus.

I've already written of the tremendous impact and legacy of Patrick Marsh, whom the Lord brought to us right when we most needed him. I've also written about my dearest friend, Buddy Davis, whom the Lord called home in 2024 after he had impacted untold numbers of people with his music, videos, and teaching. I really look at Buddy as a fourth "founder" of the ministry. I've also highlighted the brilliant Ivy League educated scientist, Dr. David Menton, whose detailed research and expertise inspired and was integral to the Fearfully and Wonderfully Made exhibit, among others. His legacy regarding the sanctity of human life continues to impact people day after day. But this book wouldn't be complete without mentioning my dear friend Dr. Tommy Mitchell who entered his heavenly inheritance in 2019.

Dr. Tommy Mitchell

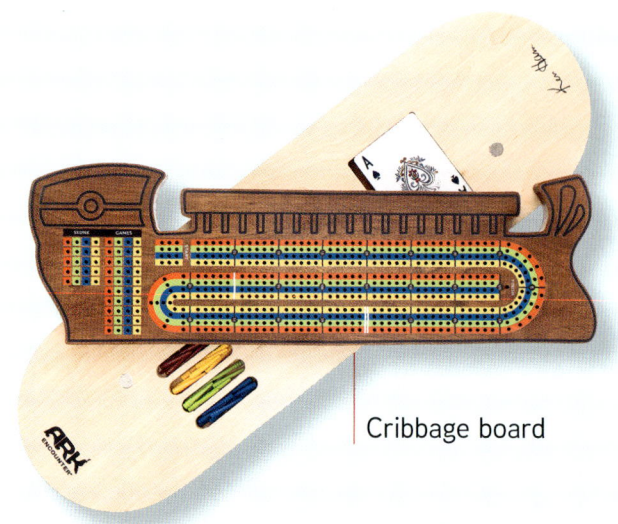
Cribbage board

Tommy was a medical doctor from Tennessee who I met in 1995 when he drove four hours to purchase several resources from our new bookstore in Florence, KY. He spearheaded a major AiG conference in 1999 and eventually joined our staff in 2006, quickly becoming one of our most effective and dynamic speakers. Everyone loved him, and he soon became one of my closest friends, stopping by my house to chat, watch science fiction programs, play cribbage, or fix my MacBook or iPhone for me. (He was brilliant with Macs. He could always fix any problem I had, even when I was on the road.) He is greatly missed by myself and everyone at AiG who was privileged to know him.

Special Mention

One final special mention, this time of a staff member who is still with us: Tim Schmitt. (You've met him in previous chapters.) He's a visionary himself, and God brought him along at just the right time to develop our gorgeous grounds, including the stunning botanical gardens at the Creation Museum and our first of its kind Plants of the Bible Conservatory that opened in late 2024. I never would have imagined we would have such beautiful grounds and zoos (they are an attraction in and of themselves), and we owe that to Tim's vision and the amazing team he's developed.

Yes, the Lord has graciously brought so many people to us, and we know He will continue to do so, allowing this ministry to continue into the future, reaching people with the message of biblical authority and the gospel.

Tim Schmitt

MINISTRY MOMENT

Bring the Plants of the Bible to Life

When we first built the zoo at the Creation Museum, it was only meant to last five years. Fast forward to almost three times that length of time and the zoo was in desperate need of being replaced. As we discussed what we could add to the zoo complex, I thought it would be so cool to have a Plants of the Bible Conservatory to help bring the Bible to life. The leadership team caught the vision and we began to design this one-of-a-kind attraction.

Four glass greenhouses, each a different climate, are climate controlled so we can grow plants that aren't widely cultivated (and certainly wouldn't normally grow around here!) to show guests plants mentioned in Scripture. It took hours and hours of extensive research to try and discover which plants described in the Bible match which modern plant. After all, the Bible doesn't use the Latin genus and species names of today!

For example, when you read "rose of Sharon" in the Bible, you might picture the Midwestern plant by the same name—even though the biblical plant is something totally different. Or the sycamore tree Zaccheaus climbed; not a sycamore like the ones we have here in America, but rather it's a fig tree. And the frankincense given to Jesus by the wise men grows in Africa, so we can teach guests about travel and trade routes in Jesus' day. It's just another way of connecting the Bible with the world around us and showing that it's a book of history about real people, real places, and, yes, even real plants!

Tim Schmitt

Opened the fall of 2025, the conservatory consists of four glass greenhouses, all climate controlled, with different climates in each greenhouse—Tropical, Subtropical, Mediterranean, and Arid. This not only will be the largest conservatory in Kentucky but will also be unique in the world in exhibiting the plants of the Bible.

There is no doubt that the Creation Museum and Ark Encounter are the world's two leading Christian themed attractions, with guests visiting from across the USA and around the world.

The master plans for both attractions show upgrades and additions proposed that we pray will be added for years to come. We praise the Lord for the millions already impacted by these world class attractions and pray that tens of millions more will be impacted over the coming years. Enhancements to the garden by our horticulture team happens on an ongoing basis.

Closing Thoughts

So much has changed over the years. When we employ staff today, they fill out an application form and receive information concerning salary and benefits. It's easy to take all that for granted. When we first started the ministry, we had no salary or benefits. Those of us who have experienced the pioneering days understand the sacrifice that has gone into building the ministry and the value of protecting every dollar. So I counsel staff, "don't just take everything for granted."

Here's another thing I want our staff to remember. Throughout this book, I've talked about "Red Sea" events. We've had many of these events, each requiring increasing steps of faith. When an organization becomes large, with financial stability from income and donations, it is easy to forget about trusting God and stepping out in faith. As organizations grow, things do change. There needs to be greater control in regard to financial integrity and so on. And it's easy to then see everything in terms of finances and forget that "without faith it's impossible to please God..." (Hebrews 11:6). It's easy to look at something totally from a financial perspective without considering the faith aspect (responsible faith) if God is burdening us to do something.

As organizations grow it's easy to rely more on human endeavors and "that you have abandoned the love you had at first" (Revelation 2:4). And it's easy to stop praying and crying out to the Lord. When we have times of plenty it's easy to forget to pray.

And I must admit, as I think about topics like succession, I have, from looking at history, concluded that God raises up special people at times to do a special work for him. There was only one Martin Luther, one Charles Spurgeon, one Martyn Lloyd-Jones, one Dwight Moody, one John Wesley, and so on. Organizations and movements are certainly built around people, but that doesn't mean they are meant to continue in the same form for the future.

Every individual has different backgrounds, life experiences, training, talents, and so on. You can't replace an individual. So as you look to the future, you have to pray and seek the Lord as to what he is directing. Maybe he will raise up some different individuals who will add to the ministry, or redirect portions of it, or maintain and expand it—really it's in the Lord's hands. At the same time, we have the responsibility to be considering all the possibilities and keeping watch for whom the Lord may be leading to the ministry or how he may be directing it for the future. And always remember, it's God's ministry, not ours. It's God's organization, not ours. We are only caretakers of what God has enabled to happen. So the question is, "what does God want for the future?" not "what do we want for the future?" It's God's agenda we need to be seeking, not our own.

Battles Within

Our family became dual citizens of both Australia and America many years ago. One of my favorite U.S. presidents is Abraham Lincoln. In most of his speeches, he mentioned God or the Bible or quoted Scripture. I once read an address he gave before the Young Men's Lyceum of Springfield, IL (one of the leading forces in the cultural activity of Springfield) on January 27, 1838.

Let me set up the context for this address. Lincoln was addressing the issue of mob law, where people took the law into their own hands, and meted out punishments of hanging and burning. A part of his address really stood out to me as a warning for all of us: our nation, churches, Christian organizations, and so on. He said this:

How, then, shall we perform it? At what point shall we expect the approach of danger? By what means shall we fortify against it? Shall we expect some transatlantic military giant to step the ocean and crush us at a blow? Never! All the armies of Europe, Asia, and Africa combined, with all the treasure of the earth (our own excepted) in their military chest; with a Bonaparte for a commander, could not by force take a drink from the Ohio, or make a track on the Blue Ridge, in a trial of a thousand years.

At what point then is the approach of danger to be expected? I answer, if it ever reach us, it must spring up amongst us. It cannot come from abroad. If destruction were our lot, we must ourselves be its author and finisher. As a nation of freemen, we must live through all time, or die by suicide."

Wow! What a profound statement. He was referring to the nation and stating that if America was going to be destroyed that it would not be from without, but it would come from within.

As I think back over the years, we have had so many battles from without, from atheist groups, etc. Some of these battles I've already detailed in this book. But, sadly, we've also had many battles from within, some minor but occasionally some quite major. The devil will use circumstances and people's weaknesses, pride, or personality, to stir up a battle within.

Mark, Ken, Mike, and Joe Boone, President of Answers in Genesis

Most churches I've visited over the years have gone through battles from within. For example, a group of people who don't like the pastor stir up trouble to force him out. Or someone who gives a lot of money to the church uses that to force decisions he wants made that are not best for the church. Another pastor thinks he should be the senior pastor, and so it goes on.

And yes, we've had our own battles from within. In fact, if a church or organization is proclaiming the truth of God's Word and the gospel, expect battles from within! They will happen.

> Be sober-minded; be watchful. Your adversary the devil prowls around like a roaring lion, seeking someone to devour (1 Peter 5:8 ESV).

One of those battles lasted a number of years with lawsuits launched against me personally and the ministry. It was one of the greatest valleys I've ever had to go through. But God taught me things—though I wish he used an easier way to do it! At one stage, I remember crying out in my sleep, "why Lord, why?" I agonized over all the false information put out on the internet that will be there till Jesus comes again. I then came to a point in my life where I said to the Lord, "I can't answer every accusation. I can't refute every attack. Lord, I need to commit this into your hands and recognize only you can protect my reputation. I need to give it all to you."

Actually, it was a turning point in my life as after this event was resolved (thank you, Lord), we had to deal with increasing attacks from people and I learned not to let such attacks get to me. I also learned you can't answer every attack and you can't try to justify yourself all the time. Over the years I've had many people ask me, "how do you stay so calm with all the attacks you get?" Well, God brought me through a valley to teach me how to do that. It really did change me. When I met Bill Nye for our debate in 2014, so many told me how amazed they were at how gracious I was to Bill with all his snide comments, etc. He didn't phase me with his attacks. I just needed to do my best to honor God and his Word and present the material with grace. People noticed.

And with all the attacks from without and within, God brought us on a journey, not just to build an amazing organization to impact the world for him, but to personally teach us many things as part of an ongoing molding and maturing process in our lives.

The glass case in the Creation Museum offices is full of dozens of awards that we have received over the years. It is a testament to the talented staff that the Lord has brought to us.

It's Just Miraculous!

Writing this book has brought back so many memories of people we love, funny happenings, challenges we've faced, people we've impacted, and victories we've celebrated. It's been a joy to remember, write, and celebrate the history of this unique ministry.

But ultimately I hope this book is a reminder that the story of the ministry of Answers in Genesis, what some people might call the "Ken Ham story," isn't really about me, Mark Looy, Mike Zovath, or any of the hundreds of people who have come and gone over the years. **It's the story of a faithful God who has marvelously, as only He can, woven together a tapestry that's impacted millions of people in ways we won't know this side of eternity.** We see bits and pieces in the testimonies I hear or receive daily. But we won't know the full extent of what God was doing until we stand before Him.

> *While we don't know everything He's done, we catch glimpses here and there of the fruit of His eternal plan of redemption. And it's nothing short of Miraculous!*
>
> *May God, and God alone, get the glory for what He has done.*

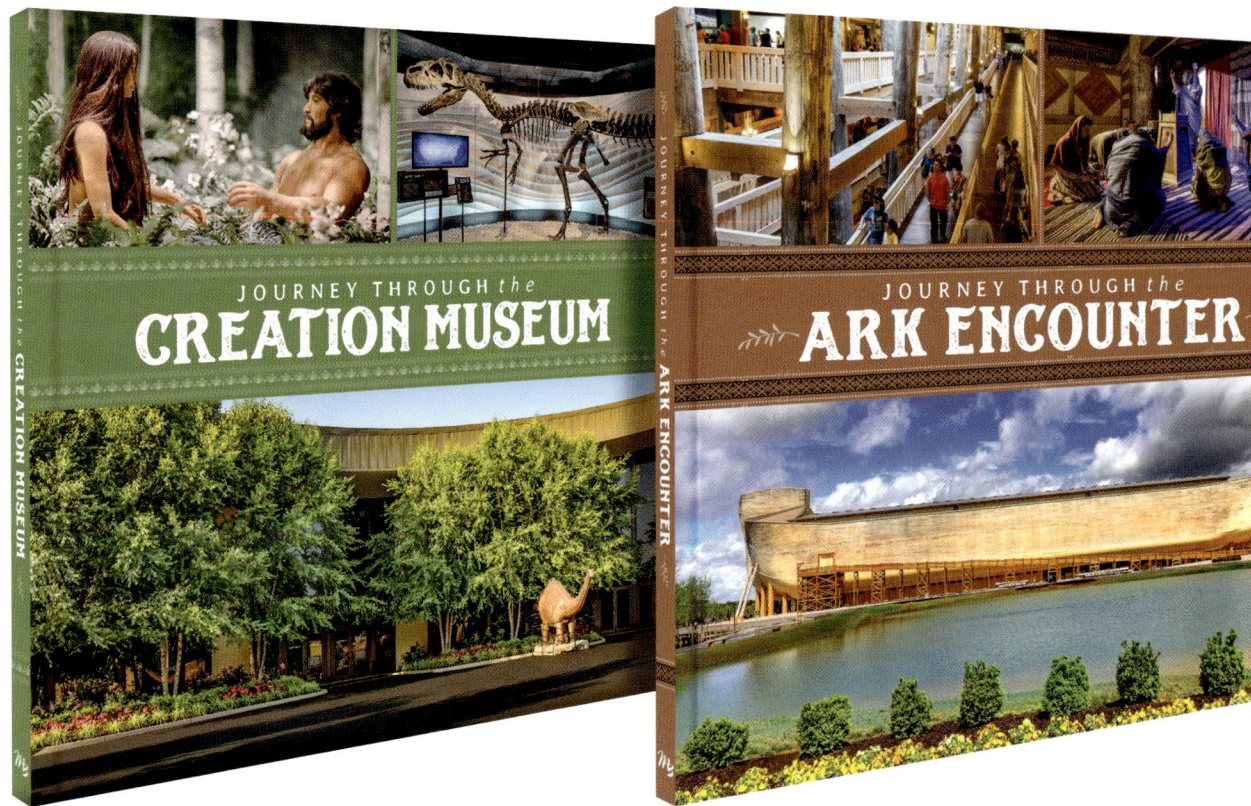

978-1-68344-147-2

Relive the awe-inspiring experience of touring the Creation Museum. Filled with beautiful photography capturing dozens of spectacular exhibits and vibrant gardens, this book will surely be read time and time again. For those who have never visited this world-class facility dedicated to upholding the authority of Scripture from the very first verse, you can now enjoy the next best thing to a visit and see why millions of people consider the Creation Museum a must-see destination.

978-1-68344-012-3

Take an amazing tour through the pages of this book as the world's true history is shared through unique, world-class exhibits. Experience the reality of Noah's Ark, an immense wooden ship built to biblical dimensions to survive the violent forces of the global Flood. See common-sense solutions that would have enabled eight people to care for the animals. Discover the Ark's remarkable animal kinds, based on a multi-year study of both living and extinct creatures.

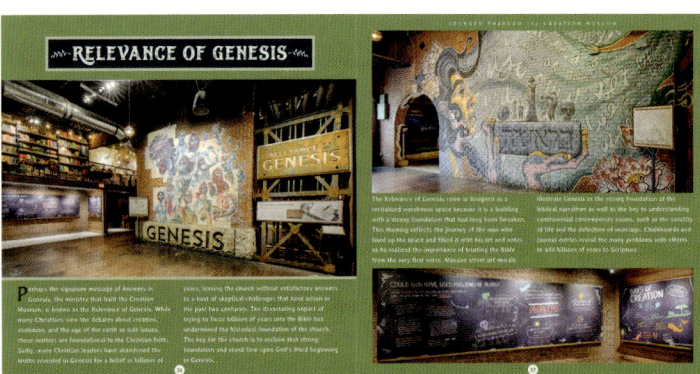

Master Books®
A Division of New Leaf Publishing Group
www.masterbooks.com

KEN HAM
Essentials

978-1-68344-399-5

In a time of cultural confusion over gender, race, marriage, science and more, the Ken Ham Essentials Book Set is an indispensable resource for Christian adults. Packed with foundational Scriptural insights, this apologetic collection offers clear answers to some of the most pressing issues Christians face today. Each of the five books included empowers parents, teachers, and leaders to stand firm in their faith, equip the next generation with confidence, and boldly proclaim the gospel amid a culture that promotes truth as subjective. Ideal as a gift for ministers, Bible teachers, and youth pastors, this set provides the timeless wisdom needed to lead with conviction and uphold God's truth in an ever-changing world.

Master Books®
A Division of New Leaf Publishing Group
www.masterbooks.com

5-Book Set
- Divided Nation
- Divine Dilemma
- Gospel Reset
- The Lie (Updated Edition)
- Will They Stand

978-1-68344-397-1

365 thought-provoking readings

Covers key topics like faith, science, defending the gospel, and building a Christ-centered home. Each reflection will equip you to navigate today's cultural challenges with confidence and deepen your understanding of Scripture. Whether used for personal devotions, family discipleship, or church use, this resource encourages spiritual growth and a strong biblical foundation in everyday life.

Master Books®
A Division of New Leaf Publishing Group
www.masterbooks.com

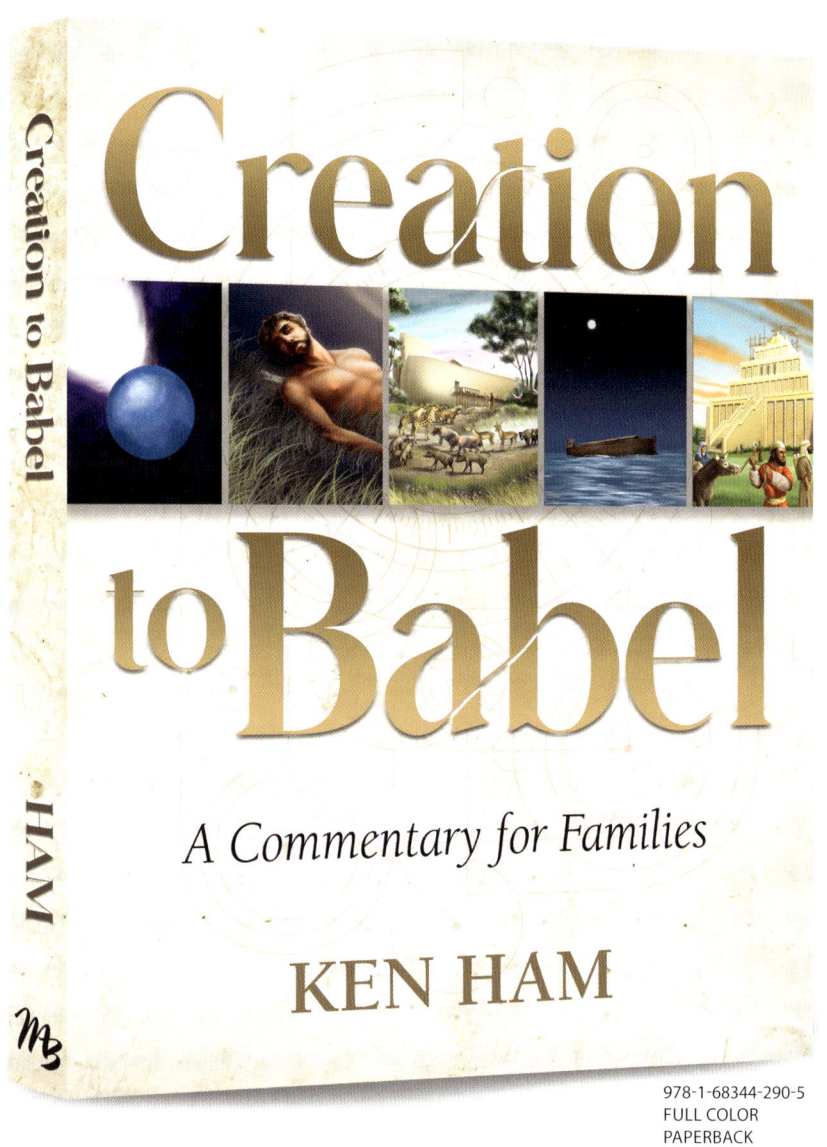

978-1-68344-290-5
FULL COLOR
PAPERBACK

Faith without a strong foundation crumbles in the face of today's relentless cultural rejections. Christians, young and old, will find the strong foundation they need in the biblical bedrock of Genesis.